Journal of the American Revolution

EDITORIAL BOARD

DON N. HAGIST, MANAGING EDITOR

J. L. BELL, ASSOCIATE EDITOR

JIM PIECUCH, ASSOCIATE EDITOR

RAY RAPHAEL, ASSOCIATE EDITOR

TODD ANDRLIK, FOUNDING EDITOR

BRUCE H. FRANKLIN, PUBLISHER

JOURNAL
OF THE
AMERICAN REVOLUTION

ANNUAL VOLUME 2023

WESTHOLME
Yardley

Compilation © 2023 Journal of the American Revolution.
All articles © 2023 by their respective authors.
Images are from the Library of Congress unless otherwise indicated.

All rights reserved under International and Pan-American Copyright Conventions. No part of this book may be reproduced in any form or by any electronic or mechanical means, including information storage and retrieval systems, without permission in writing from the publisher, except by a reviewer who may quote brief passages in a review.

Westholme Publishing, LLC
904 Edgewood Road
Yardley, Pennsylvania 19067
Visit our Web site at www.westholmepublishing.com

ISBN: 978-1-59416-404-0

Printed in the United States of America.

CONTENTS

Editor's Introduction	ix
Charles Thomson and the Delaware • JAMES M. SMITH	1
Benjamin Franklin's Unconventional Marriage to Deborah Read • NANCY RUBIN STUART	14
Governor William Franklin: "Sagorighweyoghsta" (Great Arbiter or Doer of Justice • JOSEPH E. WROBLEWSKI	28
One of the "Powers of Good in the World," Mercy Otis Warren • JAMES M. DEITCH	40
The British Soldiers Who Marched to Concord, April 19, 1775 DON N. HAGIST	46
Virginian Ned Streater, African American Minute Man PATRICK H. HANNUM	52
The 1775 Duel Between Henry Laurens and John Faucheraud Grimké • AARON J. PALMER	58
Washington's Final Retreat: Asylum ALEXANDER LENARCHYK	67
George III's (Implicit) Sanction of the American Revolution M. ANDREW HOLOWCHAK	69
Edward Hand's American Journey • DAVID PRICE	73
Jemima Howe, Frontier Pioneer to Wealthy Widow JANE STRACHAN	84
Hell's Half-Acre: The Fall of Loyalist Crean Brush ERIC WISER	96
Thomas Plumb, British Soldier, Writes Home from Rhode Island • DON N. HAGIST	111

Unraveling the Beginning and Final Phases in the Emergence of the French-American Alliance • MARVIN L. SIMNER … 114

Marinus Willett—The Exploits of an Unheralded War Hero
RICHARD J. WERTHER … 127

Point/Counterpoint, 1777 Style: Dueling Proclamations from Putman and Tryon • TODD W. BRAISTED … 136

Did Washington Swear at Charles Lee during the Battle of Monmouth? • CHRISTIAN MCBURNEY … 140

Black Drummers in a Redcoat Regiment • DON N. HAGIST … 151

Under the Banner of War: Frontier Militia and Uncontrolled Violence • TIMOTHY C. HEMMIS … 156

Rhode Island Acts to Prevent an Enslaved Family from Being Transported to the South • CHRISTIAN MCBURNEY … 167

British Soldier John Ward Wins Back His Pocketbook
DON N. HAGIST … 181

Anthony Wayne's Repulse at Bull's Ferry, July 21, 1780
JIM PIECUCH … 185

Two Hurricanes One Week Apart • BOB RUPPERT … 195

Top Ten Weather Interventions • DON N. HAGIST … 204

The Fruits of Victory: Loyalist Prisoners in the Aftermath of Kings Mountain • WILLIAM CALDWELL … 209

Top Ten Quotes by Francis Lord Rawdon
TODD W. BRAISTED … 218

Russia and the Armed Neutrality of 1780 • ERIC STERNER … 225

Prelude to Yorktown: Washington and Rochembeau in New York • BENJAMIN HUGGINS … 235

The Abdication(s) of King George III • BOB RUPPERT … 247

Jemima Howe, Facts and Fiction • JANE STRACHAN … 253

The Articles of Confederation–A Silver Lining
RICHARD WERTHER … 262

Undeceived: Who would Write the Political Story of the Revolution • JAMES M. SMITH … 272

Partisan Politics and the Laws which Shaped the First Congress • SAMUEL T. LAIR … 276

Contents

"Characters Pre-Eminent for Virtue and Ability": the First
Partisan Application of the Electoral College
SHAWN DAVID MCGHEE ... 289

Weaponizing Impeachment: Justice Chase and President
Jefferson's Battle Over the Process • AL DICKENSON ... 296

Insurrection and Speculation: How a Farmer, Financier, and
Surprising Sharper Seeded the Constitution • SCOTT M. SMITH ... 306

Natural History in Revolutionary and Post-Revolutionary
America • MATTEO GIULIANI ... 321

A Great Englishman? British Views of George Washington,
from Revolution to Rapprochement • SAM EDWARDS ... 332

Author Biographies ... *341*
Index ... *347*

EDITOR'S INTRODUCTION

Each year the editorial board for this publication selects about three dozen articles that we published during the previous year, for inclusion in our annual hardcover volume. After the selections are made, we arrange them into a roughly chronological order, from the early 1760s to the early 1800s, taking the reader on a tour of events over a four-decade time span. For the most part, the articles line up neatly along this time line, giving a sense of progression from the beginning of an era to the end.

Time may march forward in a neat straight line, but the path of history is much more complex. At any point on our nice straight timeline there were myriad events happening in parallel. Each person that marked their own aging on the timeline was involved with countless others, forming threads that weave this way and that across the overall progression. Threads unravel, and their strands intertwine with other threads. The timeline is not a line at all, but an infinitely wide band filled with winding and interlaced paths running alongside, over, under and through each other; a close look at each one reveals still others within.

Every year, writers for *Journal of the American Revolution* find new stories to tell, new paths to explore, new threads to unravel. This year saw articles on little-known aspects of well-known people about whom there is always more to discover, like Benjamin Franklin, Mercy Otis Warren, George Washington, King George III, Charles Lee, Anthony Wayne, Comte de Rochambeau, and Thomas Jefferson. There were insightful articles on people who were influential in their time but whose names are unfamiliar today, including Charles Thomson, William Franklin, Henry Laurens, Edward Hand, Marinus Willett, Lord Rawdon, and Samuel Chase. And fascinating stories about ordinary individual people whose names might be lost entirely were it not for some extraordinary event: Jemima Howe, Ned Streater, Thomas Plumb, and John Ward.

All of these people, and more, appear in the pages of this, our ninth uniform Annual Volume. They are testimony to just how broad and intricate the timeline of history really is.

Charles Thomson and the Delaware

JAMES M. SMITH

There are many, many founding fathers in the story of America's Revolution and unfortunately only a few are really known to the general public. Yet without those who are less known, there would have been no revolution.

One of those men was the official secretary of the Continental Congress, Charles Thomson. He was the sole fixture of the congress throughout its entire fifteen years of existence. All the others came and went, some were sent overseas to diplomatic assignments, many went home to their home colonies to participate in local legislatures. There was a time after the war was over when they all went home and left Charles Thomson all alone; he was the entire government for a period of time. He never left his post; he was always there. In the end, when it was all over, it was he who traveled to Mt. Vernon to inform George Washington, officially, that he had been elected to the presidency of the new government under the new constitution. He then accompanied Washington to New York, the new capital of the nation, and turned over to Washington all the official papers, journals and documents of the nation including the Great Seal.

Charles Thomson was born into an Irish family. In 1739 his mother died and his father thought he should emigrate to America. He left his daughter in Ireland with other members of the family, took his three sons and sailed for America. Charles was eight years old, the youngest. Unfortunately, his father died before the ship reached America. When the ship arrived at New Castle, Delaware, the two older brothers were able to get jobs and support themselves. The captain apprenticed Charles to a blacksmith in town who had no children of his own. That night Charles overheard the man and his wife talking about how they now had someone who would learn the trade and support them in their old age. It seems no one asked Charles about that. So, that same night,

Charles put what goods he had into a small bag, climbed out a window and left town.[1]

When he reached Philadelphia, he was able to enroll in a school run by Francis Allison, a Presbyterian minister. Mr. Alison has been recognized as one of the leading educators in early American history. Five of his students went on to be physicians, four were members of the Continental Congress, and when the new constitution was adopted and the new government formed, five went on to become either senators or members of congress. Four signed the Declaration of Independence, and some became federal judges.[2]

After graduating from Mr. Alison's school, Thomson moved back to New Castle to start his own school. He did this for a number of years, often traveling to Philadelphia where he became friends with Benjamin Franklin and his son William. Franklin had created a trust to start a new school, the Academy of Philadelphia, which eventually became the University of Pennsylvania. Under Franklin's plan it was to be a non-sectarian school. In 1750 Franklin suggested that Thomson apply there for a teaching position; he was hired at a salary of £60 a year.[3] He was originally hired as a teacher of Latin and Greek, but after a few years was also given the duties of treasurer.

Thomson spent five years at the academy but left to teach at a Quaker school, the Friends Public School of Philadelphia, as the head of the Latin Department at a salary of £150 a year.[4]

The colony of Pennsylvania was not a Royal colony, that is, it did not come under the rule of the King or Parliament. It was owned first by William Penn for the settlement of Quakers, as they were not allowed in Massachusetts or Virginia. After he died, the proprietorship of the colony was left to his heirs, all of whom lived in England. The family members appointed a governor to run the colony in their absence. He answered to the family, not to the British government. The colony was allowed to have an elected legislature as were other colonies, but the governors were always chosen by the family in Britain. This was an extremely lucrative situation for the family. Under the rules of the colony, as set up by William Penn, only the governor could negotiate with the Native Americans to buy land from them. The land then belonged to the family, not the colony. The family then had the purchase divided into lots and the lots sold to settlers. Revenue came from

1. Boyd Stanley Schlenther, *Charles Thomson, A Patriot's Story*. (Newark: University of Delaware Press, 1990), 19.
2. Ibid., 20.
3. Ibid., 7.
4. Ibid., 22-23.

taxes on land owned by settlers, not the land owned by the family—they paid no taxes. This left the tax burden solely on small land owners. The legislature of the colony decided to send Benjamin Franklin to London to petition the King and Parliament to make Pennsylvania a royal colony with a governor appointed by the King, as in other colonies. This was a long, drawn-out process that went on for years. Franklin was still in London trying to have Pennsylvania made into a Royal colony when the American Revolution began.

For over eighty years wars broke out between France and Britain. A number of battles were fought in the new world with American colonial militia units participating. The last war prior to the American Revolution, was known in America as the French and Indian War. For the first few years the war went badly for the British and Americans. The French and their Native American allies defeated a large force of British regulars and Virginia militia in the Ohio Valley under British Gen. Edward Braddock. They were now able to raid well into territories settled by English settlers. The French had built a large fort in the area now known as Pittsburg, and their Delaware and Shawnee allies owned lands between that fort and the surrounding area of western Pennsylvania. In order for new British forces to get to the French fort in Western Pennsylvania and round the great lakes, they would have to fight their way through Delaware and Shawnee lands.

As the war was going on a group of Quakers tried to establish better relations with the Delaware and Shawnee Native Americans who were the original occupiers of land in what is now Pennsylvania and New Jersey. The people known as the Delaware, a name given to them by the British, referred to themselves as the Lenape. Before the English came they lived in what is now known as New Jersey, eastern Pennsylvania, southern New York and the Maryland Eastern Shore. Prior to the English coming they had been conquered by the Six Nations; also, their population had been decimated by European diseases.[5] Over the years after the settlement of Pennsylvania by Quakers under the leadership of William Penn, English colonists bought land from the Delaware to settle. As more and more settlers came, the demand for more and more land created ever more purchases. The problem was that what was supposed to be the boundaries of the land tended to be viewed differently by the English and the Delaware. The Delaware

---

5. Joseph E. Wroblewski, "Governor William Franklin: Sagorighweyoghsta, 'Great Arbiter' or 'Doer of Justice,' *Journal of the American Revolution*, April 8, 2022, allthingsliberty.com/2022/04/governor-william-franklin-sagorighweyoghsta-great-arbiter-or-doer-of-justice/.

were constantly crying "foul" when they saw the English settling on land that they felt exceeded the boundaries they had agreed to.

The Quakers, being pacifists, felt uneasy at the cost of the French and Indian war and the taxes that were being requested of them to finance it. They felt that if the Delaware could be satisfied with respect to their complaints and properly recognized borders be agreed to by both parties, there would be no need for the war, especially if the Delaware, who were siding with the French, could be made neutral if not allies. The Quakers formed a group called the "Friendly Association." They approached Charles Thomson and asked if he would research all the records of treaty negotiations and land purchases between colonial authorities and the Delaware to determine the facts. He agreed.

He began by reviewing all the transcripts of minutes taken by colonial authorities with the goal of trying to determine exactly where the boundaries were supposed to be. He also interviewed a number of eye witnesses. He published his research in a report entitled *Causes of the Alienation of the Delaware and Shawnese Indians from the British Interests.*[6]

Thomson opened his report with the observation that "It has been to many a cause of wonder, how it comes to pass that the English have so few Indians in their interest, while the French have so many at command." He also asked "by what means and for what reason those neighboring tribes ... who, at the first arrival of the English in Pennsylvania, and for a long series of years afterwards, showed every mark of affection and kindness, should become our most bitter enemies."

Some, he said, looked upon the Native American "as faithless and perfidious." "Others," he said, "imagine there must be some causes for the change in their behavior." Native Americans, he said, "to explain the motives of their conduct, declare that the solicitations of the French, joined with the abuses they have suffered from the English, particularly in being cheated and defrauded of their land, have at length induced them to become our enemies and to make war upon us." Thomson took notice of the fact that when challenged, colonial authorities took "much pain" to present the claims of the Native Americans "as groundless, and only lame excuses for their perfidiousness." Thomson went on to explain the purpose and method of his research to find the truth.

---

6. Charles Thomson, *Causes of the Alienation of the Delaware and Shawnese Indians from the British Interest* (Philadelphia: John Campbell, 1889). All quotes from this report in this article are taken from this edition, reprint from the first publication in London by J. Wilkie in 1759.

> In order, therefore, to clear up these points, and to examine into their foundation and truth of the complaints, recourse has been had to as many of the treaties and conferences held between the Indians and this government ... It is a matter of no small consequence to know the ground of complaints made by the Indians, that in case they are false, justice may be done to the characters of those who are injured thereby; and if true, that proper remedies may be applied, and that the Crown of Great Britain may not, by the avarice and wickedness of a few be deprived of the friendship and alliance of those nations who are capable of being our most useful friends, or most dangerous enemies.
>
> It could be wished, for the sake of truth, that access had been allowed to the minutes of Council, which are the only public records kept of the transactions between the Government of Pennsylvania and the Indians, or the minutes of several conferences with the Indians had been duly taken, and regularly published, or that all the deeds granted by the Indians had been recorded in the Rolls-Office, as they ought to have been: had this been done, the matter might have been set in a fuller and clearer light. However, by perusing the following extracts taken from such treaties as could be met with, from the votes of the assembly, from the deeds as have been recorded, and from other authentic papers and letters, it will be clearly seen whether the complaints of the Indians are only invented to palliate their late conduct; whether they are objects of party; or whether their pretensions are reasonable and their demands consistent with justice.

Much of Thomson's report dealt in depth with the numerous treaties and conferences, especially conferences in 1722, 1727, 1729, 1732, 1736, 1737 and 1749, with reference to various deeds documenting purchases from the Delaware. One treaty which was much discussed between the parties was that of 1686. This deed was missing from the record and seems to be the one that started the process of buying lands from the Delaware. Colonial officials often referred to it, but never produced it, much to the chagrin of the Delaware.

The primary complaint of the Delaware was that the boundaries agreed to in the treaties were never respected by the English. A boundary was described in a treaty, be it a river or a mountain range in which one side was for the English and the other remained the possession of the Delaware. No sooner was the ink dry than English pioneers began to settle on the Delaware side of the border in ever increasing numbers. When the Delaware complained to colonial officials, the officials claimed that there were too many settlers to be removed and that therefore they needed to buy the disputed land from the Delaware and set up a new boundary. Thus, the Delaware were forced to move further and further west until they were forced onto Shawnee lands. Then, the two of them were forced into the Ohio where they bumped up against the French who were expanding their settlements and forts down from Quebec into the Ohio Valley. Thomson noted that it "was commonly the case that when the Indians complained; they had fair promises made them, but no effectual measures seem to have been taken to redress their grievances."

Thomson could find no notes or minutes of the 1737 meeting. While there were deeds going back to 1718 there were no records or minutes of the meetings to prove there were payments made to the Delaware for the land described in the deed. He concluded that the deeds were questionable if not downright fraudulent. This led to the infamous Walking Purchase. It was agreed that the boundaries would be defined by the distance a man could walk in one-and-one half days, which normally would be about forty miles. To this the Delaware agreed. What the Delaware did not know was that the Pennsylvania governor prepared ahead of time for this and even before he suggested it to the Delaware, he had a trail prepared and pathway cleared. He then arranged for runners to run in relays. When the Delaware saw this, they were furious. Instead of a forty mile boundary the English were able to declare they had an eighty mile boundary, and they refused to budge on the issue.[7] When the Delaware kept complaining of fraud the governor requested the Iroquois of the Six Nation Confederacy send representatives to the conference to speak to the Delaware as the Six Nations claimed supremacy over them. The Six Nations Confederacy, also known as the Iroquois Confederacy, consisted of the Mohawks, Oneida, Onondagas, Cayua, Seneca and Tuscarora nations.[8]

When the representatives of the Six Nations arrived at the meeting, they told the Pennsylvania governor "that they saw the Delawares had been an unruly people, and were altogether in the wrong; that they had concluded to remove them, and oblige them to go over the River Delaware, and to quit all claim to any lands on this [the east] side for the future, since they have received pay for them."

Then the representative of the Six Nations turned to the Delaware and said,

> they deserved to be taken by the hair of the head and shaked severely, till they recovered their senses and became sober—That he had seen with his eyes a deed signed by nine of their ancestors above fifty years

---

7. Brittania.com. 2/18/2022.
8. Wroblewski, "Governor William Franklin: Sagorighweyoghsta."

ago for this very land . . . But how came you to take upon you to sell lands at all? We conquered you; we made women of you: you now are women, and can no more sell land than women; nor is it fit you should have the power of selling lands, since you would abuse it. This land that you claim is gone thro' your guts; you have been furnished cloaths, meat and drink, by the goods paid you for it, and now you want it again like children as you are. But what makes you sell lands in the dark? Did you ever tell us that you had sold this land? Did we ever receive any part, even the value of a pipe shank, from you for it? You have told us a blind story, that you sent a messenger to us, to inform us of the sale, but he never came amongst us, nor we ever heard any thing about it. This is acting in the dark, and very different from the conduct our Six Nations observe in the sales of land . . .

But we find you are none of our blood; you act a dishonest part not only in this but in other matters; your ears are ever open to slanderous reports about your brethren—for all these reasons we charge you to remove instantly; we don't give you the liberty to think about it. You are women. Take the advice of a wise man, and remove immediately. You may return to the other side of Delaware where you come from; but we do not know whether, considering how you have demeaned yourselves, you will be permitted to live there, or whether you have not swallowed that land down your throats . . . We therefore assign you two places to go, either to Wyomen or Shamoken. You may go to either of these places, and then we shall have you more under our eye, and shall see how you behave. Don't deliberate, but remove away.

Thomson wrote that some of the Delaware did as they were told and moved up closer to the Six Nations, but others refused to go to where they were told; instead, they moved further west, merging with the Shawnee and into the Ohio. There they formed an alliance with the Shawnee and both found a powerful new ally in the French. The French were quite happy to give them guns, powder and clothes without making territorial demands.

Here Thomson noted the difference in how the French treated the Native Americans as opposed to the British. The English, he said,

in order to get their lands, drive them as far from them as possible, nor seem to care what becomes of them, provided they get them removed out of the way of their permanent settlements; whereas the French, considering that they can never want land in America, who enjoy the friendship of the Indians, use all the means in their power to draw as many into their alliance as possible; and to secure their affection, invite as many as can to come and live near them, and to make their towns as near the French settlements as they can. By this means they have drawn off a great number of Mohawks, and other Six Nation tribes and having settled them in towns along the banks of the river St. Lawrence, have so secured them to their interest, that even these, they can command about six or seven hundred fighting men.

Thomson noted that by 1742 even the Six Nations were beginning to complain that they were suffering from illegal land seizures by the English, and by 1744 were demanding the English remove all English settlers along the Juniata River.

By the 1750s English settlers who had remained east of the Appalachian Mountains began to spill over into western Pennsylvania and the Ohio lands. The Six Nations began to rethink their alliance with the English. Hunting grounds were being compromised and over hunted; worse, land in the Ohio was being cleared and cultivated.

Finally in 1749 Pennsylvania authorities made a purchase of lands from the Native Americans around the Susquehanna and the Juniata Rivers. More and more land was being cleared and cultivated. Thomson wrote that by 1753 the Native Americans had requested a new meeting to clear up some deeds and land grants. This meeting was to open to the Delaware, Shawnee, and Six Nations. In 1754 Thomson reported that

> a purchase of land was made by the proprietors of Pennsylvania which ruined our interest with the Indians and from then, especially those westward of us and drove them entirely into the hands of the French. . . By this the lands where the Shawnese and Ohio Indians lived and the hunting grounds of the Delaware, the Mohicans and the Tuteloes were included and consequently these nations had nothing to expect but to see themselves in in a short time, at the rate the English settled, violently driven from their lands, as the Delaware had formally been, and reduced to leave their country and seek settlement they knew not where. This engaged many of the people to give ear to the French, who declared that they did not come to deprive the Indians of their land but to hinder the English from settling westward of the Alleghany hills.

The Delaware, the Onandago, the Shawnee were never invited to the meeting, as the Pennsylvania authorities dealt directly with the Six nations. By this time the Six Nations were suspicious, so the Pennsylvania authorities pulled a ruse. According to Thomson, the governor told the Six Nations that they were buying this additional land over the mountains, not to settle, but to keep settlers out. They persuaded the Six Nations that if the government owned the land they could better accomplish this. They said they wanted to own the land simply to keep the French from settling there and building forts. The Six Nations agreed, but as soon as the land was transferred to the governor surveyors started showing up and dividing it into lots. The Six Nations, those who had been stalwarts in defending the English against other tribes in the area, had been deceived.

Around this time several tribes under the leadership of the Delaware realized that each tribe by itself could never stand up to the English or the Six Nations. They needed an alliance of their own. Several, primarily the Shawnee and the Delaware, decided to unite and elect a chief to speak for them all. They elected a man called Teedyuscung. He led them on several raids against the English on the frontiers of New York and Pennsylvania. The English called upon the Six Nations to stop the raids. The Six Nations notified the Delaware to send representatives to meet with them. When the delegates arrived the leaders of the Six Nations started to talk down to them as they had in the past, but the representatives of the Delaware stopped them short. They replied to the Six Nations,

> They looked upon themselves as men, and would acknowledge no superiority that any other nation had over them. We are men and are determined not to be ruled any longer by you as women; and we are determined to cut off all the English, except those that escape from us in ships; so say no more to us on that head, lest we make women of you as you have done us.

Having thus gotten the attention of the Six Nations, the Delaware did agree to listen to the Seneca who had backed the stance of the Delaware.

While war was ongoing between the English and the French with the Delaware and Shawnee among others siding with the French, a group of Quakers in Philadelphia talked the Pennsylvania governor into trying to discuss a real peace with the Delaware and honestly address their complaints. The Pennsylvania authorities, speaking through the Six Nations, invited the Delaware and the new confederacy to a new conference. The Delaware agreed to listen to what the English had to say and as an act of good faith agreed to return a number of captives to the English.

In the conference the Six Nations agreed to the independence of the Delaware and recognized Teedyuscung as a chief speaking for the new alliance of the four nations as well as the Six Nations.

All through 1756 and 1757 there were a series of negotiations about how and where a conference would take place and who should be invited. It was agreed that the Delaware, Shawnee, Seneca and the Six Nations would attend and that Teedyuscung would speak for them all.

As this meeting, held in Easton, Pennsylvania started, Teedyuscung did something that had never been done before at a treaty conference between Native Americans and the English. He requested that he have his own secretary present to keep notes on the speeches and agreements. Up to this time it had always been the English who had a scribe present to keep notes, who would give a copy of any agreement to the Native Americans at the end of the conference. Often those notes were incomplete or inaccurate—in one past treaty meeting the scribe had thrown down the pen and refused to write down what the chief was saying as he complained about the cheating done by the English in land transactions. The Quakers, who had meetings with Teedyuscung prior to the conference, suggested having a scribe with him. When the request was made the Pennsylvania governor refused and said that it had always been that the English had kept the notes and he saw no reason why that should change. Teedyuschung refused to meet unless he had his own scribe. The standoff lasted four days until the governor realized he needed Teedyuscung more than Teedyuscung needed him. When it was finally agreed, Teedyuscung announced that Charles Thomson would be his scribe.

The conference went on for days, but in the end it was agreed that the Delaware would make a complete list of all their complaints that would be sent to the King in England who would make the final decision. In addition to the complaints listed by the Delaware, the report of the histories of the various treaties written by Charles Thomson would be a part of papers that would be sent to London. By this time, with the war against the French going badly with the defeat of Braddock in the Ohio, the King and his ministers decided to get directly involved in dealing with the Native Americans. Teedyuscung agreed to abide by the decision of the King. But he made one additional and farsighted request of the King, besides just addressing his specific complaints. He was looking into the future and sought a way to create a final peace. What he asked for was simple but far-reaching and was a huge admission that for there to be a real peace, the culture of Native Americans had to adjust to the reality that the English were not going to ever leave the lands. He said that for the Delaware, he thought it was

> best to have a certain country fixed for our life and the lives of our children forever and as we intend to make a settlement ... and to build houses different from what we have done before, such as may last not only for a little while, but for our children and us; we desire you will assist us in making our settlements, and send us persons to instruct us

in building houses and in making such necessaries as shall be needful; and that persons be sent to instruct us in the Christian religion, which may be for our future welfare, and to instruct us into reading and writing. That our trade be established between us and such persons appointed to conduct and manage affairs as shall be agreeable to us.

This was an extraordinary request which, if carried out, had the potential of creating a lasting peace throughout the land.

With this treaty, both the English and the Delaware agreed to abide by the King's decision. The Delaware ceased their war against the English which allowed the English free passage through to the French in Ohio. The Shawnee remained loyal to the French and pulled their forces back closer to the French forts. The French abandoned their fort at what is now Pittsburgh and withdrew further into the Ohio territory.

Charles Thomson made one final note, a request to the English as well as the King. He said,

> Here the affair rests. If the proper papers and true state of case be laid before the king and council for a just determination: If the Indians be assisted in making this settlement, secured in their property and instructed in religion and the civil arts, agreeable to their request, and the trade with them regulated and set upon such a footing that they may be secure from abuse, there is not the least doubt but the alliance and friendship of the Indians may be forever secured to the British interest; but should these things be neglected, the arms of the French are open to receive them.

While working and living with the Delaware Thomson was adopted into the tribe and given the name that means "the man who tells the truth." This legend of telling the truth stuck with him throughout his time at the Continental Congress. After the American Revolution he wrote to a man who asked him about this legend and Thomson wrote back saying that "It was well known that I had resolved in spite of consequences, never to put my official signature to any account, the accuracy of which I could not vouch as a man of honor."[9] Under the rules of the Continental Congress, no document was official unless it contained signatures of both the President and the Secretary. This meant that Charles Thomson's signature was required on all official documents of the United States during the time of the Continental Congress.

After the 1757 conference Thomson organized his notes into a full report and in addition to giving the governor a copy, sent a copy to

---

9. Schlenther, *Charles Thomson*, 48-49.

Benjamin Franklin in London. Realizing the report would give great discomfort to the Penn family, Franklin had it published. He sent several copies to various crown officials, sent 250 copies back to Pennsylvania to be distributed, and put several hundred copies up for sale in Britain. He reported back to his allies in Pennsylvania that sales were brisk and said that the effect "was more positive that I expected. It will, I think, have a good effect."[10]

To what extent Charles Thomson's report may have influenced official British thinking we do not know. We do know that it was circulated in the highest circles in the British government. Benjamin Franklin confirmed this. We also know that after the French and Indian War, the King of England issued his famous Proclamation of 1763, in which he addressed Native American concerns. This proclamation specifically addressed a number of issues described in Thomson's report: settlement west of the Appalachian Mountains, insecure borders, fraudulent land grabs, porous borders, and unscrupulous traders. The Proclamation stated:

> Whereas it is just and reasonable, and essential to our interest, and the security of our colonies, that the several Nations or Tribes of Indians with whom we are connected and who live under our protection, should not be molested or disturbed in the possession of such parts of our Dominions and Territories as, not having been ceded to or purchased by us, are reserved to them . . . no [colonial authority] do presume, upon any pretense whatsoever, to grant warrants of survey, any patent for lands beyond the bounds of their respective governments . . . beyond the heads or sources of any rivers which fall into the Atlantic Ocean . . . nor any lands whatever which . . . are reserved to the said Indians or any of them.
>
> We do further declare it to be our Royal will and pleasure . . . to reserve under our sovereignty protection and dominion, for the use of the said Indians, all the lands and territories lying to the westward of the sources of the rivers which fall into the sea . . .
>
> And we do hereby strictly forbid, on pain of our displeasure all our loving subjects from making any purchase or settlements whatever or taking possession of any of the lands above reserved . . .
>
> And we do further strictly empower and require all persons who have seated themselves upon any lands . . . still reserved for the Indians as aforesaid, forthwith to remove themselves from such   settlements.
>
> And whereas great frauds and abuses have been committed in purchasing lands of the Indians . . . we do, with the advice of our Privy

---

10. Ibid., 23.

Council, strictly require that that no person or persons is to presume to make any purchase of land from the said Indians.

And we do, by the advice of our Privy Council declare and enjoin that the trade with the said Indians shall be free and open to all our subjects whatsoever provided ... they do take out a license for carrying on such trade ... and give security to observe all our regulations as we shall at anytime think fit ... taking care to insert a condition that such license shall be void and security forfeited in case the person ... shall refuse or neglect to observe such regulations.[11]

This proclamation was considered by the American colonists to be one of the "intolerable acts" and as such was given as an excuse to rebel against Britain. With American independence, the proclamation became moot and under the American flag settlers poured into the Ohio territory, pushing ever westward and leading to one hundred years of wars with Native Americans until Anglo-Americans completed their "manifest destiny" and occupied all the lands between the Atlantic and Pacific Oceans. Teedyuscung's dream of a secure place was not to be.

11. avalon.law.yale.edu/18th_century/proc1763.asp.

Benjamin Franklin's Unconventional Marriage to Deborah Read

NANCY RUBIN STUART

She was neither beautiful nor wealthy. Nor was Benjamin Franklin's wife educated or intellectual. Nevertheless in 1724 he proposed to Deborah Read while renting a room from her father, the carpenter John Read of Philadelphia. Was it simply youthful passion that attracted him or did the eighteen-year-old printer ask for Deborah's hand because she had a dowry?

Ben's Autobiography glossed over key emotional moments in his life. Written more than four decades after that proposal, it offers few hints about the depth of his attraction to Deborah. "I had a great Respect and Admiration for her, and had some Reason to believe she had the same for me," he wrote.[1] There is no mention of "love" as we perceive it today, but in the colonial era, an affectionate attraction between the partners and the man's economic abilities were the standards by which most marriages were made.

Ben's Autobiography adds that his marriage to Deborah was postponed because her newly-widowed mother, Sarah Read, thought it imprudent. He and Deborah were still teenagers; besides he was about to sail to England to buy printing equipment through the largesse of Sir William Keith, deputy governor of Pennsylvania. "A Marriage if it was to take place would be more convenient after my return, when I should be as I expected set up in my Business," Ben wrote, quoting Mrs. Read.[2] Just before sailing, he "interchanged some promises with Miss Read" to marry after his return.[3]

---

1. Benjamin Franklin, *The Autobiography of Benjamin Franklin*, Leonard W. Labaree, Ralph L. Ketcham, Helen C. Boatfield, and Helene H. Fineman, eds. (Yale University Press, New Haven, CT, and London, 1964.) 89.
2. Ibid.
3. Ibid, 92.

Soon after Ben's ship approached England he discovered Sir Keith support was non-existent. In London he found a job at Palmer's printing house which provided funds to pay his rent and that of unemployed poet friend James Ralph. Thrilled by the city's rich cultural offerings, the two young men gallivanted round the city with Ben paying the bills.

Ralph, meanwhile, having abandoned his wife and child in Philadelphia, soon acquired a mistress, a milliner identified only as Mrs. T.; being unable to find work, he took a job as a schoolmaster outside London. Emboldened by Ralph's callous attitude towards women, Ben wrote Deborah "never more than one letter, and that was to let her know I was not likely to return soon."[4]

In Ralph's absence, Mrs. T. borrowed money from Ben who "presuming on my Importance to her attempted Familiarities (another Erratum), which she repulsed with a proper Resentment."[5] After learning that, Ralph stormed back to town, denounced Ben and ended the friendship.

Soon afterwards, Ben landed a better job at the John Watts printing shop. After work he visited London's coffee houses where literary and scientific men debated the intellectual issues of the day. Somewhat later in his Autobiography, Ben mentioned that his "hard-to-be-govern'd Passion of Youth had hurried me frequently into Intrigues with low Women."[6] No dates are mentioned but they probably occurred during that trip to London.

In Philadelphia, meanwhile, the jilted Deborah spent her days weeping until her mother and friends encouraged her to allow other suitors. In August 1725 she consequently wed an English man named John Rogers, but after learning he had a wife, abruptly quit the marriage. Before long Rogers had squandered her dowry, fallen into debt and fled to the West Indies where he was allegedly killed in a brawl. That left Deborah in a strange position, neither single nor married but, since nothing could be proven, with no recourse for a divorce.

When Ben returned from England in 1726, he learned about his former sweetheart's misfortune. "I should have been much asham'd at seeing Miss Read, had not her friends . . . persuaded her to marry another," he recalled in his Autobiography.[7] Even so, "a friendly Correspondence as Neighbours and old Acqaintances, had continued between me and Mrs. Read's Family . . . I was often invited there and consulted in their Affairs wherein I sometimes was of service."[8]

4. Ibid, 96.
5. Ibid, 99.
6. Ibid, 128.
7. Ibid, 106-107. 8. Ibid, 128-129.

Ben did not explain the nature of that "service" but it was probably financial since Mrs. Read had inherited several properties from her husband's estate. During those visits Ben expressed pity for "poor Miss Read's unfortunate Situation," finding her "generaly dejected, seldom chearful and avoided Company."[9] Yet whatever guilt he felt did not stop him from courting other young women, only to be rejected by their fathers, who thought printers were poor providers.

Nevertheless, Ben's fortunes were rising. After returning to Philadelphia, he worked briefly for a merchant, then returned to his job as a printer for the cantankerous Samuel Keimer. By 1728, he and fellow printer Hugh Meredith established their own printing establishment financed by Meredith's father. A year later they bought the *Pennsylvania Gazette* from Keimer. But by July 1730, Meredith's fondness for the bottle and his father's sudden financial reversals led Ben to buy out his partner. A month after establishing the B. Franklin printing house, he admitted his guilt to Deborah's mother. To his surprise Sarah Read confessed she, too felt responsible for urging Deborah to marry Rogers.

Ben's Autobiography then simply announced, "I [took] her to wife Sept. 1, 1730."[10] Living together was the couple's only option. If Ben married Deborah in a church wedding and Rogers was still alive, the couple would be punished as bigamists. Even if Rogers was dead and Ben then married Deborah in church, he would be liable for Rogers' debts. So it was that guilt and potential legal obstacles ushered the Franklins into a common-law marriage. While unconventional, their marriage was accepted by friends and family.

In retrospect Ben wrote that Deborah proved "a good and faithful Helpmate, assisted me much by attending the Shop, we throve together and have ever mutually endavour'd to make each other happy."[11] According to his Autobiography, the marriage was a purely joyous union. Perhaps initially, it was. Soon after moving in, Deborah took over his stationary shop, added groceries and household items and transformed it into a profitable enterprise. Six weeks later Ben promoted his expectations about wedded life in a November 19, 1730 essay entitled "Rules and Maxims for Promoting Marital Happiness" in the *Pennsylvania Gazette*. Primarily directed to women, whom he believed were "better disposed to receive and practice" his advice than men, Ben urged the

9. Ibid, 129.
10. Ibid.
11. Ibid.

reader to be faithful, agreeable, cheerful and "take care ... not to overlook the word *obey*."[12]

The first test for those expectations happened the following March when Ben arrived home with a bundle covered in blankets. Within it gurgled his infant son, William, or Billy, the result of his cohabitation with another woman. Deborah was shocked—and hurt. She had already been betrayed by her first husband: now her second one had dealt her a humiliating blow.

Initially she balked, but finally agreed to care for the child because she loved Ben. Who was the mother and why couldn't she raise the child herself? Those questions have perplexed historians for two centuries. According to Franklin scholar J. A. Leo Lemay the mother may have been the wife of one of Ben's acquaintances who was away for many months.[13] If Billy's mother was a prostitute, Ben would not have claimed the infant as his son. Other historians have suggested that Ben, knowing about the child's imminent birth and needing someone to care for him, consequently married Deborah that September. That made the Franklins' common-law marriage even more unusual: a couple with a bastard son.

Other tensions appeared in the marriage. For all her warm heart, industriousness and thrift, Deborah had a prickly temper. Several contemporary accounts claim that she was quarrelsome; one neighbor even compared her to a "hedgehog" who shot quills at her during an argument over money.[14] Ben was well acquainted with Deborah's willfulness. Three years after his marriage, he amended his expectations for domestic obedience. His "A Scolding Wife" published in the July 5, 1733 *Pennsylvania Gazette* even claimed a wife's strong personality was an advantage. Although her outspoken ways could be an "inconvenience ... women of that character have generally sound and healthy constitutions, produce vigorous offspring are active in the business of the family, special good housewives, and very careful of their husband's interests."[15]

Deborah seemed to exemplify that. On October 20, 1732 she had birthed Francis, or Franky, the Franklin's first child, upon whom they

---

12. Benjamin Franklin, "Rules and Maxims for Promoting Matrimonial Happiness," www.historycarper.com/1730/10/08/rules-and-maxims-for-promoting-matrimonial-happiness/.
13. J. A. Leo Lemay, *The Life of Benjamin Franklin* (Philadelphia: University of Pennsylvania Press, 2006), 2:6.
14. Sara Broughton to Benjamin Franklin, July 3, 1766, Leonard W. Labaree et al. eds, *The Papers of Benjamin Franklin* (New Haven, CT: Yale University Press, 1959 –), 13:329.
15. "A Scolding Wife", July 5, 1733, ibid., 1:325-27.

both doted. By then Philadelphia had been ravaged by smallpox, prompting the scientific-minded Ben to urge residents to be inoculated. In 1736 the disease surfaced again but little Frankly was so sick with dysentery that Ben delayed inoculating him. In November the child contracted smallpox and died a few weeks after his fourth birthday. Ben was plunged into grief. Deborah was so devastated that she displayed the boy's portrait in the house for the rest of her life.

Seven years after Franky's death in 1743 Deborah delivered the Franklin's second child, Sarah, known as Sally. In an era of unreliable contraception most married colonial women delivered eight children on average, as Ben noted in a subsequent essay titled "Observations Concerning the Increase In Mankind."[16] Deborah's inability to produce children for those years thus seems notable. Theories again abound, among them that the Franklins were no longer intimate or happy or that Deborah's duties assisting Ben as saleswoman, bookkeeper, and hostess left little time for childbearing. Possibly Deborah had suffered miscarriages and stillbirths during the eleven years between the births of Franky and Sally.

The theory that the Franklins were neither happy nor intimate seems unlikely given Ben's poem of 1742, "I sing my plain country Joan." Presented during a Masons' meeting, Ben celebrated his wife, "the Joy of my life" for her thrift, dependability and removal of several of his duties. "She could not be a better Wife . . . so I'd stick to my Joggy alone / My dear Friends / I'd cling to my lovely ould Joan."[17]

By then, Ben's achievements were already remarkable. Among them was establishment of the successful B. Franklin printing house, the *Pennsylvania Gazette, Poor Richard's Almanack*, an intercolonial publishing empire, an appointment as clerk of the Pennsylvania Assembly, and the postmastership of Pennsylvania. In addition were Ben's civic improvements: a lending library, fire company, the American Philosophical Society, sidewalks, streetlights, and an academy of higher learning. Deborah, too, worked hard, running the store, collecting rags for paper for Ben's print shop, assisting in the post office, keeping accounts, hosting relatives, nursing the sick, and raising Billy, Franky and Sally.

By the late 1740s Ben was wealthy enough to retire but in 1753 the Crown appointed him the co-deputy postmaster general of North America. Deborah, in contrast to wives of other affluent men, kept working by assisting Ben in the intercolonial post office. She became

---

16. "Observations Concerning the Increase in Mankind, 1751," ibid., 3:255.
17. "I Sing My Plain Country Joan," 1742, ibid., 2:352-54.

Left, Portrait of Benjamin Franklin by Mason Chamberlain, 1762 (*Philadelphia Museum of Art*); portrait of Deborah Read, right, attributed to Benjamin Wilson, c. 1759 (*American Philosophical Society Library and Museum*).

so skilled that later when her husband was training his replacement William Dunlap, he insisted "I depend on your paying considerable attention to her advice" since she had "a great deal of experience" running it.[18]

Another unusual feature of their marriage was Ben's electrical experiments. During his early efforts he borrowed some of Deborah's household products, among them a salt cellar, a vinegar cruet, a cake of wax, and a pump handle. After his famous kite experiment, he placed an experimental lightning rod on the roof of the Franklin home. Despite its success he continued experimenting by rigging the rod to a wire inside the house attached to bells which rang when electricity gathered in passing clouds. For years Ben retained the bells in the house creating shrill ringing which gave Deborah headaches.

Another even more serious headache was the legal status of Pennsylvania which, unlike most other American colonies owned by the Crown, was a proprietorship whose heirs had inherited it from its founder, William Penn through a 1681 charter from Charles II. For years Penn's heirs had refused to pay taxes on their western lands and when hostilities broke out during the French and Indian War and even threatened Philadelphia, the citizens became alarmed. After the Penns repeatedly rejected pleas to pay taxes, the colony's Assembly elected Ben to settle the disagreement with the heirs in London. Naturally he

18. Benjamin Franklin to William Dunlap, April 4, 1757, ibid., 7:168.

expected Deborah to accompany him but to his surprise, she refused.

Much ink has again been spilled over her decision to remain in Philadelphia. One theory was that Deborah was traumatized by childhood memories of a 1711 voyage with her parents from England. Another held that Deborah, knowing she was a plain, provincial women, felt intimidated by the thought of meeting the urbane scientists, writers and intellectuals Ben would befriend.

Soon after his 1757 arrival in London Ben rented rooms in a townhouse on London's Craven Street owned by the widowed Margaret Stevenson. Her attentions to Ben soon went beyond her role as landlady. When he fell ill Margaret nursed him back to health. Then she outfitted Ben in English clothes, introduced him to friends, and socialized with him so often that others considered them a couple. Soon after he began rooming at Craven Street, Ben's friend, the printer William Strahan, became so concerned that wrote to Deborah.

> For my own part, I never saw a man who was, in every respect, so perfectly agreeable to me... Now madam as I know the ladies here consider him in exactly the same light I do. I think you should come over, with all convenient speed to look after your interest; not but that I think him as faithful to his Joan, as any man breathing, but who knows what repeated and strong temptation, may in time... accomplish.[19]

Strahan then became more blunt:

> I cannot take leave of you without informing you that Mr. F. has the good fortune to lodge with a very discreet good gentlewoman, who is particularly careful of him, who attended him during a very severe cold ... with an assiduity, concern, and tenderness, which perhaps only yourself could equal."[20]

Still Deborah refused. Only gradually did Ben mention Margaret by name in his letters rather than merely as his landlady. He finally did so while sending Deborah gifts—fine china, salt ladles, candle snuffers, upholstery fabrics, yards of blue cotton and fancy flowered "tissue" for a formal gown. The last of these, Ben gingerly explained, was a favorite of "Mrs. Stevenson," who sent her "compliments" to Deborah.[21]

Deborah in turn sent her husband apples, buckwheat, cranberries and nuts to remind him of home. Although her letters from this period are lost, Ben's replies indicate she sent similarly polite replies to Margaret and her young adult daughter, Polly.

---

19. William Strahan to Deborah Franklin, December 13, 1757, ibid., 7:29.
20. Ibid.
21. Benjamin Franklin to Deborah Franklin, February 19, 1758, ibid., 7:379.

To Deborah's distress, Ben's journey turned into five years during which little was settled with the Penns. While his letters to Deborah always began with "My dear child" (the eighteenth century equivalent of "sweetheart?") and often concluded with "Your loving husband," they became less frequent. In contrast she wrote regularly, often rushing to meet the next departure of the packet boats. Increasingly Ben became attached to Margaret and her intellectually curious daughter Polly, to whom he wrote more affectionately than to his own daughter, Sally.

How much Deborah understood about Ben's relationship with Margaret is unclear. By 1760 she may have suspected something, for one of her letters apparently questioned rumors that arrived from London. In response, Ben chastised his wife for believing "idle reports concerning me. Be satisfied, my dear ... I shall do nothing unworthy the character of an honest man, and one that loves his family."[22] No less disturbing were Ben's promises to return to Philadelphia that were invariably postponed. Was this, then, an eighteenth century version of a legal separation—one begun amiably enough but sealed by the formation of new personal attachments?

When Ben finally returned to Philadelphia in November 1763 Deborah was ecstatic and assumed he was home to stay. Not Ben, however, who wrote to Strahan, other friends and even Polly about wanting to return to England. Added to his restlessness were messages from Margaret, to whom Ben sent presents and letters of which he suspiciously did not keep copies in his letter book. One of Margaret's letters invited Ben to return to England and bring his "better half and dear girlie" with him.[23] Margaret's comment captures the cordial, if paradoxical, relationship she maintained with Ben.

Within the first few weeks of Ben's return home, Deborah unhappily discovered he wanted to return to London. To placate her, Ben promised to build them a new house. Located on Market Street between Third and Fourth, the new three-story brick home seemed proof of Ben's permanence in Philadelphia. According to his son Billy, the plans momentarily ended his parents' quarrels. "My mother is so entirely averse to going to sea, that I believe my father never be induced to see England again. He is now building a house," he reported to Strahan.[24]

Still, Ben intended to return to England. "It is however impossible for me to execute the resolution this ensuing summer, having many af-

---

22. Benjamin Franklin to Deborah Franklin, June 17, 1760, ibid., 9:173.
23. Margaret Stevenson to Benjamin Franklin, March [1763?], ibid., 10:427.
24. Charles Henry Hart, ed. *Letters from William Franklin to William Strahan* (Philadelphia: J. B. Lippincott, 1911), 14.

fairs to arrange, but I trust I shall see you before you look much older," he assured Strahan."[25] One of those "many affairs" was Ben's duties as the co-deputy postmaster general of North America. In April, after five months at home, he traveled to Virginia to meet his co-deputy postmaster partner, John Foxcroft, and to initiate postal reforms. Once home, he asked Deborah to accompany him on a northern postal tour, possibly to "train" her to the idea of future travel. But again Deborah refused. For all her spirit, she was reluctant to leave Philadelphia. There she felt most comfortable, the place where she was surrounded by family and friends and where, as a businesswoman, assistant postmistress and Ben's representative, she was admired as a prominent woman.

Another symbol of Ben's promised permanence in Philadelphia was his election to the Assembly and subsequent role as Speaker. In that role, he renewed his earlier idea of removing the Penns and converting Pennsylvania into a Crown colony. That, in turn, sparked hostility from those loyal to the Penns as well as Germans and Scot-Irish settlers whom he had critiqued for their hostility to the native Americans. Political cartoons, newspaper notices, and handbills soon appeared, portraying Ben as a lecherous, corrupt figure who had duped the public through diplomatic chicanery while living luxuriously as Pennsylvania's colonial agent in England.

Damaging too were attacks upon his marriage. The pamphlet *What Is Sauce for the Goose Is Sauce for the Gander* accused Ben of having exploited Billy's mother as a "most valuable slave" for the "foster mother of his latest offspring who did his dirty work."[26] That "foster mother" was Deborah, and her "dirty work" was her duties to Ben as his devoted wife. The pamphlet also accused Ben of having "piously withheld" from the mother the means to survive and had starved her to death."[27]

To those scurrilous insults, neither Deborah nor Ben publicly responded. Still, they cut deep. Even deeper was Ben's defeat for re-election. Nevertheless, with peace still threatened on Pennsylvania's frontier and the Penns' continued refusal to pay taxes for defense, Ben's allies in the Assembly again elected him their overseas agent. Once again Ben asked Deborah to join him in England. And once again she refused. An argument followed after which Ben demanded that Deborah write him only cheerful letters. If she would not travel to England with him, she had no right to complain.

25. Benjamin Franklin to William Strahan, March 28, 1763, *The Papers of Benjamin Franklin*, 10:23.
26. Claude-Anne Lopez and Eugenia W. Herbert, *The Private Franklin: The Man and His Family*, (New York: W.W. Norton, 1975), 120.
27. Ibid.

After his 1764 return to England, Ben resumed living with Margaret at her Craven Street townhouse. As earlier, he wrote Deborah occasionally and sent on more English presents. In contrast Deborah's correspondence (which was preserved) reveal a dutiful wife who kept Ben informed about local news, managed his business affairs, sent him requested goods and rarely complained. Deborah also supervised completion of their unfinished house—a highly unusual task for a colonial woman.

Once again she mentioned worrisome rumors from abroad. In reply, Ben wrote "Let no one make you uneasy with their idle or malicious stories or scribblings, but enjoy yourself and friends and the comforts of life that God has bestowed on you, with a cheerful heart."[28] Was he referring to political rumors about his efforts to petition the Crown—or to talk stirred by his renewed relationship with Margaret? To console Deborah he added, "A few months, I hope, will finish affairs here ... and bring me to retirement and repose with my little family, so suitable to my years, and which I have so long set my heart upon."[29]

Deborah, in turn, assured Ben she was avoiding any behavior that might provoke his enemies. The day of her letter, she wrote that neighbors had invited her to attend an ox roast on the river, but she had declined. "I have never said or done anything or any of our family, you may depend on it ... I partake of none of the diversions. I stay at home and flatter myself that the next packet will bring me a letter from you."[30]

Instead of socializing with others, Ben's wife focused upon completing details of their new house. "This day the man is putting up the fireplaces that came from London. The plasterer is finishing the lathing of the staircases and I am getting the lower part of the house cleaned out ready for the laying of the kitchen floor."[31] Even so, she felt insecure making decisions traditionally left to husbands. "O my child [as she also addressed Ben], there is a great odds between a man's being at home and abroad as everybody is afraid they shall do wrong so everything is left undone."[32]

Despite her lament, Deborah sensed that if the house was ever to be completed, she would have to do it. With the independence that became a necessity she purchased the empty lot next to the house, to

28. Benjamin Franklin to Deborah Franklin, February 14, 1765, *The Papers of Benjamin Franklin*, 12:62.
29. Ibid.
30. Deborah Franklin to Benjamin Franklin, February 10, 1765, ibid., 12:43.
31. Ibid.
32. Deborah Franklin to Benjamin Franklin, October 6-13, 1765, ibid., 12:292.

create what was called Franklin Court. Despite the steep price of nine hundred pounds, Ben agreed it was a sensible decision. "I am very glad you do approve of my purchase and when it will please God to restore you to your [own] house I think you will be very much pleased" she replied.[33]

The following September as colonial opposition to British tyranny rose, Ben's enemies in Philadelphia accused him of supporting the Stamp Act. On Wednesday the 16th an angry mob began forming and was heading to Franklin Court with the intent of demolishing it. Deborah soon sent for a cousin who was joined by her brother carrying a gun. "We made one room into a magazine. I ordered some sort of defense upstairs such as I could manage myself," she wrote Ben nine days later.[34] Throughout that night she stood watch with a gun, determined to defend her husband's innocence. "I was very sure you had done nothing to hurt anybody nor would I stir or show the least uneasiness, but if anyone came to disturb me I would show a proper resentment."[35] By morning eight hundred Franklin supporters had gathered and threatened the mob which soon disbanded.

Nor was that the last of Deborah's new independent spirit. By late 1767 the Franklins' daughter Sally fell in love with Richard Bache, an impoverished English merchant, and wanted to marry him. Observing her daughter's determination Deborah allowed the courtship, but Ben, horrified by the thought of his daughter marrying a debtor, opposed the marriage. After months of uncertainty, Deborah agreed to Sally's wedding on October 29 but did not mention it to Ben. After learning about it, his letters stopped for weeks. So it was that the already unconventional Franklin marriage now included a debtor son-in law.

As she did every autumn Deborah shipped new crates of local produce to London. On February 13 Ben thanked her for them but untactfully added, "I forget to tell you that a certain very great lady, the best woman in England, was graciously pleased to accept some of your nuts and to say they were excellent."[36] A "very great lady?" The "best woman in England?" Any wife reading that would cringe at those words. Perhaps Deborah did, but she seems to have stoically accepted his admiration for Margaret as the inevitable consequence of her refusals to join him in England.

Over the next six months Ben conveyed his love to Sally but never mentioned her husband. Finally in August 1768 he sent a conciliatory

---

33. Deborah Franklin to Benjamin Franklin, August 1765, ibid., 12:250.
34. Deborah Franklin to Benjamin Franklin, September 22, 1465, ibid., 12:270.
35. Ibid.
36. Benjamin Franklin to Deborah Franklin, February 13, 1768, ibid., 15:45.

letter to Richard, relieving Deborah's worries. Several months later she rejoiced again when Sally became pregnant but that winter Deborah collapsed from a stroke. On June 3 after learning she was better, Ben congratulated her on healing from "your late indisposition."[37]

Four days later Philadelphia's prominent Dr. Thomas Bond warned Ben that Deborah's health was fragile. "Your good Mrs. Franklin was affected . . . with a partial palsy in the tongue and a sudden loss of memory, but she soon recovered . . . though her constitution in general appears impaired. These are bad symptoms in advanced life and auger further injury on the nervous system."[38] Anxiously, Ben relayed that information to Dr. John Pringle, physician to the queen, then sent Deborah his advice.

Simultaneously the relentless series of tyrannical acts the British had imposed upon the colonies—The Sugar Act, the Stamp Act the Townshend Duties—had enraged colonists who wrote petitions and held boycotts and protests. In London, Ben, whose role as agent for Pennsylvania now included other colonies, worked diplomatically to win support from sympathetic members of Parliament. Despite Deborah's waning health his return to Philadelphia in that tense political climate thus seemed unfeasible.

Even so, Deborah's one repeated wish was Ben's return. "When will it be in your power to come home? How I long to see you, "she wrote. Then mindful of the gravity of his political duties, she backed off, assuring him, "I would not say one word that would give you one moment's trouble."[39]

The long years of separation had taught Deborah to expect little more from her husband than sympathetic letters. Political duties had always come before personal ones. Now since Ben's travels to England, his attachments were divided between Craven Street and Philadelphia. A muted competition for his loyalties ensued, becoming especially obvious in 1771 when Polly, who had wed a year earlier, delivered her first son. Deborah's letters had continually praised Sally's first child, Benny, whom she dubbed "kingbird." Typically they contained messages like "This morning would [have] afforded you much pleasure with my kingbird . . . as soon as he ate his breakfast he said he would go to school."[40]

By early 1773 Ben matched Deborah's praise with reports about Polly's first son. "In return for our history of your grandson, I must give

37. Benjamin Franklin to Deborah Franklin, June 3, 1769, ibid., 16:144.
38. Thomas Bond to Benjamin Franklin, June 7, 1769, ibid., 16:152.
39. Deborah Franklin to Benjamin Franklin, August 16, 1770, ibid., 17:205.
40. Deborah Franklin to Benjamin Franklin, June 10, 1772, ibid.,19:130.

you a little of the history of my godson. He is now 21 months old, very strong and healthy, begins to speak a little and even to sing. He ... grew fond of me, and would not be contented to sit down to breakfast without coming to call, *Pa*, rejoicing when he had got me into my place." Then, fearing he sounded too fond, he added, "It makes me long to be at home to play with Benny."[41]

Soon after that note, Ben was swept into an ugly political intrigue. That spring he sent copies of six letters to Thomas Cushing, Speaker of the Massachusetts House, insisting on confidentiality. Written by Governor Thomas Hutchinson and colonial secretary, Andrew Oliver, to Thomas Whately, commissioner of the royal Board of Trade, the letters disguised the governor's role provoking British hostilities in Massachusetts. Simultaneously, Hutchinson feigned sympathy for his constituents and escaped blame for the subsequent protests in Boston.

The so-called Whately letters, as Ben had warned the Speaker, must be shared with only a few political leaders. Nevertheless, Cushing and the Adamses leaked them to the newspapers, inciting riots, the burning of Hutchinson and Oliver effigies on Boston Common, and protests in other colonies. Once reports of the upheavals reached London, Ben was blamed as an "incendiary" and "the papers ... filled with invectives against me."[42]

In early January 1774 he was summoned to the "Cockpit," an octagonal inner room of the Privy Council once favored by Henry VIII for cock fights. On the 29th Ben stood calmly on the stand before a hostile audience of courtiers, Members of Parliament, dignitaries, and others who came and "seemed to enjoy highly the entertainment, and frequently burst out in loud applauses" when the caustic Solicitor General Alexander Wedderburn accuse him of inciting colonial hostility.[43] The next day Franklin was dismissed from his royal appointment as deputy general postmaster of North America.

After that Ben became a fervent supporter for American independence. Although publicly humiliated, rarely seen in public, and knowing he could best serve the colonies by returning home, Ben remained in England where he penned treatises in defense of the colonies. To Deborah, he again hedged about returning to Philadelphia. "I hoped to have been on the sea in my return by this time, but find I must stay a few weeks longer, perhaps for the summer ships. Thanks to God I con-

---

41. Benjamin Franklin to Deborah Franklin, February 2, 1773, ibid., 20:34.
42. Benjamin Franklin to Thomas Cushing, February 15 [19], 1774, ibid., 21:86.
43. Ibid.

tinue well and hearty and hope to find you so when I have the happiness once more of seeing you," he wrote that April.[44]

A week later, tragedy struck the Stevensons. "Our family here is in great distress. Poor Mrs. Hewson [Polly] has lost her husband and Mrs. Stevenson, her son-in-law. He died last Sunday morning of a fever.... She is left with two young children and a third soon expected.... All their schemes of life are now overthrown!" Ben lamented to Deborah on May 5.[45]

Two days later he realized Deborah had not written in months. "It is now a very long time indeed since I have had the pleasure of a line from you. I hope, however, that you are well as I am."[46] Ten weeks later he nervously penned, "I have had no line from you. I flatter myself it is owning not to indisposition but to the opinion of my having left England, which indeed I hope soon to do."[47] Still Ben remained in London.

By September Deborah's long silence alarmed him. "It is now nine long months since I received a letter from my dear Debby. I have supposed it owing to your continual expectation of my return. I have feared that some indisposition had rendered you unable to write. I have imagined anything rather than admit ... your kind attention towards me was abated.... you who used to be so diligent and faithful a correspondent."[48]

Ten years had passed since Deborah had seen Ben. On December 14, 1774 the sixty-six-year-old suffered another stroke. On Christmas Eve Billy wrote to Ben, "I came here on Thursday last to attend the funeral of my poor old mother who died the Monday noon ... She told me ... that she never expected to see you unless you returned this winter, for she was sure she would not live till next summer. I heartily wish you had happened to come over in the fall, as I think the disappointment in that respect, preyed a good deal on her spirits."[49]

So it was that the Franklin's marriage ended as abruptly and unconventionally as it had begun.

---

44. Benjamin Franklin to Deborah Franklin, April 28, 1774, ibid., 21:205.
45. Benjamin Franklin to Deborah Franklin, May 5, 1774, ibid., 21:208.
46. Benjamin Franklin to Deborah Franklin, May 7, 1774, ibid., 21:210.
47. Benjamin Franklin to Deborah Franklin, July 22, 1774, ibid., 21:246.
48. Benjamin Franklin to Deborah Franklin, September, 10, 1774, ibid., 21:303.
49. William Franklin to Benjamin Franklin, December 24, 1774, ibid., 21:402.

Governor William Franklin: "Sagorighweyoghsta" (Great Arbiter or Doer of Justice)

JOSEPH E. WROBLEWSKI

William Franklin, son of Benjamin Franklin, was the last Royal Governor of New Jersey, from 1763 to 1776. He is usually identified in U. S. History texts negatively as an ardent Loyalist and opponent of the American War of Independence. Historian Larry Gerlach offers a different view: "He was one of the most popular and successful of all royal governors, effectively representing both the crown and the people of New Jersey from 1763 to 1776."[1] One area of his administration that is overlooked is his actions in 1766 seeing that justice was afforded to Native Americans in New Jersey.

William Franklin took office after the French and Indian War and during Pontiac's Rebellion. Those events stirred up increased hatred for Native Americans throughout the Colonies and led to several atrocities directed towards them regardless of whether they had participated in attacks on settlers or they were non-belligerents. These acts of violence took place with disregard to the overall policy of the British Government to treat the Native American population with equanimity.

In 1766 two crimes were perpetrated against Native Americans in New Jersey that reflected this hatred: the murder in northwestern New Jersey (Sussex County) of a visiting member of the Oneida tribe; then the murder of two Lenni Lenape women who lived in Burlington County. In both cases, Governor Franklin, as the representative and chief law enforcement officer of the Crown, oversaw the capture, trial, and execution of the murderers. One result of his actions in these inci-

---

1. Larry R. Gerlach, "William Franklin: New Jersey's Last Royal Governor," *New Jersey's Revolutionary Experience*, no. 13 (Trenton: NJ Historical Commission, 1975), 5.

dents occurred at the 1768 signing of a treaty with Native Americans at Ft. Stanwyck, New York when an Oneida chief bestowed upon William Franklin the honorific "Sagorighweyoghsta" (Great Arbiter or Doer of Justice).[2]

William Franklin, born in Philadelphia in 1730, began life with a handicap: he was referred to as Benjamin Franklin's "illegitimate son" and it was to be used as a slur on his character throughout his life and political career.[3] Deborah Read, Franklin's common-law wife, raised William; she also had two children by Benjamin: son Francis Folger, born in 1732 but died of smallpox in 1736, and daughter Sarah (known as Sally) born in 1743.

Starting in 1750, Benjamin and William both agreed William would study law. He was apprenticed to a noted Philadelphia lawyer Joseph Galloway and Benjamin went so far as to secure William a future place at the Inns of Court in London where British lawyers studied to hone their skills.[4] At this time, Benjamin Franklin's political career was in its ascendancy, plus his reputation as a scientist and philosopher was also enhanced. It seems William was happy to benefit from the success of his father, accepting several positions with the colonial government through Benjamin's influence. It was during this period that William fell in love with Elizabeth Graeme, the daughter of Dr. Thomas Graeme, and they planned to marry.[5] The relationship was opposed by her parents but this did not deter the young couple's plans. The relationship, however, came to an end when William accompanied his father to England in 1757.

Benjamin Franklin had been sent to England as a representative of the Pennsylvania Assembly opposing the Proprietary rule of the Penn Family. After William completed his legal studies, both Franklins pro-

---

2. "Ratified treaty # 7: Treaty of Fort Stanwix, or The Grant from the Six Nations to the King and Agreement of Boundary — Six Nations, Shawnee, Delaware, Mingoes of Ohio, 1768," Edward O'Callaghan, ed., *Documents Relative to the Colonial History of the State of New York*, vol. 8. (Albany, NY: Weed, Parsons, and Co.,1857), 132.

3. For discussions on who his mother was and the effects of his illegitimacy see: Sheila L. Skemp, "William Franklin: His Father's Son," *The Pennsylvania Magazine of History and Biography* 109 no. 2 (1985), 145-78; Charles Henry Hart, "Who Was the Mother of Franklin's Son. An Inquiry Demonstrating That She Was Deborah Read, Wife of Benjamin Franklin," *The Pennsylvania Magazine of History and Biography*, vol. 35 no. 3 (1911): 308-14.

4. Gerlach, "William Franklin: New Jersey's Last Royal Governor," 11. Franklin was admitted to the Bar of the Middle Temple, November 1758.

5. Elizabeth Graeme was a noted American poet. For a brief review of this amazing woman's life see: History of American Women—Colonial Women, www.womenhistoryblog.com/2009/01/elizabeth-graeme-fergusson.html.

ceeded to tour throughout the British Isles, meeting with some of the most influential men both in and out of the government. Evidence suggests that William didn't devote all his time to his duties as personal secretary to his father; in 1760, an "unknown woman" presented him with a son, William Temple. Then in 1762 momentous changes occurred: Benjamin returned to America in August, William married Elizabeth Downes on September 4, and on September 9 he was named governor of New Jersey.[6]

When William Franklin arrived in New Jersey in 1763, unlike neighboring colonies, it had not been affected by hostile Native American actions in Pontiac's Rebellion. While the intense fighting between English settlers and the Native Peoples occurred mainly in Trans-Appalachia (Ohio Country), it ingrained in many Anglos an intense hatred of all Indians. Historian Clinton Weslager notes:

> Many friends or relatives of persons who had been massacred or taken into captivity by Indian war parties - particularly those who saw the mutilated bodies of loved ones lying in the smoldering ashes of burned homes - became "Indian haters" and sought reprisal. They called Indians "dogs" and "thieves" and cursed them to their faces.[7]

An example of this attitude toward all Native Americans was manifested in the actions of a group of Pennsylvanians who became known as the "Paxton Boys." They murdered a group of Native Americans referred to as "Praying Indians" near Lancaster, Pennsylvania in 1763.[8]

The first murder of a Native American during Franklin's time in office occurred in April 1766. Governor Franklin described the murder in a Proclamation:

> Whereas I have received Information from one of the principal Officers of the County of Sussex, that a most inhuman Murder and Robbery has been lately committed near Minisink, on the Body and Effects of an Indian of the Oneida nation, who had come there to trade, and had behaved himself soberly and discreetly; and that one Robert Simonds, alias Seamonds, had been charged with the same was on the

---

6. Elizabeth was the daughter of a wealthy Barbados sugar planter.
7. Clinton A. Weslager, *The Delaware Indians: A History* (New Brunswick, NJ: Rutgers University Press, 1972), 247.
8. For an excellent review of the role of the Paxton Boys, see Alden T. Vaughan, "Frontier Banditti and the Indians: The Paxton Boys' Legacy, 1763-1775," *Pennsylvania History: A Journal of Mid-Atlantic Studies* 51 no. 1 (1984): 1–29.

second day of April Instant committed to the common Goal of the County aforesaid.[9]

The Oneida were part of the original Five Nations of the Iroquois Confederacy—Mohawk, Oneida, Onondagas, Cayuga, and Seneca (in 1722 a sixth was added, Tuscarora)—that controlled much of what became New York state and the Great Lakes region. Throughout the colonial wars between the French and English, the Iroquois, for the most part, remained, neutral. During the French and Indian War (1754-1763), under the influence of Sir William Johnson, the British Indian Agent in the north who had been adopted by the Mohawks, the Mohawk and Oneida took active parts in the war on the side of the English. The killing of a friendly Oneida caused consternation to those who wished to continue friendly relations with the Iroquois.[10]

Two men, Robert Seymour and David Ray, were suspected of the murder. Seymour was described as a "base Vagabond fellow" who had deserted from the British Army.[11] He was arrested for the crime and taken to the Sussex County Jail located in the county seat, Sussex Courthouse (today Newton, New Jersey). Locals in Sussex broke him out of jail and he was hidden by his neighbors who threatened harm to anyone who tried to turn him in to the authorities. This reaction by residents eventually emboldened Seymour to come out of hiding and resume his normal life as a farmer.[12] To help bring Seymour to justice, Governor Franklin stated:

> I do promise, that the Person or Persons who shall after the Date hereof, who shall apprehend the said Robert Simmonds alias Seamons or any Person guilty of the Murder and Robbery aforesaid, shall, upon conviction of the Offender, receive from the Treasury of this Province, ONE HUNDRED DOLLARS Reward.[13]

---

9. "Extracts from American Newspapers to New Jersey," vol. VI, 1766-1767, in *Documents Relating to the Colonial History of the State of New Jersey*, vol, XXV, First Series, William Nelson, ed., (Paterson, NJ; The Call Printing & Publishing Co., 1903), 91-93.
10. For an excellent overview of the history of the Iroquois see Paul A. Wallace, "The Iroquois: A Brief Outline History," *Pennsylvania History*, Vol. 23, no. 1 (January 1956), 14 - 28.
11. Alden T. Vaughan, "Frontier Banditti," 15. Governor Franklin referred to him as Simonds or Seamons; in a number of present-day histories he is known as Robert Seymour. The governor did not mention the second person believed to be involved in the murder, David Ray.
12. Ibid., 15.
13. "Extracts from American Newspapers," 94. No mention if anyone ever received the reward.

Answering the order to rearrest Seymour, the Sheriff replied that it was useless to do so because no Sussex County jury would convict him. Franklin then ordered the Sheriff of neighboring Morris County to arrest Seymour and asked the Provincial Legislature to change the venue of the trial, which they refused. As a result, the Sussex magistrates refused to call a special court into session; instead they would wait the five months until the Provincial Circuit Court came there. Being rebuffed by local authorities, Franklin appointed a Court of Oyer and Terminer under Charles Read,[14] who held the trial in Sussex County and invited Native American observers.[15]

Although the murder occurred in April it wasn't until December 18, 1766, that a grand jury indicted Seymour on the charge of murder and David Ray for manslaughter. Ray decided to ask for the "benefit of clergy" and pled guilty. His punishment was to be branded on the hand and then released.[16] As for Seymour, despite witnesses attesting that he admitted his crime and declared "he would destroy any Indian that came in his way," he wanted his case to go to trial.[17] A description of Seymour's actions, given at the trial, was quite vivid:

> The evidence against him was—His Behavior to the Indian before they went together from the House, his being possessed of the Indian's Gun and Goods, Proof that he broke the back and Legs of the dead Body, and buried it, that he confessed the Murder to some Witnesses and declared he would destroy any Indian that came in his Way. He challeng'd several of the Jury, denied the Fact, and said he bought the Goods found on him, of a Sailor.[18]

---

14. Charles Read was the secretary for the governor and the legislature; also, he was a judge on the Provincial Supreme Court. For a brief biography of this influential individual, see: J. Granville Leach, "Colonel Charles Read," *The Pennsylvania Magazine of History and Biography*, Vol. 17, No. 2 (1893), 190-194.

15. The Court of Oyer and Terminer functioned as the court of general jurisdiction in serious criminal cases—i.e., those which required an indictment or presentment for the Crown to proceed. See: George C. Thomas III, "Colonial Criminal Law and Procedure: The Royal Colony of New Jersey 1749-57," *NYU Journal of Law and Liberty*, vol. 1, no. 2 (2005), 672.

16. Asking for the "benefit of clergy" was part of British Common Law that allowed a first-time defendant to be spared execution for a capital crime. Also, in Colonial British America, a person convicted of manslaughter who was spared execution was branded with the letter M. See: *Benefit of Clergy*, www.u-s-history.com/pages/h1250.html.

17. "Extracts from American Newspapers," 92-93. In all the newspaper accounts and histories of this event, the murdered individual's name was never given, he was only identified as an "Oneida."

18. "Extracts from American Newspapers," 271.

Seymour was found guilty but he believed that he would be freed again like he was when he was originally arrested. Governor Franklin, anticipating this possibility, ordered twenty-five militiamen to guard the prisoner night and day. A newspaper account described Seymour's last hours:

> The next Morning he was brought to the bar, and sentenced to be executed between three and four that Afternoon, at which time he was brought out, strongly guarded by Detachments from adjacent Companies of Militia—He appeared dismayed—at the Gallows, made a short Prayer, declared that he lived a very wicked Life, and was Guilty of the Fact for which he was to suffer: He was then executed.[19]

Of the Oneida observer at the trial, the Governor stated:

> An Indian of Note, of the Oneida Nation, had with some Difficulty been prevail'd upon to attend the Trial, from the first to last—he was respectfully treated, and appeared highly satisfied with the Justice of the Proceeding, which he said should represent to his Brethern.[20]

The next murder of Native Americans in New Jersey took place in June 1766 in Burlington County. As troubling as the murder of a visiting Oneida trader in Sussex County was, the murder of two local Lenni Lenape women was viewed as even more heinous.

The native people who originally lived in what was to become New Jersey were the Lenni Lenape ("true men" or "original people"); they were also known as the "Delaware," a name given to them by English settlers.[21] The Lenape were an Algonquin-speaking people who lived in what is today southern New York, through eastern Pennsylvania, all of New Jersey and Delaware, south to Maryland's Eastern Shore. The Lenape were not a single tribe under one chief; rather they were three distinct groups who spoke different dialects: the Munsee in the North, Unami in the Central Region, and the South, Unalactgio. Overriding these dialect groups were three matrilineal clans that were found in all of the regions: Turtle, Wolf, and Turkey, with the Turtle Clan having the most influence. It has been estimated that pre-European settlement

---

19. Ibid., 272.
20. Ibid.
21. The Delaware River was called by the Native Americans *Wihittuck*; in 1610 Samuel Argall, on an exploring expedition, named the bay and river after the then governor of Virginia, Thomas West, Lord De La Warre. Today tribal groups in various states refer to themselves as "Delaware Nation."

there were about 20,000 Lenni Lenape.[22] Through decimation from inter-tribal warfare (with the Susquehannock and the Iroquois Confederation), followed by the introduction of European diseases, mainly small-pox, by the start of the eighteenth century they numbered about 4,000.[23]

As European settlement encroached on Lenape land in New Jersey many began to move west to the Pennsylvania area between the Delaware and Susquehanna Rivers. Others moved farther west to the Ohio Valley area joining the Miami Confederation. Throughout this migration period, the Lenape continued to cede more and more land in New Jersey to the Europeans so that by 1750 no more than 200 to 300 Lenni Lenape in New Jersey remained living in a tribal group setting, or on their farms or near towns, usually having friendly relations with their European neighbors. As Clinton Weslager described the situation:

> Although there had been a series of movements of New Jersey Indians across the Delaware river—to settle in the Forks at Easton, Pennsylvania, to affiliate with the Moravians at (the first) Gnadenhutten, and later to join other migrants at Shamokin and Wyoming—a small group of Delawares clung tenaciously to their New Jersey homes. They no longer resided in villages but were scattered in rural areas, a few families had their own cornfields and vegetable patches. Perhaps they owned a horse or a few pigs, and some raised chickens. They fished and crabbed in season, some made splint baskets, brooms, cornhusk mats, and wooden bowls, and peddled them from door to door.[24]

Sadly, these benign relations took a turn for the worse with the coming of the French and Indian War.

In 1755 some of the Lenape who emigrated from New Jersey sided with the French and began attacking settlements in northeastern Pennsylvania between the Delaware and Susquehanna Rivers, with a few incursions into northwestern New Jersey. While the majority of European residents in central and southern New Jersey were in no danger from Indian attacks, with continued stories of "Indian massacres" they

---

22. Jean R. Sunderal and Claude Epstein put the pre-European Lenape population at 12,000. "Lenape—Colonial Land Conveyances in West Jersey: Evolving in Space and Time," *New Jersey Studies* (Summer 2018), 186.
23. See: *Native Americans: Lenni Lenape*, Penn Treaty Museum, www.penntreatymuseum.org/americans.php#lenapehistory. The article states from latest census data the number of Lenni Lenape (Delaware) is back to the 20,000 number, with largest concentration in Oklahoma.
24. Weslager, *The Delaware Indians*, 261.

became suspicious of local Lenape. By 1756 the suspicion of the motives of local Lenni Lenape went so far that Gov. Jonathan Belcher joined with Pennsylvania and offered a bounty for the scalps of "hostile Indians."[25] Eventually, with the French prospects for victory over the English in the decline, relations between the Leni Lenape and New Jersey's government were settled with the 1758 Treaty of Easton in which the Lenni Lenape basically ceded all "tribal" land claims in the colony.[26] This led to the purchase of a large tract of land in Burlington County that became the first "Indian Reservation," known as Brotherton.[27]

Moving ahead to June 1766 in relatively peaceful Burlington County, the *New York Journal or Weekly Post Boy* recorded:

> Burlington, in (N. Jersey) July 3, 1766, Two Indian Women were barbarously murdered a few Days ago, at Morristown [*sic*, Moorestown], in this County, by two Scotch-Irish strollers. One of the Murderers, named James Anin, was committed to our Gaol, the Night before last, the other, James M'Kensie, is not yet taken.[28]

The attack and murder occurred on June 26, 1766. The victims were two Lenni Lenape women identified as Catherine and Hannah, "who had long resided in the neighborhood of the place where the murder was committed."[29] The two men identified as "Scotch-Irish strollers" James Anen (aged fifty-four) and James McKinsey (aged nineteen) both had spent time on the Pennsylvania and Virginia frontier regions, an area that experienced a good deal of brutality during the warfare associated with the Pontiac's Rebellion. Supposedly the younger man,

---

25. "Extracts from American Newspapers Relating to New Jersey, Vol. IV 1756-1761," *Documents of Relating to the Colonial History of New Jersey, Vol. XX*, William Nelson, ed., (Patterson, NJ: Call Pub. & Printing, 1898), 39-41. On July 26, Belcher rescinded the bounty on Indian scalps.
26. For what transpired at the Easton Conference see: "The Minutes of a Treaty held at Easton, in Pennsylvania, in October, 1758," *Evans Early American Imprint Collection*, quod.lib.umich.edu/e/evans/N06429.0001.001/1:2.11?rgn=div2;view=fulltext.
27. For an overview of the Brotherton Reservation see: "Passing of the Indians," XVI, *Moorestown and Her Neighbors - West Jersey History Project*, www.westjerseyhistory.org. Today the Brotherton Reservation is known as Indian Mills, Shamong Township, Burlington County.
28. "Extracts from American Newspapers," vol. VI, 160. In the articles dealing with this incident the names of the accused were spelled in various ways; the consensus of the correct spelling was James Anen and James McKinsey. On July 17 a correction was published that the murders took place near Moorestown, not Morristown.
29. "Pennsylvania Gazette, August 7, 1776," *Extracts from American Newspapers*, 184 -185. The description of the events of the murders and the events surrounding them are mainly from this article.

McKinsey, had been the servant of a "Scotch" officer killed at Pittsburgh. Anen and McKinsey had met in Philadelphia and decided to travel to New York together, where McKinsey hoped to meet with the widow of his deceased master.[30] Over the next month, newspaper accounts described what happened next.

The two perpetrators arrived in the Moorestown area where they "begged for charity." While they were eating, the two Lenape women came to the same place. The "youngest of the men gave them abusive language." The women went into nearby woods where they rested; one of them had a "clean shift" and the other a "new piece of linen" they bought that day. They were seen laying near the road and it was supposed they were asleep. Three days later, Sunday, June 29, "two persons perceived the stench, and ongoing near the bodies found that they were dead; whereupon the coroner was called, whose inquest found them to be murdered by persons unknown."[31] Anen and McKinsey became the chief suspects when it was recognized that "Anen sold the shift and McKinsey the piece of linen about two miles from Moorestown" on the last day the women were seen alive. An alarm went out. Anen was apprehended and sent to the Burlington jail; McKinsey fled back to Philadelphia but was soon arrested and returned to Burlington. Each man stated that the other was the one who committed the murders.[32]

They were indicted and a court of Oyer and Terminer was held in Burlington on July 30. In the indictment it was noted that both men stated that they went over to the women "with the intent to ravish them if they refused their offer." Both admitted being present at the murders and taking the women's goods, but each continued to maintain it was the other "giving the stroke." The jury found them both guilty and they were sentenced to death by hanging. The execution took place on Friday, August 1, 1766.

When led to the gallows, the murderers provided more details of their crimes, but each man continued to blame the other. Anen "thought it a duty extirpate the heathen." McKinsey claimed that both women were knocked down by Anen, but "one of the Indians, on receiving the blow from Anen, struggled violently," so McKinsey "to put her out of her pain, sunk the hatchet in her head." A newspaper account added, "The youngest of the squaws was near the time of delivery and had marks of shocking treatment which the most savage nations on

---

30. *Extracts from American Newspapers*, 159.
31. Ibid., 160.
32. Ibid., 165.

earth could not have surpassed." To demonstrate that justice was done, "A few of the principal Indians in Jersey were desired to attend the trial and execution, which they did, and behaved with remarkable sobriety."[33]

The murders of these Native Americans in New Jersey attracted the attention of the British government. The Earl of Shelburne (William Petty) was the Secretary of State for the Southern Department that included the American Colonies. In a letter dated September 13, 1767 to Governor Franklin he wrote "that the most unprovoked violences and Murthers have been lately committed on the Indians, under the Protection of His Majesty, and whose Tribes are at Peace and Amity with His Majesty's Provinces and that the offenders have not yet been discovered and brought to Justice." Further, Shelburne ordered Franklin "that you apply yourself in the most earnest manner to remedy and prevent those Evils, which are as contrary to the Rules of good Policy as of Justice and Equity."[34]

On December 16, 1767, Governor Franklin wrote a reply to Lord Shelburne detailing the actions he took to apply "Justice and Equity" with regards to the murders:

> In answer to your Lordship's Letter of the 13th of September, relative to the Violences & Murthers which have lately committed on the Indians under the Protection of His Majesty, I can assure you Lordship that whatever may be the Case in the other Colonies nothing of the kind has been suffered to pass with Impunity in this Province.... There has been lately two Persons executed here for the Murder of two Indian Squa's, belonging to a small Tribe settled in the interior Parts of the Province, on Lands given them by the Publick.[35]

Franklin went on to describe the background of the perpetrators, noting that they "were not inhabitants of the Colony" and that he "omitted nothing in having the Villains apprehended." He further explained how the murderer of the Oneida in Sussex County was arrested and would be dealt with appropriately.[36]

---

33. Ibid., 183-185.
34. "Shelburne to Franklin, Sept. 13, 1767," *Documents Relating to the Colonial History of the State of New Jersey*, vol. IX, 1757 -1767, Fredrick W. Ricord and William Nelson, editors, (Newark, NJ: Daily Advertiser Printing, 1885), 570. Shelburne mentioned that he received the reports of the murders from "Superintendent of Indian Affairs," who was Sir William Johnson.
35. "Letter from Franklin to Shelburne Dec. 16, 1767," ibid., 575.
36. Ibid.

Governor Franklin continued in this letter to give an overview of how he dealt with Indians in these instances:

> These are only two Affairs of the kind which have happened in this Province during my Administration; & I hope these Instances of Attention and Regard to the Indians will prove an Advantage to the British Interest with them, as well as of Service to those Colonies where they have not met with the same Justice.[37]

He added that of all the colonies New Jersey probably had the least amount of dealings with Indians "as they do not pretend any and Claim to Lands within our Limits, and we have no Trade or Intercourse with them except now & then."[38]

His last words on the subject of the Indian murders were in a letter to Shelburne dated December 23, 1767:

> I have this Moment receiv'd a Letter from Judge Read, whom I sent into the County of Sussex, with a Special Commission of Oyer & Terminer to try one Seamour, the Supposed Murderer' of the Oneida Indian, in which he informs me, That he procured Indians to attend the Trial, and that Seamour was convicted and executed, a Detachment of the Militia attending the Execution to prevent a Rescue.[39]

Franklin summarized his attitude toward Native Americans in New Jersey by ending his Proclamation dealing with the murder of the Oneida with the following admonition:

> And I do likewise in the most earnest Manner recommend it to the Inhabitants of this colony, to behave with Kindness, Humanity, and Justice, to such Indians who shall visit the Frontiers in a friendly Manner, as such a Conduct will have a tendency to perpetuate the Blessings and Advantages of Peace.[40]

Gov. William Franklin's actions in applying justice in these cases of murders of Native Americans in New Jersey have been looked upon by historians as almost unique in the British colonies. Marshall Becker summarizes Franklin's resolution of dealing with the murders:

> The murders seem to have been prompted by greed spurred on by racism, rather than being related to contemporary military activities. That the perpetrators of these deeds were swiftly apprehended, tried

---

37. Ibid, 576.
38. Ibid, 578.
39. Ibid.
40. "Extracts from American Newspapers to New Jersey," 94.

and hanged may reflect the colonial government's commitment to justice for Native American inhabitants of New Jersey.[41]

Further, Alden Vaughan sees that Governor Franklin's actions in bringing justice to Native Americans were different than in the other British Colonies:

> New Jersey's handling of the two murder cases in 1766 demonstrated that not every colonist wanted to exterminate the Indians and that colonial courts on rare occasions administered impartial justice, the baneful shadow of the Paxton Boys did not reach every corner of British America. But New Jersey's record was atypical.[42]

Governor Franklin's actions in seeking and obtaining justice for Native Americans in these two cases justify the title "Sagorighweyoghsta" bestowed upon him by the Oneida.

---

41. Marshall J. Becker, "A New Jersey Haven for Some Accultured Lenape of Pennsylvania During the Indian Wars of the 1760s," *Pennsylvania History: A Journal of Mid-Atlantic Studies*, vol. 60, No. 3 (July 1993), 334.
42. Vaughan, "Frontier Banditti," 17.

One of the "Powers for Good in the World," Mercy Otis Warren

JAMES M. DEITCH

Students of history will no doubt have John Adams, Thomas Jefferson, George Washington, and Benjamin Franklin at the top of their mind when recalling the great leaders of early America and the story of American independence. The thoughtful and considered utility of the words contained within the Declaration of Independence and Constitution cannot be understated. The discourse, debate, word-smithing, and final product have been the subject of much study and discussion amongst historians and academics throughout time. But for those who seek a better understanding of the supporting actors and cast that assisted these great men in arriving at their conclusions and the cohesiveness of their message, we must dig a little deeper. Mercy Otis Warren may be one of the more overlooked influencers of her time. In an era when women were not generally considered to be sources of inspiration to great men and their efforts, Warren contributed not only to considered and educated thought, but also laid the foundation for future discussions on women's rights. At the time, she was often considered a thorn in the leaders' sides, particularly by John Adams. He would express such to his good friend, James Warren, Mercy's husband and a leader in his own right.

Mercy Otis Warren would come to be known as the "Conscience of the American Revolution." Her thoughts and writings were of caution and rebuke to the dangers this young republic might encounter should its leaders pursue independence. Her works as a historian were beautifully and elegantly written, striking the tone of the poetry she was equally known for. Yet within her writings were unmistakable cautions and warnings, and sometimes rebuke of the narrow-mindedness and dangers inherent in the aspiration of man. Her observations were astute, and her musings on the character and nature of key figures of the time are well documented and have been referenced in the historiography of the period by the likes of David McCullough, Benson Bobrick, Gordon S. Wood, and others.

So, who was Mercy Otis Warren? She was born on September 14, 1728 to Col. James Otis and Mary Allyne, a descendent of Edward Doty, a passenger on the Mayflower. She was the fifth of thirteen children. Her influences began early. Her father was a leader in the movement against British rule. Although she had no formal education, not unusual for girls during that time, she was greatly influenced by her brothers and was able to partake in their education by proxy and through the assistance of the Rev. Jonathan Russell, who provided both books and instruction. Her brother James Otis played a key role in her learning and thoughts as well. In 1754 Mercy Otis married James Warren, her second cousin and descendent of another Mayflower passenger, Richard Warren.

It was her husband's prominent role in the patriotic cause that inspired Mercy to write. James Warren did not play prominently in the war itself, although he and Mercy's brother James Otis both fought at Bunker Hill. James Warren would become president of the Massachusetts House of Representatives and later Speaker of the House, and President of the Massachusetts Provincial Congress. He recognized her gifts and encouraged her. When she could not speak her opinions, she committed them to pen and paper. Because of her skill and determination, she befriended and influenced such patriots as George Washington, Thomas Jefferson, Samuel Adams, John Hancock, and Patrick Henry. And despite the fact that she often irritated John Adams she was close with him and his wife Abigail. Adams once quipped in a letter to James Warren to inform his wife that "God Almighty has entrusted her with the Powers for the good of the World, which ... he bestows on few of the human race. That instead of being a fault to use them, it would be criminal to neglect them."[1]

Still, Mercy's persistent edge and resolution confounded the likes of Adams and others. She was impatient for the change she wanted to see in the world and expressed such to her husband regularly, causing him to lament to his friend Adams, the "People can't account for the hesitancy they observe." Mercy would lecture Adams on the ideal republican government and her vision of the future of the colonies and the union of the same. Barely controlling his anger, not with Mercy but with the situation and the lack of recognition of progress being made,

---

1. Ivy Schweitzer, *The Heath Anthology of American Literature*, Fifth edition (Independence, KY: Centage, 2011).

on April 16, 1776, he appealed to Warren, "Have you seen the privateering resolves? Are not those independence enough for my beloved constituents? Have you seen the resolves opening our ports to all nations? Is this independence enough? What more would you have?" Adams was concerned about the consequences of independence and appealed to Mercy Warren, "Patience! Patience! Patience!"[2]

Still, Mercy and her husband held their own reservations about the dangers of a new republic. In fact, the Warrens were among those who adamantly opposed the Constitution. They feared what the document might cause, specifically ambition, speculation, and vice. The cause of independence itself was fraught with problems and Mercy wrote to the Adams cautioning against the "Avidity for pleasure." James Warren complained to those who would listen and in writing that principals had given way to love of money and that "Patriotism is ridiculed. Integrity and ability are of little consequence." John Adams recognized the merit in Warren's concerns and understood the moral shift that was occurring.[3]

David Hume, the noted Scottish philosopher, historian, economist, and essayist, wrote extensively on human nature. Hume considered himself a moralist and believed that all knowledge of anything must be acquired through experience. This is relevant to Mercy's own thought processes. She struggled with the conflict between moral capacity and free will. This was Hume's own conflict, the question of liberty and necessity. Mercy Otis Warren wrote that "Ambition and avarice are the leading springs which generally actuate the restless mind. From these primary sources of corruption have arisen all the rapine and confusion, the depredation and ruin, that have spread distress over the face of the earth from the days of Nimrod to Cesar, and from Cesar to an arbitrary prince of the house of Brunswick."[4]

"It was necessary," she wrote, "to guard at every point, against the intrigues of artful or ambitious men." She believed such men were engaged in a game of deception designed to hide their true motives.[5] Her judgment of the nature and character of men is such that many historians have cited her observations in their biographical accounts. She wrote that Gen. George Washington was "the most amiable and accomplished gentlemen both in person, mind, and manners that I ever

---

2. David McCullough, *John Adams* (New York: Simon & Schuster, 2001), 105-106.
3. Ibid., 398.
4. Gordon S. Wood, *The Idea of America: Reflections on the Birth of the United States* (New York: Penguin Press, 2011), 97-98.
5. Ibid., 105.

met."[6] Although Gen. Arthur Lee was learned and capable as a military officer, she considered him to be unwise and of disagreeable character, "plain in his person even to ugliness," and morose, testy, cynical, and rude.[7] She demonstrated more generosity in her description of Martha Washington, her friend, as "affable, candid, and gentle," ideally suited to provide General Washington a softening of his private life with her ability to "smooth the rugged cares of War."[8]

James Otis and Samuel Adams were known for their boisterous rants and reviling of the British, but it was Mercy's biting wit and gift for satire that often caught the attention of both sides.[9] Robert Harvey described her, along with others including her husband, as the principal radical leaders in Boston.[10] Radical may not be an inappropriate word. Consider that in the opening pages of her monumental work on the history of the American Revolution she wrote that the "indulgence of turbulent passions have depopulated cities, laid waste the finest territories, and turned the beauty and harmony of the lower creation into an Aceldama."[11]

Mercy understood the nature of the human character and despite her cynical descriptor of history as the depository of crimes and a record of everything disgraceful and honorary to mankind, she deferred to the judgment of character as necessary to the complete understanding of history and as a precursor to the judgment of it.[12] Yet her prose is not without intensity and strength. In 1774 she described the American condition as standing with armed resolution and virtue, "but still she recoils at the idea of drawing the sword against the nation from whence she derived her origin." This was not a comment on the restraint of the nation but rather a condemnation of it. She described Britain, as an" unnatural parent, ready to plunge her dagger into the bosom of her affectionate offspring."[13] Later, she hinted that "the sword was half drawn

---

6. Benson Bobrick, *Angel in the Whirlwind: The Triumph of the American Revolution* (New York: Simon & Schuster, 1997), 130.
7. Ibid., 151.
8. Ibid., 394.
9. Harlow Giles Unger, *John Hancock: Merchant King and American Patriot* (New York: John Wiley & Sons, 2000), 85-86.
10. Robert Harvey, *A Few Bloody Noses: The Realities and Mythologies of the American Revolution* (Woodstock: Overlook Press, 2001), 105.
11. Mercy Otis Warren, *History of the Rise, Progress, and Termination of the American Revolution* (Boston: E. Larkin, 1805), 1:1. Aceldama, the fourteenth century Greek term meaning Field of Blood, was potter's field purchased with the money given to Judas for betraying Jesus Christ. Matthew 27:7-8; Acts 1:19.
12. Ibid.
13. Elizabeth F. Ellet, *Women of the American Revolution* (New York: Baker & Scribner, 1849), 1:79.

from the scabbard. Since then, it has been unsheathed ... Almost every tongue is calling on the justice of heaven to punish the disturbers of the peace, liberty, and happiness of their country."[14] Yet she fretted about her words. Abigail Adams encouraged her by reminding her that "satire in the hands of some is a very dangerous weapon; yet when it is so happily blended with benevolence, and is awakened by the love of virtue and abhorrence of vice when truth is unavoidably preserved, and ridiculous and vicious actions are alone subject, it is so far from blamable that it is certainly meritorious."[15]

In her prose, she wrote that "the study of the human character opens at once a beautiful and a deformed picture of the soul. We there find a noble principle implanted in the nature of man, that pants for distinction. This principle operates in every bosom, and when kept under the control of reason, and the influence of humanity, it produces the most benevolent effects."[16] While patriot leaders like Adams, Jefferson, and Washington focused on the business of diplomacy and war, Mercy's gift to historians was focusing on the observation of man, the nature of man, and the counsel to those who benefited from her wisdom. She was apt to keep these gentlemen focused on the seed of their origin which was to escape that which suffered them impositions, restrictions, and penalties, and leave England and later Leyden, not for wealth or fame, but for the quiet enjoyment of religion and liberty.[17] No doubt, she and her husband were rooted in the interests of their ancestors Richard Warren and Edward Doty who had arrived on the shore of Massachusetts aboard the Mayflower. In this respect she provided both anchor and rudder to the ship of liberty.

Mercy Otis Warren died on October 19, 1814 at the age of eighty-six. She is buried at Old Burial Hill in Plymouth, Massachusetts beside her husband, James Warren who preceded her in death in 1808. Her legacy is well earned and her contributions are best held within the pages of her best work on the history of the American Revolution. Her skill lied in her ability to combine the harshness of her ideas with the beauty of her words and the conceptual and contextual manner in which she presented them. Not to be overlooked is the benevolence and love in which she presented her rebuke. It is no doubt easier to reflect on her passion and intensity when one does not need to be the subject of it. Still, for the historian and academic alike, an understand-

14. Ibid., 45.
15. Ibid., 85.
16. Warren, *History*, 1:1.
17. Ibid., 2.

ing of the American Revolution would be incomplete without an understanding of her role. Her demands on those who led this new republic were without the restraint of both expectation and process. She along with her husband reflected the true nature and character of the republic in which they served and her service was with purpose and result. "Her powerful intellect and the sheer force of it provided an ascendancy over the strongest and she supplied political parties with their arguments." But perhaps she might also be known as the first of her sex in America to open the world of politics and history to those who read of such matters.[18]

18. Ibid., 105.

The British Soldiers Who Marched to Concord, April 19, 1775

DON N. HAGIST

During the night of April 18-19, 1775, a force of roughly 700 British soldiers left Boston on a mission to find and destroy rebel military stores in Concord, Massachusetts. What happened on that day is the topic of innumerable books and articles, most of which treat the soldiers as an amorphous mass of men. But they were individual people, each with a distinctive background and subsequent life. Who were they? What were they like, in terms of background, age, and military experience? What became of them?

The information in this article pertains solely to the sergeants, corporals, drummers, fifers and private men who marched on April 19. Their names were recorded on muster rolls, most of which survive in The National Archives of Great Britain.[1] The age, place of birth and other details on some of these men can be found in pension records, and details on a few others come from a host of other primary sources.[2]

The expedition to Concord consisted of eleven grenadier companies and ten light infantry companies detached from British regiments garrisoned in Boston.[3] At full strength, each had two sergeants, three corporals, one drummer and thirty-six private soldiers, and each grenadier company also had two fifers. This means that the most men who could have marched out that day was 42 sergeants, 63 corporals, 21 drummers, 22 fifers, and 756 private soldiers—904 men, not including offi-

---

1. Muster rolls are in the WO 12 collection, The National Archives (TNA), Kew, Richmond, Surrey, UK.
2. Pension records from this era consist primarily of data in: Pension Admission Books, WO 116, TNA; Soldiers' Discharges, WO 97, WO 119 and WO 121, TNA.
3. The grenadier and light infantry companies were detached from the 4th, 5th, 10th, 23rd, 38th, 43rd, 47th, 52nd, and 59th Regiments of Foot, and a battalion of Marines. The grenadier company of the 18th Regiment of Foot also participated.

cers. It is clear that not every single man of each company marched out on April 19. For example, an officer recorded that the 23rd Regiment sent out 29 grenadier and 35 light infantry "rank & file," meaning corporals and private soldiers.[4] Muster rolls survive to tell us the names of the men in most of the companies, but not exactly which ones marched out on April 19.

Using muster rolls as a guide and incorporating information from other sources, it is possible to construct a demographic profile of a large sample of grenadiers and light infantrymen involved in the first conflict of the American Revolution. The information below pertains to the companies as a whole, based on the muster rolls, bearing in mind that some of these men may not have been on the march that day. British army pension records provide most of the details, but only, of course, for those men who received pensions. Comparing these records with muster rolls for the grenadier and light infantry companies involved on April 19 yields data for almost 200 men. Additional information comes from a host of sources including American records on prisoners of war, advertisements for deserters and escapees, and an assortment of military documents.

At this writing, the nationality of 200 men has been determined:

111 English
36 Scottish
3 Welsh
49 Irish
1 American

When a man applied for a pension, his age was recorded—but not his date of birth. This makes it possible to determine each man's approximate age on April 19, 1775, knowing that it might be off by a year depending upon his date of birth and the date his age was recorded. With data available for 202 men, this inaccuracy makes little difference. Dividing the ages into groupings, we find:

Age in 1775	Number of Men
15-20 years old	5
21-25 years old	33
26-30 years old	44
31-35 years old	53
36-40 years old	40
41-45 years old	16
46-50 years old	10
51-55 years old	1

4. Frederick Mackenzie, *The Diary of Frederick Mackenzie* (Cambridge, MA: Harvard University Press, 1930), 23.

Grenadiers and light infantrymen were selected for their skill as soldiers; they were the most capable men in each British regiment. One requirement for service in these elite companies was at least a year of military experience—there were no new recruits in the grenadiers and light infantry. The length of service, as of 1775, of 240 men has been determined. We have:

Length of Service	Number of Men
1 year	3
2 to 5 years	37
6 to 10 years	91
11 to 20 years	95
21 years or more	14

Seldom were men accepted as recruits before they were seventeen years of age, and most British soldiers enlisted between the ages of twenty and twenty-five.[5] In an era when few children attended school beyond the age of about twelve, boys and young men found some sort of work before they were old enough to enlist. Some pursued trades, while others worked at whatever labor they could. Pension rolls record these avocations, using the term "labourer" for anyone who did not have a trade, regardless of education or social background—occasionally, men who met all of the qualifications for becoming an officer but who lacked the means and influence to obtain a commission entered the ranks as private soldiers, and were listed as "labourers" not because they had toiled at labor, but because they had not followed a trade before enlisting.[6]

Trades have been identified for 188 of the men who served in grenadier and light infantry companies on April 19, 1775:

95 Labourers
21 Weavers
11 Tailors
6 Carpenters
4 each: Shoemakers, Hosiers, Framework knitters, Clothiers
3 Butchers
2 each: Blacksmiths, Smiths, Coopers, Dyers, Cordwainers, Wool combers
1 each: Baker, Bleacher, Brickmaker, Button maker, Cabinet maker, Cutler, Engraver, Glover, Gunsmith, Husbandman, Malster, Mason, Musician, Nailor, Sawyer, Serge weaver,

---

5. For details on British army recruiting during this era, see Don N. Hagist, *Noble Volunteers: the British Soldiers who fought the American Revolution* (Westholme, 2020).
6. See Hagist, *Noble Volunteers*, 35, 47.

Amos Doolittle, "Plate II A View of the Town of Concord." (*New York Public Library*)

Stockenor, Stuff weaver, Tallow chandler, Toy maker, Upholsterer, Whip maker, Whitesmith, Woolcard maker

The British commander in chief reported 73 men killed, 174 wounded and 53 missing on April 19. This included casualties in the 1,500-man relief force that met the retreating grenadiers and light infantry at Lexington that afternoon. It is not possible to determine exactly how many of the casualties were from the force that had marched to Concord. Muster rolls show the names of twenty grenadiers and light infantrymen who died on April 19 or within the next few days. Tracing men through subsequent muster rolls reveals the fate of another 458 of them—again, including only those who were sergeants, corporals, drummers, fifers or private soldiers on April 19, 1775:

> 199 received pensions
> 8 received land grants in Nova Scotia
> 7 became officers
> 17 deserted
> 227 died while in service, including 120 from the Battle of Bunker Hill on June 17, 1775

A few of the men wounded on April 19 obtained brief statements from officers attesting to their wounds, statements that bolstered their cases for deserving pensions. These statements, combined with other data recorded by the pension office, allow us to create brief biographical sketches of a few soldiers.

John Mosely was born in 1744 in the town of Leicester in England. He was five-feet-six and three-quarters inches tall and joined the army in 1764. By 1775 he was in the light infantry company of the 5th Regiment of Foot, and was wounded in the left arm on April 19. He recovered quickly enough to fight at Bunker Hill just two months later, where he was wounded in the left shoulder. This wound also did not put him out of the war. In September 1777 he was on the British campaign to capture Philadelphia; he was wounded once again, this time in the right knee at the Battle of Brandywine on September 11. In spite of three wounds in two years, Mosely continued his career in the army until June 1784 when he received a pension.[7]

Born in St. Andrews, Norfolk, England, in 1731, John Smith pursued the trade of a dyer before joining the army in 1754. Serving in the 4th Regiment of Foot, he was wounded in the leg during the British capture of Martinique in 1762. He was in the regiment's grenadier company on April 19, 1775, when, at the age of forty-four, he was wounded "through his thigh." He nonetheless continued in the army until September 1788 when he received a pension for his thirty-one years of service.[8]

Mathew Haymour joined the 23rd Regiment of Foot in 1766 at the age of twenty. A "labourer" from the town of Burnley, Lancashire, he was in the regiment's grenadier company on April 19. He was wounded twice that day, in the right thigh and left foot. At Bunker Hill he was on the march again, and received a wound in the right shoulder. These wounds were not debilitating; Haymour remained in the army until 1790 and was granted a pension in recognition of his twenty-four years as a soldier.[9]

James Rennison, a native of Kendal in the county of Westmorland in northwest England, had been a weaver before he joined the army in 1759 at the age of just sixteen. At five feet six inches tall, with brown hair, hazel eyes, a swarthy complexion and "round visage," he was a corporal in the 59th Regiment's light infantry company when he was wounded in the thigh on April 19, 1775. His wound did not prevent him from taking part in the bloody Battle of Bunker Hill that June. In December, he and his comrades in the 59th received the welcome news that they were going back to Britain, having been in America for nearly ten years. But his war was not over. The regiment was sent to Gibraltar, where Rennison and his fellow soldiers endured a four-year siege, one

---

7. Discharge of John Mosely, WO 97/274/18, TNA.
8. Discharge of John Smith, WO 121/5/226, TNA.
9. Discharge of Mathew Haymour, WO 121/8/92, TNA.

of the longest in military history. In 1788 he was discharged from the army and granted a pension after twenty-nine years in the army. Doing what many men in his position did, he joined the army again, this time in the 6th Regiment of Foot. He was discharged again in 1791 and returned to the pension rolls. But he was a military man—he enlisted again, into the 95th Regiment, and served until 1797 when he was discharged once more. He joined an invalid company, an army corps of men no longer fit for overseas service who garrisoned installations in Great Britain. In 1802 he was discharged and returned to the pension rolls yet again, at the age of fifty-nine, having spent more than forty years in the army.[10]

The fighting on April 19 affected families as well as the soldiers themselves. Samuel Lee, a grenadier in the 18th Regiment of Foot, left his family in Boston when he marched to Concord. He was taken prisoner that day, and ultimately chose to remain in Concord where he remarried and lived until his death in 1790.[11] What became of his family in Boston remains unknown; probably they returned to Great Britain with other widows in August 1775. Catherine Rogers' husband Daniel was a grenadier in the 38th Regiment, and died of wounds on April 20, 1775. She remained with the regiment in America, and eventually married another soldier of the 38th, Thomas Mason, in New York in May 1777.[12]

Dennis Green of the 5th Regiment's grenadier company was wounded on April 19, hit by a musket ball that lodged in his body. The native of Mallow in County Cork, Ireland, who stood almost six feet tall, recovered from the wound, but army surgeons were unable to extract the ball. He nonetheless served for eight more years, going before the army pension board in 1783. An officer wrote that he suffered "under a Complaint, occasioned by a Musquet shot (which still remains in his Body) he received at Lexinton N. America, & is so reduced in Body that it does not seem probable he will recover) And will not by Labour be able to Provide a Maintenance for himself."[13] That bullet from the first day of the war remained with him for the rest of his life.

10. Discharges of James Rennison, WO 121/3/157, WO 121/140/371, WO 121/146/407, WO 121/154/509, TNA.
11. *Concord, Massachusetts Births, Marriages and Deaths, 1635–1850* (Boston: Thomas Todd, 1895), 420; for having a family in Boston, see Prisoners in Concord Jail, December 6, 1775, Revolutionary War Records SC1 Series 57, vol. 8, Massachusetts State Archives.
12. Muster rolls, 38th Regiment of Foot, WO 12/5171; "Marriage Licenses in New York", *New York Genealogical and Biographical Record* Vol. 47 No. 2 (April 1916), 179.
13. Discharge of Dennis Green, WO 97/271/32, TNA.

Virginian Ned Streater, African American Minute Man

PATRICK H. HANNUM

Ned Streater (also spelled Streator) was a twenty-year-old man when he first served early in the American Revolution as a member of a Virginia Minute Battalion from Nansemond County during the Battle of Great Bridge in 1775. Streater served again during the Virginia campaign of 1780-81. What makes Ned Streater unique is not his multiple tours of militia service or the fact he received no written discharge to document his service to the Patriot cause, but that he was an enslaved African-American. He is one of only three African-American soldiers identified to date who fought on the Patriot side from the State of Virginia early in the war, at the Battle of Great Bridge.[1] The most notable African-American Patriot to serve in Virginia's first Revolutionary War battle, Great Bridge, was William (Billy) Flora, a free African-American from Portsmouth, Virginia.[2] Flora was reportedly one of the three sentries on duty at the south end of the Great Bridge on the morning of December 9, 1775, when the British assault took place. Flora's story has been told many times and likely romanticized over the years.[3] Ned Streater's story is quite different, and likely never previously told. His

---

1. Ned Streater Pension Application, S7645, revwarapps.org; The others are James Bass (Pension Application S1745) and William "Billy" Flora, both free African-Americans. James Bass is listed as "Free Colored" on the 1830 federal census, but may also have had Native American lineage.
2. Norman Fuss, "Billy Flora at the Battle of Great Bridge," *Journal of the American Revolution*, October 14, 2014, allthingsliberty.com/2014/10/billy-flora-at-the-battle-of-great-bridge/.
3. William S. Forrest, *Historical and descriptive sketches of Norfolk and vicinity: including Portsmouth and the adjacent counties, during a period of two hundred years: also, sketches of Williamsburg, Hampton, Suffolk, Smithfield, and other places, with descriptions of some of the principal objects of interest in eastern Virginia* (Philadelphia: Lindsay and Blakiston, 1853), 79.

story provides insight into the military service of enslaved African-American veterans and their post-revolutionary experiences.[4]

Today, Nansemond County, Virginia is one of several extinct counties in the state. It was incorporated with the Independent City of Suffolk in 1972, and in accordance with Virginia law, when incorporated, the county ceased to exist.[5] Historical research into people and events in Nansemond County is difficult for other reasons beyond a name change. The county records were destroyed by fire on at least three separate occasions in 1734, 1779 and again in 1866.[6] This makes the content of Ned Streater's pension application particularly valuable for the study of local history because it contains official court documents and proceedings, providing insight into his service and journey to freedom. Unlike many revolutionary veterans who moved west after the revolution, Ned remained in Nansemond County linked to his enslaved status. Ned Streater's pension application was sworn and attested by Jeremiah Jones and Henry Lassiter in Nansemond County in 1833. He was successful in obtaining a pension in the amount of $112.55 that November but passed away only one month later at age seventy-eight. One is left to wonder if he actually received any of the pension funds he earned before his death.[7]

Ned Streater signed his pension statement with an X like many veterans, indicating he was illiterate, but clearly this was not any measure of his intellect. Ned was astute enough to file suit against his former owners in 1814 seeking his emancipation under existing Virginia law. His owner at the time of his revolutionary service was Willis Streater, for whom he served as a substitute in the militia. Willis Streater's (Streator's) estate documents date from 1802, but he likely died in 1792 reflecting an extended period of time to settle his estate. After Willis Streater's death, Ned Streater lived on the farm of Stephen Graham

---

4. The revolution's "darkest shadow is unquestionably slavery, the failure to end it or at least to adopt a gradual emancipation scheme … slavery remains a permeant stain on the legacy of the founders, as most of them knew it would." Joseph J. Ellis, *American Creation: Triumphs and Tragedies at the Founding of the Republic* (New York: Alfred A. Knopf, 2007), 10.
5. Emily J. Salmon and Edward D.C. Campbell, Jr., eds., *The Hornbook of Virginia History: A Ready Reference Guide to the Old Dominion's People, Places and Past* (Richmond: Library of Virginia, 1994), 167.
6. Genealogy Trails History Group, Nansemond County, Virginia, genealogytrails.com/vir/nansemond/#:~:text=Nansemond%20County%20was%20once%20located%20in%20the%20Virginia,Cittie%20in%20the%20area%20which%20became%20Nansemond%20County.
7. United States Senate, *The Pension Roll of 1835*, 4, 1968 (reprint, with index, Baltimore: Genealogical Publishing Company, 1992), 3:514; Ned Streater Pension Application, S7645.

from 1793 to 1810 and "acted as a free man being permitted to manage his own affairs and to hold property & that for other portion of the said time he was treated with great humanity and unusually indulged." After the death of Stephen Graham, Ned Streater sued for his emancipation based upon his honorable Revolutionary War service.[8] He was awarded his "freedom from bondage" and $165 in compensation for damages in May 1814.[9] As a "free man of color" Ned filed suit again in 1824 seeking compensation for his period of bondage from 1783 to 1792 and the court ordered an award of $105. The court awarded an additional $210 for the period 1792 to 1810. Virginia had finally lived up to the promises made upon his enlistment and formalized into law in 1783.[10]

The Commonwealth of Virginia passed legislation in October 1783 that emancipated slaves who successfully served as substitutes for free persons and were forced to return to servitude. The law specifically stated "that on expiration of the term of enlistment of such slaves that the former owners have attempted again to force them to return to a state of servitude, contrary to the principles of justice, and to their own solemn promise."[11] This clause implies that enslaved people who served as substitutes were often denied the freedom they were promised as a result of their service, as in Ned's case. This particular statue was passed into law shortly after the Treaty of Paris formally ended the war and highlights a recognition by Virginia's lawmakers of the military contributions of an undetermined number of Virginia's enslaved veterans. This acknowledgment of the legacy of enslaved soldiers is alone a testament to their value and contributions to the Patriot victory, however large or small their numbers.

---

8. Bins Genealogy, 1790/1800 Virginia Tax Lists Censuses, 1800, Streator, Willis (estate), Nansemond County, www.binnsgenealogy.com/VirginiaTaxListCensuses/; Ned Streater Pension Application, S7645.
9. The date of Ned Streater's lawsuit for his freedom coincides with slave escapes to the British during the War of 1812, as British warships and raiding parties patrolled the Chesapeake Bay region. Ned likely enjoyed some freedoms without having been formally emancipated as a result of his revolutionary service. Slave owners began to suppress those freedoms during this period as hundreds and possibly thousands of enslaved Virginians fled to the British fleet. See: Alan Taylor, *The Internal Enemy, Slavery and the War in Virginia, 1774-1832* (New York: W.W. Norton & Company, 2013), 268-273.
10. Ned Streater Pension Application, S7645 contains copies of his court documents from 1814 and 1824, likely the only surviving copies of these important court records.
11. William Walter Henning, *Henning's Statutes at Large, being a Collection of all the Laws of Virginia from the first session of the Legislature, in the Year 1619*, 11, 308, transcribed for the internet by Freddie L Spradlin, Torrance, CA, 2009, www.vagenweb.org/hening/vol11-15.htm.

The revolutionary era population of Virginia was about 600,000 with at least one third of that total or over 200,000 African-Americans, most enslaved.[12] While there are few surviving military records for Virginia's substitute African-Americans, service was probably more widespread than surviving records support.[13] This makes Ned Streater's pension application even more valuable for researchers attempting to define the contributions of African-American revolutionary soldiers.[14]

As with many surviving pension applications, not all the details one would like to know about a soldier's life and revolutionary service were recorded. But Ned Streater's statements and records provide enough detail for us to piece together his military service and journey to freedom as a result of it. He recalled the name of his company commander, Capt. Elvington Knott of the Princess Anne District that included Nansemond County, his home.[15] Col. William Woodford of the 2nd Virginia Regiment, in command at Great Bridge, was authorized to call up the Princess Anne District Militia as part of the campaign of 1775-1776 to liberate Virginia from royal governance.[16] Ned Streater specifically stated, "I was present at the battle of the 'Great Bridge' in Norfolk County when Fordice was killed." Capt. Charles Fordyce of the British 14th Regiment of Foot led the failed assault on the morning

---

12. Population estimates for Virginia in 1775 vary; 600,000, including 400,000 of European decent and 200,000 African-Americans, is a reasonable number, making Virginia the most populous colony/state with at least one-third of the population African-American: see, Everts B. Greene & Virginia D. Harrington, *American Population Before the Federal Census of 1790*, (Gloucester, MA, Peter Smith, 1966), 6-8, 141; Robert K. Wright, *The Continental Army* (Washington, DC: Center for Military History 1983), 94; Patrick Henry to Bernardo Galvez, January 14, 1779, in Ian Saberton, ed., *Cornwallis Papers: The Campaigns of 1780 and 1781 in the Southern Theatre of the American Revolutionary War* (Uckfield, England: The Naval & Military Press Ltd, 2010), 3:300.

13. Researchers estimate about one in six veterans lived long enough or actually filed pension applications. If we multiply the known number of cases by six, this may provide some insight into the numbers of enslaved African-Americans who served as substitutes during the American Revolution.

14. John U. Rees, *They Were Good Soldiers': African-Americans Serving in the Continental Army, 1775-1783* (Warwick, England: Heilon & Company Limited, 2019). Rees addresses the challenges faced when researching African-Americans with Revolutionary War service.

15. Capt. Elvington Knott served the Princess Anne District Minute Battalion during 1775-76 and as a militia officer later in the war. The Princess Anne District included the counties of: Princess Anne, Norfolk, Nansemond, Isle of Wight, and Norfolk Borough. E. M. Sanchez-Saavedra, *A Guide to Virginia Military Organizations in the American Revolution, 1774-1783* (Richmond: Virginia State Library, 1978), 11-12, 21.

16. Brent Tarter, "The Orderly Book of the Second Virginia Regiment: September 27, 1775-April 15, 1776," *The Virginia Magazine of History and Biography* 85, no. 2 (April 1977), 173n54.

of December 9, 1775 and died a few yards from the Patriot earthworks at the south end of the Great Bridge causeway.[17]

Considering he made his statement in 1833, his account of events fifty-eight years earlier is remarkably detailed and consistent with records of that event left by others. He continued his record of service by addressing events of 1780-81. This second period of service took place during the British occupation of Virginia by Generals Benedict Arnold, William Phillips and Charles Cornwallis. He named a number of Patriot field grade officers who were known to operate at that time period in the region.[18] He also addressed a skirmish at "Pip Pot Swamp" where he was wounded with a ball through the leg, "which deformed and very much disabled that leg."

"Pip Pot Swamp" is likely a corruption or version of the contemporary Pitchkettle Creek and marsh just north and west of modern downtown Suffolk, Virginia. Pitchkettle Creek is a tributary of the Nansemond River. Today, the area remains a marshy swamp near the creek but modern drainage systems, including several dams and resulting fresh water reservoirs, reduced the size of the swamps that once existed there.[19] Many small skirmishes during this period of British military occupation south of the James River remain unrecorded. Local militias used their familiarity with the thick marshy terrain to their advantage when confronting occupying British and Loyalist forces. Perhaps Ned's pension application provides insight into another yet-undocumented skirmish in the swampy terrain near downtown Suffolk, producing at least one casualty.[20]

---

17. Ned Streater Pension Application, S7645.
18. Among other officers, Streater named Maj. Alexander Dick who had an extensive record of Patriot service to Virginia throughout the revolution in a variety of units. See Sanchez-Saavedra, *A Guide to Virginia Military Organizations*, 122-3, 175.
19. United States Geologic Service Maps, contemporary map, maps.usgs.gov/map/, and historic 1919, ngmdb.usgs.gov/ht-bin/tv_browse.pl?id=34a98f0efd84cda083718cbffcf6ab 2d; the best revolutionary era map located to date, Library of Congress, *Plan of Princess Anne and Norfolk Counties* (1780) www.loc.gov/item/2012589670/, unfortunately lacks fine points for the target area of Nansemond County.
20. The most detailed first-hand accounts of the military actions south of the James River during early 1781 may be found in two published works. Unfortunately there are few specifics in surviving Patriot accounts of these smaller and irregular military actions and many engagements likely went completely undocumented or unnamed. See: Johann Ewald and Joseph P. Tustin, ed & trans., *Diary of the American War* (New Haven: Yale University Press, 1979), 255-316; John Graves Simcoe, *Simcoe's Military Journal: A History of the Operations of a Partisan Corps, called the Queen's Rangers* (New York: Bartlett & Welford, 1844), 158-248, ia902607.us.archive.org/2/items/simcoesmilitary00simcgoog/simcoesmilitary00simcgoog.pdf.

Ned Streater's pension application provides a glimpse into the experiences of one enslaved African-American Revolutionary War soldier from Virginia. He served two periods of service, one in 1775-76 as Virginia's Whig government used military force to ejected Lord Dunmore, the royal governor, from the colony of Virginia. His second period, during 1780-81, took place as the war once again shifted focus to the south during the British campaign to occupy Virginia. The main operating base for the British in Virginia was in Portsmouth until the move to Yorktown in August of 1781. Portsmouth borders Nansemond County, placing local militia operating there within easy reach of the occupying British forces. Ultimately, this British campaign ended with Lord Cornwallis's surrender at Yorktown, contributing to the end of major hostilities and ultimately the recognition of the United States as an independent nation.

Ned Streater's journey to liberation and independence likely parallels the path taken by other enslaved African-American veterans. The American Revolution was fought in part to implement lofty ideals concerning freedom and independence, and Ned Streater's journey is part of that story. Publicly acknowledging and expressing appreciation for all Revolutionary War veterans is an American tradition, regardless of race or ethnicity.

The 1775 Duel Between Henry Laurens and John Faucheraud Grimké

AARON J. PALMER

Charles Town, the metropolis of the South (today Charleston, South Carolina), was a leading location for duels in the late eighteenth century. One detailed example reveals much about the practice and about honor in general. In this case, an elite gentleman used every means available to him to defend his honor and police the bounds of his class. A man from a lower class violated the protocols of gentlemanly behavior, attacked the reputation of an elite, questioned that man's conduct as a political leader, and attempted to destroy his reputation. The gentleman, intimately familiar with elite protocols of honor, used them effectively to defend his political and personal reputation. This incident, which occurred during the early stages of the American Revolution, also clearly shows the difficult position occupied by conservatives who opposed questionable, extra-legal tactics that were being used for the sake of ideological conformity.

By the fall of 1775, Charles Town was in the midst of revolution. The Council of Safety had assumed executive power and the Provincial Congress had supplanted the old Commons House of Assembly. The provisional government also actively debated about how to treat royalists. Henry Laurens served as president or chair of the Council of Safety and consistently opposed persecuting royalists. As a member of the council, he was also expected to keep its proceedings in strict confidence. A bizarre incident began to unfold in October 1775, shortly after the twenty-two-year-old John Faucheraud Grimké returned to Charles Town from a trip to England. The young man was the son of John Paul Grimké, a Charles Town silversmith, skilled in making English-style silver luxuries.[1] He also owned a small plantation of about

---

1. Richard Walsh, *Charleston's Sons of Liberty: A Study of the Artisans* (Columbia: University of South Carolina Press, 1959), 11.

500 acres on Edisto Island.² Both father and son zealously opposed British policy during the imperial crisis and fought in the subsequent war. Neither ever served in the Commons House of Assembly or on the Council of Safety.³

Henry Laurens was a friend to both Grimkés, which makes the incident even more bizarre. When J.F. Grimké returned from England in October 1775, Henry Laurens planned to visit the family's home in Charles Town to "pay my respects to the young man."⁴ Laurens was running late thanks to a Council of Safety meeting, but he met J.F. Grimké in the street. Laurens asked if he had brought any letters from his son in England. He had not, but the younger Grimké did have another packet of letters he showed to Laurens when the two arrived at the Grimké home. As Henry Laurens was about the leave the house, J.P. Grimké stopped him to reveal several letter packets. They were letters the younger Grimké had been entrusted to carry from England to Charles Town, but they had already been opened and examined. J.P. Grimké explained they were sent to "suspected persons" (that is, persons suspected of supporting the royal government). The elder Grimké asked Laurens what should be done. Should the letters go to the Council of Safety or one of its committees? Should they go to the press to shame the recipients?⁵

Henry Laurens refused to become involved, saying that "I have never interfered in such matters." He only agreed to take an unopened packet of London newspapers to the printer Robert Wells, but he again refused to take the intercepted letters to Peter Timothy as the elder Grimké had requested.⁶ Peter Timothy was the printer of the *South Carolina Gazette* and served as the Council of Safety's secretary.⁷

The events that followed became increasingly bizarre and perplexing for Henry Laurens. Within days, the younger Grimké claimed that

---

2. Ibid., 18.
3. John Faucheraud Grimké was the son of John Paul Grimké and Mary Faucheraud. He was born in December 1752. Grimké attended Westminster School and the Middle Temple in London. He became involved in revolutionary activity and joined other colonists in petitioning George III against British colonial policy while in London. John Belton O'Neall, *Biographical Sketches of the Bench and Bar of South Carolina* (Charleston: S.G. Courtenay & Co., 1859), 39.
4. "Newspaper Account, October 13, 1775," *Papers of Henry Laurens* (Columbia: University of South Carolina Press, 1968-2003), 10:461. Laurens printed a detailed narrative of the incident in the *South Carolina Gazette and Country Journal*, which was operated by Robert Wells.
5. Ibid., 462.
6. Ibid.
7. "Journal of the Council of Safety for the Province of South Carolina," *Collections of the South Carolina Historical Society* (1858), 22.

Henry Laurens had actually tried to persuade his father to turn the open letters over to either the council or a local newspaper. Laurens was stunned. He had stated "by repeated declarations that I never opened letters, or concerned myself in such matters, I meant to discourage the delivery of private letters to any but the persons to whom such letters were respectively addressed."[8] Then J.F. Grimké accused Laurens of removing letters from the Grimké home without permission, presumably referring to the packet of newspapers for Wells. He did not specify what letters had been removed. J.F. Grimké refused to discuss the dispute with Laurens in any detail and bungled an attempted exchange of notes by publishing at least one of Laurens' notes in a newspaper attack piece. The younger Grimké continued to insist that Laurens had removed some of the letters from his home without permission and advised his father to turn over other letters to the provisional government or the press.[9] Laurens was at a loss. He wrote, "I should as soon have expected such a base, unmanly, ungenerous, cowardly attack from my own son as from Mr. J.F. Grimké, a lad to whom I have been a father, for whom I have done more than his own father would have done."[10] His newspaper article, printed in response to Grimké's public accusations, flatly stated that "I have done Mr. Grimké no injury. If I have not merited his bitter censures, it will become him, if he has one spark of honor, to make a concession as public as his affront has been, and as ample as it has been unjust."[11]

Laurens provides an interesting insight into honor with his response. He damned Grimké's attack as dishonorable because it was not based

---

8. "Newspaper Account, October 13, 1775," *Papers of Henry Laurens*, 10:462.
9. Ibid., 463-464.
10. Ibid., 461. Laurens did not specify what he did for Grimké. J.F. Grimké was sent to London to study at Westminster School and the Middle Temple. Given that Henry Laurens had a close friendship with the family; it is possible that Laurens assisted John Paul Grimké in financing his son's education and potential elevation in social status as a result. It is highly unlikely that a silversmith would have been able to afford such an education without the patronage of a wealthier man. Grimké's educational background is noted in E. Alfred Jones, "Two Problems in the Hall-Marking of Silver," *The Burlington Magazine for Connoisseurs* 66.387 (June 1935): 287. Bertram Wyatt-Brown suggests that such patron-client relationships were common expressions of elite power in early America. He cites George Washington and Alexander Hamilton as examples. Clientage was a way to balance "respectable modesty and political ambition." Bertram Wyatt-Brown, *The Shaping of Southern Culture: Honor, Grace, and War, 1760s-1880s* (Chapel Hill: University of North Carolina Press, 2001), 46. Laurens seems to have adopted J.F. Grimké as a client, and, as such, had a right to expect modesty and deference from the young man. Grimké clearly violated this important convention, which itself was a major affront and explains Laurens' very clear sense of betrayal.
11. "Newspaper Account, October 13, 1775," *Papers of Henry Laurens*, 10:461.

in truth or fact. Moreover, Grimké's background and behavior demonstrated his unworthiness to even make a challenge to a recognized gentleman like Laurens. Grimké broke protocol by taking the dispute public before attempting to resolve the confusion directly with Henry Laurens. Laurens also suggests that such a public attack could only be corrected by an equally public and honest apology and admission of wrong. If the young Grimké failed to do so, he would prove his lack of honor.

Laurens' honor had been called into question in a very serious way. He would have to find some other means to restore it if Grimké refused to make a public apology. Grimké either did not understand the rules of elite protocol or did not care about them, but the incident clearly points to the existence of established rules of conduct between gentlemen who had fallen into dispute. In any event, Laurens quickly brought honor to the forefront of the issue. He even went so far as to swear that, "upon my honor," he never took letters or advised their reading.[12] In the end, he was totally exasperated: "I am an oldish man, and infirm . . . yet if he will name his time, place and weapons," Laurens would duel him.[13] This terrible breach of honor could be repaired in no other way given the total failure of protocol.

The seedy politics surrounding this situation made it even more difficult for Henry Laurens. He believed that the whole thing was a scheme on the part of the young, brash J.F. Grimké to rise politically at Laurens' expense. Laurens consistently defended individual rights and opposed how some in the revolutionary movement hoped to pressure and persecute conservatives and royalists. Laurens even thought the whole affair may have been a set-up cloaked in "love of country," designed to discredit him politically.[14] David Wallace, Henry Laurens' biographer, agrees. He suggests that Grimké may have been pressured into the scheme by a "radical clique" who either wanted to discredit the more conservative and cautious Laurens or were trying to cover their own misdeed of letter-opening without council authorization.[15] Laurens even wrote his brother that J.F. Grimké would never have acted so, if he had not been pressed by a group who harbored a political

---

12. Ibid., 462.
13. Ibid., 466.
14. Ibid.
15. David Wallace, *The Life of Henry Laurens* (New York: G.P. Putnam's Sons, 1915), 216. Wallace only briefly recounts the incident as part of his narrative of the revolution. He does not study it as an affair of honor but treats it as another political episode in the larger narrative.

grudge against Laurens and his consistent opposition to opening private letters.[16]

Laurens was naturally outraged and wrote to his son that Grimké had made an "attempt to rob your father of both his reputation and his life and that without the smallest provocation on your father's part or truth or justice on his own."[17] Laurens saw this political attack as an unprovoked assault on his honor, and he believed that the real dishonor was Grimké's, for "his conduct was ungentlemanlike and unmanly— he has dishonored and disgraced himself."[18] J.F. Grimké had betrayed a close relationship for petty causes. Friends sometimes fall out. However, Laurens's newspaper account makes it clear that there were protocols and rules that gentlemen followed when reputation and honor were involved. The bitter politics grieved Laurens, but the personal betrayal, failure of protocol and attack on his honor demanded a response.

Honor was integral to one's genteel status. When attacked or challenged, especially in a dishonorable (or false) way, honor had to be defended if one still wanted to claim the title of gentleman. Why was this challenge false? Laurens disputed the facts of the case, but he really focused on his accuser's character. When protocol failed, Laurens had two weapons at his disposal: shame and ritual violence. Thus, he first set out to destroy his accuser's reputation and make it clear that J.F. Grimké had no just claim to the title of gentlemen. If such were the case, Laurens' peers would have to trust his word of honor over the word of a dishonored man, and he might be able to avoid violence. Laurens claimed he did not want any physical harm done to Grimké. Grimké was a young man, who may not have known better and was full of passion. Hence, Laurens was willing to just shame Grimké and make him to suffer the "universal censure of the people" for the sake of self-defense.[19] Laurens, as a respected gentleman, simply had to refute the charges and brush the unworthy youth aside. Unfortunately, Grimké would not let the issue die so easily, and he challenged Henry Laurens to a duel on October 16, claiming that the shame Laurens inflicted on him was also an attack on his honor that must be answered. Grimké believed himself to be a gentleman despite the "universal censure" heaped upon him. It is also possible he realized he was in over his head in having insulted a man as prominent as Laurens, and pride prevented him from backing down at this point.

16. Ibid., 217.
17. "Henry Laurens to John Laurens, October 21, 1775," *Papers of Henry Laurens*, 10:487.
18. Ibid., 489.
19. Ibid.

Laurens did not want to engage in violence, but he hoped to use the duel's rules to finally prove that J.F. Grimké had no honor. Grimké had already proven he did not understand or respect gentlemanly protocol, and now he proved that he did not understand or respect the rules of the duel. Grimké issued the challenge through Ralph Izard (whom Laurens respected), but Laurens initially refused, saying "we [Laurens and Grimké] are not upon a par and he has no right to challenge me."[20] Grimké was much younger. He was from an artisan family. A silversmith stood atop artisan ranks, but no artisan could claim elite status. J.P. Grimké had purchased land in an attempt to enter the planting class, but occupation and wealth alone did not grant one elite, gentlemanly status.[21] Grimké's dishonorable and uncouth behavior placed him beneath Laurens on the social ladder. Notably, Laurens never attacked Grimké for his wealth or profession. He focused on behavior and reputation. Despite the disparity in status between them, Laurens agreed to meet at New Market at 6:00 the next day. John Lewis Gervais, one of the witnesses, recorded a full account of the subsequent events, which provides a rare, detailed look at the ritual of the duel.[22]

The ritual began when the parties met at Mr. Gibbes's house, and Henry Laurens loaded two pistols. Grimké immediately showed his lack of knowledge and respect for the ritual by challenging the presence of John Lewis Gervais, who was there serving as Henry Laurens's "second" (i.e. representative / referee / witness). Gervais responded, "What business have I here! What business has Mr. Izard [Grimké's second] here! What! Did you come to murder Mr. Laurens!"[23] Once Grimké acknowledged Gervais's role as second, Laurens went out into the middle of the street with the loaded guns. Grimké followed, and the two took their positions in the street. Grimké commanded Laurens to fire the first shot, but Laurens insisted that Grimké take the first shot instead. Doing so was Laurens' first step in a calculated risk to avoid having to kill the young man while yet proving Grimké's shame and his own honor. Grimké agreed, took several steps closer, aimed his gun and fired. The gun fortuitously misfired, and Grimké went for another gun. By tradition, it was now Henry Laurens' turn to fire. A misfire did not grant one party a second shot. Laurens could have aimed, fired and killed Grimké on the spot (assuming his gun actually worked).[24]

20. "Henry Laurens to John Laurens, October 23, 1775," *Papers of Henry Laurens*, 10:492.
21. Walsh, *Charleston's Sons of Liberty*, 18.
22. "Henry Laurens to John Laurens, October 23, 1775," *Papers of Henry Laurens*, 10:492-493.
23. Ibid., 496.
24. Ibid., 492-493.

Laurens did not want to kill Grimké, and his gamble had paid off so far. He wanted to shame him utterly, strip him of all pretenses to honor and prove that Grimké was not a gentleman. Laurens admitted as much to his friend George Karr: "My standing up to be fired at like a Butt disdaining to take an advantage which was fairly in my hands will prove to every sensible and dispassionate man that I was willing to seal the truth with my blood."[25] Laurens said, "I give you your life Mr. Grimké," immediately after the misfire.[26] Ralph Izard insisted that it was not over. There was another pair of pistols and Laurens had to take his shot, but Laurens continued to insist that he would not take Grimké's life. An argument between Laurens, Grimké and the two seconds ensued. Finally, Laurens told Grimké that if someone must fire, Grimké could take another shot, but Ralph Izard talked Grimké out of further dishonoring himself by brazenly killing Laurens. Grimké backed down and said that he could not fire "consistent with my honor," and Laurens simply told him to go home if that was the case. Grimké, still hoping to fight, suggested they "take the sword" and leave the guns alone, but Laurens refused on account of having only one real leg.[27]

This duel was far more than two men shooting at each other. The true duel here was Laurens' bold use of the ritual to fully demonstrate Grimké's shame—a psychological duel between an old gentleman and a young fool. Laurens' refusal to fire was a deliberate attempt to shame Grimké and provoke him into behaving in a vulgar and dishonorable way. Grimké did not take an extra shot. It would have killed Laurens in cold blood outside the usual rules of the duel, which required alternating shots. Ralph Izard and John Lewis Gervais (themselves both elite and wealthy gentlemen) had to enforce the rules and persuade Grimké to back down. Even if Grimké had killed or wounded Laurens, Henry would have won the duel by proving his honor and Grimké's shame. Henry Laurens risked his life to clear his name and prove that Grimké had no legitimate claim to honor or the title of gentleman.

Laurens was older, understood the duel and won this battle. He continually refused to fire, even telling Grimké that he could "fire half a dozen shots if you please." Grimké lost his composure, hurled some "scurrilous language" at Laurens and called him a coward. This verbal assault gave Laurens the chance to prove his gentlemanly status and highlight Grimké's dishonor by responding, "I believe I have not acted like one. I have done more than you deserved." He further said that

---

25. "Henry Laurens to George Karr, October 21, 1775," *Papers of Henry Laurens*, 10:487.
26. "Henry Laurens to John Laurens, October 23, 1775," *Papers of Henry Laurens*, 10:492.
27. Ibid., 494.

Grimké was "no judge of honor for you have none." At this point, Laurens sealed Grimké's shame when Grimké challenged him to a second duel. Laurens said, "I receive no challenge from you . . . I have done more than you have a right to expect."[28] This duel went beyond personal combat and became a contest of wills and composure. Laurens successfully refused Grimké admission to elite ranks and repaired the attack on his honor by demonstrating his attacker's shame. Henry Laurens was a very wealthy man. However, he deemed his honor and reputation worth as much as his life and fortune.

A printed code of honor would not appear until the 1830s in South Carolina, when Gov. John Lyle Wilson published his "Code of Honor," which clearly stated the rules for dueling.[29] Though Laurens and Grimké dueled long before its publication, the rules Wilson laid out generally fit the pattern of the Laurens-Grimké duel, which suggests the rules were well known already in the 1770s and simply awaited a man like Wilson to chronicle them.

Laurens and Grimké employed many of Wilson's rules, though Grimké lacked knowledge or respect for those rules. According to Wilson, duels normally began with the formal passing of notes between the concerned parties. The offended party (Grimké in this case) was to send a note explaining the offense and requesting a written explanation or apology. If an apology or suitable explanation came, then some sort of public notice should be made (e.g. in a newspaper). Grimké skipped this step by going directly to the newspapers, which Laurens viewed as a breach of etiquette and an attack on his honor. Assuming the issue could not be resolved by notes and apologies, the two parties chose "seconds" or representatives who were responsible for coordinating and refereeing the duel. They were also to communicate (or pass notes) for the two parties. It was also the seconds' job to enforce the rules. For example, a second would be expected to shoot a man for gross violation (e.g. shooting out of turn). Hence, when Grimké's gun misfired, Izard was well within his rights to determine who should fire next.[30] When Wilson finally codified the rules in 1838 (and included a printed Irish honor code from 1777 in his work) they reflected the traditional operation of duels in the eighteenth century.

Laurens used the ritual to prove his initial contention that Grimké was beneath him, not a gentleman, had no honor to begin with and, thus, had no right to challenge a true gentleman to a physical contest

---

28. "Henry Laurens to John Laurens, October 23, 1775," *Papers of Henry Laurens*, 10:494.
29. Don C. Seitz, *Famous American Duels* (New York: Thomas Crowly, 1929), 33.
30. Jack K. Williams, *Dueling in the Old South* (College Station: Texas A&M University Press, 1980), 41-57.

of honor. Both parties had to be recognized, honorable gentlemen. No gentleman accepted a challenge from "one not considered his social equal."[31] Mere wealth or land ownership did not make one a gentleman. A planter like Laurens "had both the tangible qualities of possession and the intangible ones of courtly manners and a precise understanding of what was a gentleman's province and what was not."[32] Grimké's family may have been well-off and rising, but those things alone did not automatically make him a gentleman. When Grimké showed his true nature by hurling insults and issuing continual challenges, Laurens believed he had proven his point and increased Grimké's shame. He restored his own honor and prevented an unworthy man from claiming equal status

This episode involving Henry Laurens illustrates the importance of honor and reputation in lowcountry South Carolina's genteel society and how members of the elite used those concepts to defend status. It was imperative that a gentleman respond to a challenge against his honor. Courts, judges and lawyers could not help. Honor operated according to its own rules outside of any legal body or official. One could effectively defend honor by attacking the honor and reputation of the attacker. Thus Henry Laurens destroyed Mr. Grimké's reputation. To ameliorate an initial attack, he had to restore his honor by either discrediting his foe or meeting him in ritual combat. If a duel became necessary, only men of honor and equal status could participate. When a lesser man challenged Henry Laurens, he participated only to defend his power and honor, and then used the duel itself to demonstrate the dishonor and inferiority of his opponent. There was no written "code" in this period which directed how South Carolina gentlemen related to each other in terms of honor. An unofficial body of rules governed their relations, and the prime rules were that a challenge to honor could not be left unanswered and a gentleman must defend his status. Honor was a system of interchanges between individuals and the community—an encoded if unwritten system that helped define the boundaries of the elite, ruling class.[33]

---

31. Ibid., 27.
32. Ibid., 29.
33. Bertram Wyatt-Brown, *Honor and Violence in the Old South* (Oxford, UK: Oxford University Press, 1986), vii.

Washington's Final Retreat: Asylum

ALEXANDER LENARCHYK

George Washington's appointment as commander of the Continental Army filled him with doubt from the start. In his address to the Continental Congress on June 16, 1775, Washington described himself in the best light while at the same time signaling doubt. He declared himself humble to accept the position and explained that he did so to preserve the "glorious cause."[1] He could not, however, leave the phrase, "unlucky event" out of his address due to the formidable task at hand, facing off with the mother country.[2] Should Washington fail, the result would be catastrophic for him.

Washington's position in the winter of 1775-1776 put further pressure on his abilities which likely sowed the seeds of the "what if" scenario. What if the cause failed? What if he was captured? Washington described the scene in Boston as a "predicament," musing, "I have often thought, how much happier I should have been, if, instead of accepting of a command under such Circumstances I had taken my Musket upon my Shoulder & enterd the Ranks."[3] Washington hoped to deal a final and decisive blow with his dwindling army by attacking Boston which would result in an early version of urban warfare in the "crooked streets" to expel the British.[4] Perhaps he was trying to end his worries as fast as possible. In a letter to Col. Joseph Reed on January 14, 1776, Washington romanticized about retiring "to the backcountry" and living "in a wig-wam."[5] Words like these

---

1. George Washington, Address to the Continental Congress, June 16, 1775, founders.archives.gov/documents/Washington/03-01-02-0001.
2. Ibid.
3. Washington to Joseph Reed, January 14, 1776, founders.archives.gov/documents/Washington/03-03-02-0062.
4. Nathaniel Philbrick, "The Fiercest Man," *Bunker Hill* (New York: Penguin Books, 2014), 250.
5. Washington to Joseph Reed, January 14, 1776.

must have troubled Washington within. If they had leaked out, the morale of the army would have suffered because that their commander had reservations about his and the army's position. In addition, it showed the complexity of the situation in the early war period.

With doubts about the cause, the Continental Army, and his own leadership, Washington began to think about an asylum should the revolution fail. The mention of such a place of refuge must have been something personal to Washington. Perhaps he mentioned it more in private conversations, but in writing we only have a short glimpse. On February 28, 1776, he sent a letter from Cambridge, Massachusetts to his nephew Burwell Basset. Washington thanked him for taking care of his land affairs on the Ohio.[6] Washington then mentioned "my interest in which I shall be more Careful of as in the worst event, they will serve for an Asylum."[7] What sort of an asylum? Was Washington planning on hiding out in the lands he well knew from his expeditions as a surveyor and service during the French and Indian War?[8]

Although the mention of a potential asylum is there, Washington cannot be blamed for it or thought of in an ill light. He accepted a task that would buckle the knees of most men. Having an escape in the event of the revolution's failure was probably on the mind of most generals and enlisted men of the Continental Army.

---

6. Washington to Burwell Basset, February 38, 1776, founders.archives.gov/documents/Washington/03-03-02-0280.
7. Ibid.
8. Peter Stark, *Young Washington* (New York: HarperCollins Publishers, 2018), 27-31.

George III's (Implicit) Sanction of the American Revolution

❧ M. ANDREW HOLOWCHAK ☙

In *Summary View of the Rights of British America* (1774), Jefferson wrote of King George III's unwillingness to use his "negative" to veto unjust proposals. Two years later, Jefferson echoed this sentiment in his first draft of Declaration of Independence. Here, Jefferson listed a "long train of abuses & usurpations," at the hand of King George III. Those, he added, were "begun at a distinguished period, & pursuing invariably the same object." Those abuses were indicative of "arbitrary power," and he considered it the right, even duty, of those oppressed to throw off such discretionary abuse of authority and establish a new government, by consent of the people, in accordance of the will of the people.

The abuses Jefferson delineated in his draft of the Declaration are many, at least twenty-five, some complaints listed being compound claims. The last, and that to which he devoted the most ink, was the introduction of slavery into the colonies.

> He [King George III] has waged cruel war against human nature itself, violating its most sacred rights of life & liberty in the persons of a distant people who never offended him, captivating & carrying them into slavery in another hemisphere, or to incur miserable death in their transportation thither. This piratical warfare, the opprobrium of <u>infidel</u> powers, is the warfare of the <u>Christian</u> king of Great Britain. <u>Determined</u> to keep open a market where MEN should be bought & sold, he has prostituted his negative for suppressing every legislative attempt to prohibit or to restrain this execrable commerce: and that this assemblage of horrors might want no fact of distinguished die, he is now exciting those very people to rise in arms among us, and to purchase that liberty of which <u>he</u> has deprived them, & murdering the people upon whom he also obtruded them; thus paying off former crimes committed

against the <u>liberties</u> of one people, with crimes which he urges them to commit against the <u>lives</u> of another.

Some things are worth underscoring in Jefferson's passage on slavery.

First, there is Jefferson's use of capital letters for the word men. Nowhere else in his draft did he employ capitals. That shows philosophically and unequivocally that Jefferson considered Blacks as men, not as chattel, and that argues decisively against the naïve view, articulated by many in the secondary literature, that the Declaration was not meant to include Blacks. In Jefferson's eyes, by simple tautology, as human beings, slaves in the colonies deserved the same rights as all other men.

Second, Jefferson accused the king of religious hypocrisy. George III was a "Christian king," yet he was guilty of "piratical warfare:" taking people, who had done nothing to offend him, and conveying them like cattle to America. The king, of course, did not introduce slavery to America, nor did Jefferson accuse him of such. That occurred in 1619, when Dutch merchants brought some twenty Africans as indentured servants, to Jamestown, Virginia. Those who settled in America quickly found that transatlantic slavery provided a cheaper and more abundant labor source than other indentured servants, mostly penurious Europeans, and so the practice continued. Yet the king, Jefferson asserted, had "prostituted his negative"—that is, he had availed himself of none of presumably numerous legislative opportunities to nullify or even moderate the slave trade. George III could have put an end to the transatlantic slave trade, but he did not.

Most importantly, Jefferson drew an impassioned, if dubious comparison between the plight of the slaves and that of the colonists. In Jefferson's eyes, while colonists made slaves of the Blacks brought to the colonies, King George, through abuses and usurpations, made slaves of his colonial subjects. He viewed the arbitrary hand with which the colonies were governed by England, under the auspices of Parliament and King George III, as akin to arbitrary and brutal conditions of captivity under which slaves in the colonies suffered. Thus, Jefferson considered there existed two levels of slaves: colonists, who were not deserving of the same rights and treatments of other British citizens perhaps because of their "voluntary" transplantation, and transplanted Blacks, who were the property of the colonists, or the slaves of the "slaves."

Yet George III encouraged these "slaves of the slaves," Blacks who had been stripped of their humanity by being stripped of their rights, to rise up in revolt against their white masters by joining the British in the Revolutionary War. His inducement was freedom from oppression—a condition for which he, through his own refusal to act, was deemed in large part responsible by Jefferson. Nonetheless, by the same argument, the colonists, stripped of their humanity by being stripped of their rights, considered themselves entitled to rise up against the king, as George III, in his overtures to enslaved Blacks, implicitly sanctioned in a generic argument that any people deprived of their rights had a moral duty to revolt. Thus, the king himself implicitly justified a wholesale colonial revolution.

In constructing the layered argument in the passage and in underscoring the king's hypocrisy, Jefferson may have reflected on the hypocrisy of colonists who kept enslaved people. That the king might have been partially responsible for the transplantation of enslaved people to the continent did not exculpate colonists for keeping slaves.

Finally, the undue length and the placement of the passage in Jefferson's first draft are revelatory. There are 168 words in the passage. No other grievance comes near to it in length. That argues for the strength of Jefferson's conviction that slavery was opprobrious. Moreover, that Jefferson positioned the lengthy grievance in the last place indicates that he considered the grievance his *coup de grace*.

Those things noted, there is something strained in the passage. Carl Becker in his *The Declaration of Independence* writes: "The passage is clear, precise, carefully balanced. It employs the most tremendous words—'murder,' 'piratical warfare,' 'prostituted,' and 'miserable death.' But in spite of every effort, the passage somehow leaves us cold." It is "calm and quiescent," lacking in warmth, and fails to move us. Readers get a sense of "labored effort"—that is, of "deliberate striving for an effect that does not come."

Becker is right but fails to recognize the reason: the hypocrisy of the colonists, Jefferson included. He blamed the king for sanctioning slavery by not stopping the exportation of enslaved people to America, but he nowise addressed the issue of the colonists, freed Blacks among them, putting transmigrated Blacks to work as slaves. The guilt here must be shared.

That stated, we must acknowledge the entrenchment of slavery at the time—the year was no longer 1619—and the South's economic dependency on it. The issue of eradication of the vile institution held serious and enormous short-term economic implications for the nascent country, hence the broad-based reluctance to take action.

Jefferson's anti-slavery passage was excised by Congress and so it did not appear in the Declaration of Independence. The reason was that slavery, widely practiced in the South, was a divisive issue and the Declaration of Independence and its redress of grievances to the King and parliament required that all states form a united front. To include this lengthy grievance, Jefferson wisely anticipated, would likely have created unnecessary division among members of Congress at a time when their common cause demanded cohesion.

Jefferson expressed regret that the excised passage was not included in the final draft. He said in notes on the Continental Congress: "the clause ... reprobating the enslaving the inhabitants of Africa, was struck out in complaisance to South Carolina & Georgia, who had never attempted to restrain the importation of slaves, and who on the contrary still wished to continue it. Our Northern brethren also I believe felt a little tender under those censures; for tho' their people have very few slaves themselves yet they had been pretty considerable carriers of them to others."

His hypocrisy aside, Jefferson deserves acknowledgement for articulating his anti-slavery views in his draft of the document, even if the paragraph was axed. By doing so, he stuck out his neck, so to speak, placing himself at odds with most others from the South, his own state especially, on slavery. The passage did reach the hands of others in the Congress and Jefferson's opposition to slavery became widely known by members. In that regard, the excised passage was not without effect and ought not now to be without effect. Yet today's scholars often conveniently overlook the risk Jefferson took in crafting that passage.

Edward Hand's American Journey

DAVID PRICE

It has been said of Edward Hand that he was "the stuff of which the hard core" of Washington's army was made.[1] Indeed, he may have been the most unsung Patriot military hero of the American Revolution. On the second day of 1777, Hand organized a remarkable defensive action along the road from Princeton to Trenton, New Jersey, against an Anglo-German force that heavily outnumbered his contingent. In the process, he may very well have prevented the destruction of Washington's army and facilitated one of the most remarkable military maneuvers in history. The rebel troops halted the enemy thrust at the Battle of Assunpink Creek, or Second Battle of Trenton, and then counterattacked at Princeton in the capstone engagement of the "Ten Crucial Days" winter campaign of 1776-1777, which reversed the military momentum that had previously favored His Majesty's forces.

COMING TO AMERICA

The son of John and Dorothy Hand was the descendent of English ancestors who probably came to Ireland in the sixteenth or seventeenth century. Edward was born on December 31, 1744 in Clydruff, a small village west of Dublin, but little is known about his formative years. He moved to Dublin and pursued medical studies at Trinity College while in his early twenties; however, no record exists of his having matriculated.[2] Hand enlisted as a surgeon's mate (assistant physician) in the 18th (Royal Irish) Regiment of Foot in 1767. For someone who aspired to be a physician in Ireland, this type of military service was preferred to the alternate route available for medical training, that of a five-year apprenticeship with a Dublin physician; and in the eighteenth

---

1. Richard Ketchum, *The Winter Soldiers* (New York: Doubleday & Company, Inc., 1973), 341.
2. Michael Williams Craig, *General Edward Hand: Winter's Doctor* (Lancaster, PA: Rock Ford Plantation, 1984), 1.

century, Trinity graduates often occupied positions in the medical department of the British army.[3]

Hand sailed with his regiment for North America on May 19, 1767 and reached Philadelphia in July after a journey of three thousand miles across an ocean noted for its severe weather. He investigated Native American medical practices and horticulture during his frontier duty at Fort Pitt (the site of Pittsburgh today) and profited from several land transactions. These enabled the young soldier to purchase an ensign's commission in 1772, and he became a supply officer at Fort Pitt. However, Hand eventually became disenchanted with British colonial policy, which reminded him of what the Irish viewed as England's overbearing posture. Many of Hand's fellow migrants from the British Isles, including the Irish and Scots-Irish, came to the New World bitterly resentful of the British government. They felt abused by edicts from London—forcing Presbyterians to pay taxes to the Church of England; excluding Presbyterians from the military, the civil service, and teaching; restricting Irish trade with other English colonies; and limiting Irish wool exports to only England or Wales—to the point where their loyalty to the Crown had lapsed. Indeed, sympathy for the Revolutionary cause among those of Irish descent was such that they, in particular the Scots-Irish, would in time constitute a significant presence in the Continental Army.[4]

Hand's sympathy for the colonial perspective on their relations with Britain led him to sell his officer's commission and resign from the army in 1774. He settled in Lancaster, Pennsylvania—a community of about three thousand people—and turned to the practice of medicine. The newcomer met Katherine Ewing (1751-1805), whom he married in 1775, and they went on to have three daughters (only one of whom lived to adulthood) and a son. The former soldier established himself as a competent physician and industrious vestryman, and an active and responsible man of public affairs.[5] As the colonies' dispute with Britain deepened, Hand was exposed to opinions in newspapers and various tracts in support of the Patriot cause that he could relate to his own experience. The views expressed recalled those of his fellow Anglo-Irishmen in their dispute with Parliament during Hand's time as a student in Dublin and presumably appealed to him.

---

3. Richard Reuben Forry, *Edward Hand: His Role in the American Revolution* (Durham, NC: Duke University Press, 1976), 20.
4. Michael Stephenson, *Patriot Battles: How the War of Independence Was Fought* (New York: Harper Perennial, 2008), 29-30.
5. Forry, *Edward Hand*, 53.

GOING TO WAR

Upon the Revolution's outbreak, the soldier-turned-physician helped organize a local militia unit known as the Lancaster County Associators and was subsequently commissioned a lieutenant colonel in command of a rifle unit known as the 1st Pennsylvania Continental Regiment. Because of his military and medical experience, Hand was welcomed by rebel organizers when he enlisted in the cause. After Hand's promotion to colonel, his regiment joined the newly designated Continental Army in Cambridge, Massachusetts, just outside Boston, in August 1775. Hand's unit constituted the first detachment of soldiers to join the rebel forces from beyond the boundaries of New England; and Dr. James Thacher, a Continental Army surgeon, observed of the newcomers, "Several companies of riflemen, amounting, it is said, to more than fourteen hundred men, have arrived here from Pennsylvania and Maryland; a distance of from five hundred to seven hundred miles. They are remarkably stout and hardy men; many of them exceeding six feet in height. They are dressed in white frocks, or rifle shirts, and round hats. These men are remarkable for the accuracy of their aim; striking a mark with great certainty at two hundred yards distance. At a review, a company of them, while on a quick advance, fired their balls into objects of seven inches diameter, at the distance of two hundred and fifty yards." Thacher reported that these sharpshooters "are now stationed on our lines, and their shot have frequently proved fatal to British officers and soldiers, who expose them selves to view, even at more than double the distance of common musket shot."[6]

The members of Hand's 1st Pennsylvania Regiment carried an American-made long rifle that posed a lethal threat to enemy combatants. In addition to their skilled marksmanship, these soldiers were noted for their utility, as they could be employed effectively in a variety of tactical settings: as snipers or scouts, in joint operations with regular troops, or as light infantry units were in European armies.[7] The colonel made a considerable effort to properly equip his men and instill in them a sense of esprit de corps. He ordered a silk standard or color for the regiment—made in Philadelphia and delivered to his unit by the fall of 1776—which he described as "a deep green ground, the device a tiger partly enclosed by toils, attempting the pass, defended by a hunter

---

6. James Thacher, *A Military Journal During the American Revolutionary War, from 1775 to 1783, Describing Interesting Events and Transactions of This Period, with Numerous Historical Facts and Anecdotes, from the Original Manuscript* (Boston: Richardson and Lord, 1823), 37-38.
7. Forry, *Edward Hand*, 66.

armed with a spear . . . on a crimson field the motto Domari nolo," a Latin expression for refusing to yield or be subdued.[8]

Rifles were made mostly in Pennsylvania and used there and in the Chesapeake colonies by men who hunted for much of their fresh meat, but anecdotal information about this firearm's accuracy spread far and wide. Its long barrel was etched or "rifled" with seven or eight internal grooves, unlike smooth-bore muskets, and the effect was to make the rifle accurate at a range of about two hundred and perhaps even three hundred yards, several times the range of a musket.[9] The singular nature of these instruments was recognized by the Continental Congress when it established the Continental Army in June 1775 in support of New England's uprising against the British troops in Boston. Rifles were scarce in the colonies and, while popular in the more rural areas, largely unknown around Boston. John Adams informed his wife Abigail that the Continental Congress in which he served "is really in earnest in defending the Country. They have voted Ten Companies of Rifle Men to be sent from Pennsylvania, Maryland and Virginia, to join the Army before Boston. These are an excellent Species of Light Infantry. They use a peculiar Kind of [Firearm ca]ll'd a Rifle—it has . . . Grooves within the Barrell, and carries a Ball, with great Exactness to great Distances. They are the most accurate Marksmen in the World."[10]

Hand's riflemen repeatedly demonstrated what their long rifles could do in the face of superior enemy numbers. One of the more memorable displays occurred on October 12, 1776, when Maj. Gen. William Howe, the British army's commander, landed four thousand troops at Throgs Neck above Manhattan Island in an effort to trap Washington's force there by sealing off the main crossing to the mainland. A small detachment of Hand's Pennsylvanians frustrated the British army and held them while another 1,500 American infantry came to their support, forcing the redcoats to abandon the effort and seek a better landing site, which they found at Pell's Point a few days later, but too late to prevent Washington's escape from Manhattan. Under orders from Maj. Gen. William Heath, Hand and a detachment of riflemen tore up the bridge that connected Throgs Neck to the main-

---

8. James L. Kochan and Don Troiani, *Don Troiani's Soldiers of the American Revolution* (Guilford, CT: Stackpole Books, 2007), 91-92.
9. John Ferling, *Almost a Miracle: The American Victory in the War of Independence* (New York: Oxford University Press, 2007), 89.
10. John Adams to Abigail Adams, June 11-17, 1775, in Margaret A. Hogan, and C. James Taylor, eds., *My Dearest Friend: Letters of Abigail and John Adams* (Cambridge, MA: The Belknap Press of Harvard University Press, 2007), 59.

land and concealed themselves behind a long pile of cord wood near its western end. According to General Heath, "Col Hand's riflemen took up the planks of the bridge, as had been directed, and commenced a firing with their rifles."[11] The British withdrew to the top of the nearest hill and dug in there, abandoning their objective. As historian Christopher Ward put it (dramatically, if not hyperbolically), some twenty-five American riflemen behind a wood-pile temporarily stopped the British army.[12]

By the end of 1776, Hand's regiment had fought in nearly every important engagement since joining Washington's army.[13] They were at the Battle of Long Island in August and endured the near-disastrous New York campaign and long retreat across New Jersey to Pennsylvania that autumn. Serving in the brigade commanded by Brig. Gen. Matthias-Alexis de Roche Fermoy, a French volunteer in the Patriot cause from Martinique, Hand's soldiers were consolidated with the German Continental Regiment under Col. Nicholas Haussegger and engaged the Hessian brigade at the First Battle of Trenton on December 26. Their charge toward the road leading to Princeton, northeast of the town, foiled an attempt by Col. Johann Rall's troops to escape in that direction by skirting the Continentals' left flank and helped seal the fate of the enemy garrison.

THE ROAD TO ASSUNPINK CREEK

Washington dispatched a body of soldiers halfway up the road to Princeton on New Year's Eve, Hand's thirty-second birthday, to disrupt the enemy's anticipated advance toward Trenton. He knew he could not defeat the large force that would be marching down from Princeton under Lt. Gen. Charles Earl Cornwallis, but hoped his outnumbered troops would make the enemy pay dearly for any success they achieved. This forward deployment of rebel units included about a thousand men commanded by General Fermoy and comprised Hand's regiment, Haussegger's regiment, a Virginia Continental brigade, and a pair of field guns manned by the 2nd Company of the Pennsylvania State Artillery.[13] Before sunrise on New Year's Day 1777, the troops under Fermoy's command occupied a position called Eight Mile Run—known as Shipetaukin Creek today—about six miles south of Nassau Hall in

---

11. William Heath, *Memoirs of Major-General William Heath*, William Abbatt, ed. (New York: William Abbatt, 1901. Reprint: Sagwan Press, 2015), 62.
12. Christopher L. Ward, *The Delaware Continentals, 1776-1783* (Wilmington, DE: The Historical Society of Delaware, 1941), 76.
13. Ketchum, *The Winter Soldiers*, 341.

Princeton, which housed the College of New Jersey (after 1896, Princeton University). The rebel pickets there skirmished with British and Hessian patrols, who pushed the outnumbered Americans back but at a heavy cost.

On the morning of January 2, the lead elements of General Cornwallis's column—the Hessian jägers (riflemen)—began to encounter scattered resistance before they had ventured far from Princeton, as small parties of rebel skirmishers began a harassing fire. Proceeding along the Princeton Road, Cornwallis's vanguard encountered its initial resistance at Eight Mile Run, and by mid-morning, the advancing column had begun to enter into a daylong series of running battles. A mile below Maidenhead (after 1816, Lawrence Township), the Princeton Road crossed a stream called Five Mile Run, known as Little Shabakunk Creek today, where the rebels offered only token resistance. A mile beyond that was a larger waterway known as Big Shabakunk Creek. In the woods behind this larger stream, some three miles north of Trenton, the bulk of Fermoy's men waited. As the enemy approached, General Fermoy suddenly mounted his horse without speaking a word to anyone and fled towards Trenton, thereby leaving his command to Colonel Hand as the next senior officer present. That may have been the best possible development for the Patriot cause under the circumstances.

When the flank and advance guards of Cornwallis's force approached the Big Shabakunk Creek, rebel snipers unleashed a deadly fire that broke the enemy vanguard and sent it reeling backwards into their main body, creating great confusion among these troops. Hand was "determined to waste as much time as possible for the enemy at this point."[14] The longer it took the British commander to get to Trenton, the less time he would have to attack Washington's army arrayed behind the Assunpink Creek before the onset of darkness limited his tactical options. Hand's riflemen used to their advantage every kind of wooded cover as they forced Cornwallis's main body to halt repeatedly while troops from the advance guard were deployed to drive off the unseen rebels. The soldiers under Hand's command fell back in the face of superior numbers but fought a stubborn delaying action for most of the afternoon. They utilized every tactical means available to hinder the enemy: cannon fire, ambushes, irregular warfare, and regular infantry maneuvers.[15] Hand's small force held off the enemy until about

---

14. James Wilkinson, *Memoirs of My Own Times*. Vol. 1 (Philadelphia: Abraham Small, 1816. Reprint: Sagwan Press, 2015), 137.
15. Forry, *Edward Hand*, 107.

3 p.m.[16] Then, facing continued heavy pressure and outnumbered by more than six to one, they began a slow withdrawal in good order toward Trenton.

At a ravine called Stockton Hollow, about half a mile north of Trenton, the rebel skirmishers made their final stand with about six hundred men. Washington, accompanied by Maj. Gen. Nathanael Greene and Brig. Gen. Henry Knox, rode out from town to personally encourage the skirmishers' continued resistance and emphasized the importance of delaying the enemy until nightfall. The commander in chief thanked the defenders for their efforts, "gave orders for as obstinate a stand as could be made on that ground, without hazarding the [artillery] pieces, and retired to marshal his troops for action, behind the Assunpink."[17] When the full weight of the imperial force was brought to bear on this last point of resistance, Hand was forced to give ground to avoid being outflanked. Daylight was fading as the British and Hessians entered Trenton, and Hand's men retreated in an orderly manner through the town toward the Assunpink Creek bridge held by Washington's main body.[18]

As daylight faded, the British and Hessians launched a series of probes in an effort to secure the bridge and exploit any possible weakness in Washington's defenses; however, they were beaten back with heavy losses each time. When darkness fully descended, the two sides exchanged cannon fire to little effect for some time. Cornwallis called for reinforcements from his units in Princeton and Maidenhead and made plans to continue his assault in the morning, but the Battle of Assunpink Creek was over. His Lordship's opportunity to continue the engagement was lost when the American army vacated its position overnight and marched around the enemy's left flank to Princeton under the cover of darkness. There, on January 3, Hand's riflemen assisted in overcoming an outnumbered redcoat contingent's spirited resistance to win the final Patriot victory in their remarkable winter offensive.

ON THE RISE

Hand earned a series of promotions as the Revolution unfolded. He became a brigadier general in April 1777 and was assigned to command the American troops at Fort Pitt, where the threat posed by hostile tribes and the lack of support from local militia made life challenging.

---

16. Henry Knox to Lucy Flucker Knox, January 7, 1777, in William S. Stryker, *The Battles of Trenton and Princeton* (Boston: Houghton, Mifflin and Company, 1898), 449.
17. Wilkinson, *Memoirs*, 138.
18. Ibid.

Hand advised Washington that "the Western Indians are united against us" and "the Militia are [called] and Promise to turn out on an Expedition that must for the Security of the Frontiers, be Carried in to the Indian Country, but they cant be induced to do duty here."[19] The commander in chief replied: "I am sorry your force is not more adequate to the uses you have for it, and that such coldness appears in the neighbouring inhabitants as to preclude the assistance you had a right to expect from them."[20] Hand subsequently reported to Washington, "When I last did myself the Honour to write to your Excy I fully Expected to be able to penetrate the Indian Country. But Alas! I was disappointed the Whole force I was Able to Collect, including Draughts from, Hampshire, Berckley, Dunmore, Loudon, Frederick & Augusta Did not exceed 800 men—I am therefore obliged to Content myself with Stationing Small Detachments on the Frontiers to prevent as Much as possible the Inroads of the Savages & rely on the Successes of Our Arms to the Northward, & Your Excellys Operations for the Rest."[21]

Notwithstanding such difficulties, when Hand wrote his wife, Katherine, from the fort in December 1777 (the letter being addressed to "My Dearest Kitty," the nickname he conferred upon her), the general reported: "Every thing is quiet here now. God grant it may continue so, and that I may soon have the Happiness to fold you & our Dear little Babes in my longing arms."[22] Hand was relieved of his assignment at the fort in August 1778, in accordance with his wishes, and wrote Washington from Lancaster on the 25th "that I last Evening arrived here from Fort Pitt & in a very few days intend to wait on the board of war to give that Honorable Body a State of Affairs on the Western frontiers & settle the Accounts of that Departmt during my Command there."[23]

---

19. Edward Hand to George Washington, September 15, 1777, https://founders.archives.gov/?q=Correspondent%3A%22Hand%2C%20Edward%22%20Correspondent%3A%22Washington%2C%20George%22&s=1111311111&r=6.
20. Washington to Hand, October 13, 1777, https://founders.archives.gov/?q=Correspondent%3A%22Hand%2C%20Edward%22%20Correspondent%3A%22Washington%2C%20George%22&s=1111311111&r=8.
21. Hand to Washington, November 9, 1777, https://founders.archives.gov/?q=Correspondent%3A%22Hand%2C%20Edward%22%20Correspondent%3A%22Washington%2C%20George%22&s=1111311111&r=9.
22. Hand to Katherine Ewing Hand, December 17, 1777, in the *Edward Hand Papers* (Collection 261), Historical Society of Pennsylvania.
23. Hand to Washington, August 25, 1778, https://founders.archives.gov/?q=Correspondent%3A%22Hand%2C%20Edward%22%20Correspondent%3A%22Washington%2C%20George%22&s=1111311111&r=10.

In October, Washington ordered Hand to relieve Brig. Gen. John Stark on the northern frontier: "You are forthwith to proceed to Albany and take the command at that place and its dependencies—The forts on the frontiers, and all the Troops employed there will be comprehended under your general command and direction.... The principal objects of your attention will be the defence of the frontiers, from the depredations of the Enemy, and the annoyance of their settlements, as much as circumstances will permit; in which you will be aided by the militia of the Country."[24] Upon arriving in Albany, Hand informed Washington that, "As the Greater part of the Troops on the Frontier are Almost naked, and the Winter Approaching, I intend Send[ing] an Officer from each Corps to head Quarters for a Supply of Cloat[h]ing for them."[25] Hand was occupied with defending against raids by hostile Indian tribes in New York's Mohawk Valley, a threat magnified by the Cherry Valley Massacre that November, and he led a brigade as part of the expedition under Maj. Gen. John Sullivan against the Iroquois of the Six Nations that was launched in mid-1779 at Washington's direction.

When the campaign against the Iroquois ended, Hand returned to Lancaster for the winter but was summoned to camp at Morristown, New Jersey, by the commander in chief in February 1780 and served as President of court martials. He left that desk job in June to lead a contingent of five hundred men against a small army of Hessian troops advancing towards Morristown, but the enemy force aborted its effort and withdrew at news of an anticipated landing of French troops at Newport, Rhode Island. That September, Hand was ordered to serve on a board with several of the army's highest-ranking officers in order to render a verdict on the ill-fated British Major John André, who would be hanged as a spy for assisting Benedict Arnold's attempted surrender of the fort at West Point.

On January 8, 1781, Hand was selected as adjutant general (chief administrative officer) of the Continental Army by a vote of Congress—the last man to occupy that position during the war. He replaced Col. Alexander Scammell, who had notified Washington in November of his desire to resign the office, which prompted the commanding gen-

24. Washington to Hand, October 19, 1778, https://founders.archives.gov/?q=Correspondent%3A%22Hand%2C%20Edward%22%20Correspondent%3A%22Washington%2C%20George%22&s=1113111111&r=13.
25. Hand to Washington, October 29, 1778, https://founders.archives.gov/?q=Correspondent%3A%22Hand%2C%20Edward%22%20Correspondent%3A%22Washington%2C%20George%22&s=1113111111&r=16.

eral to recommend Hand to the President of Congress. Washington's letter of January 23 to Scammell's successor broke the news: "I have the pleasure to congratulate you, on your appointment as Adjutant General to the Army. This has been announced to me two days ago officially from Congress."[26] As adjutant general, Hand served at Washington's side and assumed responsibility for the transmission of most general orders to the army, personnel administration, supervision of outposts, and security matters. When General Cornwallis's besieged force capitulated to the Franco-American army at Yorktown, Virginia, on October 19, 1781, Hand accompanied General Washington and the French commander, the Comte de Rochambeau, as they rode out to one of the captured British redoubts to receive the official document of surrender.[27]

With the formal termination of hostilities by the Treaty of Paris in September 1783, Hand was made a brevet major general in recognition of his service. Four months later, Washington wrote his former comrade-in-arms to express "my entire approbation for your public conduct, particularly in the execution of the important duties of Adjutant General" and to convey "how much reason I have had to be satisfied with the great Zeal, attention, and ability manifested by you in conducting the business of your Department; and how happy I should be in oppertunities of demonstrating my sincere regard & esteem for you." The letter included an implicit invitation to visit Washington's Virginia home at Mount Vernon: "It is unnecessary I hope to add with what pleasure I should see you at this place."[28]

AFTERWARDS

Hand's tenure as adjutant general of the army ended on November 3, 1783, and he returned to Lancaster, Pennsylvania, where in 1794 he would build Rock Ford, a Georgian-style brick mansion on several hundred acres of land he had purchased. He lived there, along with his family and their servants and laborers—both enslaved and free, for the remainder of his life. Hand practiced medicine, served as a member of the Congress of Confederation (1784-1785) and the Pennsylvania Assembly (1785-1786), and subsequently as a delegate to the Pennsylvania

---

26. Washington to Hand, January 23, 1781, https://founders.archives.gov/?q=Correspondent%3A%22Hand%2C%20Edward%22%20Correspondent%3A%22Washington%2C%20George%22&s=1111311111&r=65.
27. Craig, *General Edward Hand*, 95.
28. Washington to Hand, January 14, 1784, https://founders.archives.gov/?q=Correspondent%3A%22Hand%2C%20Edward%22%20Correspondent%3A%22Washington%2C%20George%22&s=1111311111&r=87.

Constitutional Convention (1790). Tradition has it that he played host to President Washington when the latter visited Lancaster in 1791. At his death on September 3, 1802 at age fifty-seven (attributed to cholera morbus, a term then applied to various cholera-like symptoms), Hand was interred in St. James Episcopal Cemetery in Lancaster.

Today, the site of Edward Hand's last home—known as Historic Rock Ford—comprises thirty-three acres at the southeastern edge of Lancaster City and is enveloped by Lancaster County Central Park. The mansion, a registered National Historic Landmark recorded in the Historic American Building Survey, is regarded as one of the most important examples of Georgian domestic architecture in Pennsylvania and the most intact building in Lancaster County from before 1800. It features an exceptional display of period furnishings and decorative arts, and is complemented by the John J. Snyder, Jr. Gallery of Early Lancaster County Decorative Arts situated in a reconstructed eighteenth-century barn.[29] In their efforts to educate the public about Hand's life and legacy and the realities of eighteenth-century American life, the Rock Ford staff and volunteers have made this site a fitting shrine to a young nation's spirit and enterprise.

For the past sixty years, the actions of Hand and his skirmishers against General Cornwallis's army on the second day of 1777 have been celebrated each January in an event sponsored by Lawrence Township, New Jersey, to highlight its role (as Maidenhead) in the War of Independence. Since 1981, the part of Colonel Hand has been performed by township resident Bill Agress, joined by other re-enactors, history enthusiasts, Boy Scouts, township officials, and local residents. After a ceremony at the municipal building, they march south along Route 206 (which Hand's men would have known as the Princeton Road, the Princeton-Trenton Road, or the Post Road) to Notre Dame High School adjacent to Shabakunk Creek, where Hand orchestrated his soldiers' delaying action.

Upon final reflection, Edward Hand's defining moment will always be that January day when his outnumbered force, and unusually mild temperatures and rain that turned the road to Trenton into a muddy morass, impeded the advance of a formidable adversary. As has been written elsewhere, one might say the weather was guided by the hand of fate and the defenders by the Hand of Pennsylvania.[30]

---

29. https://historicrockford.org.
30. David Price, *The Road to Assunpink Creek: Liberty's Desperate Hour and the Ten Crucial Days of the American Revolution* (Lawrenceville, NJ: Knox Press, 2019), 194.

Jemima Howe, Frontier Pioneer to Wealthy Widow

JANE STRACHAN

Jemima Howe (1724–1805) reflects the strength it took to endure the harsh realities of the Vermont frontier during the American colonial and Revolutionary War eras. Although recognized as the "fair captive" then and now, Jemima was far from a damsel in distress. During her full life, she outlived three husbands and five of her nine children, was a witness to divided loyalties in her own home during the American Revolution, and through her tenacity and wit became a wealthy widow and financial matriarch to her family. Because Jemima Howe is only known to a few historians and experts on Indian captivity narratives, it is time to bring her back to life as a remarkable woman of her time.

Jemima Sartwell was born in Groton, Massachusetts on March 7, 1724, the fourth generation of her paternal family from Somersetshire, England who settled in the area west of Boston. Jemima's great-grandfather, Richard Sawtell, was an early proprietor and selectman of Watertown, Massachusetts and later the first town clerk of Groton. Her father, Josiah Sartwell, was born in Groton where he married his second wife and Jemima's mother, Lydia Nutting. Having served as a soldier and sustaining wounds likely during Dummer's War, in 1738 Josiah received a military grant of 100 acres just west of the Connecticut River in present day Vernon, the most southeasterly town in Vermont bordering New Hampshire.[1] This is where Jemima Howe would spend

---

1. *Massachusetts: Vital Records, 1620–1850*, AmericanAncestors.org, Groton, births, 209. *The New England Historical and Genealogical Register* (Boston: New England Historic Genealogical Society, 1847–1972), 126:3–4, 8, 14–15. Herbert Williams Denio, "Massachusetts Land Grants in Vermont," *Publications of the Colonial Society of Massachusetts* (Cambridge: John Wilson and Son, 1920), 24:40–41. Samuel A. Green, *Groton During the Indian Wars* (Cambridge: John Wilson and Son, 1883), 147. Sartwell, Sawtell and Sawtelle are among the most often used spellings of the surname and of which Richard is the forbear, in *Genealogical and Family History of the State of Maine*, ed. George Thomas Little (New York: Lewis Historical Publishing. Co., 1909), 1:421.

most of her years, in the frontier wilderness of the Connecticut River Valley where the dark shadows of international and local wars and politics loomed large over her and her family.

During the late 1730s and early 1740s, Jemima's family and neighbors built a chain of more than a dozen forts—or, more accurately, twenty-foot by thirty-eight-foot log cabins packed with multiple, large families—to defend against French-instigated Abenaki attacks. The earliest and most northerly link in the chain was Fort No. 4 located in present-day Charleston, New Hampshire on the east side of the Connecticut River. Just south of Brattleboro, Vermont was Fort Dummer; a few miles farther south stood the fort named after Jemima's father and built in 1737; and Orlando Bridgman's Fort rested another one-half mile south of that.[2]

Despite these community efforts to protect family and home, the constant threat of attacks and actual captivity by the French and their allied-Indians were a part of Jemima Howe's life. Her uncle, Obadiah Sartwell, was captured and returned by Indians in 1747 only to be killed two years later while hoeing the field near Fort No. 4. Her younger brother Jonathan was captured near Fort Hinsdale and brought to Montreal where he died. Her second father-in-law, Nehemiah Howe, was captured in 1745 near Fort Dummer and died in a Quebec prison two years later, just before his expected release.[3] For Jemima, the story continued.

Jemima Sartwell married her first husband, William Phipps, an early settler in the Connecticut River Valley, most likely in 1740 at age sixteen and soon bore him two daughters—Mary, and then Submit two years later. On July 5, 1745, William Phipps was killed at Great Meadow, present-day Putney, Vermont, in a skirmish with French-allied Indians.[4]

---

2. Benjamin H. Hall, *History of Eastern Vermont, from its Earliest Settlement to the Close of the Eighteenth Century, with a Biographical Chapter and Appendixes* (New York: D. Appleton & Co., 1858), 1:26–27. Abby Maria Hemenway, *Vermont Historical Gazetteer. A Local History of All the Towns in the State, Civil, Educational, Biographical, Religious and Military* (Brandon, Vt.: Published by Mrs. Carrie E. H. Page, 1891), 5:277.
3. Emma Lewis Coleman, *New England Captives Carried to Canada: Between 1677 and 1760 during the French and Indian Wars* (Portland, Me.: Heritage, 1926), 2:183–184, 186 (Obadiah Sartwell) and 2:198 (Jonathan Sartwell). Nehemiah How, *A Narrative of the Captivity of Nehemiah How, who was Taken by the Indians at the Great Meadow Fort Above Fort-Dummer, where he was an Inhabitant, October 11th, 1745* (Boston: N.E., 1748), excerpted from Samuel G. Drake, *Indian Captivities, or Life in the Wigwam* (Auburn, MA: Derby and Miller, 1852), 127–128.
4. James Axtell, "Sawtelle, Jemima," in *Dictionary of Canadian Biography*, vol. 5, University of Toronto/Université Laval, 2003–, www.biographi.ca/en/bio/sawtelle_jemima_5E.html.

Not long after, the young and, by all accounts, beautiful widow Jemima married her second husband, Caleb Howe, originally from Grafton, Massachusetts. From a grant chartered in 1753 by the provincial governor of New Hampshire, the Howe family became early settlers of Hinsdale, New Hampshire which then spanned both sides of the Connecticut River. They lived on the west bank of the river in what is today Vernon, Vermont.[5]

Caleb Howe was active in military and local government affairs. He was a captain in Phineas Steven's Company and a sergeant at the often-besieged Fort No. 4. At the first proprietors' meeting for Hinsdale he was elected constable. Soon after, he was appointed tithingman and to a committee to search for the town's minister.[6] Jemima and Caleb had five sons born every other year from 1747 through 1755: William, Moses, Squire, Caleb, and Josiah.[7]

When the French and Indian War broke out in 1754, Indian attacks around the Connecticut River Valley were once again more frequent. The Howe family and several neighbors took refuge at Fort Bridgman. On June 27, 1755, Caleb Howe, his two oldest sons, William and Moses, and neighbors Hilkiah Grout and Benjamin Gaffield were attacked by a dozen Abenaki while returning to the fort. Caleb was pierced with a spear, scalped, and died the next day. His two sons were captured. Hilkiah Grout escaped, while Benjamin Gaffield drowned in the river trying to flee. Jemima and her remaining five children, as well as Mrs. Grout and Mrs. Gaffield and their four children, were seized from the unmanned fort.[8]

Although there are no known records written by Jemima, primary sources can help us piece together certain facts about the difficulties

---

5. *Massachusetts: Vital Records, 1620–1850*, AmericanAncestors.org, Grafton, births, 73. *The Provincial and State Papers of New Hampshire. State of New Hampshire, Town Charters, Granted within the Present Limits of New Hampshire, Vol. XXV, Town Charters*, ed. Albert Stillman Batchellor (Concord, NH: Edward N. Pearson, 1895), 2:115–119.

6. *Hinsdale, New Hampshire, Town Records, 1753–1836*, FamilySearch.org, 1:3–7 (DGS 5510738, images 8–10).

7. Harlan L. Howe, "Jemima (Sartwell) (Phipps) (Howe) Tute," *The Howe, Willard, Sartwell Families of Vernon, Vt.* (Manuscript, n.d.) held at Brooks Memorial Library, Brattleboro, Vermont. Daniel Wait Howe, *Howe Genealogies* (Haverhill, MA: Record Publishing Co., 1929), 45–46. For son Caleb Howe, see, *UK, Pension Applications for Widows and Family of Military Officers, 1776–1881* online database, Ancestry.com in "Loyal American and Canadian Corps," doc. no. H.25 (pp.179–186), W.O. 42/61, from The National Archives, Kew, UK.

8. Axtell, "Sawtelle, Jemima," *Dictionary of Canadian Biography*, vol. 5, 2003. *Women's Indian Captivity Narratives*, ed. Kathryn Zabelle Derounian-Stola (New York: Penguin Books, 1998), 96–97.

she endured during her three years of captivity. One of the most well-known sources is from Hinsdale's first and long-serving Congregational chaplain Rev. Bunker Gay, a graduate of Harvard College and neighbor of the Howes. At least some of our knowledge about Jemima's captivity comes from her telling her own story—her oral history—to Reverend Gay who published *A Genuine and Correct Account of the Captivity, Sufferings and Deliverance of Mrs. Jemima Howe* in 1792. Although Reverend Gay has been criticized for being overly "sentimental" to "boost sales and enhance readability," there is some degree of credibility to his narrative, thus making it noteworthy.[9]

Jemima and her young family endured a tedious march for eight days to Crown Point, at the narrows of Lake Champlain about fifteen miles north of Fort Ticonderoga, where they remained for a week. They then proceeded by canoe to St. Francis, the Abenaki First Nations reserve called Odanak in Quebec, at the confluence of the St. Francois and St. Lawrence Rivers about midway between Montreal and Quebec City. Their Abenaki captors separated Jemima from her children, who were likewise separated from one another.[10]

Early that winter, Jemima was taken on an arduous trip to Montreal for ransom, but there was no market for a mother with an infant. Soon after, Jemima's infant was taken from her and brought to the northern shore of Lake Champlain by her captors while she and her Abenaki family, which included a so-called sister and her husband, roamed from one place to another during the harsh winter months. With great difficulty, Jemima managed a few brief glimpses of her emaciated sons Caleb and Squire and soon learned that her infant had starved to death.[11]

After nearly a year in captivity, Jemima's Indian sister's husband sold her to a Frenchman, Joachim de Saccapee, captain of the fort at St. Johns on the Richelieu River, not far from Montreal. While there, she had considerable liberty and became a missionary to other captives brought to St. John's. This freedom didn't come without its downsides. Saccapee and his young adult son became "excessively fond" of Jemima, who required a "large stock of prudence" to maintain her virtue. She prevailed on Col. Peter Schuyler, a wealthy New Jersey landowner, who had the ear of the French-Canadian Gov. Pierre de Rigaud, Marquis de Vaudreuil-Cavagnial. Although a prisoner himself, Colonel Schuyler used his time on parole to help countless prisoners of war and civilian

9. Derounian-Stodola, *Women's Indian Captivity Narratives*, xix.
10. Ibid., 97–101.
11. Ibid., 98–101.

captives, like Jemima. Colonel Schuyler informed the governor of the disgrace the Saccapees tried to inflict upon the beautiful widow. Using his political position as governor, Marquis de Vaudreuil sent the young Saccapee away on military assignment and chastised the father. Upon hearing that her daughter Mary might soon be married to an Indian, Jemima again prevailed on Governor Marquis de Vaudreuil whose wife, Jeanne Charlotte de Fleury Deschambault, arranged for Jemima's daughters to be placed in a Montreal nunnery.[12]

In addition to Reverend Gay's narrative of Jemima's story, first-hand accounts shed further light on her plight as word of her captivity reached various corners of New England. Several influential men had met with her and attempted to have her and her children ransomed and brought back home.

Early in 1758, Rev. Ebenezer Hinsdale, from a wealthy Deerfield, Massachusetts family and for whom the town and fort were named, and friend and neighbor of the Howes, felt duty-bound to write New Hampshire Governor Wentworth to appeal for a ransom for Jemima Howe and her children. Reverend Hinsdale heard that a petition had been filed with the general court on her behalf, as well as the other captured women, and hoped the governor would support their "redemption."[13]

Reverend Hinsdale's letter to Governor Wentworth included two enclosures. One was a plea from Dr. Benjamin Stukes, surgeon of the New Jersey troops stationed in upstate New York and on parole when he and Colonel Schuyler met Mrs. Howe at Fort St. Johns. Dr. Stukes wrote that Mrs. Howe had been sold to the captain of the fort there and was "in miserable circumstances." The surgeon reminded the governor that to provide relief for her would be "well pleasing in the sight of God."[14]

Reverend Hinsdale's package to the governor also included an extract of a letter from Col. Nathan Whiting, a successful merchant in New Haven who had first-hand military knowledge of the difficulties facing the Connecticut River Valley frontier and especially Fort No. 4. Colonel Whiting, who had been with Colonel Schuyler in Canada, confirmed Jemima Howe's bleak predicament. He wrote that Colonel Schuyler had given his "parole of honor" to do everything possible to

---

12. Axtell, "Sawtelle, Jemima," *Dictionary of Canadian Biography*, vol. 5, 2003; Derounian-Stodola, *Women's Indian Captivity Narratives*, 101–103.
13. Reverend Hinsdale was the chaplain at Fort Dummer. *Collections of the New-Hampshire Historical Society* (Concord, N.H.: Printed by Asa McFarland for the Society, 1837), 5:256–257.
14. Ibid., 5:256–257.

secure her exchange upon his return from parole back to Canada in the spring of 1758.[15]

Finally, near the end of the year, ransom money was paid by New Hampshire in the amounts of £600 for Jemima Howe, £800 for her eldest son William, and £1,200 for sons Squire and Caleb.[16] The list of prisoners to be released was negotiated and signed in duplicate by Colonel Schuyler and Governor Marquis de Vaudreuil. Colonel Schuyler, Dr. Stukes, Captain-Major Israel Putnam who had been captured by French-allied Indians late that summer, and more than one hundred prisoners, including Jemima and her three sons, were soon exchanged and released.[17]

Once back in Vernon, Jemima Howe focused on the plight of her daughters who were still in Canada and candidates to be converted to Catholicism. Again, with help from Jeanne-Charlotte de Fleury Deschambault, Submit and Mary were brought to the Ursuline convent in Quebec a year apart, one in the fall of 1756 and the other the following year.[18]

Another long-term captive, Susannah Johnson, who had been taken from Fort No. 4 and knew the Phipps sisters, met with them at the Ursuline convent, noting they were "beautiful, cheerful and well-taught" under the special care and tutelage of Mother Superior, Esther Wheelwright, who had been captured by French Canadians and Wabanaki from her home in Wells, Massachusetts (now Maine) at the age of seven.[19]

In late June 1759, not long before the British assault on Quebec, the Marquis de Vaudreuil's wife had the two sisters placed in the Congregation of Notre-Dame in Montreal.[20] Eventually, Mary was married to Cron Lewis, a French aide to Conte d'Estaing, a match likely arranged by the governor and his wife. Sometime after 1760, Jemima

---

15. Ibid., 5:257–258.
16. Coleman, *New England Captives Carried to Canada*, 2:317.
17. *Documents Relative to the Colonial History of the State of New York*, ed. E.B. O'Callaghan et al., 15 vols. (Albany: Weed, Parsons and Company, 1853–87), 10:882–884 for the list of prisoners to be exchanged.
18. Pole culturel du Monastèe des Ursulines. MQ/1K/7/1/2/2. Livre des entrés et sorties des pensionnaires1719 à 1838, no. 2.
19. *Narrative of the Captivity of Mrs. Johnson, Containing an Account of her Sufferings during Four Years with the Indians and French, Fourth Ed.* (Lowell, MA: Published by Daniel Bixby, 1834), 67. Ann M. Little, *The Many Captivities of Esther Wheelwright* (New Haven: Yale University Press, 2016), 186–187.
20. Pole culturel du Monastèe des Ursulines. MQ/1K/7/1/2/2. Livre des entrés et sorties des pensionnaires 1719 à 1838, no. 2, noting that Submit and Mary left the convent on June 26, 1759; Little, *The Many Captivities of Esther Wheelwright*, 186–187 and 276, n. 31.

returned to Canada determined to bring her daughters back home, only to learn that Mary was already in France; Mary was never seen again by her family.[21]

Now Jemima was resolute in her efforts to bring Submit home, but the young girl required considerable coaxing to leave the convent. Another young captive, Frances Noble, recalled the "grief and lamentations" of Submit who was now well-indoctrinated into Catholicism and being forced to return to what would have been a strange, long-forgotten place and people. Jemima enlisted the support of Thomas Gage, the British military governor of Montreal, who ordered the Congregation of Notre-Dame to persuade Submit to return home with her mother, which she finally did.[22] Moses Howe also returned home around the same time although there are no records showing exactly how or when.

Survivor that she was, Jemima continued to move forward. She married her third husband, Amos Tute, originally from Deerfield, Massachusetts, an early settler of Vernon and six years her junior. Jemima and Amos had two boys. The oldest was Jonathan, who died at a young age due to a smallpox vaccination administered by his father, and Amos Jr. who lived but three years. Tute, a politician and landowner, lived until age sixty, making this relationship a lasting one for Jemima.[23]

During this time, Jemima Tute and her family were swept up in the decades-long, acrimonious and, at times, deadly land grant controversies between the provinces of New York and New Hampshire over possession of land that is now Vermont. In 1768, the situation worsened with politicians and landowners jockeying for position, often disrupting allegiances within families caught in the middle.[24] That same year, New York Gov. Cadwallader Colden appointed Amos Tute coroner of Cumberland County. His affiliation was Pro-New York. Jemima's son Squire, however, was Pro-Vermont.[25]

---

21. Coleman, *New England Captives Carried to Canada*, 2:320.
22. Samuel Gardner Drake, *Tragedies of the Wilderness; or True and Authentic Narratives of Captives who have been Carried Away by the Indians from the Various Frontier Settlements of the United States, from the Earliest to the Present Time* (Boston: Antiquarian Bookstore and Institute, 1841), "Captivity of Frances Noble," 165–172, 169. Axtell, "Sawtelle, Jemima," *Dictionary of Canadian Biography*, vol. 5, 2003.
23. H. L. Howe, *The Howe, Willard, Sartwell Families*.
24. Hemenway, *Vermont Historical Gazetteer*, 5:1–3.
25. Hall, *History of Eastern Vermont*, 2:767. *Early Vermont Settlers Index Cards,1750–1784* online database, AmericanAncestors.org, citing *Legacy of Dissent: Religion and Politics by Revolutionary Vermont, 1749–1784* (Worcester, MA: D.A. Smith, 1980), for Amos Tute in "Civil Enemy Officers" and "Pro-New Yorkers" index cards and Squire Howe in "General Eastern Vermont" and "Pro-Vermont" index cards.

Amid this long-term local strife, Jemima faced a major blow to her and the family she had tried for so long to hold together. The American Revolution brought a house divided between her Patriot and Loyalist sons, Squire and Caleb.

Squire spent most of his military career in the artillery, beginning in late 1775 at Ticonderoga as a gunner and then as a bombardier in Col. Richard Gridley's and Col. Henry Knox's artillery regiments.[26] After this early training, Squire served in the Rhode Island artillery in Col. Robert Elliot's Regiment, working his way up to captain lieutenant in 1780.[27]

Loyalist Caleb was an ensign and then a lieutenant in Lt. Col. John Graves Simcoe's Queen's Rangers, serving in Capt. James Murray's Company from late 1777 and for the next six years. As a Queen's Ranger serving under the disciplined Simcoe, Caleb would have been self-reliant, well-versed in the methods of light infantry, the effective use of the bayonet, and precision shooting.[28]

In the Revolutionary War widow's pension application filed by Squire's wife, Martha (Field) Howe wrote that her husband often told her of the many difficult battles he was in during the war, including meeting Caleb "face to face in a bloody engagement," and heard them speak later about their "feelings towards each other when they met as enemies." Squire Howe, Jr., submitted an affidavit for the pension record, writing that his father was at the siege of Yorktown and the surrender of Cornwallis on October 19, 1781. Maj. Mathias Joy, a neighbor of the Howes, also provided sworn testimony that Squire was a "substantial friend to the cause of liberty" who left his new bride Martha in the spring of 1781 and finally returned home some six months later after Cornwallis's surrender.[29]

---

26. "Squire How/e" in *U.S. Compiled Revolutionary War Service Records, 1775–1783* online database, Ancestry.com, citing NARA Record Group 93, Publication *M881*, NARA Roll 77.
27. Joseph Jencks Smith, *Civil and Military List of Rhode Island 1647–1800* (Providence, RI: Preston and Bounds Co., 1900), 343, 355, 357, 371, 394.
28. Murtie June Clark, *Loyalists in the Southern Campaign of the Revolutionary War* (Baltimore: Genealogical Publishing Company, 1999), 2:465–489 (passim), 562, 586, and 627. John Graves Simcoe, *Simcoe's Military Journal. A History of the Operations of a Partisan Corps, Called the Queen's Rangers, Commanded by Lieut. Col., J. G. Simcoe, During the War of the American Revolution* (New York: Bartlett & Welford, 1844), viii.
29. Martha Howe widow's pension application no. W.21431, for Squire Howe's service, *Revolutionary War Pension and Bounty-Land Warrant Application Files* (NARA microfilm publication M804, 2,670 rolls), Records of the Department of Veterans Affairs, Record Group 15, National Archives, Washington, D.C.

Although there are no known military records for Squire Howe during his time away from home that year, these pension documents combined with the two brothers' numerous military records and type of training suggest they may have been in the front lines during the siege of Yorktown.[30]

It could be, for example, that Brig. Gen. Henry Knox of the 2nd Continental Army Regiment at Yorktown, knew first-hand of Squire's long history in the artillery and ensured that his expertise was put to good use. If so, Squire's rank may have meant an assignment to command from the batteries and redoubts surrounding Yorktown in rotating twenty-four-hour shifts, bombarding British trenches using mortars and howitzers.[31]

Caleb's records are much more definitive. He was stationed at Redoubt Number One at Gloucester Point about 1,500 yards across the York River from Yorktown. As the Americans and French tightened the noose around Yorktown, Caleb may have served as a sentry to prevent communications leaks across the river into enemy hands at Yorktown, a guard to secure Cornwallis's potential escape route north from Gloucester Point, or in small skirmishes like the aborted attack on the French who had taken several redoubts at Gloucester.[32]

After the British surrender and the capture of Cornwallis, Caleb became a prisoner of war along with more than 300 Queen's Rangers. As an officer, he commanded fifty men with loaded knapsacks who marched north through the Blue Ridge Mountains and across the Shenandoah River to prison camps in Pennsylvania and eventually to Long Island.[33] In 1785, Caleb was granted land in Parr Town, now St. John, in New Brunswick where he remained with his wife Esther (Fairweather) and son Charles and daughter Submit, until his death in 1810.[34]

---

30. "*Revolutionary War Service, 1775–1783*," at *Military Resources: American Revolution* online resource at the National Archives (archives.gov). The Department of War attempted to reconstruct the Revolutionary War records destroyed in fires of 1800 and 1814; however, many service records were lost, perhaps including those of Squire Howe.
31. William W. Reynolds, "The American Gunners at Yorktown," *The Journal of the American Revolution*, May 9, 2017, allthingsliberty.com/2017/05/american-gunners-yorktown/#_edn21.
32. Donald J. Gara, *The Queen's American Rangers* (Yardley, PA: Westholme, 2016), 316–317, 320–325. Banastre Tarleton, *A History of the Campaigns in the Southern Provinces of North America* (London: Printed for T. Cadell, 1787), 376–389.
33. Gara, *The Queen's American Rangers*, 343–352.
34. *UK, Pension Applications for Widows and Family of Military Officers, 1776–1881* online database, Ancestry.com, for Caleb Howe. See also, *Index to New Brunswick Land Grants, 1784–1997* (RS686) online database, Provincial Archives of New Brunswick, archives.gnb.ca.

It is impossible to know for certain if, and, if so, to pinpoint exactly where Squire and Caleb fought face-to-face as Martha Howe wrote. It is certain, however, that the long-term effects of captivity on Jemima and her young children and the division within her family brought on by the Revolution were profound and clearly on her mind for the rest of her life.

In Jemima's will, she wrote that Caleb would have one year to claim his inheritance for land, realizing she would likely never see him again once he had been exiled to Canada as a Loyalist.[35] Her probate records, including her will and codicil, dated 1797 and 1798 respectively, show that she helped her children financially, with notes totaling more than £1,800 outstanding from Moses, Squire, Caleb and grandson William Howe, and bequeathed nearly 350 acres of real estate, appraised at £3,000, equally to them. She also amassed personal property, comprised of items such as glassware, pewter, a gold locket with 117 gold beads, a gold ring, silk gown, and considerable livestock, valued at more than £3,000. Her clothing and furniture were to be divided equally among granddaughters Polly (Mary) and Charlotte Willard and the remainder of her personal estate among her two granddaughters and Jonathan Willard, all children of Submit who died in 1781.[36]

In other ways, Jemima carried the weight of family responsibility on her perpetually strong shoulders. When her daughter Submit died, she left behind three children under the age of four. Granddaughter Mary was the oldest with two of her own children passing while Jemima was still alive. Jemima, now the family matriarch, took care of them all.[37]

Amos Tute died in April 1790. According to Jemima and the other heirs of his estate, Amos was not of sound mind when he signed his will the day before he died. The Probate Court agreed.[38] Accordingly, Jemima inherited her dower's share of Amos's real estate, which was valued at £1,495, including the north portion of the Sartwell Farm, sixty acres in Hinsdale and a farm from Arad Hunt, Esq., as well as £575 in personal property.[39]

---

35. *Vermont (Marlboro District), Probate Records* at FamilySearch.org, Jemima Tute's will and codicil at 3:29–32 (DGS no. 7714773, images 34–36).
36. *Vermont (Marlboro District), Probate Records*, at FamilySearch.org, Jemima Tute inventory at 3:51–54 (DGS no. 7714773, images 45–47) and div. of estate at 3:70–72 (DGS no. 7714773, images 55–56). H. L. Howe, *The Howe, Willard, Sartwell Families*.
37. H. L. Howe, *The Howe, Willard, Sartwell Families*.
38. Ibid.; *Vermont (Marlboro District), Probate Records* at FamilySearch.org, court petition at 1:167 (DGS no. 7714772, image 116) and purported will at 1:356–357 (DGS no. 7714772, image 212).
39. *Vermont (Marlboro District), Probate Records* at FamilySearch.org, Amos Tute inventory at 1:226–231 (DGS no. 7714772, images 146–149), div. of estate at 1:235–240 (DGS no. 7714772, images 151–153) and acct. summary at 2:229 (DGS no. 7714772, image 353).

Nearing the end of Jemima's life, she amassed a fine estate, some of it likely from her dower's share from Amos, but some coming from her own determination and innate smarts. She had become a peer of some of the most powerful gentlemen in the area, acknowledged by them or not. In addition to the outstanding notes to her sons, there were nearly £700 in notes outstanding to a dozen neighbors, including Micah Townsend, a Princeton-educated attorney and Vermont Secretary of State from 1781 to 1788, and to Arad Hunt, Esq. and his brother, Lt. Gov. Jonathan Hunt, both major land speculators responsible for accelerating the early growth of southeastern Vermont.[40] Local tax records also show that she was engaged in selling and buying property.[41]

The year following Jemima's death in 1805, her homestead and 225 acres of land were posted for sale. It was comprised of a dwelling house, a large barn and corn house, an orchard with fruit trees and a new orchard with one hundred trees. Seventy of these acres were handsomely situated on the bank of her beloved Connecticut River.[42]

Jemima Howe was an original, an indomitable pioneering woman who overcame the perils of the frontier right in her own backyard, in a hostile foreign country and against a tyrannical foe in the cause of liberty. She may never have known if her strength came from within or from the unspoken attraction of the Connecticut River Valley itself.[43] Perhaps it was both. And just perhaps there was even more to her remarkable story.

The prolific New England historical novelist, Marguerite Allis, wrote a well-regarded story of Jemima Howe's event-filled life. At the end of the novel, Allis described Jemima, a woman nearing the end of her time, holding a newly-minted silver dollar of the United States of America, a gift from her favorite son, Squire. For Jemima, the hard coin

---

40. *Vermont (Marlboro District), Probate Records* at FamilySearch.org, Jemima Tute inventory at 3:51–54 (DGS no. 7714773, images 45–47). *Early Vermont Settlers Index Cards, 1750–1784* online database, AmericanAncestors.org, Micah Townsend in "Civil Enemy Officers" and "Pro-New Yorkers" index cards, and Arad Hunt in "Pro-New Yorkers" index card. Hall, *Eastern Vermont*, 700–706. Clark Jillson, *Green Leaves from Whitingham, Vermont: A History of the Town* (Worcester, MA: Printed at the Private Press of the Author, 1894), 72–73, 78.
41. *Cheshire Co., New Hampshire, Land Records* at FamilySearch.org, 24:78–79 (DGS no. 7836177, images 44–45), 53:10 (DGS no. 8291333, image 14). *Vernon, Vermont Town Records, 1763–1908* at FamilySearch.org, 1:306–307 (DGS no. 7919211, image 191).
42. "Advertisement," *Advertisement Reporter* 4 (published as *The Reporter* in Brattleboro, VT) (March 1, 1806) no. 159, 1 at America's Historical Newspapers.
43. Marguerite Allis, *Not Without Peril* (1941; repr., Charlestown, N.H.: Old Fort No 4 Associates, 2004), 31.

was a symbol of what she, her entire family, friends and neighbors had put into the land along the Connecticut River: "steadfastness and courage, disappointment, frustration, blood, bitterness and death" and a lasting will for freedom. Such is her heritage, the real story of the "high priestess of the River."[44]

---

44. Ibid., 402–404.

Hell's Half-Acre: The Fall of Loyalist Crean Brush

ERIC WISER

On October 18, 1777, New York provincial assemblyman, and Tory, Crean Brush, penned his final will and testament from prison in Boston. After nineteen months of confinement bound in irons, and "in a state of body and mind so debilitated by misfortune," Brush made provisions for his wife Margaret, stepdaughter Frances, and biological daughter in Ireland, Elizabeth.[1]

Brush was captured at sea during the British evacuation of Boston in March 1776. Destined for Nova Scotia and captured by rebel privateers off Cape Ann, the ship carrying Brush contained a cargo of goods he had confiscated from Boston merchants.

Three weeks after writing his will, Brush turned the tables on his captors and escaped. His daughter Elizabeth told the British government, that with "the assistance of a faithful friend he effected his escape ... in the disguise of an Indian."[2] An early American biographer tells it differently:

> On Wednesday, the 5th of November following, Mrs. Brush, as was her custom, visited her husband in his cell, and remained with him several hours. The time for locking up the prisoners for the night having come, she was requested to terminate her visit. As the turnkey stood at the door, waiting for her appearance, a tall figure in woman's garb passed out of the cell, walked with deliberation to the outer door, and disappeared in the darkness ... Mr. Brush had escaped in his wife's clothing.[3]

---

1. The Will of Crean Brush, New Hampshire, Probate Court (Cheshire County); Probate Place: Cheshire, New Hampshire, case 101, vol. 1-2, 1771-1793.
2. Elizabeth Martha Brush to the Earl of Carlisle, November 19, 1782, *American Loyalist Claims Commission, 1776-1835*, AO13/63, Kew, Surrey, The National Archives of the United Kingdom (TNA).
3. Benjamin H. Hall, *History of Eastern Vermont, from its earliest settlement to the close of the eighteenth century* (New York: D. Appleton & Co., 1858), 624.

Having slipped past the jail guards, Brush managed a journey from Boston to British-controlled New York City, his first home in America after immigrating from the Kingdom of Ireland in 1762.⁴

Crean Brush was born in Northern Ireland to landed gentry in Tyrone County around 1725. By the 1760s he was a lawyer and widower with a daughter, Elizabeth. Leaving her in the care of his sister Rebecca and brother-in-law Arthur Clarke, Brush left a comfortable life for grand opportunities in North America.⁵

Brush practiced law in New York City with Irish lawyer John Kelly and plied his craft on deeds, powers of attorney and wills. Shortly after establishing himself, Brush obtained employment as a law clerk in the office of the colony's Deputy Secretary, Goldsboro Banyar.⁶

Brush's personal life changed quickly. In August 1765, he married Margaret Schoolcraft in Manhattan's Collegiate Dutch Reformed Church. Margaret hailed from a Schoharie Valley family and brought to the marriage her deceased sister's illegitimate, six-year-old daughter Frances Montressor, whom she was raising as her own child.⁷

Gov. William, Lord Tryon said Brush "conducted himself with diligence and integrity" while working for Banyar. It was in this capacity that Brush installed himself into the patronage machine of New York. Banyar, like Brush, was a lawyer born in the British Isles, the former in London, long tenured with three decades in provincial government, with "a hand in virtually every land transaction . . . building valuable relationships and a considerable fortune."⁸ Brush and Banyar formed a close friendship which provided the former with a path to becoming a land baron.

---

4. Elizabeth Brush to the Earl of Carlisle, *American Loyalist Claims Commission*, TNA; Evidence of the foregoing Memorial of Thomas Norman and Elizabeth Martha his Wife Daughter of Crean Brush, January 19, 1788, *American Loyalist Claims Commission, 1776-1835*, AO12/30, TNA.

5. John J. Duffy and Eugene A. Coyle, "Crean Brush vs. Ethan Allen: A Winner's Tale," *Vermont History*, Vol. 70, Summer/Fall (2002), 104; Certificate of Arthur Clarke, *American Loyalist Claims Commission, 1776-1835*, AO13/63, TNA.

6. Duffy and Coyle, *Winner's Tale*, 104; Crean Brush Account Books, 1765-1766, New York Historical Society, https://digitalcollections.nyhistory.org/islandora/object/islandora%3A106621; Certificate of Lord William Tryon, February 10, 1784, *American Loyalist Claims Commission, 1776-1835*, AO13/63, TNA.

7. The Archives of the Reformed Church in America, New Brunswick, New Jersey, *Collegiate Church, Ecclesiastical Records, Baptisms, Members, Marriages, 1639-1774*; John J. Duffy and Eugene A. Coyle, "Crean Brush vs. Ethan Allen: A Winner's Tale," *Vermont History*, Vol. 70, Summer/Fall (2002), 104.

8. Certificate of Lord William Tryon, *American Loyalist Claims Commission, 1776-1835*, AO13/63, TNA; Biographical Note, *Goldsboro Banyar and Banyar Family Papers 1727-1904*, New-York Historical Society Museum & Library, http://dlib.nyu.edu/findingaids/html/nyhs/banyar/bioghist.html.

In 1772, Brush moved his family 200 miles northeast of New York City to the village of Westminster. Located on the Connecticut River, Westminster was the seat of government for newly formed Cumberland County with its 4,024 people and 774 heads of families.[9] Brush brought his habit for ostentatious dress and purchased a home in Westminster "north of the meeting-house, and was the only building in the town whose four sides faced the cardinal points." The move was accomplished during legislative action establishing governance in the county – Brush was groomed and poised to be a major player.[10]

Brush's connections paid-off. He was chosen commissioner of the court, county clerk, and surrogate of the court. As surrogate, he represented the colonial secretary and held power to administer oaths and oversee probate matters. Brush was involved in Cumberland's division of townships into districts, and a circular bearing his name summarizing the changes was posted throughout the county.[11]

Toward the end of his first year in Westminster, a petition from freeholders in Cumberland County called for representation in New York's general assembly. They elected Crean Brush and Samuel Wells of Brattleboro as assemblymen.[12]

Brush and Wells arrived in New York City in January 1773, and Brush was admitted to the assembly at City Hall on the afternoon of February 2. The very next day he presented a spate of business related to Cumberland County, proposing amendments to existing legislation regulating highways, inns and taverns, and "a bill for raising the sum of £250, in the county of Cumberland, towards finishing the courthouse and gaol already erected in the said county."[13]

Cumberland, Charlotte, and Gloucester Counties were recent creations from Albany County. Albany consisted of territory between the Hudson River and Lake Champlain in the west, and the Connecticut

---

9. An Inventory of Lands belonging to the Estate of the late Crean Brush of Cumberland County, *American Loyalist Claims Commission, 1776-1835*, AO13/116, TNA; Jay Mack Holbrook, *Vermont Census of 1771* (Oxford, MA: Holbrook Research Center, 1982), Table 9, Cumberland County Population in 1771 and 1791.
10. Hall, *Eastern Vermont*, 604-605; Session] Begun the 7th of January, 1772, and ended, by prorogation, the 24th of March Following, *Journal of the Votes and Proceedings of the General Assembly of the Colony of New York, from 1766 to 1776, inclusive* (New York: J. Buel, 1820), 64, 70, 110 (JVGA).
11. Hall, *Eastern Vermont*, Appendix G – Division of Cumberland County into Districts, 743-744.
12. [Session] Begun the 5th of January, 1773, and ended, by prorogation, the 8th of March Following, 41, JVGA, 41; Hall, *Eastern Vermont*, Cumberland County Civil List: 767.
13. [Session] Begun the 5th of January, 1773, JVGA, 42-44, 65.

River to the east. The Green Mountains bisected the region, and settlement accelerated after Britain's victory in the French and Indian War. New York's claim was supported by a 1684 grant from King James to his brother the Duke of York. In 1764, the Crown elicited delight from New York by confirming the Connecticut River boundary.[14]

The New Hampshire government had also been issuing land warrants in the same region. An impressive 138 chartered townships had been created on the west side of the Connecticut River which were divided and sub-divided, changing hands, in many cases trimmed to sizes sufficient for single-family sustenance farming. A chaotic tangle of competing land ownership between "Yorkers" and "New Hampshire Grant" holders pervaded the mountains, fields and forests, resulting in distrust and violence.[15]

The New York and New Hampshire governors executed their grants differently but were equally motivated by fees augmenting their salaries. A patent - a survey and organization of unsettled land - was an asset for speculative gain or tenant income. Land ownership was power, and those with authority over it were fodder for bribes and for rewarding allies, friends and relatives. The beneficiaries of patents were groups called "proprietors" who were obligated to pay Crown taxes called "quit rents." Crean Brush was a proprietor in several New York patents and owned well over 30,000 acres in Charlotte, Cumberland, and Gloucester counties.[16]

Between April 1765 and June 1776, over 2,000,000 patented acres were granted by New York governors in the New Hampshire Grant region. New Hampshire governor John Wentworth issued 3,000,000 acres west of the Connecticut River and to himself 65,000 acres. Both colonies issued grants to land speculators, though Wentworth was willing to grant land to any group willing to pay his cheap fees, allowing speculators to make a profit while offering affordable prices. Yeoman farmers poured in from New England, while New York patents were largely granted to New York City lawyers, merchants and speculators.[17]

---

14. Holbrook, *Vermont Census*, Table 3, Origin of Vermont Counties; Representation of the Lords of Trade on the New Hampshire Grants, December 3, 1772, in E.B. O'Callaghan ed., *Documents Relative to the Colonial History of New York* (Albany: Weed, Parsons and Company, 1857), 8:330-337 (DRCNY).
15. Charles A. Jellison, *Ethan Allen: Frontier Rebel* (Syracuse: University of Syracuse), 19-21.
16. Irving Mark, *Agrarian Conflicts in Colonial New York: 1711-1775*, (New York: Ira J. Friedman, Inc., 1965), 19; An Inventory of Lands belonging to the Estate of the late Crean Brush, TNA; Hall, *Eastern Vermont*, 605.
17. Jellison, *Frontier Rebel*, 20, 22; Mark, *Agrarian Conflicts*, 22.

In 1765, New York ruled the New Hampshire Grants illegal, requiring their owners to pay half-fees to validate claims that didn't overlap with a New York patent. In response, a petition representing 600 New Hampshire Grant holders seeking a redress of grievances reached the Crown. A King in Council ruled that New York could no longer patent land in the New Hampshire Grant region. In April 1767, the governor of New York received tersely worded instructions: "His Majesty Commands you make no grants of these Lands and that you do not molest any person in the quiet possession of [Wentworth's] Grant, who can produce good and valid Deeds."[18]

The Crown rebuked New York's land practices, issuing an acreage limit. Governor Tryon argued against the ceiling, explaining that large grants to "Gentleman of weight and consideration" were a bulwark against "the general levelling spirit" in the colonies. Compliance with the 1767 temporary ban on patents in the New Hampshire Grant region was largely ignored.[19]

In the provincial assembly, Crean Brush offered his persuasive writing skills to help establish New York dominance of the Green Mountain region. Brush barely warmed his seat in the assembly when he joined Philip Schuyler to draft a definitive document enumerating New York's claim to the Connecticut River boundary. Intended for the colony's agent Edmund Burke, the copious and detailed document was called *A State of the Right of the Colony of New-York, with respect to its eastern boundary on Connecticut River, so far as concerns the late encroachments under the government of New-Hampshire*. The piece was read before the assembly on March 8, 1773, and subsequently sent to London.

In March 1774, Brush was serving on the assembly's Committee of Grievances when it received a petition from a subject in Charlotte County "complaining of many Acts of Outrage and Cruelty, and Oppression committed against their Persons and Properties by the Bennington Mob, and the Dangers and Injuries to which they are daily exposed." The petition asked the assembly to "take them under their Protection, and secure them against future Violence."

The yeoman farmers of the New Hampshire Grants made common cause with speculators to protect their homes and property. New York surveyors caught on New Hampshire Grant properties were driven off by their owners and neighbors. Ethan Allen, owner of a New Hamp-

---

18. Jellison, *Frontier Rebel*, 23-24; Earl of Shelburne to Governor Moore, April 11, 1767, DRCNY, 8:917.

19. Mark, *Agrarian Conflicts*, 25, 31; Governor Tryon to the Earl of Hillsborough, April 11, 1772, DRCNY, 8:293-294; Frederick Franklyn Van de Water, *Vermont: The Reluctant Republic, 1724-1791* (New York: The John Day Company, 1941), 56.

shire Grant investment enterprise called the Onion River Land Company, led the Green Mountain Boys in an information and armed resistance effort against New York. Allen and his men were declared insurgents by New York's governor and legislature. The "Bennington Mob" was accused of throwing the region into turmoil through acts of property destruction, intimidation, and violence. Brush co-drafted the infamous bill known as the "12 Bloody Acts," that made riotous assemblies of three or more individuals a felony, made any sheriff or magistrate killing a rioter in the act of apprehending free of penalty, and called for the arrest of Allen and other leaders of the Green Mountain Boys.[20]

In May, Ethan Allen sent Brush and Wells a warning with a postscript threatening the former:

> I have sundry ways received intelligence of your hatred and malice toward the N. Hampshire Settlers on the west side of the Green Mountains and particularly towards me. The report you made on behalf of Mr. Clinton is noticed by the Green M Boys. They have also took a retrospective view of a number of learned attorneys and gentleman (by birth) interested in the lands (by N. York Title) on which they dwell deluding the Assembly Part of the Members ... I know it was the Land Schemers [who] Influenced the Assembly to pass the 12 Bloody Acts ... Wells and You are but busie Understrappers to a Number of more Overgrown Villains which can Murther by Law without remorse. But I have to inform that the Green Mountain Boys will not tamely resign their necks to the halter to be hanged by your cursed fraternity of land jockeys who would better adorn a halter than we, therefore as you regard your own lives be careful not to invade ours for what measure you meet it shall be measured against you ...
>
> P.S. Mr. Brush Sir
>
> As a testimony of gratitude for the many unmerited kindnesses, and services, you have done us the last session at New York &c &c we intend shortly visiting your abode, where we hope to have the honor of presenting you the beech seal ...
>
> To be yours sincerely,
> Green Mountain Boys[21]

---

20. Mark, *Agrarian Conflicts*, 196; Jellison, *Frontier Rebel*, 44-45, *Hartford Courant*, June 21, 1774; An Act for preventing tumultuous and riotous Assemblies, March 9, 1774, in William Slade, ed., *Vermont State Papers* (Middlebury: J. W. Copeland, 1823), 42-48.
21. Ethan Allen to Crean Brush and Samuel Wells, May 19, 1774, in John J. Duffy, ed., *Ethan Allen and His Kin: Correspondence, 1772-1819* (Hanover, NH: University Press of New England, 1998), 16-17.

In addition to fighting the Bennington Mob, the conservatives in New York's government were grappling with colonial resistance efforts promulgated by the First Continental Congress. Lt. Gov. Colden told the assembly at the start of the 1775 session: "We cannot sufficiently lament the present disordered state of the colonies ... If your constituents are discontented and apprehensive, examine their complaints with calmness and deliberation."[22]

Whigs in Brush's constituency networked to undermine Royal authority, and Congress was the catalyst. Meetings of patriots representing townships across Cumberland met in Westminster at various times from Fall 1775 through Winter 1776, forming a Cumberland Committee of Correspondence and encouraging support for the resolutions of Congress.[23]

On February 17, 1775, Suffolk County assemblyman Nathaniel Woodhull made a motion "that thanks of this house be given" to representatives of Congress "for their faithful and judicious discharge of the trust reposed in them by the good people of this colony."[24] Woodhull's motion was debated and voted down; Brush and Wells voted against it. The same scenario played out a few days later when assemblyman and congressional delegate Philip Livingston proposed a formal thanks to the colony's merchants and citizens for their "public spirited, and patriotic" conduct in carrying out Congress's nonimportation association. Once again, Brush and Wells voted in the negative.

On February 23, Brush seized an opportunity for going on the record opposing Congress. A motion was made by a Livingston ally for appointment of delegates to the next Congress in Philadelphia on May 10.[25] Brush articulated his belief in a speech to the assembly that a proper avenue for the colony's redress of grievances existed within the established framework:

> I again freely repeat my opinion ... As the proposed Congress is to be a continuation of the last, and is to meet in consequence of their vote declaring the necessity of holding it, by nominating Delegates for it we shall, in effect, recognize the last Congress, and make ourselves, parties to all the measures then agreed upon. If this will be the consequence, as I conceive it clearly will, of the present motion, no other reason can

---

22. [Session] Begun the 10th of January, 1775, and ended, by prorogation, the 3rd of April Following, JVGA, 4, 85, 100.
23. The Pingrey Papers, *History of Windsor County Vermont*, ed., Lewis Cass Aldrich and Frank R. Holmes (Syracuse: D. Mason and Co., 1891), 47-49 (HWCV).
24. [Session] Begun the 10th of January, 1775, JVGA, 38.
25. [Session] Begun the 10th of January, 1775, JVGA, 40, 44-45.

be necessary why this House should not agree to it; because we have already determined not to consider the Proceedings of that Congress, much less espouse its principles or adopt its measures. But, sir, we are the legal and constitutional Representatives of the people; to us the care of their liberties is, in the most sacred manner, entrusted; and I think it would be a breach of our trust to delegate that most important charge to any body of men, whose powers are circumscribed by no law . . . I hope this House will have too much prudence, as well as virtue, to give a sanction to an assembly who would sap our Constitution, and may probably involve this once happy country in all the horrors of a civil war. However, let their determination be as it will, I shall have the satisfaction of doing my duty, in declaring my dissent to the motion now before the House.[26]

Brush and others defeated the proposal 17–9.[27]

On March 13, 1775, Crean Brush was with the assembly when armed conflict exploded near his home at Westminster. An armed mob of eighty persons occupied the county courthouse to prevent the next day's business. The anger stemmed from eviction and foreclosure actions scheduled at the courthouse. Sheriff William Paterson of Cumberland County arrived with a posse, and after failing to disperse the mob peacefully, fired warning shots. The mob returned fire, wounding a judge. In subsequent fighting one rioter was killed and nine wounded. The court defiantly held business the next day, and "a number of persons partly of the said County (Cumberland) and partly from the Provinces of Massachusetts Bay and New Hampshire assembled, surrounded the Court House." The judges and clerks were imprisoned in the county jail.[28]

"The Westminster Massacre" caused Lieutenant Governor Cadwallader Colden to excoriate the assembly to "strengthen the hands of civil authority," and warned that "negligence of government will ever produce a contempt of authority." The assembly debated whether to provide support for re-establishment of peace in Cumberland County. The measure passed on a faction-line vote with Brush in the affirmative.

26. Speech of Mr. Brush, of Cumberland County, on this question, February 23, 1775, Peter Force, *American Archives*, Northern Illinois Digital Library, https://digital.lib.niu.edu/islandora/object/niu-amarch%3A98782.
27. [Session] Begun the 10th of January, 1775, JVGA, 44-45.
28. Hall, *History of Eastern Vermont*, 184-186; Jellison, *Frontier Rebel*, 98-99; Colonel Wells and Crean Brush, representatives of Cumberland County report of a violent riot in their county during which Justice Butterfield was wounded, *New York Colony Council Minutes*, March 21, 1775, NYSA_A1895-78_V026_06, New York State Archives, https://digitalcollections.archives.nysed.gov/index.php/Detail/objects/85117.

Brush made a motion for funds to supplement the effort, which also passed.

Open war after the Battles of Lexington and Concord made Brush's residence in Westminster untenable. Added to his corrupt "Yorker" status was a perception that Brush was an unrepentant Tory and Gov. Tryon sycophant. Not only did he oppose Congress vehemently, in October 1774 Brush had called for the arrest of Dummerstown farmer Leonard Spaulding for high treason after he spoke out against the British Quebec Act which legitimized Catholicism in Canada. Outrage led to Spaulding's release and left simmering anger toward Brush and the county magistrates.[29]

Crean Brush, with "utmost difficulty and hazard of his life," fled with his wife to Boston. His property in and around Westminster was confiscated. Brush's library, law books and furniture were "scattered among the households of the neighborhood." Brush's co-assemblyman, Samuel Wells, had deeper roots in his community and tried to remain in Brattleboro, enduring harassment from an aggrieved Leonard Spaulding. Unable to stay neutral, Wells became a spy for the British. He was found out and fled, dying in Canada after the war. Among Wells' creditors at the time of his death was the Estate of Crean Brush.[30]

Brush did not sit idle within British lines at Boston. He approached commander in chief Gen. Thomas Gage for employment. In October 1775 Gage told Brush that "the inhabitants have expressed some fears concerning the safety of goods especially as a great part of the houses will necessarily be occupied by His Majesty's Troops and the followers of the Army as Barracks during the winter season." Gage offered Brush a wage to collect and catalogue personal property of loyal Bostonians leaving the city.[31]

On January 10, 1776, Brush looked requested more belligerent service when he asked for permission to conquer the New Hampshire Grant region, proposing:

> one body under his command to occupy proper posts on the Connecticut River, and open a line of communication from whence westward towards Lake Champlain . . . your memorialist's intimate knowledge of that frontier enables him to ensure your excellency that such an es-

---

29. The Pingrey Papers, HWCV, 49-50.
30. The Memorial of Thomas Norman and Elizabeth Martha Brush, *American Loyalist Claims Commission, 1776-1835*, AO13/63, TNA; Hall, *Eastern Vermont*, 628, 724-725.
31. Thomas Gage to Elizabeth Martha Norman, December 5, 1783. *American Loyalist Claims Commission, 1776-1835*, AO13/63, TNA; Thomas Gage to Crean Brush, October 1, 1775, in William B. Clark et al., eds. *Naval Documents of the American Revolution*, 13 volumes (Washington, DC: Government Printing Office, 1964-2019), 2:263-264 (NDAR).

tablishment in that country will become absolutely necessary for the purpose of reducing to obedience, and bringing to justice, a dangerous gang of lawless banditti, who, without the least pretext of title, have by violence, pressed themselves of a large tract of interior territory, between the Connecticut River on the East, and the waters of the Hudson's River and Lake Champlain on the West, in open defiance of government.[32]

Nothing came of this request, but Gen. James Robertson recommended Brush to Gage's replacement, Gen. William Howe. Howe considered Brush a "Loyal & Zealous Subject," and employed him in work that earned the Loyalist animosity in Boston.[33] Within a tense atmosphere surrounding the army's imminent departure (which included fears the town would be burned), Howe posted a circular throughout the town:

> As Linen and Woolen Goods are Articles much wanted by the Rebels, and would aid and assist them in their Rebellion, the Commander-in-Chief that all good Subjects will use their utmost Endeavors to all such Articles convey'd from this Place; Any who have not Opportunity to convey their Goods under their own Care, may deliver them on Board the Minerva at Hubbard's Wharf, to Crean Brush, Esq; mark'd with their Names, who will give a Certificate of the Delivery, and will oblige himself to return them to the Owners, all unavoidable Accidents accepted.
> If after this Notice and Person secrets or keeps in his Possession such Articles, he will be treated as a Favourer of the Rebels.[34]

Brush was empowered to question merchants and search their property upon suspicion of noncompliance. He was given a small band for muscle including Irish immigrant Richard Hill—a Loyalist living on 900 acres near Westminster purchased from Brush. Hill served in the sheriff's posse that engaged the rioters in the Westminster Massacre. Hill's home was plundered by the mob, causing him to flee with his family to the British army at Boston.[35]

---

32. Hall, *Eastern Vermont*, 611-612.
33. William Howe to Elizabeth Martha Norman, December 13, 1783, *American Loyalist Claims Commission, 1776-1835*, AO13/63, TNA.
34. Proclamation from Gen. William Howe to the People of Boston, March 10, 1776. *Papers of the Continental Congress*, M247, Roll 88, Record Group 360, NARA.
35. Certificate of William Paterson, Sheriff of Cumberland County for Richard Hill, March 18, 1780, *American Loyalist Claims Commission, 1776-1835*, AO13/13, TNA; The Claim of Richard Hill, Esq., a loyalist from the Township of Westminster, County of Cumberland, *American Loyalist Claims Commission, 1776-1835*, AO13/13, TNA; Crean Brush to William Howe, March 26, 1776, NDAR, 4:522-523; Hall, *Eastern Vermont*, 611-612.

A day after Howe's proclamation, merchant Samuel Dashwood was at his home and shop whereby his account, a sword wielding Crean Brush forced his way through the back door. Dashwood and his family watched the unwelcome visitor brazenly move through the home. Brush opened the front door to the shop, allowing his men to enter. The raid lasted two hours, and according to Dashwood was served "with great force and violence," and "terror of myself and family." Dashwood also claimed Brush threatened that "if any person should presume to interrupt . . . they would thrust their bayonets into such a person." Nine large trunks and two large chests of silks and cloth were carried away.[36]

Merchant John Rowe recorded the visit Brush paid:

> This morning I rose early and very luckily went to my warehouse – when I came there, I found Mr. Crean Brush with an order and party from the Gen. who was just going to break open the Warehouse which I prevented . . . They took from me to the Value of Twenty Two hundred & Sixty Pounds Sterling . . . in Linens, Checks & Woolens. This Party behaved very Insolently and with Great Rapacity.[37]

Brush carried out similar confiscations on merchants Samuel Austin, Cyrus Baldwin, John Barrett, Samuel Partridge, and John Scollay. Austin wrote that Brush "did by force and Arms, with near Twenty Soldiers, with their Guns and Bayonets enter my House and took from me in goods and merchandise. I apprehend it needless to say anything about the rude and insulting behavior of the officer (Crean Brush) who took my goods." Brush's confiscations surely brought a measure of satisfaction – Austin, Baldwin, Barrett, Dashwood, Partridge, and Scollay were Sons of Liberty.[38]

Brush was determined to head off complaints of his raids, explaining to General Robertson:

> These People your Memorialist are irritated against him but your Memorialist begs leave to assure your Honor he is fully able to prove that his Conduct toward them was governed with politeness coolness & moderation true it is that when attempts were made to engage his

---

36. Samuel Dashwood Deposition on goods seized by British troops. *Papers of the Continental Congress*, M247, Roll 88, Record Group 360, NARA.
37. John Rowe, *Letters and Diary of John Rowe: Boston Merchant 1759-1762 1764-1779*, ed. Annie Rowe Cunningham (Boston: W.B. Clarke Co., 1903), 301-302.
38. Samuel Austin to John Adams, December 23, 1785, https://founders.archives.gov/documents/Adams/06-18-02-0032; Col. William Palfrey, *An Alphabetical List of the Sons of Liberty who din'd at Liberty Tree*, Dorchester, August 14, 1769, Massachusetts Historical Society Collections Online, http://masshist.org/database/8.

attention in tedious dissertations on Magna Charta & the rights of British Subjects with intent to retard him in the execution of his Office he did interrupt such Harangues & with an Irony which inflamed their resentments complimented them on their Eloquence which had in Town Meetings been so successful as to throw all America into confusion but that I was upon Business which I was determined to execute without interruption.

With only a week to complete his assignment, Brush worked on little sleep and faced a scarcity of rolling stock: "The goods I received from the stores taken on board and stowed away with all the care and attention my peculiar situation would possibly admit." Brush loaded the goods on the ships *Peggy, Polly,* and brig *Elizabeth* which "had but two boys and a man onboard none of them mariners and ignorant of stowing goods which were however put away the best manner they could."[39]

Elizabeth departed Nantasket Roads at the entrance of Boston Harbor on the afternoon of March 21, 1776, carrying sixty-three passengers including Brush, his accomplices and their families, thirteen British soldiers and four enslaved people. The voyage of Capt. John Ramsey's ship was tension filled.[40]

A British major added to Brush's burden by placing nineteen barrels of flour in his care. The crew broke into one of the barrels and Brush harangued them. Brush was resting below decks when an angry crew member threatened him. They fought verbally, causing Captain Ramsey to lose patience and promise Brush imprisonment if he "uttered three words more."[41]

On March 29, *Elizabeth* became separated from her escort and was fallen upon by the Yankee privateer *Hancock* fifty miles east of Cape Ann. *Hancock* closed on Capt. Ramsey's ship and fired a broadside *Elizabeth* answered with small arms fire. Two more privateers arrived convincing Ramsey to surrender his vessel in the late afternoon.[42]

Elizabeth was brought into Portsmouth, New Hampshire. Brush was interrogated, and his inventories, orders and sealed letters were taken. Gen. George Washington was informed that the prisoners "were examined by the General Court, who were all committed to prison Yesterday, Brush in Irons."

---

39. Crean Brush to James Robertson, March 25, 1776, NDAR, 4:501-502.
40. Joshua Wentworth to Stephen Moylan, April 15, 1776, NDAR, 4:522-523, 828-830.
41. NDAR, 4:501-502.
42. Extract of Letter from Cambridge dated April 7, 1776, NDAR, 4:694; *Journal of the Continental Congress,* October 14, 1776, NDAR, 6:1263-1265.

Brush was uniquely singled out for irons and taken to the notorious jail in Boston. The confiscations were not viewed by the merchants as military exigency, but rather as malicious theft. The merchants were left to pursue their own restitution. This included legal action in New Hampshire's maritime court for claims on *Elizabeth's* captured cargo and later lobbying Congress and its agents in London. Merchant Samuel Austin, who was also a Boston selectman, confronted General Howe before the evacuation and received unequivocal assurances his property would be returned. Almost ten-years later, in December 1785, Austin was still trying to recover his losses when he wrote an impassioned letter to then ambassador to Great Britain, John Adams. Austin informed Adams that the confiscated goods on the ships aside from *Elizabeth* that arrived in Canada, were sold at auction in Halifax. Austin derisively stated: "the King has had my money, and I suppose it has been applied for his use." Stationed in London after a long, bitter war, and busy negotiating significant matters on behalf of the new nation, Adams doubted Austin and his fellow merchants would ever be fully-compensated, and frankly told them so. Based on silence to that effect in the historical record, Adams appears to have been proven correct.[43]

Sworn affidavits condemned Brush in addition to the certificates he had given the merchants. The exhausted lawyer must have thought it possible he would never leave the Boston jail alive. Brush penned his will, reaffirming for posterity his loyalty to the Crown by dating the document "the 18th year of his Majesty's Reign." His estate was divided between his wife Margaret, stepdaughter Frances, and natural daughter Elizabeth. The bequeathment consisted of debts he was owed but was principally tied up in his vast landholdings.[44]

Brush escaped, but according to most accounts died by suicide in New York City just months later. The May 21, 1778 edition of *The Independent Chronicle and the Universal Advertiser* of Boston reported that Brush "retired to his chamber, where, with a pistol, he besmeared the room with his brains."[45]

Brush's daughter in Ireland applied to the Loyalist Claims Commission for relief. The certificates supporting Elizabeth's application avoided specific mention of how he died. General Robertson stated

---

43. John Gizzard Frazer to George Washington, April 14, 1776, NDAR, 4:808; Samuel Austin to John Adams, December 23, 1785, 06-18-02-0032; John Adams to Samuel Austin, May 25, 1786, https://founders.archives.gov/documents/Adams/06-18-02-0163.
44. Acts of NH and MA, *Papers of the Continental Congress*, M247, Roll 88, Record Group 360, NARA; Isaac Smith, Sr. to John Adams, April 6, 1776, NDAR, 4:676; Will of Crean Brush.
45. Hall, *Eastern Vermont*, 626.

that "his endeavors drew on him the resentment of all who wished for Rebellion & Revolt," and that "his life was rendered miserable, and his death occasioned by misfortune."[46]

In the first half of the nineteenth century, a legend persisted that Brush cut his own throat with a razor in a New York law office.[47] Cumberland County Loyalist Timothy Lovell, in sworn testimony in a lawsuit brought by Brush's Estate for the recovery of debts, said he was fetching firewood for Brush at his residence-in-exile in New York City, when he returned to find him dead with his throat cut.

Historians Patrick J. Duffy and Nicholas Muller speculate that Ethan Allen murdered Brush. In 1777, Allen, who hated Loyalists and especially Brush, was a prisoner of war on parole and free to walk the New York City streets until the British sent him to Long Island. Allen broke his parole in August, was brought back to the city and imprisoned in the provost. It is possible that Allen ran into Brush or was told his whereabouts. Brush died while Allen was in the provost, but Duffy and Muller, citing the frequency of escapes from that provost, believe Allen may have slipped out, killed Brush and returned.

The strangest twist in Brush's story was his stepdaughter Frances's marriage to Ethan Allen. In February 1784, Frances, at twenty-four a widow with a young child, and widower Allen at forty-six, married in Westminster. This effectively made Allen a co-beneficiary to Brush's estate.[48]

Brush's wife Margaret remarried and lived the rest of her life in Westminster. In the wake of her father's death, Elizabeth Brush applied to the Loyalist Claims Commission for financial assistance, supported by written statements of Brush's loyalty and service on behalf of the Crown from Gage, Howe, Robertson and Tryon.

In 1782, Elizabeth Brush married Thomas Norman of Drogheda, near Dublin. Norman used his modest inheritance to purchase a commission in the British Army and was financially ruined by a lawsuit. As a result, he vigorously assisted in recovering his late father-in-law's estate.[49] Elizabeth owned one-third of her father's estate and purchased the other two-thirds from Margaret and Frances, becoming the sole heir. Attorneys including Brush's friends John Kelly and Goldsboro

---

46. James Robertson to Elizabeth Brush, February 1, 1784, *American Loyalist Claims Commission, 1776-1835*, AO13/63, TNA.
47. Hall, *Eastern Vermont*, 625.
48. Duffy and Muller, *Inventing Ethan Allen*, 129-133, 142-146.
49. Henry Dogherty to the Loyalist Claims Commission, February 10, 1784, *American Loyalist Claims Commission, 1776-1835*, AO13/63, TNA.

Banyar tried to recover Crean Brush's debts and land. Some land in New York proper was recoverable, but the land in Vermont was "irrevocably lost" to confiscation. The Normans, along with other claimants, recovered a cash settlement from Vermont.

Elizabeth and Thomas Norman had four children and moved to the United States, first living in Westminster, then permanently settling in Caldwell, New York on land formerly owned by Crean Brush.[50]

---

50. Hall, *Eastern Vermont*, 623-626.

Thomas Plumb, British Soldier Writes Home from Rhode Island

DON N. HAGIST

"Dear Brother," wrote Thomas Plumb from Newport, Rhode Island on February 22, 1777, "this comes with my kind Love to you and hope these lines will find you, my Wife, Child & all Enquiring Friends in as good Health as they do Leave me at this Present time."[1] Plumb had been in Rhode Island for almost three months, and it was important to let his family and friends know that he was in good health and spirits. He was a soldier, a British soldier, in a war that had been raging in America for almost two full years.

Plumb had joined the 22nd Regiment of Foot at the end of December 1765, according to the regiment's muster rolls.[2] He may have enlisted with a recruiting party anywhere from a few weeks to several months prior, before arriving at the regiment's post at Chatham Barracks near London. The regiment had recently returned from several years in America, and was recruiting and training new career soldiers for what was to be almost a decade of service in England, Scotland and Ireland.

By the time the regiment arrived in Boston, Massachusetts just days after the battle of Bunker Hill, Thomas Plumb was a well-seasoned professional soldier. With his regiment he endured a difficult winter in besieged Boston, followed by two months of reorganization in Halifax, Nova Scotia before landing on Staten Island in June 1776 and quickly securing the region around the City of New York during the ensuing months. By the time the regiment landed, unopposed, in Newport on

---

1. Thomas Plumb to Alexander Johns, February 22, 1777, Intercepted mails and papers, America, 1777–1779. HCA 30.272, The National Archives of Great Britain.
2. Muster rolls, 22nd Regiment of Foot, WO 12/3871, The National Archives of Great Britain.

December 8, 1776, Plumb was a veteran of several battles and skirmishes, and many dangerous days and nights at war. After his opening comment of his good health, he wrote, "I thank God for it."

"I am Resolved to Relate our present state and situation in this country at the present time," he continued, with the freestyle spelling and punctuation typical of the era. Although the town of Newport was on an island, much of the shoreline was very close to the mainland. This afforded ample opportunities for rebel raiders to harass British soldiers on duty at the island's many outposts. "Our duty is very hard Upon the Accounts as we receive from the Rebels daily such as we are not in sight of as we are day & night within musket shot of each other," Plumb wrote. He ended this sentence with a phrase that has the final word obscured by a tear in the page: "& they are as numerous as Motes in the Sun" is likely what he wrote, assuming he used a metaphor common during the era, but only the S is legible. "But we still keeps them in constant employ," he assured his brother, "but the cowardly rascals will not stand their ground But watching all Oppertunitys by lying in Ambush behind some trees which is the cause of us looseing so many men but thank God where we loose 10 they loose 100."

Plumb's next sentence referred to the campaign he had been on in New York during August, September and October, where British troops repeatedly routed American forces around the City of New York. "But as we routed them from so many places so that they are in the greatest consternation," he wrote, "possibly they may give us a field day for it early this spring." He was optimistic that a decisive fight was in the offing, that the rebel army would have no choice but to fight a major battle in the open. "I do not doubt but they will," he continued, "as they are almost surrounded by our troops and they must fight or die." He closed this long paragraph, the one begun "Dear Brother," with his opinion of Americans as soldiers—although they were "numerous as Motes," he doubted their will to fight: "But had they the heart as we Britoners have we should stand no chance with them." He saw American soldiers as willing to harass, but not fight in a pitched battle, based on his own observations so far during the war.

That Thomas Plumb wrote a letter is not, in itself, surprising. The rate of literacy among British soldiers is not known, but the army valued education; surviving documents indicate that over half of British soldiers could at least sign their names.[3] For those who wrote letters, the army provided opportunities to send them home; "A Man of war will

---

3. Don N. Hagist, *Noble Volunteers: the British Soldiers who fought the American Revolution* (Yardley, PA: Westholme, 2020), 35-36, 151-153.

sail for England very soon; the Deputy Adjutant General will take care of all letters which may be sent to him," read general orders in Rhode Island on January 3, 1777, and similar orders on later dates.[4] Very few letters from soldiers are known to survive – as unofficial, personal correspondence, no duplicate copies were retained in government records. Thomas Plumb's letter, and a number of other letters from Rhode Island, apparently were captured in transit, and eventually deposited in a large collection of "intercepted mails and papers" in the National Archives of Great Britain. The letter never reached his family, and there is no way to know whether he wrote others that did.

Thomas Plumb ended his short, one-paragraph letter with the sentimental closure, "No more but my kind respects to my loveing Wife & Child Uncle Wood, Molly & little William and all Enquireing friends." He signed it with two lines, "Thomas Plumb Soldier 22d Regiment" "Captn McDonalds Company." An additional note in the margin had one word blotted out by the wax seal used to close the letter: "Your [illegible] by the first opportunity."

Thomas Plumb may have written more letters home, but he never saw his family again. He was killed on August 29, 1778 in the Battle of Rhode Island.[5]

---

4. Don N. Hagist, *General Orders, Rhode Island, December 1776–January 1778* (Bowie, MD: Heritage Books, 2001), 17.
5. Muster rolls, 22nd Regiment of Foot, WO 12/3872, The National Archives of Great Britain.

Unraveling the Beginning and Final Phases in the Emergence of the French–American Alliance

MARVIN L. SIMNER

It is widely acknowledged that the military alliance between the United States and France, established in 1778, was responsible not only for a number of American victories over the British, but also for the end of the Revolutionary War. While much has been written about this topic as well as the events that occurred between 1777 and 1778, which led to the alliance, far less is known about the factors that took place in 1775 and 1776 that contributed to the initial need for the alliance, as well as the factors that culminated in the eventual signing of the alliance.

BACKGROUND

Between June 5, 1775, when George Washington became Commanding General of the Continental Army and the end of that year, the British and Americans had engaged in seventeen important battles, skirmishes, and naval confrontations, of which twelve were won by the Americans.[1] Although from a military perspective the Continental Army was a reasonably effective fighting force, the colonies not only had hoped to free themselves from England's dominance either by winning the war or through negotiations, but also had hoped to become an effective trading partner with many European nations. With these dual objectives in mind, in the latter part of 1775, they began to court France, an acknowledged world power, for additional military support as well as for the political acceptance they needed to gain the trust required by these other nations.

1. Harry Karapalides, *Dates of the American Revolution*, (Shippensburg, PA: Burd Street Press, 1998), 36-52.

Without some acknowledgement of their legitimacy, the colonies were merely rebels, traitors, and pirates; recognition [by France] would transform them from criminals to statesmen, diplomats, and privateers. Other European powers would quickly follow French recognition. It would afford the Americans opportunities for trade relations, loans, and alliances through Europe that were essential to securing and maintaining independence.[2]

In addition to these dual objectives, though, the immediate reason for pursuing France in 1775 was the introduction on November 20 of the Prohibitory Act by Lord North, an act which is said to have been an instrument tantamount to a declaration of war between Britain and its American colonies.[3] While John Adams felt that the Act "throws the thirteen Colonies out of the Royal Protection, levels all Distinctions and makes us independent in spite of all our supplications and Entreaties," Adams also felt obliged to conclude his remarks by stating that, "it is very odd that Americans should hesitate at accepting such a gift."[4] In short, although Adams firmly believed that now was the time for the colonies to declare independence, the problem he clearly recognized was that the mood in Congress in 1775 was simply not compatible with need to "accept such a gift." As these events developed, the expansion of hostilities gradually prompted the colonies to seek French assistance, beginning with an unsuccessful attempt in 1775 to circumvent the British naval blockade.

THE BRITISH NAVAL BLOCKADE

All American Vessels found on the Coast of Great Britain or Ireland are to be seized & confiscated on the first Day of January [1776]—all American Vessels sailing into or out of the ports of America after the first of March are to be seized & confiscated- all foreign Vessels trading to America after the first of June to be seized.... All Captures made by British Ships of War or by the Officers of the Kings Troops in America [will be] adjudged by this Act to be lawful Prizes and as such Courts of Admiralty to proceed in their Condemnation.

This British naval order stemmed from provisions near the end of the Prohibitory Act and was found in "Some Newspapers and private Letters...stowed away by a Passenger in the Bottom of a Barrel of

---

2. Joel R. Paul, *Unlikely Allies* (New York: Riverhead Books, 2009), 130.
3. Thomas Fleming, *1776 Year of Illusions* (New York: W.W. Norton and Company,1975), 78.
4. David Armitage, *The Declaration of Independence: A Global History* (Cambridge, MA: Harvard University Press, 2007), 14.

Bread...which escaped Search."⁵ The information eventually was received by the Maryland Council of Safety in a letter dated February 27, 1776.

Though not mentioned by name in any of the Congressional minutes that took place following Lord North's introduction of the Act, Congress must already have been aware of these provisions, since as early as January 6, 1776, it had also approved a resolution to compensate American seamen who took part in the capture of any British ships "as lawful prizes" of war.

> That the Commander in chief [of any American naval vessels] have one twentieth part of the said allotted prize-money... [and that the] captain of any single ship have two twentieth parts for his share... that surgeons, chaplains, pursers, boatswains, gunners, carpenters, masters' mates, and the secretary of the fleet, share together two twentieth parts and one half of one twentieth part divided amongst them equally... (and the rest of the ship's company) at the time of the capture receive eight twentieths, and one half of a twentieth, be divided among them equally.⁶

Indeed, owing to this British "declaration of war," the North Atlantic in 1776 had truly become a virtual highway for British military vessels. Between December 31, 1775, and December 31, 1776, 895 ships had sailed from England transporting British troops along with their provisions to the North American colonies.⁷ In fact, to cope with this problem, as early as January, 1776, Congress had purchased eight ships and ordered thirteen others that "could carry as many as 120 guns and crews up to 1,000."⁸ In the case of any American ships destined to leave American ports, Congress had also issued messages for the ship owners to warn their captains "to take every possible precaution to avoid all British men of war and cutters on the voyage."⁹

In view of what was obviously becoming a steadily worsening military and maritime situation, it is not surprising that as early as September 18, 1775, Congress had formed a committee known initially as the Secret Committee, the sole purpose of which was to establish overseas contracts for "the importation and delivery of quantities of gun-

---

5. Letters of Delegates to Congress, 3:308-309.
6. *Journals of the Continental Congress*, 4: 36-37.
7. David Syrett, *Shipping and the American War 1775-83* (The Athlone Press, University of London, 1970), 249.
8. James K. Martin and Mark E. Lender, *A Respectable Army: The Military Origins of the Republic, 1763-1789* (Wheeling, IL: Harlan Davidson, 2006), 144.
9. *Journals of the Continental Congress*, 4: 108.

power ... brass field pieces, six pounders ... twenty thousand good plain double bridled musket locks ... and ten thousand strand of good arms."[10]

THE EVOLUTION OF THE SECRET COMMITTEE

Although the Secret Committee's original mandate was solely to procure military supplies, shortly after it was established, and as a result of the blockade, its mandate was broadened to cope with what had become an extremely serious financial problem for many local merchants who were engaged in domestic as well as foreign trade. To help overcome this problem the committee's name was changed to the Secret Committee on Trade because it was also asked to consider how best to establish trade connections on both sides of the Atlantic. As an example of domestic trade, on October 2 the Secret Committee introduced the following recommendation:

> To encourage the internal Commerce of these Colonies, your Committee thinks Provision should be had to facilitate Land Carriage, and therefore are of the opinion that it should recommend by this Congress to the several provincial Conventions and Assembles, to put their Roads in good Repair, and particularly the great Roads that lead from Colony to Colony.[11]

Next, the Secret Committee was asked to devise a plan "for carrying on a trade with the Indians, and the ways and means for procuring goods proper for that trade."[12] Such action was considered essential to prevent the Indians from joining forces with the British as well as to maintain the Indian's longstanding wish to remain neutral throughout the war.[13] Owing to this further increase in responsibility, the committee's name then became the Secret Committee on Trade and Commerce.

In essence, and with this final role in mind, the overall mandate of the Secret Committee needed to satisfy three major goals: (1) obtain foreign military assistance, (2) establish foreign and domestic commercial trade connections, and (3) enhance Indian trade relations. To achieve these goals, all of which stemmed in one way or another from the Prohibitory Act, a nine-member panel was selected with Thomas

---

10. Ibid., 2: 253.
11. Ibid., 3: 269.
12. Ibid., 3: 366.
13. Milton C. Van Vlack, *Silas Deane, Revolutionary War Diplomat and Politician* (Jefferson, NC: McFarland & Company, 2013), 77-78; Barbara A. Mann, *George Washington's War on Native America* (Westport, CN: Praeger, 2005), 10.

Willing as chair. Since the focus of two of the three committee goals was on trade and commerce, it is not surprising that of this number, six of the committee members (John Alsop, Philip Livingston, Silas Deane, Samuel Ward, and John Langdon), along with the committee chair, were all highly successful merchants, many of whom also had developed considerable experience forming important overseas trading connections. Although Willing resigned shortly after the panel was formed, he was replaced by Robert Morris who was Willing's partner in one of the largest and most successful overseas shipping companies in the colonies.

The first overture of the Secret Committee took place on December 12, 1775. During a meeting held in America with the French foreign minister, the comte de Vergennes, the committee was told that "France is well disposed to you; if she should give you aid, as she may, it will be on just and equitable terms. Make your proposals and I will present them." The committee was also told not to move forward until Vergennes let them know when and how it would be best to proceed.[14] With these thoughts in mind the committee then began to develop plans to initiate talks not only with France but also with other European governments who might be interested in establishing military and trade relations with the united colonies.

Because of its highly sensitive mission, Congress had resolved that the business of the committee needed "to be conducted with as much secrecy as the nature of the service will possibly admit," which meant that many of its records were destroyed.[15] For this reason, much of the following was distilled from the personal letters of the committee members who played a central role in the unfolding events: Morris and Deane. While Morris, as committee chair, remained in America and served as Deane's major contact, Deane was selected to implement the committee's overseas plans. Among the reasons given for Deane, he was well known to all of the other members of the committee, had many foreign contacts as the result of his highly successful commercial business in Connecticut, and, perhaps of even greater importance, Deane was the only committee member who was not an elected delegate to Congress.

> On your arrival in France you will [appear] . . . in the Character of a Merchant, which we wish you continually to retain among the French in general, it being probable that the Court of France may not like it

---

14. George Bancroft, *History of the United States from the Discovery of the American Continent, Vol. 8* (Boston, MA: Little Brown and Co, 1853), 216.
15. *Journals of the Continental Congress*, 2: 254.

should it be known publicly, that any [congressional] Agent from the Colonies is in that Country [to conduct business].[16]

The first set of instructions Deane received appeared in a letter from Morris, dated February 19, 1776.

> We deliver you herewith one part of a Contract made with the Secret Committee of Congress for exporting Produce of these Colonies to Europe & Importing from France Certain Articles suitable for the Indians . . . We [also] deliver to you herewith Sundry letters of introduction to respectable Houses in France which we hope will place you in the respectable light you deserve to appear & put you on a footing to purchase the Goods wanted on the very best terms . . . We think it prudent thus to divide the remittances that none of the Houses may know the Extent of your Commission but each of them will have orders to Account with you for the Amount of what comes into their hands for this purpose . . . The Vessel [we hired to deliver the goods] is on Monthly pay. Therefore, the sooner you dispatch her back the better & you will give this captain . . . suitable directions for approaching this Coast on their return [to avoid the blockade].[17]

The same letter also contained the following information, which indicates how purchasing arrangements were to be made.

> That the sum of $200,000 in continental money now advanced and paid by the said Committee of Secrecy to the said John Alsop, Francis Lewis, Philip Livingston, Silas Deane and Robert Morris, shall be laid out by them in the produce of these Colonies and shipped on board proper vessels, to be by them chartered for that purpose, to some proper port or ports in Europe (Great Britain and British Isles excepted) and there disposed of on the best terms . . . (the proceeds from the sales of this produce should then be used to purchase) such goods, wares or merchandise as the Committee of Secrecy shall direct and shipped for the United Colonies to be landed in some convenient harbor or place within the same and notice thereof given as soon as conveniently may be to the said Committee of Secrecy.

Deane then received a second set of instructions from Morris that he was to implement when he arrived in Paris. To maintain the secrecy of his visit, he was told to inform those whom he would initially meet that he was only in Paris as a tourist ("it is scarce necessary to pretend any other business at Paris, than the gratifying of that Curiosity which

---

16. Letters of the Delegates to Congress, 3: 321.
17. Ibid., 3:314-315.

draws Numbers thither yearly, merely to see so famous a City") and that only when the time seemed most appropriate was he to request a meeting with the French foreign minister.

INITIATING THE ALLIANCE

Deane was also told that upon meeting Vergennes, his message should be flattering, convincing, and contain no information that would allow anyone to know that he and Vergennes had previously met in America. The words in Morris' letter were carefully crafted and designed to convey these exact points.

> you had been dispatched by the Authority [of Congress] to apply to some European Power for a supply [of arms] ... if we should [as there is great appearance we shall] come to a total Separation from Great Britain, France would be looked upon as the Power, whose Friendship it would be fittest for us to obtain & cultivate ... it is likely that a great part of our Commerce will naturally fall to the Share of France, especially if she favors us in this Application as that will be a means of gaining & securing the friendship of the Colonies—And, that as our Trade rapidly increasing with our Increase of People & in a greater proportion, her part of it will be extremely valuable ... That the supply we at present want is Clothing & Arms for 25,000 Men, with a suitable Quantity of Ammunition & 100 field pieces ... That we mean to pay for the same by Remittances to France, Spain, Portugal & the French Islands, as soon as our Navigation can be protected by ourselves or Friends.[18]

The last set of instructions to Deane prior to his departure also dealt with arrangements that had been made for his passage from the colonies to France. Although scheduled to leave Philadelphia on March 8, due to many unforeseen delays, Deane finally set sail on May 3 and arrived at Bordeaux on June 6.[19]

Once in France Deane received a further set of instructions from Morris dated July 8, 1776. It was only at this point that Deane was able to make clear to Vergennes, that to satisfy a major condition as stipulated by France for receiving French military aid, the united colonies had finally broken away from Britain through the ratification of the Declaration of Independence and therefore was now able to negotiate on its own terms with all foreign nations.

> With this [letter] you will receive the Declaration of Congress for a final separation from Great Britain ... You will immediately commu-

18. Ibid., 3: 322.
19. Ibid., 3: 315, see note 2.

nicate the piece to the Court of France, and send copies of it to the other Courts of Europe. It may be well also to procure a good translation of it into French, and get it published in the gazettes. It is probable that, in a few days, instruction will be formed in Congress directing you to sound the Court of France on the subject of mutual commerce between her and these States. It is expected you will send the vessel back as soon as possible with the fullest intelligence of the state of affairs, and of everything that may affect the interest of the United States. And we desire that she may be armed and prepared for defense in the return.[20]

On October 1 Morris wrote again, but this time he informed Deane that the committee had received nothing further from him since his departure at the beginning of May. Throughout the letter Morris expressed his considerable anguish over this lack of communication coupled with his concern over this lengthy passage of time.

It would be very agreeable and useful to hear from you just now in order to form more certain the designs of the French Court respecting us and our Contest especially as we learn by various ways they [the British] are fitting out a considerable Squadron... they may now strike at New York. Twenty Sail of the line would take the whole Fleet there consisting of between 4 & 500 Sail of Men of War, Transports, Stores, Ships, and prizes... alas we fear the Court of France will let slip the glorious opportunity and go to war by halves as we have done. We say go to war because we are of the opinion (that) they must take part in the war sooner or later and the longer they are about it, the worse terms will they come in upon...The Fleet under Ld. Howe you know is vastly Superior to anything we have in the Navy way; consequently wherever Ships can move they must command; therefore it was long foreseen that we could not hold either Long Island or New York.[21]

Adding to his concerns, in an earlier letter Morris had also described to Deane the devastating impact that the blockade itself was having on all colonial commercial shipping.

I [Morris] have bought a considerable quantity of Tobacco but cannot get suitable Vessels to carry it. You cannot conceive of the many disappointments we have met in this respect... So many of the American Ships have been taken, lost, sold, [or] employed abroad [as the result of the blockade] that they are now very scarce in every part of the

---

20. Ibid., 4: 406.
21. Ibid., 5: 278-279.

Continent which I consider a great misfortune, for ship building does not go on as formerly.[22]

In addition to the blockade, and contrary to the previous year, of the twelve battles and skirmishes waged between the British and the American forces between August 27 and mid-December, 1776, the British were victorious in all but two and in a number of these, the American losses, in contrast to the British, were often substantial. For example, on August 27 the British defeated Washington at the Battle of Brooklyn. Whereas the British suffered 337 wounded or missing and 63 killed, the Americans suffered 1,079 wounded or missing and 970 killed. Then on December 1, under Washington's command, the Americans arrived at the Delaware River, crossed into Buck Country, Pennsylvania, and shortly thereafter it was anticipated by the Americans that Philadelphia would soon be attacked. In view of these events it is fitting that this period has been referred to as "one of the lowest points of the war for the patriots."[23]

On October 23, to prevent an anticipated invasion of New York, Morris further requested Dean "to procure Eight Line of Battle Ships either by Hire or purchase. We hope you will meet immediate success in this application and that you may be able to influence the Courts of France & Spain to send a large Fleet at their own Expense to Act in Concert with these Ships." Although at first glance this last request by Morris may seem surprising because it called upon France as well as Spain to now engage in an act of war against Britain, the request was clearly in line with Article 4 in a September 24, 1776, congressionally-approved "Plan for a Treaty" to be negotiated by the Americans with France. It is also the case that despite the very large number of articles in the plan, it was only this article, along with Article 3[24] that the treaty negotiators were informed "must be insisted upon" during the course of negotiations.[25] In short, because the plan was approved by Congress in September 1776 and because France's initial offer of assistance to the colonies in their dispute with England took place in December 1775, Congress must have expected France to become active in the colonies' military engagements once the Declaration of Independence had been ratified.

As the events outlined above steadily unfolded, it is not surprising that the members of Congress found themselves in an increasingly des-

---

22. Ibid., 5: 147-148.
23. Karapalides, *Dates of the American Revolution*, 75.
24. *Journals of the Continental Congress*, see 5: 769.
25. Ibid., 5: 814.

perate situation. With no other help to call upon, it is also perhaps not surprising that on December 11 Congress approved the following Resolve.

> That it be recommended to all the United States, as soon as possible, to appoint a day of solemn fasting and humiliation; to implore of Almighty God the forgiveness of the many sins prevailing among all [military] ranks, and to beg the countenance and assistance of his Providence in the prosecution of the present just and necessary war. . . .It is left to each state to issue out proclamations fixing the days that appear most proper within their several bounds.

To ensure that this message was clearly understood by all concerned, the Resolve also called upon the members of the military itself, including the military hierarchy, to act in accordance with the Almighty's wishes:

> all members of the United States and particularly the officers civil and military under them, [to practice] the exercise of repentance and reformation; and further, require of them the strict observation of the articles of war, and particularly, that part of the said articles, which forbids profane swearing, and all immorality.[26]

Finally, on December 30, 1776, Congress issued its last attempt of the year to avoid total defeat by providing France with the following enticement to come to its aid: "should the Independence of America be supported [by France], Great Britain . . . would at once be deprived of one third of her power and Commerce; and that this in a great Measure would be added to the Kingdom of France." In the event this enticement failed to achieve its objective, Congress then also threatened France with the consequences that would result if it did not immediately enter the war on behalf of the Americans colonies.

> in Case Great Britain should succeed against America, a military Government will be established here [in America] and the Americans already trained to arms, will, however unwilling, be forced into the Service of his Britannic Majesty, whereby his [Majesty's] power will be greatly augmented and may hereafter be employed [to take over] the French and Spanish islands in the West Indies.[27]

Unfortunately, given the prevailing international climate in 1776 as dictated by Britain and Spain, France elected to offer only secret finan-

---

26. Ibid., 6:1022.
27. Ibid., 6: 1055.

cial and limited material aid in support of the colonies, and not the type of aid being requested by Congress. Therefore, France refused to go beyond what it felt, at that time, was most appropriate in satisfying its own best interests and chose to remain officially out of the war.[28]

CULMINATING THE ALLIANCE

The situation described above suddenly changed in the fall of 1777. On October 31, Congress sent a letter with the following information to its delegates in Paris.

> We have the pleasure to enclose the capitulation, by which General Burgoyne and his Whole army surrendered themselves [at Saratoga as] prisoners of war ... We rely on your wisdom and care to make the best and most immediate use of this intelligence to depress our enemies and produce essential aid to our cause in Europe.[29]

With this information in mind, the American delegates in France who "were attempting to play upon fears [told the French representatives] that an accommodation between Great Britain and the revolting colonies was [now] possible and even imminent."[30] The significance of these two factors and the anxiety they must have generated among the French was fully captured in the following words by Bemis.[31]

> The fear that the British Ministry, staggering under the blow of Saratoga, was about to offer to the Colonies peace terms generous but short of independence had an immediate effect in France. Anxious lest such terms might be accepted by the war-weary Americans ... the French Ministry felt that if something were not done quickly, the long-awaited chance, at last at hand, for sundering the British Empire might pass and be gone forever.

The Treaty of Amity and Commerce along with the Treaty of Alliance, both of which together are often referred to as the French Alliance, were finally signed on February 6, 1778. A question that still remained, though, was how would the Kingdom of France cover the costs associated with supplying all the military aid America needed to win the war? Anne-Robert Jacques Turgot, France's Minister of Finance, repeatedly warned the King that "the first gunshot will drive the

---

28. James Pritchard,1994, French strategy and the American Revolution: A reappraisal, *Naval War College Review*, Vol 47, Issue 4 (1994), 87-89.
29. Letters of the Delegates to Congress, 1777, 215-216.
30. Gerald S. Brown, *The American Secretary* (Ann Arbor, MI: University of Michigan Press, 1963), 151.
31. Samuel F. Bemis, *The Diplomacy of the American Revolution* (Bloomington, IN: Indiana University Press,1965), 60.

state to bankruptcy."³² The answer can be found in the following material.

>On July 16, 1782, Benjamin Franklin, Minister Plenipotentiary of the United States of North America, agreed and certified that the sums advanced by His Majesty to the Congress of the United States... under the title of a loan, in the years 1778, 1779, 1780, 1781 and the present 1782, (to repay) the sum of eighteen million livers, money of France ... on the 1st of January, 1788, at the house of the Grand Banker at Paris ... with interest at five per cent per annum.³³

To prevent a French financial catastrophe it appears that Congress had authorized Franklin to underwrite a series of French loans to cover the cost of the French military help it needed to achieve victory over Great Britain. While on the surface it would seem that France was taking a considerable risk in agreeing to this procedure, the reality of the situation suggests that it had no other choice. If the United States had lost the war, France's fears of a British takeover of its territory could very well have been realized, whereas, if the United States won, the loans would have been repaid and France would have been able to maintain its position as a European power. Although the agreement was indeed a gamble, it was a gamble that France was simply forced to take.

Despite the fact that the Alliance had been signed on February 6, 1778, it is equally important to note that, due to the naval blockade, Congress had received no further word on this matter from its overseas delegates since May, 1777. As a result, Congress was faced with an additional problem as expressed on April 30, 1778, in a letter to its Paris representatives.

>We have read a letter written by a friend dated Feb. 13, 1778, in which we are told that "you had concluded a Treaty with France and Spain which was on the Water towards us." Imagine how solicitous we are to know the truth of this before we receive any proposals from Britain in consequence of the scheme in Ld. North's speech and the two Draughts of Bills now sent to you.³⁴

---

32. Richard J. Werther, "Opposing the Franco-American Alliance: the Case of Anne-Robert Jacques Turgot. allthingsliberty.com/2020/06/opposing-the-Franco-American Alliance: the-case-of-Anne-Robert Jacques Turgot.
33. Contract between the King and the Thirteen United States of North America, signed at Versailles July 16, 1782," Avalon.law.yale.edu/18th century'fr 1782.asp https://avalon.law.yale.edu/18th century/fr-1782.asp.
34. Letter of the Delegates to Congress, 9:547.

The "proposals" in this letter referred to the terms for reconciliation that Lord North had authorized in March 1778 for the Carlisle Peace Commission to use as a means for negotiating an end to the war with America. The difficulty Congress now faced, however, stemmed not only from Lord North's proposals, but also from two Congressional counterproposals drafted by Samuel Huntington and by Henry Drayton, respectively.[35] Henry Laurens, who at the time was president of the Congress, was extremely troubled over this issue and expressed his personal concern in a letter to his son.

> Some of our people here have been exceedingly desirous of throwing abroad in addition to the Resolutions an intimation of the willingness of Americans to treat with G Britain upon terms not inconsistent with the Independence of these States or with Treaties with foreign powers. I am averse. We have made an excellent move on the Table—rest until we see or learn the motions on the other side—the whole World must know we are disposed to treat of Peace & to conclude one upon honorable terms. To Publish [anything on this matter at present is] therefor unnecessary [and] it would be dangerous to Act, encourage our Enemies & alarm our friends.[36]

Stated more succinctly, Laurens' concern stemmed from the possibility of reaching too hasty a conclusion without a full understanding of the overall ramifications in the different sets of proposals. To behave in this manner would simply not have been in the best interests of the United States.

Although Congress did debate the matter at the end of April, as the result of the fact that Silas Deane had arrived at York on May 2, the debate only lasted two days.[37] With official versions of the Treaty of Alliance and the Treaty of Amity and Commerce now in hand, Deane was able to show that the French Alliance had indeed been signed in February, which meant that closure had been achieved and no further debate was required. For the members of Congress, their long sought-after goal of French military aid could now finally be considered as secure.

---

35. Ibid., 9:468, 9:552-553.
36. Ibid., 9: 515.
37. Ibid., 9:553, see note 1.

Marinus Willett: The Exploits of an Unheralded War Hero

RICHARD WERTHER

Marinus Willett was born the son of a Quaker, Edward Willett, on July 31, 1740, in Jamaica, Long Island (now part of Queens). After spending his early years on a farm in Jamaica, he relocated to a place known then as Cedar Grove, along the East River and now part of New York City. This place, where his grandfather Samuel Willett, Sheriff of Queens County, died at age ninety-three, became the virtual Willet headquarters for his lifetime.[1]

He became a wealthy merchant and property owner at a young age. During the French and Indian War, Willett, at age eighteen, was appointed a lieutenant in Oliver De Lancey's New York Regiment, serving in numerous campaigns, among them actions on Ticonderoga (not so successful) and Frontenac (highly successful).[2] These contrasting experiences gave him some sense of the British military and its inconsistent leadership. At this point, feeling ill from the strains of the war effort, he was done with fighting for now, returned to New York, and soon married the first of what would be three wives.

Soon after, the war of words began heating up between the British and the colonies. Though his whole family were devout loyalists, Willett joined the New York chapter of the Sons of Liberty, joining agitators such as John Lamb and Isaac Sears. While Willett does not appear to have been much in the speechmaking department, he was there when the mob needed to exert itself. Such was the case when he helped liberate six hundred muskets from a local arsenal in April 1775. Later,

---

1. John Schuyler, *Institution of the Society of the Cincinnati - Proceedings of its general meetings and from the transactions of the New York State Society* (New York, D. Taylor, 1886), 347.
2. Mark Mayo Boatner, *Cassell's Biographical Dictionary of the American War of Independence* (London, Cassell, 1966), 1207.

when the British were hauling away their remaining weapons to load them on the ship *Asia*, the Sons thought the weapons were destined for Boston to interfere in the action occurring there. It was Willett's good fortune to meet the military procession at Broadway and Beaver streets, and he revved up the crowd enough to enlist their aid to capture all the carts of equipment. This equipment would later be used by the first troops raised in New York.[3] He participated in one more theft of British arms. Borrowing a sloop with some friends they raided the arsenal at Turtle Bay on the east shore of Manhattan and made off with more weapons.[4]

Once the Revolution started, Willett signed on as a captain in Alexander McDougall's 1st New York Regiment. His initial involvement was in Gen. Richard Montgomery's ill-fated attack on Canada. He was left in command of St. Johns on the Richelieu River while Montgomery made his unsuccessful push on Quebec. Returning to New York City, he was involved in a number of minor skirmishes, but things wouldn't really start to get interesting until he was transferred to Fort Stanwix in May 1777.

At Stanwix, Willett was under the command of Col. Peter Gansevoort. The fort had been little used since the French and Indian War and, in Gansevoort's assessment, was in such a state of disrepair that it was barely defensible. Willett commanded a fort in ruins with a small number of men, many too ill to work and stretched thin in both repairing the fort and protecting the region from numerous Native American attacks.[5] It was largely Willet's job to see that this changed. A French officer, Capt. B. De La Marquise, was engaged for the work. Willett did not much like his work, but politics dictated that he be retained. Eventually, though, Gansevoort was forced to arrest Marquise and ship him back to Albany due to his subpar efforts to rehabilitate the fort. It was August before Fort Stanwix was in what its officers considered a state of defense, and none too soon.

With British Col. Barry St. Leger's forces on the way, a siege was anticipated, and a siege is what they got. St. Leger's forces arrived at the fort on August 4. Gen. Nicholas Herkimer's forces were the closest with the potential to provide relief, but as we shall see, those hopes were

---

3. Frederick L. Bronner, "Marinus Willett," *New York History*, Vol. 17, No. 3 (July 1936), 274-275.
4. Larry Lowenthal, *Marinus Willett – Defender of the Northern Frontier* (Fleischmanns, NY: Purple Mountain Press, 2000), 8.
5. Harry Schenawolf, "Battle of Oriskany and Siege of Fort Stanwix—Brutal Civil War that Helped Save a Nation," www.revolutionarywarjournal.com/battle-of-oriskany-and-siege-of-fort-stanwix-brutal-civil-war-that-helped-save-a-nation/.

dashed. Herkimer did draw off St. Leger's troops, but at a high cost. A prearranged signal to call for Herkimer to assist the fort failed to click, and Herkimer's forces walked into a trap set by St. Leger in what would become the Battle of Oriskany. Herkimer's forces were cut to pieces in the resulting ambush. This included the general himself who, mortally wounded, allegedly sat against a tree and smoked his pipe as the battle raged around him.

Back at Stanwix, Willett had a plan, and it worked to perfection. By now the majority of the Loyalists, British, and German troops were absent. A sizable number had been committed against Herkimer while others were still miles away working on the wilderness road. On August 5, Willett decided to exit the fort and see what damage he could do. Dividing his force into two groups, Willett moved quickly against his two primary targets: the camps of General St. Leger and Sir John Johnson. Willett was hoping to kill or capture either one or both of the commanders.[6] After driving off the stragglers defending the camps, including Johnson who fled in his nightshirt, Willett had free run at both camps. He made off with three wagonloads of supplies, including five British flags, the baggage of Sir John Johnson with all his papers, the baggage of a number of other officers with memoranda, journals, and orderly books containing all the information which could be desired.

Willett's sortie had struck a blow not only to British morale, but especially to that of their Native American allies. The Americans had also lucked out by the confiscation of Johnson's papers. They detailed not only the British forces they faced, but St. Leger's and Gen. John Burgoyne's campaign intelligence including their critical supply lines.[7] Retiring victoriously back to Fort Stanwix, Willett and his raiders cheered loudly—the raid had been a total success, with their only casualties two men slightly wounded. In their final mockery of the British, the flags that had been captured by the raiders were hoisted right underneath the American flag.

The only negative was the question of why Willett's forces did not proceed to Oriskany to see if they could assist the outmanned Herkimer. St. Leger's troops had been informed that their camp was being raided and a portion peeled off to try to defend it. Could Willet likewise have heard what was happening at Oriskany? Willett apparently did not know the militia had engaged the enemy, which would

---

6. Michael O. Logusz, *With Musket and Tomahawk Volume II: The Mohawk Valley Campaign in the Wilderness War Of 1777* (Havertown, PA, Casemate Publishers, 2012), 151.
7. Schenawolf, "Battle of Oriskany and Siege of Fort Stanwix."

explain why he didn't immediately march to their aid. It is doubtful whether the forces under Willett's command would have changed the outcome at Oriskany. Willett's sortie into the camps was a complete success, while Oriskany was a huge loss.

St. Leger's troops, though traveling a little lighter than before, nevertheless continued the siege. In fact, on August 9 they sent Capt. William Ancrum into the fort under a flag of truce to demand the fort's surrender. Gansevoort, though he knew he was in trouble in the event of a prolonged siege, refused to budge. Willett spoke for him at the meeting, and did not mince words, saying in part:

> For my part, I declare, before I would consent to deliver this garrison to such a murdering set as your army, by your own account, consists of, I would suffer my body to be filled with splinters, and set on fire, as you know has at times been practiced, by such hordes of women and children killers, as belong to your army.

Before Ancrum could respond, Willett's officers gave a loud round of applause. Colonel Gansevoort immediately added that he had no intention of surrendering, and Ancrum was sent on his way.[8]

The bravado displayed by Gansevoort and Willet did not hide the fact that they were in a tough spot should the siege be prolonged. To get out of it, they needed something to happen. Willett would again provide the heroics. On August 10 at around 10 p.m.—in a howling and raging storm and in total darkness—Lieutenant Colonel Willett, accompanied by Lt. George Stockwell, slipped out of Fort Stanwix through a sally port and raced into a marsh. To move rapidly, each man was armed with only a short spear and tomahawk.[9] Stockwell was a good hunter and was well acquainted with the Indian method of travelling in the wilderness. Proceeding silently along the marsh, they reached the Mohawk river which they crossed by crawling over a log, amazingly undetected by the enemy's sentinels who were still close by.[10] They passed by night through the besiegers' works, and made their way for fifty miles through pathless woods and unexplored morasses, in order to summon some help and bring relief to the fort.[11] Even the British grudgingly complimented this gutsy maneuver, with one pub-

---

8. Logusz, *With Musket and Tomahawk*, 181. William Ancrum was a captain in the 34th Regiment of Foot; some accounts of his interaction with Willett give his rank as major.
9. Ibid., 182.
10. William M. Willett, *Narrative Of The Military Actions Or Colonel Marinus Willett, Taken Chiefly From His Own Manuscript* (New York: G. & C. & H. Carvill, 1831), 59.
11. Logusz, *With Musket and Tomahawk*, 183.

Marinus Willett: The Exploits of an Unheralded War Hero [131]

Marinus Willett by Ralph Earl, ca. 1791. (*Metropolitan Museum of Art*)

lication writing of their escape from the fort, "such action deserves the praise even of an enemy"[12]

After traveling fifty miles in about two days, they arrived at Fort Dayton near German Flatts. Eventually they met up with Benedict Arnold while the general was marching the 1st and 4th New York regiments west towards Fort Dayton. Willett accompanied Arnold to Fort Dayton where the relief force was assembling before the push to Fort Stanwix.[13] As a deception, Arnold sent a mentally impaired Tory named Hon Yost Schuyler ahead to Stanwix carrying a message that Arnold was approaching with an overwhelming force.[14] St. Leger intercepted the message and believed it. His demoralized Indian forces were more than ready to believe it. As a result, St. Leger ordered a general retreat to begin the night of August 22 by removing the sick and wounded to Wood Creek.[15] With his Native American allies giving up

---

12. J. Seeley and J. Wright, *The Annual Register or a View of the History, Politics, and Literature for the year 1777* (London, Longmans, Green, et al., 1835), 161.
13. Schenawolf, "Battle of Oriskany and Siege of Fort Stanwix."
14. Lowenthal, *Marinus Willett*, 35.
15. Schenawolf, "Battle of Oriskany and Siege of Fort Stanwix."

and heading home in droves, and Arnold's "overwhelming force" approaching, it seemed the only option. Thanks in large part to Willett and Stockwell's daring clandestine escape, the siege was broken.

The end of the siege freed up both sides of what became an encounter that would impact Willet both now and later. As described by Dr. William Petry (1733–1806) of German Flats, chairman of the Tryon County Committee of Safety and a surgeon in the Tryon County militia:

> Yesterday Morning one Mr. [Walter N.] Butler, Son to Colonel [John] Butler and said to be an officer in the British Army came to Mr. Shoemaker's [proprietor of a tavern], two Miles from Fort Dayton, accompanied by about fourteen white Men and as many Indians all armed under pretence of a Flag of Truce ... He was Yesterday inviting the Inhabitants to lay down their Arms and repair to the Royal Standard. While with him he used us very uncivilly indeed, condemning and ridiculing all our Measures as rebellious and tyrannical. His Conversation was much taken up in magnifying the Enemies Strength and the most insolent threats imaginable."[16]

This was the notorious Walter Butler, not a British regular but a loyalist and co-leader of a force known as Butler's Rangers. Butler seemed unaware, or did not care, that the Rebel Fort Dayton was close by and that his antics might cause some commotion. They did and after some discussion Butler and his crew were taken into custody. Arnold, still in the area, was briefed on the arrest and arranged a court martial on August 20, with Lieutenant Colonel Willett serving as judge advocate and Butler, a lawyer by trade, defending himself. The court martial found three of the accused guilty of spying or desertion and they were sentenced to death.[17] However, a number of officers belonging to the 1st New York regiment who had known Butler prior to the war petitioned to have his sentence commuted, and Arnold granted their petition. Butler was instead imprisoned in Albany. He escaped from there the following winter and became afterwards a severe scourge to the inhabitants of the Mohawk Valley and beyond.[18] As fate would have it, Willett and Butler would meet again before the war was over.

In 1778, Gansevoort released Willett to join Washington's army, and he did so for the Battle of Monmouth, where he witnessed Washing-

---

16. Philip Schuyler to George Washington, August 17, 1777, footnote 1, founders.archives.gov/documents/Washington/03-11-02-0008.
17. Schenawolf, "Battle of Oriskany and Siege of Fort Stanwix."
18. Willett, *Narrative*, 62.

ton's bravery and his rebuke of Gen. Charles Lee's retreat. "I have seen him in a variety of situations," Willett would write, "and none in which he did not appear great, but never did I see him when he exhibited such greatness as on this day."[19] Willett remained away from the upstate New York and with or close to Washington from 1778 through 1780.

Meanwhile, in Willett's absence, battles along the Mohawk raged in 1778 as the forces traded raids in which civilians were killed, each one ramping up both emotions and anxiety among the residents. One particularly egregious action came in November 1778 when Butler's Rangers, led by Walter Butler, along with some British regulars and their Indian allies, made an attack on a settlement in Cherry Valley, New York. Butler was either unable or unwilling to control his Indian allies (the stories vary depending on to whom he was writing), and the result was a massacre in which roughly seventy people including women and children were slaughtered, and many scalps taken. This attack ratcheted Butler's infamy to a new level and made him a marked man.

Willett finally returned to the Mohawk Valley in early 1781 with the assignment from Gov. George Clinton to keep things under control with the Indians and the British. As a little boost to his confidence he had a commendation from General Washington, written late in 1780: "It will give me great pleasure to see an officer of your merit retained in service, but your determination to submit cheerfully to any regulations which may be deemed necessary for the public good, is very laudable, and the surest mark of a disinterested, virtuous Citizen."[20] He needed it, as he had his work cut out for him. Headquartered in Albany, he had a force under him that was insufficient in both skill and number (fewer than 400) to cover the area he needed to control.

He distributed his forces among the various towns and hoped nothing resembling Cherry Valley would erupt. "I can promise to do everything in my power, for the relief of the people, of whom I had some knowledge in their prosperous days; and am now acquainted with in the time of their great distress; a people whose case I most sincerely commiserate" he wrote to Washington.[21] Skirmishes broke out, but major engagements were few. In one battle, Willet's forces were outnumbered two to one yet emerged victorious with five killed compared to forty of the enemy.

---

19. Lowenthal, *Marinus Willett*, 40.
20. Washington to Marinus Willett, October 24, 1780, in footnote 2 to Willett to Washington, October 18, 1780, founders.archives.gov/documents/Washington/03-28-02-0328.
21. Lowenthal, *Marinus Willett*, 59.

In late October 1781, Willett was frantically pursuing a force led by British Maj. John Ross and including Walter Butler. He was determined to destroy them if he could, so that never again would such savage warfare be brought to the Mohawk Valley.[22] The weather turned cold, and the campaigning season was drawing to a close, but Willett was determined. He rallied some 400 men and was joined by about sixty friendly Oneida Indians. Estimates of the British forces were round 600, so again he was outnumbered. In a driving snow storm, carrying provisions for just five days, he led his men out on the track of the much-hated Butler who he knew was amongst Ross's force.[23] As darkness closed in, Ross, in fear of meeting the same fate as Burgoyne at Saratoga, began a rapid retreat.[24]

Willett finally caught up with the rearguard of the Loyalist army at Canada Creek in eastern New York. What happened next remains the source of some disagreement. Some sources say the conflict was prefaced with verbal exchanges: One witness remembered Butler taunting, "Shoot and be damned," and another, "kiss [my] posterior."[25] Knowing Butler, all could be true. As a mist came down across the water, there was a burst of firing, with several men hit on each side. The enemy fire slackened and ceased, and after a pause the Continental scouts, the Oneidas, some troops, and finally Colonel Willett forded the chilling creek. There were several bodies on the opposite bank. One of them wore a gold-laced hat. They pulled it off and saw a bullet hole in the head, then someone, possibly Willett himself, recognized the man as Walter Butler, seriously wounded but still alive. An Oneida warrior proceeded to end that by scalping him.[26] Willett had achieved his goals: Butler was dead and so severely was this victory over Major Ross felt, that not only through the rest of the winter but during the following campaign of 1782, no considerable force of the enemy, in one body, at any time appeared.[27]

Willett was just forty-three years old when the war ended, with a sterling war record and still, as it turned out, more than half his life still ahead of him. There was much yet to do. His strong reputation with Washington landed him an assignment in 1790 to persuade the Creek

---

22. Fred J. Cook, *What Manner of Men: Forgotten Heroes of the American Revolution* (New York: Morrow, 1959). 171.
23. Ibid.
24. Lowenthal, *Marinus Willett*, 66.
25. Gavin K. Watt, *Gavin K. Watt's Revolutionary Canadian History 6-Book Bundle: A Dirty Trifling Piece of Business* (Toronto: Dundurn Press, 2017), 37.
26. Howard Swiggett, *War Out of Niagara – Walter Butler and the Tory Rangers* (New York: Columbia University Press, 1933), 242.
27. Willett, *Narrative*, 89.

Indians and their leader, Alexander McGillivray, to continue treaty efforts. The Creeks were causing trouble to the settlers of Kentucky and Tennessee. Willett was successful and a delegation of Creeks under McGillivray visited New York City, then capital of the United States, resulting in the Treaty of New York.[28]

As was the case with many of the former New York "Liberty Boys," he aligned himself with the Anti-Federalist party. He was appointed by New York Governor Clinton to two terms as Sheriff of New York City, from 1784-1787 and 1790-1795. Ironically, this put him in charge of suppressing any actions like the ones he was in the middle of as a Son of Liberty.[29]

In 1797, he was appointed the city's mayor, serving just one year. In the 1820s, he served as president of the Electoral College. With the ascendancy of Alexander Hamilton, Philip Schuyler, John Jay and the New York Federalists, his role in politics started to wane. During the last years of his life, Colonel Willett mingled little in public affairs. In 1824 he was a member of the delegation that met with the Marquis de Lafayette, who he had known from the Battle of Monmouth in 1778, on the latter's return trip to America. Lafayette later visited him at Cedar Grove.[30]

Surrounded by his family and friends, Willett yielded slowly, but not reluctantly, to the gradual progress of aging. Very interested in social services and the needs of citizens, Willett established relief centers and a city medical clinic and hospital to assist the needy. He donated much of his own money for this center and was involved with it until his peaceful death on August 23, 1830, at the age of ninety-one.[31] He laid in state at his home for two days and more than 10,000 paid their respects.[32]

Of the numerous epitaphs written in the New York papers following his death, the one in the *New York Evening Post* probably summed it up the best: "Col. Willett distinguished himself by his bravery and good conduct in the war of the Revolution. His courage, prowess, and presence of mind were particularly displayed in conflicts with the Indians who took part with Great Britain. He was a man of great integrity, frankness, and decision of character in private life."[33] The *New York Mirror* put it most succinctly, stating that "His biography is inseparably interwoven with the history of our country's glory."[34]

28. Bronner, "Marinus Willett," 278.
29. Ibid.
30. Lowenthal, *Marinus Willett*, 91.
31. Logusz, *With Musket and Tomahawk*, 52.
32. Lowenthal, *Marinus Willett*, 92.
33. Willett, *Narrative*, 159-160.
34. Ibid., 158.

Point/Counterpoint, 1777 Style: Dueling Proclamations from Putman and Tryon

TODD W. BRAISTED

As the year 1777 drew to a close, the region around the city of New York had been under British control for a year. Although the British position was strong, the recent surrender of a British army at Saratoga dramatically changed the prospects of the war ending any time soon. Troops in the New York garrison settled in for another winter at war.

The north end of the island of Manhattan was separated from the mainland only by a narrow waterway. The British post at Kingsbridge guarded the only bridge across, and Maj. Gen. William Tryon commanded troops stationed there. Some distance away, American troops under Maj. Gen. Israel Putnam kept a close watch British activities at Kingsbridge. The front lines were static but ever tense at this strategic location.

The soldiers under General Tryon's command included troops from the British regular army, Loyalist troops raised in America for the war, and auxiliary troops from German states—popularly called Hessians. American commanders were keenly aware that these latter troops did not have the same vested interest in the war as their British and Loyalist comrades, and had suffered several setbacks in the previous twelve months. It was to this disinterest that General Putnam hoped to appeal.

On the morning of November 30 two officers brought Tryon separate copies of the same proclamation, written in German, their troops had found near the front lines.[1] It was an appeal to German soldiers. Tryon's interpreter, Anthony Fiva, quickly translated it:

---

1. William Tryon to Henry Clinton, November 30, 1777, University of Michigan, William L. Clements Library, Sir Henry Clinton Papers, Volume 27, item 45.

By the Honorable Israel Putnam Major General & Commander in Chief of the United American Forces, On their different Stations, at the White Plains.
Proclamation

Whereas, The King of Great Britain, has found means, that a great part of the Subjects of the Prince of Hesse Cassel, and other German Princes have been sent Over to America, in order to force the Inhabitants thereof to his absolute Will, to destroy and deprive them of their natural Property and Liberty.

And Whereas, it is known that these Troops have been forc'd against their Inclination, to leave their native country, to take part in a War which they can reap no benefit by, and wash their hands in the blood of its inhabitants, who never did them any harm, and with whom they have no manner of controversy, they being also treated by the Troops of the proud King of Great Britain, with the utmost contempt, whose commander always Exposeth them to the most dangerous Posts, in Order that the lives of the British Troops may be spared, and so Glory in the victories gain'd by the German Troops for them, with the loss of their blood.

And Whereas, the King of Great Britain, and the above German Princes, have Renewed their alliances, that their Troops shall not return to their native country, Untill the present War be ended. I thought it fit & convenient to declare to the Officers and Soldiers of the above Troops in British pay, That the Inhabitants of the United American States, are willing to Receive them, as Brethren and Inhabitants of America, and every one of those who are willing and any way inclined to enjoy a quiet and peaceable life, free from hazards and dangers, In a contest which no ways concerns them. Therefore the best Encouragement is hereby offer'd to any of them who have any trade and upon such terms they never can meet with in any other Country. And as further Encouragement to these Troops, they may be assur'd that at the end of this War, they shall at public cost be sent over again to Germany, as soon as required, or Enjoy the same priveledges as the Inhabitants of this once happy country, if they have a mind to Stay. They shall likewise faithfully be paid for their arms, or any other things belonging to them, as they may be valued.

Given under my Hand at Head Quarters the 16th day of November 1777.
L.S. Israel Putnam
Translated from the Original German
By A. Fiva, Interpreter to His
Excelly. M. Genl. Tryon.[2]

---

2. University of Michigan, William L. Clements Library, Sir Henry Clinton Papers, Volume 27, item 46.

Tryon sent Fiva to ask commanders of German regiments in the area whether more copies of the proclamation had been found. More importantly, Tryon wanted to know if the German officers were concerned that it would cause unrest among the soldiery. The officers assured Tryon that "they were unanimous of opinion that not a Hesse man would be seduced with it." They also requested that Tryon make a "contrary proclamation" and post it in the newspapers. Tryon thought such a proclamation should come from the commander in chief in New York, Gen. Henry Clinton, and sent a letter to him with Putnam's proclamation enclosed.

The German regimental officers, however, chose not to wait for Clinton's response. They took it upon themselves to write a response, a declaration, that Tryon sent to Clinton for his approval:[3]

Declaration

It is not the first time that the Rebel Generals have made it their Study to mislead the Hessian and other foreign Troops in British Pay, and to induce them by insiduous arts to desertion, under the fair Promises, that they should be received well, rewarded with Land and other advantages to their perfect ease and Satisfaction; They began this Game last year at Staten Island, tryed it afterwards at Rhode Island, and now Old Putnam appears by his Proclamation upon the stage, endeavouring to inveigle these Troops from their Duty, and in plausible terms aims if possible to create a jealousy between them and the English, in hopes to gain his point by such base means: But of what benefit have all these invitations been to the Rebels? Have the Hessians deserted? or have those who have fell into Rebel hands join'd their armies? No, except some few villains who are Strangers both to the Hessians and their Country: The Rebel Armies cannot boast of having done them much injury in this way. Besides what reason can the Hessians have to enter the Rebel Service, when it is generally known they are well maintained, receive their ordinary pay & Provision punctually, and are provided with every necessary they stand in need of; can the knowledge they have of the miserable, pitifull, and wretched condition of the Rebel Soldiery, be an inducement for Hessians to Desert; while Deserters or Prisoners from the Rebels, without clothing, Shoes, or other necessaries, appear every day before their face, some of whom have confessed that their men Struggle under worse circumstances than Death itself.

It is in vain then to persuade the Hessians to be guilty of Desertion, or to breed a Jealousy between them and the English, since they live

---

3. Tryon to Clinton, December 4, 1777, University of Michigan, William L. Clements Library, Sir Henry Clinton Papers, Volume 27, item 53.

with one another like Brethren, and certainly will continue so to do, through the course of this War.

The Reasons the Prince their Master has to join His Troops to those of the British, rests on Stronger grounds of Policy, than a Carpenter, Butcher, Farmer, or any other who does not study the Laws of States or of Nations, can possibly conceive.

The Hessians are in particular a faithful and Obedient People to their Prince, and Country; It is impossible then to Seduce them like those Fanaticks among the Rebel Army's, by motives of so base a nature; They never will Desert their Prince, their Country, their honor or whatever else is Dear to them, (and sell their Souls to the Devil) for the sake of a Plantation.

The best they can do for the Rebels is to give them this Salutary advice, Let them Lay down their Arms, open their Eyes, and see the fatal consequences of the unnatural War they are engaged in; They have been deceived, Tyrannized over by Committee men: Their Country is ruined.

Rouze then every one of you, suffer Yourselves no longer to be mislead. Your Leaders intend only the destruction of yourselves, your families, and extreme misery to your Country.

Rise up then in vengeance against your real Ennemies, Congresses & Committee's, at least, endeavour to come to us, or to the English your natural Brethren, and you shall be received with open arms. This is the best time for your Submission; Since you may depend upon it, next Spring there will be such a Powerfull army of Russians and Hanoverians come over to subdue you, as will make it impossible for you to resist, then it will be too late to implore mercy, you then must wait that Dreadfull punishment Denounced against such who have obstinately persisted in their Revolt against their Parent State and lawfull Sovereign; consider well, before this horrid Scene appears of the Rashness of your ways, of the madness and Guilt of your measures, and be persuaded that on your repentance and Submission only, You can be entitled to invite the Stedfast Hessians to your Friendship.
By The Hessian Corps
encamped at Kings Bridge[4]

It is doubtful many were swayed on either side, although a few may have taken up the offer. This is but one of many examples of the psychological warfare employed by both sides during the American Revolution.

---

4. Enclosed in Tryon to Clinton, December 4, 1777.

Did Washington Swear at Charles Lee during the Battle of Monmouth?

CHRISTIAN MCBURNEY

The scene is one of the most famous in the annals of the American Revolutionary War. The commander in chief of the Continental Army, Gen. George Washington, confronts his second-in-command, Charles Lee, in the midst of a retreat by Continental Army forces during the Battle of Monmouth Court House on June 28, 1778. Washington arrives at the battlefield riding his white steed; Lee rides up to meet him on his brown horse. Washington asks, in an angry voice, what is the meaning of the retreating soldiers he sees? A baffled Lee, expecting praise instead of sharp words, stammers a response. The two men exchange harsh words and then ride off to organize defenses against oncoming enemy forces. Legendary for his composure, at this moment Washington lost it.

But did Washington use swear words in speaking with Lee during that verbal confrontation? Many popular histories of the war and battle say he did. Two sources indicate Washington swore, one from a story told by Maj. Gen. Charles Scott and the other from a story told by Maj. Gen. the Marquis de Lafayette. Both recollections were made decades after the battle by generals who were likely not present at the meeting and who held a grudge against Lee.

On the other hand, we have testimony from the court-martial trial of Charles Lee by several officers who were present at the fateful verbal encounter. The testimony was taken within a few weeks of the day of battle. This testimony has far more credibility than Scott's and Lee's post-war recollections. A close review of the testimony indicates that Washington likely did not swear and that Scott's and Lafayette's recollections made years after the event are not credible.

Here is a quick review of the background facts.[1]

On June 26, 1778, Lee was given command of many of the Continental Army's best troops with orders from Washington to attack the rear of British general Henry Clinton's column near Monmouth Court House in Monmouth County, New Jersey. The next day, Washington gave Lee somewhat vague orders to attack the rear guard of Clinton's force. Washington and his following army, six miles away, would then march to arrive at the scene of battle to support Lee.

Lee intended to attack the enemy's rear guard on June 28, but instead he retreated in the face of Clinton's bold move to reverse his march with some 6,000 troops. Crucially, two of Lee's subordinate brigadier generals, Charles Scott and William Maxwell—without orders and without informing Lee—moved more than half of his command off the field. Faced with the possible destruction of the balance of his force, Lee ordered a general retreat while conducting a skillful delaying action.

Many historians have been quick to malign Lee's performance at Monmouth. Many of his contemporaries did so too. After the battle, Lee was convicted by court-martial for not attacking and for retreating in the face of the enemy. I believe this was a miscarriage of justice, for the evidence shows Lee was unfairly convicted and had, in fact, by retreating, performed an important service to the Patriot cause by saving his troops from possible destruction. The guilty verdict was more the result of Lee's having insulted Washington, which made the matter a political contest between the army's two top generals—only one of whom could prevail.

After the court-martial, Lee faced a host of threats to duel. He actually did duel one of Washington's most loyal aides, Lt. Col. John Laurens; the contestants fired pistols at each other at close range and Lee was slightly wounded. Lee then barely avoided duels demanded by generals Baron von Steuben and Anthony Wayne. One of Lee's aides tried to provoke another of Washington's talented aides, Alexander Hamilton, to a duel. In the end, Congress upheld Lee's sentence to be suspended from the Continental Army for one year; Lee never returned to his position.

At his court-martial, Lee tried to put the blame for the retreat of his force at Monmouth where it properly belonged—on Charles Scott. A gruff and rough frontier leader from Virginia with a strong person-

---

1. For a complete discussion, see Christian McBurney, *George Washington's Nemesis: The Outrageous Treason and Unfair Court-Martial of Major General Charles Lee during the Revolutionary War* (El Dorado Hills, CA: Savas Beatie, 2020).

ality, Scott resisted and tried to turn the blame onto Lee. He succeeded. He got to Washington first after the battle and unfairly blamed Lee for the initial retreat of Lee's force.

Scott's grudge against Lee for exposing his unwarranted retrograde movement at the court-martial trial continued for many years after the war. As an elderly man in the early nineteenth century, when asked if General Washington ever swore, Scott concocted a fanciful story about Washington at their first meeting during the Monmouth battle:

> Yes, once. It was at Monmouth and on a day that would have made any man swear. Yes, sir, he swore on that day till the leaves shook on the trees, charming, delightful. Never have I enjoyed such swearing before or since. Sir, on that ever-memorable day, he swore like an angel from heaven.[2]

Scott likely was not an eyewitness to the exchange since at the time of the incident he was commanding his brigade more than a half-mile away. His story is completely refuted by the court-martial testimony at Lee's trial, yet many historians continue to repeat the story as if it were or could be accurate.

Unlike Washington, Scott was known for using crude language. In 1792, when Washington was considering whom to appoint as commander of the United States Army in the Northwest Territory, according to historian Mary Stockwell, he considered General Scott but "dismissed him as a drunkard better known for his foul mouth than for any bravery on the battlefield."[3] The authors of *Rebels and Redcoats* wrote that Scott was "a connoisseur of profanity" who "was always quick to display his own and to admire invention in that of others."[4]

Indeed, Scott's remarks were in response to a friend of his who was trying to cure Scott of his habit of employing profanity. The friend asked if Washington ever swore, hoping to show that Scott should follow his pristine example. Thus, Scott's story insulted both Washington and Lee, and was an attempt to put himself in a better light by bringing Washington down to his level. He also insulted the Christian religion by suggesting that angels swear. It was a remarkable performance by the conniving Scott.

---

2. Quoted in George Washington Parke Custis, *Recollections of Private Memoirs of Washington* (New York, NY: Derby & Jackson, 1860), 413-14.
3. Mary Stockwell, *Unlikely General: "Mad" Anthony Wayne and the Battle for America* (New Haven, CT: Yale University Press, 2018), 19.
4. George F. Scheer and Hugh F. Rankin, *Rebels and Redcoats* (Cleveland, OH: The World Publishing Company, 1957), 330.

George Washington confronting Charles Lee during the Battle of Monmouth, June 28, 1778. (*New York Public Library*)

In addition, Scott had a motive to criticize Lee. Scott wanted to deflect criticism of the generalship in the first part of the battle from him, where it rightly belonged, to Lee. At his court-martial, Lee blamed Scott.

Scott's best biographer, Harry Ward, wrote that there was no evidence that Scott was present at the famous meeting between the Continental Army's top two generals, and that Scott's story was "unsubstantiated." Ward added, "For Lee to be made a scapegoat was a face-saving measure for Scott, whose own distant retreat was inexplicable and a major cause for the failure of the attack during the first phase of the battle."[5]

Lafayette, during his return trip to the United States in 1824, first told the story that at the famous confrontation at Monmouth, Washington ended the conversation by calling Lee "a damned poltroon." Lafayette's story apparently first appeared in Henry B. Dawson's history of United States battles, published in 1858. According to Dawson, Lafayette told the story on the piazza of Vice President Daniel D. Tomkins's residence at Staten Island the morning of August 15, 1824. It was the Frenchman's first stop on his triumphant 1824-1825 tour.

5. Harry Ward, *Charles Scott and the "Spirit of '76"* (Charlottesville, VA: University Press of Virginia, 1988), 50, 52.

Dawson added in a footnote, "General Lafayette referred to it as the only instance wherein he had heard the general swear."[6]

Lafayette's story, told some forty-six years after the battle and at a time when Lee's reputation was poor, is not credible.

As with many recollections of Revolutionary War veterans written in their later years, Lafayette's are not always accurate and are best used when there is corroborating evidence from other sources. In his memoir of the war written in 1779, within a year of the battle, Lafayette did not mention any swearing. Instead, he appropriately focused on the one phrase the made the commander in chief most angry: "'you know,' Lee said to him, 'that all that [attacking the enemy] was against my advice.'"[7]

In addition, Lafayette and Lee, while they respected each other during the battle, had been antagonists. When Lee arrived at Valley Forge from his long captivity, Lafayette objected to Lee's criticisms of Washington and of the Continental Army's training. Lafayette, using the third person, wrote candidly of his relationship with Lee, "as one of them was a violent Anglomaniac [Lee] and the other a French enthusiast [Lafayette], their relationship was never peaceful."[8] Lafayette's views of Lee must be understood in this context. In addition, Lafayette was not present at the Washington-Lee meeting.

Mark Edward Lender and Garry Wheeler Stone, in their seminal work on the battle of Monmouth Court House, agree that both Scott's and Lafayette's recollections were "nonsense."[9]

---

6. Henry B. Dawson, *Battles of the United States by Sea and Land, Embracing Those of the Revolutionary and Indian Wars, the War of 1812, and the Mexican War, with Important Official Documents*, 2 vols. (New York, NY: Johnson, Fry & Company, 1858), 1:408. Historian J. L. Bell also found that Dawson's version is the first time that Lafayette's story appeared in a publication. See J. L. Bell, "Charles Lee a 'Damn'd Poltroon'?," Boston 1775 blog, November 20, 2010, boston1775.blogspot.com/2010/11/charles-lee-damned-poltroon.html. Bell adds, "Dawson cited that conversation without specifying how he came to know about it. Tompkins died in 1825. Dawson was born in Britain in 1821 and arrived in New York in 1834. So there must have been some intervening figures." None of the early histories of the Revolutionary War claim that Washington swore. Interestingly, Benson Lossing, in his history of the Revolutionary War published in 1850, did not bring up the story, despite his penchant for including myths in his accounts of the war's battles. Rather, Lossing wrote that Lee was "stung, not so much by these *words* as by the *manner* of Washington." Benson J. Lossing, *The Pictorial Field-Book of the Revolution*, 2 vols. (New York: Harper and Brothers, 1860) (originally published in 1850), 2:153.
7. *Lafayette's Memoir of 1779*, in Stanley J. Idzerda, ed., *Lafayette in the Age of the American Revolution: Selected Letters and Papers, 1776-1790*, 5 vols. (Ithaca, NY: Cornell University Press, 1977-83), 2:11.
8. Ibid., 2:9.
9. Mark Edward Lender and Garry Wheeler Stone, *Fatal Sunday: George Washington, the Monmouth Campaign, and the Politics of Battle* (Norman, OK: University of Oklahoma Press, 2016), 290.

There is one more source to consider. Private Joseph Plumb Martin, who was half-a-mile away with Scott's detachment, wrote that he witnessed the confrontation but that he was "too far off" to hear the exchange. Martin claimed that some of the soldiers who were closer to the generals had told him that they had distinctly heard Washington say "d—n him." He conceded that he was not sure whether Washington had expressed those words since "it was very unlike him, but he seemed at the instant to be in a great passion; his looks, if not his words seemed to indicate as much." As will soon be seen, Martin's observations in the prior sentence are credible, while what he heard others claim Washington said, not so much.

Here is the real story. Washington's arrival on the battlefield came at a confusing time for Lee's detachment, with some regiments retreating and a few others organizing to make a stand. Lee made matters worse by failing to keep his commander properly informed of developments. Early in the battle, before the retreat, Lee had sent a messenger to inform Washington of his plans to cut off the rear guard of the enemy, about 1,500 to 2,000 troops. The messenger, a volunteer aide of Washington's, Dr. James McHenry, informed Washington of Lee's "fixed and firm tone" that his plan would certainly succeed.[10] McHenry's report may have raised Washington's expectations, so that when the Virginian saw disorganized elements retreating, he became even more bitter than he otherwise would have been.

While Washington and his aides discussed how to dispose of his arriving troops, they stopped a civilian riding toward them and asked him for news from the front. The man responded that a fifer walking nearby told him the army was retreating. When asked whether he served in the Continental Army, the fifer responded in the affirmative and added, "the Continental troops that had been advancing were now retreating." The fifer's response "exceedingly surprised" Washington and he appeared "to discredit the account." He threatened the fifer with a whipping if he spread his views to any other person and put him under the guard of a cavalryman.[11] Moving fifty yards forward, Washington and his party met more stragglers with similar accounts.[12] An exasperated

---

10. James McHenry testimony, in Charles Lee, *Proceedings of a General Court Martial, Held at Brunswick, in the State of New-Jersey, by Order of His Excellency General Washington, Commander in Chief of the Army of the United States of America, for the Trial of Major General Lee, July 4, 1778, Major General Lord Stirling, President* ("*Lee Court-Martial*"), in *The Lee Papers, 1754-1811*, in *Collections of the New-York Historical Society for the Years 1871-1874*, 4 vols. (New-York Historical Society, 1872-75) ("*Lee Papers*"), 3:78.
11. Robert Harrison testimony, in ibid., 72; Tench Tilghman testimony, in ibid., 79-80.
12. Robert Harrison testimony, in ibid., 72.

Washington sent two of his aides, lieutenant colonels Robert Harrison and John Fitzgerald, forward to gain information at the front.[13]

Washington met the first columns of retreating troops, Grayson's and Patton's Regiments, and inquired of their officers the reasons for the retreat. None of them had a good answer. The 2nd New Jersey Regiment, in Maxwell's Brigade, appeared on the scene, with its officers expressing displeasure at the retreat. When the commander in chief asked Col. Israel Shreve about "the meaning of the retreat," the officer smiled, despite British soldiers burning down his house in southern New Jersey on June 24, and responded that "he did not know." Maj. Richard Howell, in the rear of the 2nd New Jersey and brigade major for Maxwell's Brigade, "expressed himself with great warmth at the troops coming off, and said he had never seen the like." Understandably, as one of his aides recalled, Washington "was exceedingly alarmed, finding the advance corps falling back upon the main body, without the least notice given to him."[14]

Washington, his temper simmering to a boil, spied Lee on some heights fronting the Middle Ravine and rode up to him, as Lee rode down to meet his commander.[15] The time was about 12:45 p.m. and an encounter that would have grave implications for Lee's career was about to occur.

The facts of the famous meeting are not in dispute. They are based on first-hand witness testimony at Lee's court-martial held less than a month after the battle ended.

Upon reaching Lee, Washington demanded, in an angry voice, "I desire to know, sir, what is the reason for this disorder and confusion?"[16] The commander in chief's "severe" tone shocked Lee, who had been expecting "congratulation and applause" for avoiding a crushing defeat.[17] According to the most credible account, from Washington's aide-de-camp, Lt. Col. Tench Tilghman, Lee stammered in return, "Sir? Sir?" After recovering, the subordinate insisted, "from a variety of contradictory intelligence, and from his orders not being obeyed, matters were thrown into confusion, and he did not choose to beard the British army with troops in such a situation. He said besides, the thing was against his own opinion."[18] Tilghman added, "When General Lee mentioned that his orders had been disobeyed, he mentioned General

13. John Fitzgerald testimony, in ibid., 68.
14. Tench Tilghman testimony, in ibid., 80-81.
15. John Brooks testimony, in ibid., 147.
16. Charles Lee closing statement, in ibid., 191.
17. Ibid.
18. Tench Tilghman testimony, in ibid., 80-81.

Scott particularly; he said General Scott had quitted a very advantageous position without orders." Tilghman further recalled, "General Washington answered, whatever [your] opinion might have been," he "expected [my] orders would have been obeyed," and then rode on toward the rear of the retreating troops, leaving a dazed Lee behind.[19]

John Brooks, temporary adjutant general for Lee's division, was also at the side of the two generals and had similar recollections to those of Tilghman. He described the commander in chief as speaking in a tone of "considerable warmth."[20] James McHenry, an aide to Washington, testified at Lee's court-martial trial that Washington twice asked Lee why he was retreating, mentioning that Lee's replies seemed confused and hesitant and Lee himself was embarrassed.[21] Another of Washington's aides, Richard Kidder Meade, and one of Lee's aides, John Mercer, both testified at the trial about the meeting, saying nothing inconsistent with these prior recollections.[22]

The two most detailed recollections are by Tilghman and, in his closing statement at his court-martial, Lee. As did Tilghman, Lee said he specifically mentioned Scott's withdrawing without orders.[23]

On the one hand, Lee had no time to properly explain his detachment's predicament and Washington lacked time to use courtesies. On the other hand, Washington fumed with anger, initially at the unexpected retreat. He became more heated at Lee's insolence in the midst of battle raising with him that he never supported the attack on Clinton's rear guard in the first place. Washington's harsh tone was, however, worse than the actual words he used with Lee.

Robert Harrison, returning from the front, repeated to Washington the remarks of several indignant regimental commanders who in the confusion of battle did not know why their regiments had been ordered to retreat. When asked by Harrison the reason for the retreat, Col. Matthias Ogden of the New Jersey Continentals, in Maxwell's Brigade, snarled, "By God! They are flying from a shadow."[24] Historian Theodore Thayer astutely noted of the opinions of these officers, "Here is good evidence of the fighting quality of the regimental officers, if not of their military sagacity."[25] Ironically, the New Jersey officers who

19. Ibid., 81.
20. John Brooks testimony, in ibid., 147.
21. James McHenry testimony, in ibid., 78.
22. Richard Kidder Meade testimony, in ibid., 64, and John Mercer testimony in ibid., 112.
23. Charles Lee closing statement, in ibid., 191.
24. Robert Harrison testimony, in ibid., 73; Tench Tilghman testimony, in ibid., 80.
25. Theodore Thayer, *The Making of a Scapegoat: Washington and Lee at Monmouth* (Port Washington, NY: Kennikat Press, 1976), 52.

complained of the retreat did not realize that it was due in large part to their own commander, General Maxwell.

Knowing Lee's views on the fighting abilities of the Continental soldier and seeing his well-trained soldiers retreating, Washington must have thought Lee had timidly avoided contact with the enemy. Harrison added the shocking news that the British vanguard was only fifteen minutes away.[26] Washington moved forward, issuing orders to Anthony Wayne to take troops to post at the nearby Point of Woods. Finally, the commander in chief simmered down and asked Lee to lead the defense at the Hedgerow, which Lee had already started prior to his superior's arrival. Lee agreed and said he would not be the last to leave the field.

Lee's defense at the Hedgerow provided valuable time for the Continentals brought forward by Washington to organize their defenses at Perrine Hill. The fierce action at the Hedgerow also served to exhaust Clinton's lead attacking force.[27]

Seeing Washington's strong position on Perrine Hill, Clinton called off his attack and gave orders for his advance units to retreat. Washington responded by sending forward relatively small groups of attackers against some British troops who lingered too long close to Perrine Hill. The Americans charged and inflicted some damage before the last British units retreated to their camp. One of the longest battles of the war was over.[28]

The night after the battle, Lee wrote to his ally in Congress, Richard Henry Lee, a relatively accurate account of the battle. The beleaguered Lee insisted he had been forced to retreat since his detachment had been "outnumbered," with the British cavalry numerous times on the verge of "turning completely our flanks." Had he not retreated in the face of Clinton's superior forces, the "army and perhaps America, would have been ruined." Moreover, his troops conducted the retreat with "great honor" and "coolness." "Not a man or officer hastened his step, but one regiment regularly filed off from the front to the rear of the other." But rather than receiving deserved laurels, "the thanks I received from his Excellency were of a singular nature."[29]

Lee in particular simmered from what he considered Washington's ill treatment of him on the battlefield. The commander in chief, during their first meeting in the battle, had upbraided him in front of fellow-

---

26. Tench Tilghman testimony, *Lee Court-Martial*, in *Lee Papers*, 3:81.
27. See McBurney, *George Washington's Nemesis*, 152.
28. Ibid., Chapter 8.
29. Charles Lee to Richard Henry Lee, June 28 (possibly 29), 1778, in *Lee Papers*, 2:430.

officers as if he was some tyro of a general. Lee later admitted, "I confess I was disconcerted, astonished and confounded by the words and the manner in which his Excellency accosted me."[30] It is easy to imagine Lee, in a local tavern or around a campfire, railing about his plight before a small crowd of sympathetic aides and other admirers.

Had Lee met privately with Washington and addressed these matters face-to-face, the two men likely would have ironed out their differences. Lee could have offered a full explanation of the day's events, swallowed his pride, and allowed the matter to drop. The fact was, at their first meeting on the battlefield, both men misunderstood the situation. Washington did not know that Lee had received bad intelligence, that some of his officers had retreated without orders, and that his force faced Clinton's entire first division, not just a relatively small rear guard. In turn, Lee later learned that Washington, prior to their first meeting during the battle, had seen for himself elements of Lee's detachment that appeared to be in a disorganized state and without instructions on where to march. Lee appreciated how his commander must have felt at that time. He had also failed to keep his commander properly informed of his retreat. If he had met with Washington, Lee could have explained that the bulk of his troops remained in cohesive units.

Perhaps Washington himself privately admitted he had let his temper on the battlefield get out of control without knowing all the facts. But the proud Virginian refused to call Lee to his tent and admit it. Lee also refused to come to Washington to explain his battlefield conduct.

Lee could not let the matter drop. He decided to send his commander a strong letter complaining of the "use of so very singular expressions as you did on my coming up to the ground where you had taken post."[31] This first letter was also replete with threats and insults, despite his knowing it would likely be made public. He followed this letter up with two more insulting letters to Washington. In doing so, Lee repeated his penchant for impulsive conduct. It was a foolish and grave error he would soon—and long—come to regret. It ultimately led to his court martial and suspension from the army.

Revealingly, Lee never claimed in these letters or otherwise during his lifetime that Washington swore at him. Indeed, in his closing state-

---

30. Charles Lee closing statement, *Lee Court-Martial*, in ibid., 3:191.
31. Charles Lee to George Washington, July 1 [should be June 30], 1778, in Dorothy Twohig, Philander D. Chase, Theodore J. Crackel, W. W. Abbot, and Edward G. Lengel, eds., *The Papers of George Washington, Revolutionary War Series*, 24 vols. (Charlottesville, VA: University of Virginia Press, 1985-2016), 15:594-95.

ment at his court-martial, Lee admitted that "the manner" in which Washington "expressed" his words to Lee "was much stronger and more severe than the expressions themselves."[32] Lee's best biographer, John R. Alden, wrote of Lafayette's story, "It is certain Lee never would have permitted any man to use such language toward him without demanding an apology or satisfaction on the dueling ground; and there is no record showing he demanded that Washington retract a personal insult."[33]

Moreover, Washington's response to Lee's initial letter does not indicate that he swore at Lee. Washington wrote, "I am not conscious of having made use of any very singular expressions at the time of my meeting with you, as you intimate. What I recollect to have said was dictated by duty and warranted by the occasion."[34]

The sharp words exchanged by the Continental Army's two top commanders on the field of battle at Monmouth Court House had fateful consequences for Lee. But the view that Washington swore at Lee during the battle is likely wrong and needs to change, as well as the popular view of Lee failing to achieve a victory that was in his grasp at the battle of Monmouth Court House. Sometimes retreat is the best course of action. Fortunately, the Continental force was in the hands of an experienced general who, to his mortification, concluded that retreat was advisable, if not mandated, by the circumstances. In retreating, Lee may have saved the Continental Army.

---

32. Charles Lee closing statement, *Lee Court-Martial*, in *Lee Papers*, 3:191.
33. John R. Alden, *General Charles Lee, Traitor or Patriot?* (Baton Rouge, LA: Louisiana State University Press, 1951), 343n29.
34. Washington to Charles Lee, June 30, 1778, in Twohig et al., *Papers of George Washington*, 15:595.

Black Drummers in a Redcoat Regiment

DON N. HAGIST

When British soldiers arrived in Boston in 1768 as part of the British government's efforts to maintain peace in the colony of Massachusetts, local citizens resented the military presence for several reasons. First and foremost was the implication that the army, in spite of their mission to maintain order, were in fact oppressors sent by a government that was, while not foreign, wildly out of touch with the needs and interests of American colonists. Also, colonists paid taxes to their own colonial governments; most of those governments in turn maintained militias that provided defense when needed.

The two regiments posted in Boston, while generally unwelcome, did provide a measure of entertainment with their military rituals—posting guards, drilling, and marching about for various reasons. One facet of military discipline was particularly startling to onlookers: "In the Morning nine or ten Soldiers of Colonel Carr's Regiment for sundry Misdemeanors, were severely whipt on the Common," reported a local newspaper. In an era where corporal punishment itself was not unusual, there was something besides the severity of these lashings that brought journalistic commentary. The drummers in Colonel Carr's regiment, the 29th Regiment of Foot, were in today's parlance African-American. The newspaper report continued, "To behold Britons scourged by Negro Drummers, was a new and very disagreeable Spectacle!"[1]

Most soldiers in most British regiments, as far as can be told from the scant records available, were from England, Scotland, Ireland and Wales, and were ethnically White. The 29th Regiment differed from most in having a tradition of employing Black men as drummers.

---

1. *Boston Evening Post*, October 6, 1768.

Drummers, paid 50 percent more than private soldiers, were an important component of the military system, using their instruments to signal events throughout the day from reveille in the morning to "taptoo" in the evening. Drums provided cadence for marching in step and for teaching the precisely-timed movements with which soldiers handled their weapons. In battle, "the noise of the Artillery and Musketry generally renders it impossible to use any Signals by the Drum," wrote Gen. William Howe in February 1776 when he ordered regiments "not to use the drum or fife for marching or signals when in the field."[2] Drums nonetheless conveyed important signals such as "advance" and "cease fire."[3]

Boys could begin drumming for the army in their early teens as long as they were physically able to manage the instrument and bear the fatigue of military life. Some later set the instrument aside in favor of a musket, but many men continued as drummers for their entire military careers which, for British soldiers, often spanned thirty years or more.[4]

According to regimental histories, in 1759 eight or ten Black drummers were sent from the West Indies to the commanding officer of the 29th Regiment, starting a regimental tradition that continued well into the 1800s.[5] When the 29th landed in Boston, there were nine drummers in its ranks, one in each of nine companies. No records survive to tell us whether any of these men were among those who started in 1759. Muster rolls record the names of the drummers present in 1768 but provide no information about their ethnicity: John Archer, John Bacchus, Lushington Barrett, Joseph Blenheim, Thomas Othello, Joseph Provance, John Russell, James Sharlow, and Thomas Walker.[6]

Some of these names—Bacchus, Othello, Provence, Sharlow (or Charloe)—are not typical of British soldiers and suggest a Caribbean

---

2. Bennet Cuthbertson, *A System for the Compleat Interior Management and Œconomy of a Battalion of Infantry* (Dublin, 1768), 169; General orders, February 6, 1776, William Howe, *General Sir William Howe's Orderly Book*, ed. B. F. Stevens (Port Washington, NY: Kennikat Press, 1980), 209.

3. For more on drums in battle during the American Revolution, see Don N. Hagist, *Noble Volunteers: the British Soldiers who fought the American Revolution* (Yardley, PA: Westholme, 2020), 209-213, and Matthew H. Spring, *With Zeal and Bayonets Only: The British Army on Campaign in North America, 1775–1783* (Norman, OK: University of Oklahoma Press, 2008), 157-160.

4. See Hagist, *Noble Volunteers*, 47-50.

5. J. D. Ellis, "Drummers for the Devil? The Black Soldiers of the 29th (Worcestershire) Regiment of Foot, 1759-1843," *Journal of the Society for Army Historical Research* 80 (2002), 187.

6. Muster rolls, 29th Regiment of Foot, WO 12/4493, The National Archives, Kew, UK (TNA).

heritage. For those who received pensions when they were discharged from the service their ages, length of service and places of birth were recorded. Bacchus was fifty-four years old when he obtained a pension in July 1783 after serving twenty years, and was born in Jamaica. Sharlow, born in St. Kitts, went to the pension board on the same day as Bacchus, at the age of sixty-one after twenty-nine years in the army.[7] Joseph Provance, from St. Domingo, served until 1790 when he was fifty years old with thirty-five years as a drummer.[8]

Others sources reveal the heritage of two more of the 29th's 1768 drummers. Lushington Barrett was still with the regiment in Worcester, England in 1788. Parish records described him as "Drummer of the 29th Foote a Negroe" when a daughter was born to him and his wife Susan; he died a few months later.[9] In early March 1770 as several soldiers of the 29th scuffled with Boston ropewalk workers, a local justice of the peace called out to Thomas Walker, "You black rascal, what have you to do with white men's quarrels?"[10]

After the infamous Boston Massacre later that month, the 29th Regiment left Boston for New Jersey, then went on to Florida before returning to England in 1773. An inspecting officer in 1774 noted that the regiment's "10 drummers are negroes." Among them were men with "British-sounding" names, but information recorded when they eventually received pensions reveals that they were of African or West Indian descent. James Fitzgerald was forty-two years old when he was discharged from the army and received a pension in July 1771; his birthplace was recorded as "Africa."[11] James Macnell, pensioned in December 1777, was born in Antigua and spent twenty-one of his thirty-eight years in the army.[12] Robert Baird, fifty-four years old with twenty-six years of service in March 1792, was from Kingston, Jamaica.[13]

The outbreak of war saw the 29th Regiment preparing to voyage once again to America. Changes in the established size of infantry reg-

---

7. "Examinations of Invalid Soldiers," July 17, 1783, Pension Admission Books, WO 116/8, TNA.
8. Discharge of Joseph Provance, WO 121/9/340, TNA.
9. www.explorethepast.co.uk/2020/10/black-history-month-black-presence-in-worcestershire/.
10. Ellen Chase, *The Beginnings of the American Revolution based on Contemporary Letters, Diaries and Other Documents* (New York: Baker and Taylor, 1910), 1:173.
11. "Examinations of Invalid Soldiers," July 30, 1771, Pension Admission Books, WO 116/6, TNA.
12. "Examinations of Invalid Soldiers," December 9, 1777, Pension Admission Books, WO 116/7, TNA.
13. Discharge of Robert Baird, WO 121/13/169, TNA.

iments meant that they now needed twenty drummers to be at their full complement. Posted at Chatham Barracks outside London, they continued to find and recruit Black men. Fifteen-year-old Thomas York, who "lately lived in London as a servant," enlisted on March 17, 1775 but deserted at the end of the following month. An advertisement seeking his return described him as "a Black, born on the Coast of Guinea, with Wool, round Visage, flat Nose, thick Lips, bow-legged, and stout made."[14] Thomas Smith, sixteen years old and born in "Bengal, East Indies," enlisted on March 25.[15] That August John Jubo enlisted at the age of fourteen; when he received a pension just six years and seven months later due to being "lame," his place of birth was listed as "Africa." Thomas Othello junior was added to the rolls in the same company as his father on April 1.

The regiment sailed for America in early 1776. Thomas Walker was with the grenadier company on board the warship *Isis* when it arrived at Quebec in May, relieving a siege that had lasted all winter.[16] The regiment participated in the Battle of Three Rivers on June 8, where drummer Thomas Smith was wounded in the thigh.[17] The British army routed American forces from Canada in a campaign that eventually led to the Battle of Valcour Island on Lake Champlain. In this battle men of the 29th Regiment fought on ships and gunboats. Drummer Samuel Young, who had joined the regiment in March 1775, was killed.[18]

The regiment spent the winter of 1776-1777 in Quebec, where an American prisoner of war noted that "The drummers of the 29th Regiment are black men."[19] Eight companies of the 29th remained in Canada until the late 1780s, seeing sporadic fighting during the war but mostly manning various garrisons from the northern end of Lake Champlain to Montreal. Thomas Othello, who had been with the regiment in Boston, drowned in 1777 in unknown circumstances.[20] The following year fourteen-year-old Joseph Othello, certainly another of Thomas's sons, was appointed as a drummer. He, too, saw difficult service; when he left the army in April 1788 he suffered from "his limbs

---

14. Muster rolls, 29th Regiment of Foot, WO 12/4493; *St. James's Chronicle* (London), May 9, 1775.
15. Discharge of Thomas Smith, WO 121/35/127, TNA.
16. Muster book, HMS *Isis*, ADM 36/7911, TNA.
17. Discharge of Thomas Smith, WO 121/35/127, TNA.
18. Muster rolls, 29th Regiment of Foot, WO 12/4493, TNA.
19. *Rhode Islanders Record the Revolution: the Journals of William Humphrey and Zuriel Waterman*, N. N. Shipton and D. Swain, ed. (Providence: Rhode Island Historical Society, 1984), 39.
20. Muster rolls, 29th Regiment of Foot, WO 12/4493.

being crushed by a fall in America"; his discharge indicates that he was born in "Cumberland in America."[21]

Even after the war, Black men with American connections joined the ranks of the 29th's drummers. Walter Othello, probably another of Thomas Othello's sons, joined as a drummer in 1784, serving until 1796.[22] Thomas Retford, from Sunbury, Georgia, enlisted on December 13, 1784 and served until January 9, 1812. His discharge form filled out that year gave his age as fifty-seven, and described him as five feet eight inches tall with "black wooly hair," black eyes and black complexion; he signed his own name on the form.[23]

Not all of the 29th served out the American War in Canada. In 1777 two companies, the grenadiers and light infantry, were part of Gen. John Burgoyne's army that advanced southward on Lake Champlain with the goal of reaching Albany. Faced with overwhelming opposition, the army capitulated on October and became prisoners of war. Among the prisoners was Thomas Walker, the drummer called a "Black rascal" in Boston back in 1768, now in the 29th's grenadier company. With the other prisoners he spent the winter of 1777-1778 in crude barracks outside Boston, then marched several hundred miles to Virginia. In 1781 they were moved once again, this time to Lancaster, Pennsylvania. By the time they arrived there, Walker was one of only four men in the company remaining. The years of captivity and long marches apparently had taken their toll on Walker; he died while a prisoner of war in Lancaster in July 1781.[24]

---

21. Discharge of Joseph Othello, WO 121/3/289, TNA.
22. Ellis, "Drummers for the Devil," 201.
23. Discharge of Thomas Retford, WO 121/117/183, TNA.
24. "List of British Prisoners Brought to Lancaster by Major Baily the 16th June 1781," July 18, 1781, Peter Force Papers series 9 reel 106 p. 675-685, Library of Congress.

Under the Banner of War: Frontier Militia and Uncontrolled Violence

TIMOTHY C. HEMMIS

In 1777, the third year of the American War for Independence, little had gone in the favor of the Patriots especially in the borderlands. They controlled Fort Pitt and several other outposts, but they were far from the main fighting; the region was considered a backwater theater. British governor of Detroit Henry Hamilton issued a proclamation that encouraged Native Americans to attack rebel settlers in the region.[1] Hamilton's proclamation created a panic among frontiersmen as they remembered Pontiac's Rebellion in 1763-1764 and the more recent Lord Dunmore's War in 1774. The British hoped the renewing of an Indian war would force the rebels to send valuable resources to the western borderlands, ultimately weakening American forces in the east. Hamilton's Proclamation reignited the racial hatred of the frontiersmen against Native Americans, and they used the banner of war to exact revenge against their enemies—indigenous and Anglo alike.

Despite the remote nature of the frontier, Fort Pitt and junction of three rivers that it overlooked was a strategic position controlling commerce and travel that would be important for the young republic. The Second Continental Congress, even before Thomas Jefferson penned the Declaration of Independence, understood the importance of the Western Department. Congress wanted a military and Native American diplomat that knew the region and people. In April 1776, they commissioned merchant George Morgan to be a colonel in the Con-

---

1. "Hamilton's Proclamation, June 24, 1777" in *Frontier Defense on the Upper Ohio, 1777-1778*, Reuben Gold Thwaites and Louise Phelps Kellogg (Madison: Wisconsin Historical Society, 1912), 14.

tinental Army and chief Indian agent at Fort Pitt. Morgan himself had no military experience, other than working with the British Army before the American Revolution. His personal experiences with the British Army included dealing with corrupted officers like Lt. Colonel John Wilkins, who acted like tyrants, so it is no wonder Morgan joined the American cause. In addition to Morgan, Gen. George Washington sent Gen. Edward Hand to Fort Pitt along with about 3,000 militiamen to secure the American frontier. Hand, born in Ireland, was a doctor who served in the British Army as a surgeon's mate during the Seven Years' War. With a shortage of experienced officers, Hand rose quickly through the ranks of the Continental Army. He went to Fort Pitt to secure the region and protect it from British and Native American attacks, and to also keep the peace in local matters.

Years prior during Lord Dunmore's War, in 1774, the local population became embroiled in civil conflict. The personal grudges and rumors created a volatile atmosphere even before Hand arrived. Additionally white settlers, especially the ones that experienced Pontiac's Rebellion, painted anyone friendly to any Native American group as a Tory. Their patriotic fervor overshadowed their racial prejudice against indigenous people. These frontiersmen also distrusted the Continental Army as they felt the elite officers worked with Native Americans rather than enacting their own brand of justice—genocidal justice.

As Fort Pitt and the surrounding areas were on the periphery of the action during the War for Independence, this episode is often ignored in the larger narrative of the American Revolution. The frontier militias believed that Continental leaders such as Col. George Morgan and even General Hand secretly worked with the British as they openly met with Delaware and Shawnee leaders. Because the details of the meetings were secret, many militiamen suspected treason.

In late December 1777, General Hand returned to Fort Pitt from Fort Randolph to learn of the arrest of Morgan, the Indian Agent for Congress. Hand was also accused of being in a Loyalist plot to hand over Fort Pitt to the British. More Patriot leaders became embroiled in the alleged Tory plot. In addition to Morgan and Hand, the militia suspected Col. John Campbell, Capt. Alexander McKee, and Simon Girty of being in league with the Native Americans and British.[2]

Many suspected George Morgan because he had a close relationship with Capt. Half Pipe and Capt. White Eyes of the Delaware. Often

---

2. "Loyalists at Fort Pitt," ibid., 184-185.

Morgan left Fort Pitt for extended periods of time to meet with Indian leaders as he represented the United States in diplomacy.[3] Those trips seemed curious to the militia, as Indian attacks did not seem to stop. News of Morgan's suspicious movement led to locals asking Congress to investigate his actions. On October 22, 1777, Congress resolved to set up a committee of inquiry to examine Morgan's alleged corruption.[4] During the time of the investigation Morgan refrained, as much as he could, from performing his duties as an Indian diplomat.

Local militia Col. Zachwell Morgan, the namesake of modern Morgantown, West Virginia, was the leader who brought charges of conspiracy against the suspected Tories. Frontier militias patrolled the region and reported all Loyalist and Native American activities. Additionally, there was a string of indigenous leaders' murders that took place throughout the summer and into the fall. Frontier militiamen were the main culprits for these killings, which threatened the peace that Morgan and other American officials had brokered with local tribes.

One such case was the murder of Cornstalk, a pro-American Shawnee leader, who was mistakenly captured at Fort Randolph. During Cornstalk's and several other Shawnees' imprisonment, a militia man named Robert Gilmore was killed during a hunting trip. The local militia at Fort Randolph believed the culprits to be Indians and with little thought they executed their captives including Cornstalk; "seven or eight bullets [were] fired into him, and his son was shot dead" too. We know about Cornstalk's murder because of Capt. John Stuart's account, where he claimed "I have no doubt if he had been spared but he would have been friendly to the Americans for nothing could have induced him to make the visit to the garrison at that critical time."[5] Reports from militia officers Capt. Matthew Arbuckle and Captain Stuart suggest that they told their men to stand down, but they refused to listen to orders and continued to murder the four Shawnee prisoners. At the very least these officers deflected blame to their own soldiers.

News of Cornstalk's murder spread throughout the region and to Virginia. Cornstalk's death put the relationship between the young republic and the tribes on rocky ground. Additionally, frontier militias and Continentals had a tumultuous relationship as neither trusted the other. The militias had their own objectives and often disobeyed orders. General Hand had to restore order and investigate the incident at Fort Randolph.

3. "Loyalists at Fort Pitt," ibid., 186.
4. *Journals of the Continental Congress 1774-1789* (Washington, DC: Government Printing Office, 1904-1937), 9:831.
5. "The Murder of Cornstalk" in *Frontier Defense on the Upper Ohio*, 160.

During Hand's absence from Fort Pitt, militia Col. Zachwell Morgan took it upon himself to detain Col. George Morgan. The news of George Morgan's arrest reached General Hand and pushed him to hastily return to Fort Pitt in late December. Upon his arrival he discovered that the militia continued to harass suspected Tories. Hand offered George Morgan to stay with him at Fort Pitt, but he refused; he preferred house arrest because he was "very busy."[6] Morgan's refusal made him look more guilty to the local militia.

Other suspected Tories, including Colonel Campbell, took up Hand's offer to stay with him, while Alexander McKee remained under house arrest and Simon Girty was sent to the "common guard-house." Hand reported that during the testimonies of witnesses only one man mentioned Morgan as part of a plot. Because of the lack of evidence, Hand freed Morgan, although he still was under a congressional investigation until he was cleared on April 7, 1778. The committee acquitted Girty, but McKee had been paroled as there was some minor evidence of wrongdoing. Hand believed that Captain Arbuckle of the militia (the same one from Fort Randolph) had a feud with McKee and wanted him out of the picture.[7]

Eventually both McKee and Girty would defect to the British side after their poor treatment by the American militia. The others that remained loyal to the Patriot cause like Morgan would still be under suspicion despite being cleared of wrongdoing. Simply put, it was Morgan's pro-Indian stance that made him an enemy to the frontiersmen.

With the Tory plot accusations behind him, Morgan returned his duties as an Indian agent for the United States. He went to counsel the Shawnee after the murders of Cornstalk and others at Fort Randolph. Morgan relayed, "When I look toward you or at the Kenawa River I am ashamed of the Conduct of our young foolish Men."[8] The Indian agent's diplomacy worked and the Shawnee held fast to their friendship with the United States. Morgan recorded in a letter to the Moravian missionary David Zeisberger that "it rejoices me exceedingly to hear that Captain Pipe, Captain White Eyes, Captain Killbuck, and all the other wise Delaware Chief resolve to remain our Friends."[9] Morgan's diplomacy was a delicate balancing act that seemed to work.

---

6. "Loyalists at Fort Pitt," ibid., 184-185.
7. Ibid., 184-186.
8. "Conciliating the Shawnee, George Morgan, March 25, 1778," ibid., 234.
9. George Morgan to David Zeisberger, March 27, 1778, George Morgan Letterbook, Volume III, Carnegie Library Pittsburgh.

Unfortunately, at the same time Morgan worked to patch up the relationship between the Delaware, Shawnee, and the United States, General Hand led 500 militiamen from Westmoreland County on an ill-advised mission westward into Indian territory. Almost from the start Hand's campaign was a failure. Plagued by bad weather and high water, at Beaver creek scouts reported that a native settlement was nearby, and the militia proceeded to attack the village. The undisciplined militia indiscriminately killed the indigenous peoples at the settlement. Hand recalled that "But to my great Mortification found only one Man with some women and Children . . . the Men were so Impetuous that I could not prevent their Killing the Man and one of the women."[10] The disastrous expedition climaxed when Hand realized the militia had attacked a friendly Delaware, village killing members of Capt. Half Pipe's family. Hand's disgraced mission led to him to ask to be recalled. Later that spring, Washington recalled him and replaced him with a new more aggressive commander.

In May 1778, Gen. Lachlan McIntosh became the commander of the Western Department for the Continental Army, becoming Hand's superior. McIntosh, a Scot from Georgia who killed Button Gwinnett over a political feud in 1777, traveled to the American west to find it in disarray in August 1778; his predecessor could not control the militias or the Native Americans (friendly or hostile).[11] McIntosh believed that a new westward campaign to capture Fort Detroit could bring him glory and honor, and ultimately put an end to the Indian war provoked by Hamilton's Proclamation. The problems with any campaign in the west, though, were logistics and getting enough volunteers.

McIntosh intended for a new expedition, but in order to accomplish this feat he needed allies among the Native American tribes. One thing stood in his way: George Morgan's diplomacy. Morgan kept the peace because he acknowledged the Native Americans' wish to be neutral in martial activities. The Indian stance was not one that McIntosh wanted, and he sought to renegotiate the peace with the Shawnee and Delaware without Morgan present.

When Morgan was away from Fort Pitt in September 1778, McIntosh welcomed Delaware leadership in order to hammer out a new treaty that included military support for an attack on the British at Detroit. Captains White Eyes, Half Pipe, and John Killbuck were in attendance

---

10. Edward Hand to Jasper Ewing, March 7, 1778, "One hundred and forty-five letters from Gen. Hand to Jasper Yeates, dealing with the American revolution," digitalcollections.nypl.org/items/c09184da-bbf6-a756-e040-e00a18 06216b.
11. Harvey H. Jackson, *Lachlan McIntosh and the Politics of Revolutionary Georgia* (Athens: University of Georgia Press, 2003), 74.

with General McIntosh and Colonels Daniel Brodhead and William Crawford. With Morgan's absence, the Delaware were taken advantage of as they believed the treaty only suggested to give free passage to the army and permission to build new forts in their territory. However, it was a military alliance that also promised the creation of a fourteenth state, a Lenape state with representation in Congress.[12] Like many other Native American treaties through history, the Fort Pitt Treaty of 1778 would be routinely ignored by the United States government.

Almost immediately Morgan and McIntosh were at odds with each other. Morgan's pro-Indian stance and his role as the deputy commissary general for the western department put him in an awkward position with the commander. In late 1778, McIntosh launched a campaign to attack Fort Detroit. He and the militia left Fort Pitt and ventured to Fort McIntosh and then to Fort Laurens. Along with the American forces was Capt. White Eyes as a guide. Unfortunately, White Eyes died only a few days into the expedition. Official reports suggest he developed smallpox and died. Other accounts contradict the official report by saying the militia assassinated the Delaware leader. Even George Morgan did not believe the official report; years later he told Congress he believed that White Eyes was "treacherously put to Death, at the moment of his greatest Exertions to serve the United States."[13] Whether or not McIntosh knew about the murder of White Eyes will never be known, but reports that militiamen were the culprits make the most sense. As shown by the earlier execution of Cornstalk, frontier militias put little value in native lives. As McIntosh's mission failed to achieve its desired effect the militia's frustration could have led to White Eyes' murder.

The feud between the two officers grew into a political spat that caught the attention of congressman Governour Morris and Gen. George Washington. McIntosh believed that Morgan kept "almost all his public business in this Dept. a profound Secrete from me among his other Schemes." The commander considered Morgan to be corrupt and to have his own agenda contrary to his own. McIntosh illustrated his perspective to Washington, writing, "I cannot help observing here sir, of this Gentleman & others who have Separate Views & Connections, & a Variety of Lucrative Offices to bestow, Independent as they think of any person who Commands in the Department."[14] In the same

12. Treaty With the Delawares: 1778, avalon.law.yale.edu/18th_century/del1778.asp.
13. George Morgan to the President of Congress, May 12, 1784, Papers of the Continental Congress, NARA, RG 360, M247, item 163, roll 180, pages 365-367, fold3.com.
14. Lachlan McIntosh to George Washington, March 12, 1779, founders.archives.gov/documents/Washington/03-19-02-0457.

letter, McIntosh asked Washington to reassign him, as the Western Department was a difficult assignment because of Morgan, the Native Americans, and the militias. Additionally, McIntosh was almost universally hated by his troops and native allies alike.[15] McIntosh, like Hand, could not control the militia.

Colonel Daniel Brodhead took over command of the Western Department. Despite McIntosh's recall, American relations with the Delaware and Shawnee were precarious at best. Morgan's progress with the Shawnee and Delaware all but evaporated with General Hand's infamous campaign, the Fort Pitt Treaty of 1778, McIntosh's aborted expedition to take Detroit, and White Eyes' assassination. Only John Killbuck's band remained loyal to the United States, but even he often pleaded with American officials to forgive his foolish brethren. Despite his loyalty to the Americans, he often felt uneasy at Fort Pitt because of the militia who threatened his life.[16]

After Colonel Brodhead took command he attempted to repair the diplomatic damages on the frontier, but General Washington ordered him to maintain the outposts of Fort McIntosh and Fort Laurens, which were in Delaware and Shawnee territory.[17] Washington also expressed his interest in continuing the fight against the western tribes. Washington relayed to Brodhead, "it is my wish however, as soon as it may be in our power to chastise the Western savages, by an expedition into their country."[18] Washington reminded that "It is of Importance most certainly to preserve the friendship of the Indians who have not taken up the Hatchet," but they did not have presents or gifts to award their native allies.[19] Washington did not see the Delaware and Shawnee as enemies like the local militias did.

Unfortunately, like McIntosh, Brodhead had a hard time keeping discipline among the militia. Brodhead blamed local settlers who often sold liquor to the soldiers, which led to fights and even murders. One such incident occurred when a private from the 13th Virginia Regiment "maliciously killed one of the best young Men of the Delaware Nation."

---

15. Daniel Brodhead to Washington, January 16, 1779, founders.archives.gov/documents/Washington/03-19-02-0008.
16. David Zeisberger, *Diary of David Zeisberger*, Eugene F. Bliss, ed. (Cincinnati: R. Clarke & Co, 1885), 420.
17. Washington to Brodhead, May 3, 1779, founders.archives.gov/documents/Washington/03-20-02-0268.
18. Washington to Brodhead, April 21, 1779, founders.archives.gov/documents/Washington/03-20-02-0132.
19. Washington to Brodhead, May 3, 1779, founders.archives.gov/documents/Washington/03-20-02-0268.

Brodhead did not have enough field officers to conduct a proper trial and did not want to hand him over to civilian magistrates because he feared that the soldier would escape punishment.[20] Eventually, the court martial acquitted Pvt. James Beham of the murder on June 9, 1779.

The war in the borderlands was a different kind of conflict, one of retribution and attrition. Since the Treaty of 1778 the number of friendly Native American bands began to shrink, and the Patriot army on the American frontier really did not have much support. When Brodhead took over command of the Western department he had few regular soldiers, which meant that he had to rely on local militiamen who were often more focused on revenge than on any larger military objective.

Washington's orders were to chastise the western tribes, but he also sent Gen. John Sullivan into Iroquoia to punish those tribes who decided to aid the British. Sullivan's infamous campaign was a seek and destroy mission into Indian country. Colonel Brodhead sought out glory to advance his career, so he wanted to link up with Sullivan's army as they ventured into Iroquoia. With about 600 men, mostly militia, Brodhead left Fort Pitt on August 11, 1779, to harass the Seneca north of Pittsburgh near modern Warren, Pennsylvania. Brodhead exclaimed to Washington that "It would give me great pleasure to Co-operate with Genl Sullivan but I Shall be into the Seneca Towns a long time before he can receive an account of my Movement." Brodhead moved into Seneca lands long before Sullivan arrived. But he believed if his mission against the Seneca was successful, he could then go link up with Sullivan "to reduce Detroit and its dependencies."[21] Ultimately, Brodhead dreamed of taking Detroit, even if his army really did not have the capability.

When Brodhead's advance party consisting of fifteen Americans and eight Delaware "discovered between 30 & 40 warriors landing from their canoes . . . [they] prepared for action."[22] A firefight ensued with limited success. Despite this small skirmish at Thompson's Island, Brodhead's campaign north only burnt abandoned villages and cornfields and did not have any significant outcome. By mid-September 1779, the Americans returned to Fort Pitt without linking up with Sul-

---

20. Brodhead to Washington, May 3, 1779, founders.archives.gov/documents/Washington/03-20-02-0269.
21. Brodhead to Washington, July 31–August 4, 1779, founders.archives.gov/documents/Washington/03-21-02-0599.
22. "Extract from *Maryland Journal*, October, 26, 1779," in Louise Phelps Kellogg, *Frontier Retreat on the Upper Ohio, 1779-1781* (Madison: Wisconsin Historical Society, 1981), 57.

livan's army and without going to Detroit. For Brodhead, this mission was a failure.

In the following years, Brodhead remained commander of the Western Department and continued to use the militia to launch a campaign against the Turtle Clan of the Delaware in Ohio, whose leader White Eyes had been assassinated. Under White Eyes they wanted to maintain their neutrality in the conflict, but rumors swirled that they were joining the defected Half Pipe and his British allies. Attacks and raids on American settlements by Native Americans, such as an incident in March 1780 at "Sugar Camp upon Raccoon Creek in Yoghagania County" where five men were murdered and "three Girls & three lads" were taken prisoners, only fueled more rage. Frontiersmen "conjectured that the Delawares perpetrated this Murder, but it is possible it may have been done by other Indians."[23] These raids prompted Brodhead to support Col. George Rogers Clark and his campaign against Native Americans further west with the old objective of taking Detroit.

With reports of the Delaware treachery, Brodhead with about 300 men, a mix of regulars and militia, set out to Coshocton in Ohio. There they hoped to convince the Delaware to remain with the United States but militiaman Martin Wetzel murdered a Lenape leader, spoiling the peace council. Frontiersmen like Wetzel wanted revenge against raids and murders. Eventually the Americans refocused their objectives and Brodhead and his men attacked and destroyed the villages of Coschocton and Lichtenau, where they captured fifteen warriors and executed them.[24] For Brodhead this campaign was to punish hostile Indians, so he spared most of the Moravian Christian villages.

Again, this campaign did not satisfy Brodhead as he wanted to connect with Colonel Clark to take Detroit. Despite his obsession with Detroit his men, mostly frontiersmen, were satisfied with murdering, pillaging, and razing Indian villages close to their homesteads. As Brodhead returned his force to Fort Pitt, renewed Indians raids descended on the Pennsylvania borderlands. Many of the county militias were not successful in protecting settlers and they wished to take the war to the natives.[25] 1780 and 1781 witnessed persistent Indian attacks on settlements and the militia had little success defending them. Additionally, supplies ran low for the army, but Brodhead continued to plan an ex-

23. Brodhead to Washington, March 18, 1780, founders.archives.gov/documents/Washington/03-25-02-0059.
24. Randolph C. Downes, *Council Fires on the Upper Ohio: A Narrative of Indian Affairs in the Upper Ohio Valley Until 1795* (Pittsburgh: University of Pittsburgh Press, 1977), 265.
25. Brodhead to Washington, May 30, 1780, founders.archives.gov/documents/Washington/03-26-02-0164.

pedition to Sandusky for the autumn of 1781. He wrote, "The Country appears to be desirous to promote it; and I intend to command it if they the Militia & Volunteers do not suffer themselves to be induced into a belief that I have no right to command."[26] Brodhead and his second in command Colonel John Gibson squabbled over the direction of their mission in the Western Department. This feud led to Brodhead's removal from command. Brigadier General William Irvine replaced him at Fort Pitt in November 1781.

Without orders from Brodhead the army command was in disarray. Militia Col. David Williamson of Washington County led his men to the Moravian Indian villages that Brodhead visited in 1780. They discovered the villages were mostly abandoned and they captured the remaining Indians, who were Christians. The prisoners were taken to Fort Pitt and released once they learned they were Moravian.[27] Their release continued to upset the local population, as they believed the Moravian Indians were involved in the recent raids. Historian Eric Sterner has argued that was one of the major motivations for the Gnadenhutten massacre.[28]

Angry at the continued attacks, the Pennsylvania militia returned to the pacifist Moravian Indian villages to punish any Indian they found. The vengeful militia under Williamson entered the village of Gnadenhutten on March 7, 1782, as many of the villagers tended their fields. Williamson convinced the villagers that they just wanted to take them to Fort Pitt for safety as an attack was imminent. What happened next was one of the most brutal acts in American history. The Pennsylvania and Virginia militia rounded up the Indians and informed them they were sentenced to death.[29] They used a cooper's mallet to execute the Delaware men, women, and children. On that late winter day, ninety-six Christian Indians were brutally executed while the militia plundered and razed the village. The violence continued as the frontier remained an open battlefield with little knowledge of who was a friend or foe.

Later in the spring, Col. William Crawford and Colonel Williamson raised a force of Pennsylvania militia to attack the hostile Wyandot and

26. Brodhead to Washington, August 23, 1781, founders.archives.gov/documents/Washington/99-01-02-06764.
27. David Curtis Skaggs, and Larry L. Nelson, *The Sixty Years' War for the Great Lakes, 1754-1814* (East Lansing: Michigan State University Press, 2010), 197.
28. Eric Sterner, *Anatomy of a Massacre: The Destruction of Gnadenhutten, 1782* (Yardley, PA: Westholme, 2021).
29. Not all militiamen were in favor of the mass execution. A few returned home because they did not agree with the actions in Gnadenhutten.

remaining Lenape that resided in Sandusky. Their plan was to attack Indian villages and towns near Sandusky, however, without a clear plan they were outnumbered and had to retreat. During the hastily retreat, Crawford and some men were captured by some Delaware. They ritually tortured and burnt Crawford at the stake in revenge for the Gnadenhutten massacre just a few weeks earlier.

The militia continued to attack any Indian they came across as they believed that all Native Americans were the enemy. Since it was the periphery of the Revolutionary war, there was little martial order, and Continental Army officers lacked any authority over the militia. Hand, McIntosh, Brodhead, and Irvine all failed in their objectives as they could not control discipline among their troops, especially those of the local militia. Under the banner of war, the militia's unsanctioned violence prolonged hostilities on the frontier which claimed many innocent victims—Native and Anglo alike. With the Treaty of Paris in 1783, a tentative peace returned to the borderlands, but war would return in 1790 in the form of the Northwest Indian Wars.

Rhode Island Acts to Prevent an Enslaved Family from Being Transported to the South

CHRISTIAN MCBURNEY

The American Revolution spurred the world's first significant movement to abolish slavery and the African slave trade.[1] Before then, there was virtually no antislavery activity in any of the thirteen colonies of North America, or for that matter, anywhere else in the world. There was some limited antislavery dialogue in England, but its abolitionist movement would not get serious until 1787. Meanwhile, in the first three quarters of the eighteenth century, Great Britain, supported by Parliament, was the world's leading African slave trading country.[2]

By contrast, in the thirteen North American colonies, from about 1764 to 1775, Patriots loudly proclaiming infringements on their liberties by the British Crown could not help but see enslaved people who lived in their midst as possessing almost no rights. Along with the rising desire to free themselves from British rule, some white people in the Northern colonies, and even a few in the Southern colonies, began to feel the first stirrings of antislavery thought.

1. Christian M. McBurney, "The First Efforts to Limit the African Slave Trade Arise in the American Revolution: Part 1 of 3, The New England Colonies," *Journal of the American Revolution*, September 14-15, 2020, www.allthingsliberty.com/2020/09/the-first-efforts-to-limit-the-african-slave-trade-arise-in-the-american-revolution-part-1-of-3-the-new-england-colonies/; "Part 2 of 3, The Middle and Southern Colonies," www.allthingsliberty.com/2020/09/the-first-efforts-to-limit-the-african-slave-trade-arise-in-the-american-revolution-part-2-of-3-the-middle-and-southern-colonies/; "Part 3 of 3, Congress Bans the African Slave Trade," www.allthingsliberty.com/2020/09/the-first-efforts-to-limit-the-african-slave-trade-arise-in-the-american-revolution-part-3-of-3-congress-bans-the-african-slave-trade/.
2. Christian M. McBurney, *Dark Voyage: An American Privateer's War on Britain's African Slave Trade* (Yardley, PA: Westholme, 2022), 4-9.

With the coming of the movement for political independence against Great Britain and the need to unite in conducting the difficult, existential war against the British, the legislatures in the new states of the United States mostly set aside for later consideration controversial matters such as emancipation. They wanted to avoid topics that would divide them and thus weaken the war effort. Only winning the war could secure independence. Winning the war was also the surest way for the enslaved in the North to achieve freedom.

For example, in response to a petition by some enslaved men in Massachusetts, in June 1777, the Massachusetts legislature drafted a bill for "preventing the practice of holding persons in Slavery." Concerned about how such a law might alienate the slave states in the South, a committee was appointed to prepare a letter asking the Continental Congress whether the state enacting the bill would harm the war effort. Even before the letter was sent, the state legislature shut down efforts to pass the bill.[3]

Even though he personally opposed slavery, John Adams worked behind the scenes to quash the bill. He wrote to James Warren on June 22, 1777, that if the emancipation bill was passed, "it should have a bad effect on the Union of the United Colonies. A letter to Congress on the subject was proposed and reported, but I endeavored to divert that, supposing it would embarrass and perhaps be attended with worse consequences than passing the Act." Fifteen days later, Adams wrote, "The bill for freeing the Negroes, I hope will sleep for a time. We have causes enough of Jealousy, Discord and Division, and this bill will certainly add to the number."[4]

Rhode Island adopted a similar path. Rhode Island saw its own antislavery movement arise in the years before the American Revolution, even though the colony continued to dominate the North American slave trade (mostly from Newport) and had the highest percentage of blacks of any New England colony (about six percent).[5]

By the eve of the American Revolution, Stephen Hopkins and Moses Brown of Providence, and the Reverend Samuel Hopkins (no relation) of Newport, had become a powerful triumvirate in Rhode Island opposing both the slave trade and the institution of slavery. The three men knew that because Rhode Island did not have a royal governor, its legislature, the General Assembly, could enact antislavery bills

---

3. Benjamin Quarles, *The Negro in the American Revolution* (New York: W. W. Norton & Co., 1973), 47.
4. Quoted in ibid., note 53.
5. McBurney, *An American Privateer*, 10-11, 17.

without the need for royal approval, and that because the colony was so small, officials in London might overlook the laws.

On May 17, 1774, the town meeting of Providence recommended a stoppage of "all trade with Great Britain, Ireland, Africa and the West Indies." The ban would have prohibited Rhode Islanders from carrying African captives to British-controlled Caribbean islands (which was where most Rhode Island slave ship captains carried them). The town meeting further instructed its representatives to the Rhode Island General Assembly to obtain an act banning the importation of enslaved people and to free all enslaved persons born in the colony after they reached maturity.[6]

The General Assembly at least complied with one request, banishing the importation of African captives in June of that same year. This was one of the first times in world history—perhaps the first—that a legislature adopted a material measure restricting the transatlantic slave trade.

The act's recital, likely penned by Stephen Hopkins, was impressive, even if it likely referred to the gradual emancipation proposal that was not adopted:

> Whereas, the inhabitants of America are generally engaged in the preservation of their own rights and liberties, among which, that of personal freedom must be considered as the greatest; as those who are desirous of enjoying all the advantages of liberty themselves should be willing to extend personal liberty to others.[7]

The two Hopkinses and Brown were disappointed that the General Assembly did not pass legislation gradually emancipating Rhode Island's enslaved population. With the need to unite in the long war against a powerful British military, Rhode Island joined the other new states of the United States in generally setting aside for later consideration controversial matters such as emancipation. Rhode Island would not enact its gradual emancipation bill until 1784, the year after the Revolutionary War ended.

On occasion, circumstances forced state legislatures, even during wartime, to confront the slavery issue. For example, due to the difficulty

---

6. William R. Staples, *Annals of Providence: From Its First Settlement to the Organization of the City* (Providence, RI: privately printed, 1843), 235-36; Mack Thompson, *Moses Brown, Reluctant Reformer* (Chapel Hill, NC: University of North Carolina Press, 1962), 96-99.

7. General Assembly Resolution, June 1774 Session, in John R. Bartlett, ed., *Records of the Colony of Rhode Island and Providence Plantations*, 10 vols (Providence, RI: A. C. Greene & Bros., 1856-65), 7:251-52.

in meeting enlistment demands for the state's two Continental regiments, the Rhode Island General Assembly in February 1778 enacted a law permitting enslaved men who enlisted in the First Rhode Island Continental Regiment for the duration of the war to gain their freedom. About one hundred enslaved men earned their freedom in this manner.[8]

The General Assembly again addressed slavery in Rhode Island due to an incident in 1779, when an enslaved woman, Abigail (also called Nab), from South Kingstown, Rhode Island, forced their hand.

The story begins in the spring of 1779 with John Rice, of Hartford, in Orange County, in North Carolina, travelling to New England. His aim: to purchase enslaved people and bring them back to his home state. Whether he wanted to use the enslaved people on his own farm in North Carolina or to resell them at a profit to other farmers in North Carolina is not known. Because of a resolution passed by the Continental Congress, North Carolina was not allowed to import any captives from Africa or any other place.

Rice was an ambitious twenty-five-year-old. A stranger in New England, he carried in his pocket a letter of recommendation from John Penn, a delegate to the Continental Congress from North Carolina, who wrote that Rice "is esteemed as a young man of character." Penn added that he hoped Rice would "tak[e] care to behave well."[9]

Rice must have suspected he would face opposition if he announced that he hailed from North Carolina and wanted to purchase enslaved people and bring them back there. While slavery in Rhode Island and the rest of New England on occasion could be harsh, the conditions of enslaved people in Maryland, Virginia and North Carolina, and especially in South Carolina and Georgia, were known to be much worse. Of course, slavery anywhere was horrible and had to be enforced by local laws and terror. But conditions of servitude in the South were more brutal than those in the North, particularly compared to conditions in New England. In addition, some thought it cruel to take enslaved people away from their families. Accordingly, Rice told people he encountered that he hailed from Hartford—in Connecticut.

Perhaps Rice thought he could obtain some "deals" in Rhode Island. At the time, the British army occupied Newport and the rest of Aquidneck Island, as well as Jamestown. With the Royal Navy capturing

---

8. General Assembly Resolution, Feb. 1778 Session, in ibid., 8:358-60.
9. John Penn Letter of Recommendation for John Rice, November 27, 1779, Beriah Brown Papers, mss 109, box 4, folder 7, Rhode Island Historical Society (Beriah Brown Papers).

American trading vessels by the score, trade was depressed. So called "Narragansett Planters" in King's County had less ability to profit from keeping enslaved people. In addition, astute slaveholders might have seen the writing on the wall—that slavery would soon end in the state. One solution was to obtain some money by selling them. Since the market within Rhode Island was poor due to hard economic times, a likely buyer would be from out-of-state.

On May 13, 1779, John Rice appeared at the farm of Carder Hazard of South Kingstown. Hazard, a second son, reportedly was tall and "uncommonly handsome." He was a moderately successful farmer and a slave owner whose first wife hailed from the South. At the time he was one of five justices on the King's County Court of Common Pleas, having served several terms in that position.[10]

Hazard agreed to sell Rice four of his enslaved females: Abigail and three of her young daughters, Mary, Jane and Milly. The eldest of the three girls was just seven years old. Rice must have been desperate to buy as he paid the $3,000 purchase price not only in depreciated Continental paper money, but also with "hard money"—scarce and valuable Spanish milled coins.[11]

It is not known if Hazard knew that Rice intended to take Abigail and her children to North Carolina. I suspect he did know. Rice told him and Abigail that he was taking them to Hartford, Connecticut. But Abigail later found out that that statement was a lie and instead that Rice planned to take her and her daughters to North Carolina.[12]

The identity of the father of Abigail's children is never mentioned in the record. It is possible he was one of Carder Hazard's enslaved men. In November 1777, three of Hazard's enslaved men—Jacob, Pharoah, and Quaco—were spotted helping to unload a British warship that had accidentally run ashore near Point Judith. Perhaps it was Jacob,

---

10. Bartlett, ed., *Records of the Colony of Rhode Island*, 8:5 (1776), 220 (1777), 389 (1778), and 563 (1779) (selection of Carder Hazard as justice and years); Caroline E. Robinson, *The Hazard Family of Rhode Island* (Boston: privately printed, 1895), 55-56.
11. Petition of John Rice of North Carolina to the General Assembly of the State of Rhode Island, October 28, 1779, Rhode Island Petitions, vol. 17, fol. 118, Rhode Island State Archives (John Rice Petition). Most of the details of the episode involving John Rice and Abigail are from the prior source and Statement of John Rice to the Court of Common Pleas, King's County, undated (probably late 1779 or early 1780), in the Beriah Brown Papers (John Rice Court Submission).
12. Affidavit of Denison Billings, September 28, 1781, attached to Petition of Lodowick Stanton to the General Assembly, October 29, 1781, Petitions to the General Assembly, Rhode Island State Archives (Billings Affidavit).

who on July 6, 1778 enlisted in the 1st Rhode Island Regiment of Continentals, thereby earning his freedom, but who was away on military duty.[13]

Rice was eager to travel to other states in New England, probably Connecticut and/or Massachusetts, to search for more enslaved people to buy. He did not want to have Abigail and her young children tag along with him. So he left Abigail and her children behind at Carder Hazard's farm until he returned to fetch them.

On June 18, Rice returned to South Kingstown (probably in current day Narragansett) to pick up Abigail and her girls in order to transport them to the South in a wagon he had acquired. Other enslaved people whom Rice had purchased out of state were already in the wagon.

Rice hired two men to drive the wagon, thirty-year-old Lodowick Stanton of Charlestown and John Cross of Westerly. The thirty-year-old Stanton was the son of Colonel Joseph Stanton of Charlestown, a prominent farmer and slave holder. But because thirty-year-old Lodowick was the third son and sixth child, and his father was still living on the main family farm, it appears he was not a substantial farmer. Most successful farmers would not have hired themselves out as a wagon driver. Cross was a peddler and small-time merchant.[14]

The next day, Rice and his party, including his wagon filled with enslaved men, women and children, rode southwest, probably mostly along the Old Post Road. Cross took one of Abigail's children on his horse, and Stanton drove the wagon carrying Abigail and her two other children.

---

13. For Carder Hazard's enslaved men helping to unload HMS *Syren*, see Deposition of Martin Murphy, undated, William Davis Miller Papers, Mss 629, sub-group 12, box 2, folders 7 and Mss 673, series 4, sub-series C, box 3, folder 57, Rhode Island Historical Society; Christian McBurney, "'Strange Mismanagement': The Capture of HMS Syren," *Journal of the American Revolution*, April 10, 2014, allthingsliberty.com/2014/04/strange-mismanagement-the-capture-of-hms-syren/. For Jacob Hazard, with Carder Hazard of South Kingstown as his owner, enlisting as recruit number 60, see An Account of the Negro Slaves Enlisted into the Continental Battalions, 1778, in General Treasurer's Accounts Alphabetical Book, No. 6 (1761-1781), Rhode Island State Archives.

14. For Lodowick Stanton, see *William A. Stanton, A Record, Genealogical, Biographical, Statistical, of Thomas Stanton, of His Descendants, 1635-1891* (Albany, NY: Munsell's Sons, 1891), 426 and 432. Lodowick was married to Thankful in 1772. Ibid., 43. Stanton moved to Pittsfield, Massachusetts, and died there in 1818. Ibid. He was reported to have a 150-acre farm in Charlestown on which he kept thirty cows. See Thomas W. Bicknell, *The History of the State of Rhode Island and Providence Plantations*, vol. 2 (New York, NY: American Historical Society, 1920), 482. For John Cross as a tin peddler from Westerly, see Joseph W. Blaine, ed., *Nailer Tom's Diary, A Preliminary Index* (Newport, RI: privately printed, 1971), 51.

During the day's ride, which was about thirteen miles, Abigail raised with Lodowick Rice's intention of taking her and her daughters to North Carolina. Abigail expressed her strong opposition against it and asked Lodowick if he could help her and her children avoid that fate so that they could remain in Rhode Island. According to a friend of Lodowick's, Abigail even reportedly "begged" Stanton to purchase her. The friend said that Stanton told him that he "really pitied her" and that "if it was in his power she should not be carried out of the country."[15]

The party arrived in the early afternoon at Stanton's house in Charlestown. Stanton discussed his plans with his wife, Thankful, who must have agreed to cooperate with her husband to aid Abigail. Stanton then walked into the room where Rice was resting and announced that he wanted to purchase Abigail and her youngest daughter, Milly. This was a surprising offer, since Stanton did not appear to be a wealthy man and is not reported to have held any enslaved people. Stanton may have figured that this was the only way to keep the two in Rhode Island. Rice refused. Stanton pressed him again, but Rice's denial was firm.

Stanton left Rice and went to a back room to speak with Abigail, who must have known about Stanton's offer to purchase her. The two agreed on another plan. Abigail then approached Rice and said that she wanted to stay nearby at John Cross's house for the night. Her third child was likely already at Cross's house. Lodowick Stanton then said he would be a surety for Abigail's return. Thankful, in a friendly manner, next offered for Rice to spend the night at their house for free. Rice accepted the offer, and although he feared that Abigail might never return to him, he apparently agreed that she (and presumably her children) could spend the night nearby at Cross's house. In the meantime, Stanton departed his house, claiming that he had business at a nearby mill. In reality, he was making plans with Cross and likely other locals to assist Abigail and her daughters.

Shortly after sundown, the Stantons informed Rice that they were going to bed for the night. Rice decided to get a good sleep as well; he was weary from the trip. But Lodowick must have sneaked away from his house at night to assist Abigail and her children.[16]

The next morning Rice awoke and was informed that Abigail and her daughters were nowhere to be found. Stanton was not a good liar. At first he said that they had all gone to Block Island. Then he blamed John Cross for their disappearance.

15. Billings Affidavit.
16. Same sources as in note 11 above.

In a petition Rice later submitted to the General Assembly, he stated: "In making enquiry for his Negroes, [he] has great reasons to believe that a number of people had combined against him to deprive him of his property." In addition, Rice wrote that he "was informed his person was in danger if he ... pursued after" Abigail and her children. Stanton and likely John Cross, among others, kept Abigail and her children hidden at their own expense for several weeks.

A frustrated Rice continued on to Stonington, Connecticut, where he entered into a power of attorney authorizing a Stonington attorney, Joshua Randall, to recover his lost "property." After travelling around New England to find more enslaved people to purchase, on September 11 Rice arrived at New London, Connecticut, expecting to find Abigail and her children there. He was disappointed.[17]

Rice was informed of the proceedings involving Abigail and her girls at the August 1779 session of the General Assembly at Providence. Some white men from southern Rhode Island, likely including Lodowick Stanton, approached the General Assembly and informed its members of Abigail's circumstances. In response, the General Assembly passed the following resolution:

> Whereas, it is represented unto this Assembly, that Joshua Randall, of Stonington, in the state of Connecticut, as factor for one John Rice, calling himself of Hartford, in the state of Connecticut, aforesaid, purchased of Carder Hazard, of South Kingstown, Esq., a negro woman, and three children, to reside with the said John Rice, at Hartford [meaning in Connecticut]; but that since it appeareth that the said woman and children were purchased to be carried to the state of North Carolina; wherefore—
>
> It is voted and resolved, that the sheriff of the county of Kings forthwith take the said negro woman and her children into his possession; and that they remain with the said sheriff until further orders of this Assembly.[18]

Perhaps hearing of Rice's arrival at nearby New London, the General Assembly, then meeting at the courthouse at East Greenwich, again took up Abigail's cause. On September 15, the Lower House of the General Assembly ordered Joshua Randall of Stonington to sell "the Negro woman and her 3 children" to a Rhode Island resident or

---

17. Ibid.
18. General Assembly Resolutions, August 1779 Session, in Bartlett, ed., *Records of the Colony of Rhode Island*, 8:576; General Assembly Resolutions, August 26, 1779, Rhode Island Resolves and Acts ("*R.I. Acts*"), Rhode Island State Archives, August 1779, 7.

residents whose "humanity shall be approved of by Carder Hazard of South Kingstown, the original owner of said slaves," that in the meantime Abigail and her children should continue to be held in the custody of the Sheriff of King's County, Beriah Brown of North Kingstown, and that Rice pay Brown for the cost of the food and other expenses incurred in maintaining Abigail and her children until the sale was completed.[19]

The General Assembly might have decided to void the sale by Carder Hazard, forcing him to return all of the purchase price to Rice. But it did not take that course, possibly believing that it could not interfere with a private contract, or preferring to be severe with an out-of-state slaver.

An outraged Rice, learning about the proceedings at East Greenwich, rushed to the town, arriving on the morning of September 17, but he was too late. The General Assembly had resolved not to conduct any more private business.[20]

Rice complained, in his petition, that "such a noise is made and propagated by designing men" about his character that he "must lose his said property unless" the Lower House reversed itself. On October 28, Rice submitted his petition to the General Assembly, then meeting in session at the courthouse in Little Rest (still standing in what is now Kingston, in South Kingstown), and asked for the General Assembly to grant him appropriate relief.[21]

The General Assembly did not look kindly upon Rice's petition or request for relief, refusing to change its position. Instead, it passed new legislation prohibiting the sale of enslaved people to out-of-state buyers without the consent of the enslaved people.

This article is the first time that the legislation's recital and other parts of the act have been set forth in a publication. Historians previously relied on John Russell Bartlett's *Records of the State of Rhode Island and Providence Plantations in New England*, but volume eight of that work gives only the act's name and purpose.[22] For the full text of the Act, one must consult the Rhode Island State Archives or the hard-to-find published work, *Rhode Island Resolves and Acts*.

The General Assembly included with the legislation a remarkable recital:

---

19. General Assembly Resolutions, September 1779 Session, in Bartlett, ed., *Records of the Colony of Rhode Island*, 8: 586.
20. Same sources cited in note 11 above.
21. Ibid.
22. Bartlett, ed., *Records of the Colony of Rhode Island*, 8:618.

Whereas tolerating Strangers to purchase Negroes, or Mulatto Slaves in this State, and carry them off either by Land or Water, against their consent, to perpetuate their Slavery in foreign Parts remote from their Friends and Acquaintance[s], is against the Rights of human Nature, and tends greatly to aggravate the Condition of Slavery, which this General Assembly is disposed to alleviate, till some favorable Occasion may offer for its total Abolition.[23]

This recital is extraordinary for two reasons. First is the rationale provided for it: that it was cruel for an enslaved Rhode Islander to be carried away to a different state far from the person's family and friends. Previously, most historians have concluded that the main rationale for legislation such as this (which was adopted in several northern states) was the legislators' determination that the conditions of enslavement were harsher in the South than in the North.

In addition, the recital refers to the disposition of the General Assembly to lessen the harshness of the conditions of enslavement until "some favorable occasion may offer for its total Abolition." The occasion, no doubt, was a successful end to the war of independence against Great Britain. As stated, Rhode Island did enact a gradual emancipation act in 1784, the year after the war's end.

Back in the General Assembly's August 1779 session, David Howell, Welcome Arnold and Rouse J. Helme had been appointed a committee to draft this bill. (David Howell of Providence was the first name to appear in a list of members of the Providence Abolition Society, formed in June 1790,[24] and he took an active role in leading it. One suspects he drafted the above recital.)

Remarkably, the legislation included a provision that if an enslaved person complained to a Justice of the Peace in any town in the state, and it was proven, that there had been an attempt to sell such enslaved person and have the person carried outside the state without such person's consent, in violation of the act, the Justice of the Peace was required to provide the enslaved person "a Certificate, of his or her total Emancipation; by Virtue of which such slave or slaves shall become forever thereafter as perfectly liberated . . . as though he or they had never been in Bondage."[25]

This part of the legislation is evidence that the members of the General Assembly would have liked to have emancipated Abigail and her daughters. However, they must have felt it was not fair to apply the law

---

23. *R.I. Acts*, October 1779, 6.
24. Ibid., June 1790, 6.
25. Ibid., October 1779, 7.

retroactively without having given John Rice notice of the act before applying it.

In addition, if any slave buyer was convicted in court of violating the law, such person would be required to pay a fine equal to the value of the enslaved person or persons that the convicted person attempted to sell. And one-half of such fine was to be paid to the "Informer" whose information led to the conviction.

At this writing, I am not aware of any cases that applied the emancipation provision or the provision imposing a fine on slaveholders who attempted to sell an enslaved person out of state.

The law contained another provision that must have been made at the insistence of Rhode Island slaveholders. A Rhode Island slaveholder could sell outside the state an enslaved person who had "become notoriously unfaithful and villainous." To do so, the slaveholder had to obtain a judgment in the county court that the enslaved man or woman satisfied this standard—not an easy burden to fulfill. It is not clear if an enslaved man or woman would be considered "unfaithful and villainous" if he or she tried to free himself or herself by running away.[26]

John Rice must have been dumb-founded about the legislation. To make matters worse for Rice, on the same day that he submitted his petition and the law was passed, Abigail and her three children were sold to two Rhode Islanders. Lodowick Stanton purchased Abigail and her daughter Milly. The other two girls, Mary and Jane, were purchased by Col. Joseph Noyes, a prominent militia officer and farmer from Westerly whose farm was located near the coast.[27]

In the Rhode Island censuses of 1774 and 1782, and the federal censuses of 1790 and 1800, Lodowick Stanton is not reported as having any black persons living in his household, either enslaved or free.[28] Interestingly, those census records do not indicate that his oldest brother, Joseph Stanton, Jr., who would be elected as one of the state's first U.S. Senators in 1790, ever held any enslaved people. Joseph Stanton, Jr. was also an original member of the Providence Abolition Society. Did Lodowick purchase Abigail and Milly for humanitarian purposes? Or was he from

---

26. Ibid.
27. Lodowick Stanton Bond, December 13, 1779, and Joseph Noyes Bond, December 13, 1779, in Beriah Brown Papers, infra.; John Rice Petition, infra.
28. John R. Bartlett, ed., *Census of the Inhabitants of the Colony of Rhode Island and Providence Plantations Taken by the Order of the General Assembly, in the Year 1774* (Providence, RI: Knowles, Anthony & Co., 1858), 153; Jay Mack Holbrook, ed., *Rhode Island 1782 Census* (Oxford, MA: Holbrook Research Institute, 1979), 118.; Bureau of the Census, *Heads of Families at the First Census of the United States Taken in the Year 1790, Rhode Island* (Washington, DC: Government Printing Office, 1908), 40; 1800 Federal Census, Charlestown, Rhode Island, National Archives, Washington, D.C.

the start motivated to purchase Abigail and one of her daughters to enslave them? It will never be known with certainty, but his conduct with Rice on the day before Abigail's escape, the census information, and his oldest brother's activities, constitute evidence that it was the former.

By contrast, Joseph Noyes was reported to have five black persons in his household in the 1774 census and three in the 1782 census, all of whom were likely enslaved. In the 1790 census, Noyes is listed as having seven enslaved persons residing in his household; in the 1800 census, none are reported.[29]

The General Assembly required both Stanton and Noyes to sign a bond obligating them to "not send said Negroes or either of them out of this State." The penalty for failing to comply with this obligation was $10,000.[30]

For Abigail, the outcome was mixed. On the positive side, neither she nor any of her children was transported to North Carolina. In addition, her actions helped spur legislation in the General Assembly that could be applied to help other enslaved people in Rhode Island. On the other hand, tragically, her family was divided. Stanton could not afford to purchase all of Abigail's children. Stanton's and Noyes's farms were not too far away from each other, but still, she could not see Mary and Jane on a daily basis. (It is possible Noyes allowed Abigail to look after the two young girls he had purchased until they became old enough to work at his farm or house).

The General Assembly's 1779 legislation did not apply retroactively the provisions allowing an enslaved person who filed a complaint about being sold out of state to be declared free. If it had, Abigail could have gone free. In addition, Rhode Island's gradual emancipation legislation, enacted in 1784, technically applied only to persons born of enslaved mothers after the date of the act.[31] That was too late for Abigail (and her children) too.

In actuality, the institution of slavery in Rhode Island was weakened at a more accelerated rate than the gradual emancipation law envisioned. In 1774, there were likely more than 3,000 enslaved persons in

---

29. Bartlett, ed., *R.I. 1774 Census*, 72; Holbrook, ed., *R.I. 1782 Census*, 89; Bureau of the Census, *1790 Census, Rhode Island*, 50; 1800 Federal Census, Westerly, Rhode Island, National Archives.
30. Same bonds cited in note 27 above.
31. General Assembly Resolutions, February 1784 and October 1785 Sessions, in Bartlett, ed., *Records of the Colony of Rhode Island*, 10:7-8 and 132-33. For more on the emancipation legislation and the transition from slavery to freedom in Rhode Island, see Joanne Pope Melish, *Disowning Slavery, Gradual Emancipation and "Race" in New England,1780-1860* (Cornell University Press, 1998), 66-69, 71-73, 76, 93-94, 98-103, and 206-08.

Rhode Island, but by 1790 there were only 948, and by 1800, just 380. Most enslaved persons in Rhode Island had been freed, either by manumission by their owners, by their owners through negotiations with the enslaved adults, or by the enslaved persons freeing themselves via running away. Some slave holders stubbornly held on, but many of those who remained enslaved were elderly, who may not have been able to support themselves if freed, and children born after 1784 who would eventually become free. It is likely the case that Abigail's children were not freed until they attained age twenty-one or later so that they could work to support themselves—and in the meantime repay their owners with free labor for supporting them during their years as minors.

Rice remained bitter about his situation. He appears to have received the same purchase price from Stanton and Noyes, but he lost money because he was paid in Continental paper money that continued to depreciate in value. Moreover, he had to reimburse Beriah Brown £100 for the state's expenses of maintaining Abigail and her children and pay the fees of his Stonington attorney.[32]

Both Stanton and Rice had to appear together to sign Stanton's bond. Rice became enraged when Stanton again claimed that he had no role in Abigail's escape. According to Rice, "with my naked hand I knocked him down and don't know but believe I struck him again." Stanton lodged a suit against Rice in the King's County Court of Common Pleas, charging him with assault and seeking damages.[33] In a letter to the court, Rice defended himself. First, he claimed that the General Assembly had disgraced itself by taking away his "Negroes." He even added some awful lines of poetry, including the following verses:

> By a set of arbitrary knaves
> I am deprived of lawful slaves

Rice concluded his letter by stating, "if the Honorable Court thinks I ought to pay anything for flogging a man of his character, I stand ready to do it, to the amount of any sum the Court pleases to inflict." The defendant signed his name, "J. Rice, Infamous Carolinian."[34] Rice had to leave the state without being paid for Stanton's purchase of Abigail and Milly.[35] Stanton apparently managed to keep the money frozen until the suit was resolved.

32. John Rice Court Submission; same source as in note 19 above.
33. John Rice Court Submission.
34. Ibid.
35. Power of Attorney, December 30, 1779, John Rice to Beriah Brown, Beriah Brown Papers, infra. In his instructions, Rice informed Sheriff Brown where he could send any money due to Rice if Rice was not able to collect it.

The court had the matter investigated by an impressive triumvirate: Henry Marchant, just back from serving as one of Rhode Island's delegates to the Continental Congress; James Mitchell Varnum, a retired brigadier general of the Continental Army; and Freeman Perry of Charlestown. They recommended a verdict in Stanton's favor, and the court agreed. The court ordered Rice to pay Stanton £30 in damages and for Rice to pay court costs of more than £50. Presumably, Rice's agent, Sheriff Brown, sent the remaining funds to the slave trader in North Carolina.[36]

Unfortunately, there is a sad end to Abigail's story. Shockingly, almost two years after he purchased Abigail and one of her children, Lodowick Stanton submitted a petition to the General Assembly asking that he be permitted to sell them to a Connecticut buyer. In the petition, Stanton claimed that Abigail had made "repeated urgings and requests" for him to purchase her so she would not carried to North Carolina. Stanton said that Abigail informed him that she tried but could not find a buyer from South Kingstown. Based on her requests, and Abigail "faithfully promising to behave," Stanton wrote, he was "induced" to purchase Abigail and one of her daughters, Milly. Stanton wrote that Abigail "behaved herself well for a short time" and was "kindly treated," but then she "began to disobey the orders of her master and mistress," and started to steal their property and lie to them. Stanton said he no longer felt his property was safe in her presence. He requested permission to sell Abigail and her daughter to a Captain Samuel Belden from New London.[37]

Stanton attached to his petition an affidavit from Denison Billings, a friend of Stanton's. Billings described Abigail as taking "delight in being saucy to her master and mistress." Billings said that Abigail was caught several times taking one of Stanton's horses to ride at night to South Kingstown and back. Billings even claimed to have heard a rumor that Abigail "behaved so badly" that "the Negro man who used to keep her ... would not have anything [more] to do with her."[38] Stanton was unwilling to lose money by freeing Abigail and Milly. The General Assembly granted Stanton's petition,[39] the only time this writer is aware of that this provision of the 1779 law was utilized.

The record does not provide Abigail's side of the story. She probably was simply fed up with being enslaved.

---

36. Court Record of Decisions, Court of Common Pleas, King's County, Feb. 1780 Session, 395 (Stanton v. Rice), Archives at the Judicial Records Center, Rhode Island.
37. Petition of Lodowick Stanton to the General Assembly, October 29, 1781, Petitions to the General Assembly, Rhode Island State Archives (Stanton Petition).
38. Billings Affidavit.
39. Stanton Petition.

British Soldier John Ward Wins Back His Pocketbook

⋙ DON N. HAGIST ⋘

We expect writers for the *Journal of the American Revolution* to use primary sources—things written as close as possible to the time of the events that they describe. Sometimes even primary sources contain inaccuracies that can be spotted and resolved only by cross-referencing other primary sources. One example lies in the records of a criminal trial held in April 1779 at the sessions house of the Lord Mayor and Sheriffs of the City of London and of Middlesex, known as the Old Bailey.[1]

The defendant was John Ward, who had just been discharged from the British army in America and had come to the London area to go before the army's pension examining board that sat at Chelsea Hospital. This was a common path for soldiers who had ended their careers. If a man served in the army for so long that he was no longer able to earn a living in another line of work, or if he had incurred a disability through military service, the government awarded him a pension. But he had to appear in person before the examining board, a group of army officers who determined that his circumstances did, in fact, qualify him for a pension.[2]

The trial proceedings identify Ward as "a soldier in General Burgoyne's regiment" who had "been lately discharged on coming home from America." General John Burgoyne was already famous for the failed campaign he had led in America in 1777. Like many British gen-

---

1. Trial of John Close, www.oldbaileyonline.org/browse.jsp?id=t17790404-9&div=t17790404-9.
2. For details on British army pensions during this era, see Don N. Hagist, *Noble Volunteers: the British Soldiers who fought the American Revolution* (Yardley, PA: Westholme, 2020), 244-248.

eral officers, Burgoyne was also the commanding officer of an army regiment; his regiment, the 16th Light Dragoons, had just returned to England from service in America. A search of the regiment's muster rolls, however, reveals no man named John Ward.[3]

Fortunately, the trial proceedings contain enough evidence to resolve the discrepancy. An innkeeper testified that "John Ward, with several others belonging to the 74th regiment of foot" stayed with him in March 1779 after returning from America. The pension examining board kept records of everyone who appeared before them, which reveal that nine men of the 74th Regiment, including John Ward, stood before the board on June 17, 1779.[4]

The admission book shows that Ward was Irish, a Belfast native born in 1725 who had spent over seventeen years in the army and been wounded in the arm during that long career. He probably enlisted before or during the Seven Years War, and then was discharged when peace brought reductions in the size of the army. Part way through the American Revolution he answered the call for volunteers to join a new regiment authorized in December 1777 and raised largely in the Scottish county of Argyll: the 74th Regiment of Foot, sometimes called the Argyll Highlanders. Like many new-raised regiments, its ranks were filled by a mix of new recruits and experienced veterans; men like Ward, with prior military experience, insured that the corps would quickly be ready for the demands of foreign service in spite of being newly created.

The regiment recruited throughout the first half of 1778, and sailed for Nova Scotia that August. Once in Halifax, Ward's age and injuries apparently caught up with him; he may have been wounded somehow during his brief time in the 74th Regiment, or had a lingering disability from a wound received in the past. Before the regiment went to a war zone, he and a few others from the 74th were "invalided"—discharged because they were not deemed capable of the rigors of wartime service. On February 16, 1779 he and the other invalids, still in Halifax, embarked on the warship *Iris* for the journey home.[5]

When Ward disembarked from *Iris* in Portsmouth on March 20, he probably thought he had fought his last fight. He and his comrades set

---

3. Muster rolls, 16th Light Dragoons, WO 12/1246, The National Archives, Kew, UK (TNA).
4. "Examinations of Invalid Soldiers," June 17, 1779, Pension Admission Book, WO 116/7, TNA. There is no obvious explanation for the statement that Ward was in "Burgoyne's regiment"; there is no apparent connection between General Burgoyne and the 74th Regiment, or any indication that men were transferred from Burgoyne's regiment to the 74th.
5. Muster books, HMS *Iris*, ADM 36/10046, TNA.

off for London, where they arrived five days later. They took rooms for the night at an inn called Sign of the Angel in Chapel-street, Westminster. There, according to Ward "we laid down our knapsacks, and drank pretty heartily."[6]

Lodging in the same place was John Close, a soldier in the 3rd Regiment of Foot Guards, soldiers serving in the London area to protect the Royal family and their properties. Close ate and drank with the newly-arrived veterans, and said he was an Irishman like Ward. The next morning, Ward and his comrades went to the War Office and received billets for quarters in Chelsea, where they would go before the pension board. Returning to the tavern, they met up again with Close, who accompanied them to Chelsea that afternoon.

After finding their quarters in Chelsea, Ward and Close went to a local tavern, ate, and drank some beer. Ward drew out his leather pocketbook which contained about two months' pay that he had received when he was discharged, and paid the bill. He then left Close and returned to the previous night's tavern where he wanted to spend some money because the owner had given him a free meal the night before. Close arrived later on. Some time and two pots of beer later, Close agreed to walk Ward, now somewhat tipsy, back to Chelsea.

Along the way, Close pulled Ward off the road. In the darkness he grabbed Ward's lame arm, which had no strength due to its wound, leaving Ward unable to effectively resist. Close reached into Ward's breast pocket and took the pocketbook full of cash that he had seen earlier that day. Ward, with the coolness of a veteran soldier, asked for the pocketbook back. He did not to pursue or cry out when Close went off into the night. He knew where Close lived, knew he could identify him, realized that he might leave town if he feared pursuit, and recognized that his own lameness and inebriated state rendered him unable to best Close in a confrontation. Ward knew his best chance at recovering the pocketbook was to remain calm.

John Close returned to his own quarters at the Sign of the Angel early the next morning, and went to his room to prepare for his duties as a soldier that day. Soon after, John Ward and several of his comrades arrived and told the tavern owner what Close had done. The owner summoned Close, who denied the charge, but while Close talked with his accusers the tavern owner went to his room and found the pocket book hidden in a closet.

---

6. This and all subsequent information is from the Trial of John Close, unless otherwise stated.

John Close was brought to trial at the Old Bailey the following week, on April 4, 1779. John Ward told his story and described exactly how much money was in the pocketbook. The tavern keeper from Sign of the Angel testified, as did the keepers of two other taverns where Close had spent money freely on the night of the theft. The pocketbook was shown to the court.

Close offered only a brief defense, claiming that Ward had given him money but offering no explanation of how he came to possess the pocketbook. He called on his sergeant as a character witness, but the sergeant said only that Close had been in the regiment for a year, and that he knew nothing else of him. This was no defense at all, and the court found Close guilty of theft. He was sentenced to "navigation," a year of hard labor dredging the Thames River to improve its navigability.

The court records do not state whether John Ward recovered all of his money, but he did finally go before the examining board on June 17 and was awarded a pension.[7]

---

7. The trial record of John Ward's testimony includes the sentence, "I came home in the Hallifax." This incorrect ship name is easy to reconcile, given that *Iris* brought Ward from Halifax, Nova Scotia; apparently the court recorder understood Ward incorrectly.

Anthony Wayne's Repulse at Bull's Ferry, July 21, 1780

JIM PIECUCH

General Anthony Wayne was one of the most capable generals in the Continental Army and is perhaps best remembered for his successful surprise attack that captured the British post at Stony Point, New York, on July 16, 1779. Wayne also suffered his share of reverses, most notably at Paoli, Pennsylvania, on the night of September 20-21, 1777, when his 2,500 troops were soundly defeated after being caught unaware by Gen. Charles Grey with 1,200 British regulars. As painful as this debacle was, Wayne later suffered another stinging defeat on July 21, 1780, when a handful of Loyalist militia holding a blockhouse at Bull's Ferry, New Jersey, repulsed Wayne's much larger force of Continentals. Although the battle did not alter the overall strategic situation, it proved embarrassing to the Americans, while the British and Loyalists exulted in their triumph. The event prompted Major John André, Gen. Sir Henry Clinton's aide-de-camp, to compose and publish a lengthy poem, *Cow-chace*, ridiculing Wayne and other American officers.

After the failed British efforts to strike a serious blow against George Washington's army at Connecticut Farms and Springfield, New Jersey, in June 1780, Washington believed that Clinton, having recently returned to New York following his capture of Charleston, South Carolina, would move against the American post at West Point on the Hudson River. Washington therefore in late June moved most of his troops to Preakness, New Jersey, where they would be in a better position to respond to such a threat. On July 6, Washington called a council of war to consider proposals for future operations. Wayne, whose boldness sometimes bordered on recklessness, suggested an attack on New York, but the idea was rejected because the army lacked the strength for an undertaking of that magnitude.[1]

---

1. Paul David Nelson, *Anthony Wayne: Soldier of the Early Republic* (Bloomington: Indiana University Press, 1985), 108.

Wayne, encamped with his Pennsylvania Continentals at Totowa, New Jersey, and always eager for action, informed Washington on July 19 that he intended to march the next afternoon with his two brigades, four pieces of artillery, and Col. Stephen Moylan's 4th Light Dragoons "for the purpose of destroying the blockhouse near Bulls Ferry," about four miles north of Hoboken, "and securing the cows, horses . . . in Bergen Neck between the Hackensack and North [Hudson] Rivers from Newbridge and Liberty Pole southward." Wayne stated that he would send parties out before dawn on July 20 to occupy positions where they could observe any British attempts to send reinforcements across the Hudson River. One hundred men and an artillery piece would hold New Bridge, while two infantry regiments "with a few horse" would take post at possible landing sites, one regiment going "to the beach opposite Kings Bridge, the other to Fort Lee." Should the British attempt a landing at either site, these troops would inform Wayne and defend their positions. Based on his "knowledge of the ground," Wayne declared that a British landing "is an event more to be wished than dreaded." Once these detachments had reached their assigned locations, the rest of the American force would "move in two columns to Bulls Ferry—one on the summit of the mountain—the other with the artillery and horses along the open road." The cavalry would at the same time "push with rapidity towards bergen town & when they reach as low as is necessary, or prudent, begin & Drive off every Species of Cattle & horses moving back with Velocity—whilst another party are advanced to cover them."[2]

Washington replied the next day, authorizing Wayne to employ the 1st and 2nd Pennsylvania Brigades and Moylan's dragoons "upon the execution of the Business planned." The commander in chief advised Wayne to dispatch a few of the dragoons that afternoon "to patrol all night, and see that the Enemy do not, in the course of the night, throw over any troops to form an ambuscade." Washington suggested that the mounted troops "inquire as they go, for Deserters," to conceal the true purpose of their foray.[3]

At 3 p.m. on July 20, Wayne set out with his two infantry brigades, Moylan's dragoons, and four artillery pieces "& arrived a little in the rear of New Bridge at 9. in the Evening." The Americans rested for four hours, resuming their march at 1 a.m. on July 21. The units as-

---

2. Anthony Wayne to George Washington, July 19, 1780, www.founders.archives.gov/documents/Washington/99-01-02-02573.
3. Washington to Wayne, July 20, 1780, founders.archives.gov/documents/Washington/99-01-02-02587.

signed to guard against prospective British landings, the 6th and 7th Pennsylvania regiments, were detached along the way. Wayne ordered these troops to conceal themselves and "wait the Landing of the Enemy—& then at the point of the bayonet—to dispute the pass in the Gorge of the Mountain at every expence of blood" until they were reinforced. The main force continued marching, then separated according to plan, with Gen. James Irvine moving "along the Summit of the Mountain" with part of his 2nd Brigade and the 1st Brigade under Col. Richard Humpton, the artillery, and Moylan's dragoons taking "the common road." Where the road forked with one branch going toward Bergen and Paulus Hook, Wayne left the cavalry and some infantry "to receive the Enemy if they attempted anything from that Quarter."[4]

Upon reaching their objective, Wayne and his officers examined the blockhouse and surrounding terrain. The structure, they found, was "surrounded by an Abbatis & Stockade to the perpendicular Rocks" along the Hudson River, "with a kind of Ditch or parapet serving as a Covered way." As they scouted the enemy position, Wayne claimed that the British could be seen "in motion on York Island," increasing his optimism that they would cross the river and fall into his ambush.[5]

The Continentals deployed for the attack on the blockhouse. Irvine halted north of the post, "in a position from which he could move to any point where the Enemy should attempt to land—either in the Vicinity of" Bull's Ferry or farther north at Fort Lee. The 1st Pennsylvania Regiment occupied "a hollow way on the north side the block house," and the 10th Pennsylvania took a position in a similar terrain feature south of the fortification. Wayne ordered the men "to keep up a Constant fire into the port holes" of the blockhouse to cover the artillery and the 2nd Pennsylvania as they advanced from the west.[6] Apparently Wayne had little respect for the defenders; he had often reviled Loyalists, once referring to them as "Refugees & a wretched banditti of Robbers horse thieves & c."[7]

There were about seventy Loyalists in the blockhouse, a militia company of the Loyal Refugee Volunteers commanded by Capt. Thomas Ward. They had constructed the blockhouse as protection against American attacks while they cut firewood for the British garrison in New York City, a task they performed in exchange for pay and provisions. Two "small Guns" were mounted in the blockhouse, probably

---

4. Wayne to Washington, July 22, 1780, www.founders.archives.gov/documents/Washington/99-01-02-02629.
5. Ibid.
6. Ibid.
7. Nelson, *Anthony Wayne*, 109.

swivel guns capable of firing both solid iron balls about one inch in diameter as well as grape shot.[8] Clinton, who visited the blockhouse after the battle, described it as "a trifling work," intended to protect the Loyalists "against such straggling parties of militia as might be disposed to molest them, not imagining they could ever become an object to a more formidable enemy."[9] The Loyalists must have received warning of Wayne's approach, either from their own scouts or local residents, as they had time to take shelter in their fortifications before the American force arrived.

The covering fire from the regiments north and south of the blockhouse enabled the American artillery to deploy at a distance of only sixty yards from the structure. None of the accounts mention the type of guns employed, but they were probably six-pounders, the most common fieldpieces used by both armies. At approximately 11 a.m. the artillery "Commenced a Constant fire," Wayne reported, "which was returned by the Enemy & continued without Intermission . . . until After 12 OClock." Despite the intensity of the fire, Wayne claimed "we found that our Artillery had made but little Impression (altho' well & Gallantly served) the metal not being of Sufficient weight to traverse the loggs of the Block house."[10]

Wayne may have been too far from the fortification to observe the effect of the fire, or his view may have been obscured by smoke, as in actuality the artillery had badly damaged the blockhouse. Clinton noted that the structure "was pierced by fifty-two Shot in one face only and the two small Guns that were in it dismounted."[11]

During the bombardment, Wayne received two dispatches from one of his officers, Zebulon Pike (father of the famous explorer of the same name), who was at Closter observing the movements of British troops. The first dispatch, written in the early morning, stated that about 3,000 men had boarded a dozen vessels and appeared to be sailing downriver to New York City. In the second, composed at 9 a.m., Pike wrote that while he could not see the British force on Valentine's Hill on the New York side of the Hudson, in his opinion they had left that position, as he had observed "about two thousand of the Enemy together with a

---

8. Walter T. Dornfest, *Military Loyalists of the American Revolution: Officers and Regiments, 1775-1783* (Jefferson, NC: McFarland & Co., 2011), 351; H. H. Burleigh, "The Block House in Bergen Wood," www.uelac.org/PDF/The-Block-House-in-Bergen-Wood.pdf.
9. Henry Clinton, *The American Rebellion: Sir Henry Clinton's Narrative of His Campaigns, 1775-1782, With an Appendix of Original Documents*, William B. Willcox, ed. (New Haven, CT: Yale University Press, 1954), 200-201.
10. Wayne to Washington, July 22, 1780.
11. Quoted in Burleigh, "Block House."

number of Waggons which appears to be loaded with baggage." Some eight hundred men of this force had embarked aboard ships and the boarding continued.[12] After receiving these messages, and having himself seen what he believed were "many vessels and boats moving up with troops from New York," Wayne reconsidered his attack on the blockhouse.[13] He hastily convened a council of war, where he and his officers "unanimously Determined . . . to withdraw the artillery & fall back by easy degrees" to New Bridge, "to prevent the Disagreeable consequences of being shut up in Bergen Neck," Wayne explained.[14] He portrayed the decision more favorably in a subsequent letter to Washington, insisting that the approach of a British relief force "made it necessary to Relinquish a lesser for a much greater Object," the chance to lure the reinforcements into an ambush "and Deciding the fortune of the day in the defiles thro' which they must pass before they could gain possession of the strong Grounds."[15]

Wayne ordered his troops to break off the action, but instead of obeying, they attacked the blockhouse. "Such was the Enthusiastic bravery of all ranks of Officers & men," Wayne stated, "that the first Regiment no longer capable of restraint (rather than leave a post in their rear) rushed with Impetuosity over the Abbatis & advanced to the Stockades . . . altho' they had no means of forcing an Entry—the contagion spread to the Second" regiment which joined the assault. The 10th Pennsylvania also attempted to attack, "as the same Gallant spirit pervaded the whole," and Wayne noted that it was fortunate "that the Ground would not admit of the further advance of the 10th Regiment," because it prevented their suffering as many casualties as the other two units. Only "by very great efforts of the Officers" of the 1st and 2nd Pennsylvania were those regiments "at last restrained." Once the officers had gotten the infantry under control, the artillery was withdrawn for the anticipated clash with British reinforcements. The men in the infantry regiments collected their wounded and dead comrades and carried them off the field, "except three that lay dead under the stockades."[16]

British accounts provided few details of the Loyalists' defense. Clinton wrote that in the face of "a tremendous fire of musketry and can-

12. Zebulon Pike to Wayne, July 21, 1780 (two letters), enclosures in Wayne to Washington, July 21, 1780, *Founders Online*, National Archives, www.founders.archives.gov/documents/Washington/99-01-02-02606.
13. Wayne to Washington, July 22, 1780.
14. Wayne to Washington, July 21, 1780.
15. Wayne to Washington, July 22, 1780.
16. Ibid.

non," the "gallant band" of Loyalists "defended themselves with activity and spirit; and after sustaining the enemy's fire for some hours," they repulsed "an assault on their works."[17] In his postwar Loyalist Claim, Ward remarked only that "the Post at Bull's Ferry was attacked by General Wayne with a large Body Picked American Troops who after a very severe engagement were forced to retire."[18]

While Wayne got his troops on the road and moving northward, Moylan's dragoons drove their captured cattle toward New Bridge. An infantry detachment attacked the landing on the riverbank, below the blockhouse, and Wayne reported they "destroyed the Sloop & Wood boats" found there, capturing "a Capt. & Mate with two Sailers—some others were killed" as they tried to escape by swimming. The detachment "pushed forward to oppose the troops from Voluntines hill that we expected to land at the rear at New Bridge." However, "in this project we were Disappointed, the enemy thought proper to remain in a less hostile position—than that of the Jersy shore," Wayne lamented.[19]

On July 25, the *Pennsylvania Packet* newspaper published an account of the American operations that sought to portray those events in as favorable a light as possible. According to the *Packet*, the purpose of Wayne's movement had been to collect and carry off "the cattle in Bergen County, New Jersey, which were exposed to the enemy." Having completed that task, Wayne was returning to his camp when he "visited a block-house in the vicinity of Bergen town, built and garrisoned by a number of refugees to prevent the disagreeable necessity of being forced into the British seaservice." The blockhouse proving to be invulnerable to artillery fire, the 1st and 2nd Pennsylvania regiments "were ordered to attempt it by assault." They succeeded in "forcing their way through the abattis and pickets," though "a retreat was indispensably necessary" after the attackers found there was "no other entrance into the block-house but a subterranean passage," so narrow that it could only be traversed in single file.[20] Although the article contradicted much of the information in Wayne's reports, it did display the imaginative talent of its author.

The *Packet* included one apparently factual detail that Wayne did not mention: that a Lieutenant Moody and six men were captured on their return from Sussex. The statement supports information provided by Clinton, also omitted by Wayne, that "the Exertions of the Refugees

17. Clinton, *American Rebellion*, 201.
18. Quoted in Burleigh, "Block House."
19. Wayne to Washington, July 22, 1780.
20. Quoted in Burleigh, "Block House."

did not cease after having resisted so great a force. They followed the Enemy, seized their Stragglers and rescued from them the Cattle they were driving from the neighbouring district." Clinton reported that six Loyalists were killed and fifteen wounded in the engagement, "the far greater part in the Blockhouse." According to the *Packet*, American casualties were sixty-nine killed and wounded, in addition to the seven men captured.[21] In his official return, Wayne listed a total of sixty-four killed and wounded, making no mention of prisoners.[22]

Wayne was clearly stung by his failure to capture the blockhouse, telling Washington that "should my Conduct & that of the troops under my Command meet your Excellency's Approbation—it will much Alleviate the pain I experience in not having it in my power to carry the Whole of the plan into Execution—which was only prevented by the most Malicious fortune."[23] Shortly afterward, Wayne wrote to Pennsylvania's chief executive, Joseph Reed, and claimed that his raid had probably thwarted Clinton's plan to attack the French in Rhode Island. Wayne believed that his operation had delayed the British departure from New York, allowing the French to make preparations adequate to defeat any attack. Wayne added that he had written Reed "to put the quietus on rumors by his detractors that he had rushed headlong into a useless, wasteful skirmish merely to embellish his own military reputation and that the assault really was worthless from start to finish." Reed responded that he did not believe that Wayne had acted improperly, nor would any sensible person doubt that Wayne had done his duty.[24]

For his part, Clinton did believe that his "preparations for this expedition" to Rhode Island "had caused a movement in Mr. Washington's army, with a view, it is supposed of diverting me from my object or at least retarding its taking place." These efforts, Clinton asserted, caused no disruption, as "the route I had chosen putting within my reach the quickest intelligence of his motions, I knew I could regulate mine according to them at a moment, and they of course suffered no interruption from them. None, however, appeared to have a serious tendency but one," the attack at Bull's Ferry, and there Clinton remarked that "the issue turned out exceedingly honorable to a small body of loyal refugees." He praised the blockhouse's defenders, declaring that "such rare and exalted bravery merited every encouragement in my power,

21. Ibid.
22. Wayne to Washington, July 22, 1780.
23. Ibid.
24. Nelson, *Anthony Wayne*, 111.

and I did not fail to distinguish it at the time by suitable commendations and rewards, to which I had soon after the satisfaction to add the fullest approbation of their sovereign."[25] Clinton was referring to a letter he sent to Lord George Germain, Secretary of State for the American Department, on August 20 describing the action and lauding the Loyalists' bravery. In his reply, Germain wrote that "the very extraordinary Instance of Courage shown by the seventy loyal Refugees in the Affair of Bulls Ferry . . . is a pleasing Proof of the Spirit and Resolution with which Men in their Circumstances will act against their Oppressors, and how great advantages the King's Service may derive from employing those of approved Fidelity." Germain added that he had informed George III of the Loyalists' valor, and that the king was pleased with their "intrepid Behaviour."[26]

Major John André left the official commentary on the action to others, preferring instead to commemorate the Loyalists' success in verse. André's poem, *Cow-chace, in Three Cantos*, may not have been a literary masterpiece, but it was skillfully composed to ridicule Wayne and other American officers with an almost savage intensity. No opportunity for criticism was overlooked, no insult omitted. The poem opened with the following lines:

> To drive the kine, one summer's morn,/The TANNER took his way;/The calf shall rue that it unborn/The jumbling of that day.
> And *Wayne* descending Steers shall know,/and tauntingly deride,/And call to mind in ev'ry low/The tanning of his hide.
> Yet *Bergen* Cows still ruminate/Unconscious in the stall,/What mighty means were used to get/And lose them after all.[27]

The mentions of "tanner" and "tanning" were references to Wayne's prewar occupation. André went on to describe how the Americans arrived at their objective, "All wond'rous proud in arms" and waited while Wayne spoke: "When Wayne, who thought he'd time enough,/Thus speechified the whole." André then provided an imaginary oration from Wayne that included his intention to attack the "paltry Refugees," "level" their blockhouse, "And deal a horrid slaughter;/We'll drive the scoundrels to the devil,/And ravish wife and daughter." Yet while the attack was underway, Wayne allegedly said that he would go and round up the cattle, implying that he wanted no part of the fight. Collecting

---

25. Clinton, *American Rebellion*, 200-201.
26. Quoted in Burleigh, "Block House."
27. John André, *Cow-chace, in Three Cantos, Published on Occasion of the Rebel General Wayne's Attack of the Refugees Block-house on Hudson's River, on Friday the 21st of July, 1780* (New York: James Rivington, 1780), 3.

cows, André had Wayne declare, was "The serious operation" while the battle with the Loyalists was "only demonstration."[28]

In addition, André jabbed American Maj. Gen. William Alexander, who claimed to be a Scottish nobleman and preferred to be called Lord Stirling. It was a bizarre affectation for someone fighting to overthrow monarchical rule, and André wrote "Let none uncandidly infer,/That *Stirling* wanted spunk,/The self-made Peer had sure been there,/But that the Peer was drunk." Although there is no evidence to suggest that Major Henry "Light Horse Harry" Lee participated in the operation, André could not resist the chance to lampoon him as well, writing that the battle at the blockhouse raged "Whilst valiant *Lee*, with courage wild,/Most bravely did oppose/The tears of woman and of child,/Who begg'd he'd leave the cows." Wayne, according to André, did not even bother with the cattle roundup. Instead, he fell "a prey to female charms,/His soul took more delight in." As a result, "So *Roman Anthony*, they say,/Disgrac'd th'imperial banner,/And for a gipsy lost a day,/Like *Anthony* the TANNER."[29]

As "The mighty *Lee*" stood in his stirrups "And drove the terror-smitten cows," the troops who had attacked the blockhouse came fleeing down the road in panic, running all the way to New Bridge. André claimed that Wayne had lost his horse, which carried the general's "military speeches" and "corn-stalk whisky for his grog." In the final stanza, intended as sarcasm but incredibly prophetic, André chided that "I tremble" if Wayne "Should ever catch the poet."[30]

Wayne's biographer Paul David Nelson observed that André's poem was "widely read by both British and Americans, and General Wayne suffered not a few pangs of indignity" as a result. However, though it was not Wayne who captured him, on September 23 (ironically the same day that the last portion of *Cow-chace* was published), André was taken prisoner by American militia as he was returning from West Point; he had gone there to confer with Benedict Arnold regarding the latter's plan to hand over that post to the British. André was hanged as a spy on October 2.[31]

Wayne's reputation survived the defeat at Bull's Ferry and the poetic insults André had hurled at him, and he continued to earn fame for his military exploits. His opponents, the defenders of the blockhouse, were largely forgotten. Captain Ward became a major and was awarded a

---

28. Ibid., 4, 5, 6.
29. Ibid., 8, 12, 13, 15.
30. Ibid., 15-17, 18.
31. Nelson, *Anthony Wayne*, 111.

pension by the British government after the war, and nearly twenty of his militiamen who had participated in the battle received land grants in Canada and settled there after the British evacuated New York.[32] Although the outcome of the engagement did not affect the future course of the war, the battle at Bull's Ferry deserves attention as one of the most fascinating David-versus-Goliath-type incidents of the Revolution.

32. Burleigh, "Block House."

Two Hurricanes One Week Apart in 1780

❧ BOB RUPPERT ❧

The most common storm that the British navy and army encountered at sea and on land during the American War of Independence was the nor'easter.

Nor'easters usually develop in the latitudes between Georgia and New Jersey within 100 miles east or west of the East Coast. These storms Progress generally northeastward and typically attain maximum intensity near New England and the Maritime Provinces of Canada. They nearly always bring precipitation in the form of heavy rain or snow, as well as winds of gale force, rough seas, and occasionally, coastal flooding.... During winter the polar jet stream transports cold Arctic air southward across the plains of Canada and the United States, then eastward toward the Atlantic Ocean where warm air from the Gulf of Mexico and the Atlantic try to move northward. The warm waters of the Gulf Stream help keep the coastal waters relatively mild during the winter, which in turn helps warm the cold winter air over the water. This difference in temperature between the warm air over the water and the cold Artic Air over the land is the fuel that feeds the nor'easter.[1]

A nor'easter probably played a role in General Clinton's voyage from New York to Charleston (January–June of 1776), the evacuation of Brooklyn Heights (August 29, 1776), the Battle of Newport (August 9, 1778), and General Clinton's second voyage from New York to Charleston (December 26, 1779–February 1, 1780). However, none of these storms came close to what occurred in the Caribbean in October 1780 when two hurricanes struck almost all of the islands, one week

---

1. "What is a Noreaster," in the Winter Resources of the Safety National Program, National Weather Service, and Atmosphere Administration.

apart. The first struck Jamaica, Cuba, and the Bahamas and the second struck the smaller islands, from Barbados to Puerto Rico.

SAVANNA-LA-MAR HURRICANE

Jamaica was the home to half of the British fleet in the Caribbean. The fleet, moored at Port Royal Harbor and Montego Bay, was under the command of Vice-Admiral Sir Peter Parker. It was his fleet that would be battered by the first hurricane.[2] On the morning of October 3, the weather at the town of Savanna-la-Mar on the island of Jamaica was clear with a slight breeze; by midday everything changed. According to Governor Colonel John Darling,

> The sky all of a sudden became very much overcast, an uncommon elevation of the sea immediately followed. Whilst the unhappy settlers ... were observing this extraordinary phenomenon, the sea broke suddenly in upon the town, and on its retreat swept everything away with it, so as not to leave the smallest vestige of Man, Beast or House behind.[3]

In clergyman George Wilson Bridges' account,

> Not a tree, or bush, or cane was to be seen: Universal desolation prevailed, and the wretched victims of violated nature, who would obtain no such shelter, and who had no time to fly to the protecting rocks, were either crushed beneath the falling ruins, or swept away, and never heard from anymore.[4]

The town and surrounding plantations were completely destroyed. In the town of Lucea, 20 miles to the north 400 people were killed. The water washed away all but two houses and all of the trees. Still further north in the town at Montego Bay, an additional 360 people were killed. Two ships that were outside of Port Royal harbor and Montego Bay disappeared in the storm without a trace. They were the 20-gun *Scarborough* and the 10-gun *Victor*.

On October 4, the hurricane moved on to the island of Cuba. The strong winds caused the 14-gun *Barbadoes* to founder. On the 5, the 44-gun *Phoenix* was wrecked off the coast of Cape Cruz, Cuba just before it would have foundered, killing two hundred of her crew.[5]

---

2. This was a hurricane that was born in the Gulf of Mexico rather than near the Cape Verde Islands off the coast of Africa.
3. "Hurricane of 1780," old.jamaica-gleaner.com/pages/history/story008.html.
4. Kerry A. Emanuel, *Divine Wind – The History and Science of Hurricanes* (New York: Oxford University Press, 2005), 63-4.
5. In sailing terms, wrecked means the ship's hull lacked integrity, and foundered means took on water and sank. T. Southey, *The Chronological History of the West Indies* (London: Longman, Rees, Orme, Brown and Green, 1827), 2:471.

Just before the arrival of the hurricane, Parker ordered Rear-Admiral Joshua Rowley and his squadron to escort some merchant ships part of the way to Europe. On October 6, as they were about to leave the waters of the Caribbean, the front of the hurricane overtook the squadron near the city of San Domingo. The 74-gun *Thunderer* foundered and her entire crew was lost; the 64-gun *Stirling Castle* was wrecked on the coast and all but 50 of her crew were lost. The 74-gun Ships of the Line, *Berwick, Grafton, Hector, Ruby, Trident* and the *Bristol*, lost most of their masts and riggings. Four were forced to throw some of their cannons and carronades overboard to stabilize their ships.[6]

SAN CALIXTO II HURRICANE

Unlike the first hurricane, this one began, as most Caribbean hurricanes do, off the west coast of Africa between the Tropic of Cancer and the Equator in the Atlantic Ocean. The combination of trans-Atlantic currents and winds blow the storm east to west and ultimately become the prevailing winds in the Caribbean. Using today's terms, a hurricane starts out as a tropical disturbance then develops into a tropical depression,[7] followed by tropical storm,[8] and finally a hurricane.[9] In the southeastern portion of the Caribbean is a series of islands starting with Tobago that extend northward in an arc formation to the island of Puerto Rico. The eastern most island in the series, 153 miles north of Tobago, is Barbados. It was here that the hurricane landed first.

On October 9, winds began steadily to increase in the morning; in the afternoon ships in Bridgetown's Carlisle Bay began to break their moorings; and by early evening winds were nearing full force. Dr. Gilbert Blane in a letter to his friend, Dr. William Hunter, claimed that the force of wind "was thought to be at its greatest at midnight... A ship was driven on shore against one of the buildings of the Naval Hospital, which by this shock, and by impetuosity of the wind and sea, was entirely destroyed and swept away."[10] All of the houses and forts

---

6. "Log of the HMS *Berwick*," in William Reid, *An Attempt to Develop the Law of Storms by Means of Facts* (London: John Weale, 1838), 298-99; "Log of the HMS *Grafton*," ibid., 296; "Log of the HMS *Hector*," ibid., 302-03; "Log of the HMS *Ruby*," ibid., 306; and "Log of the HMS *Trident*," ibid., 297.
7. A tropical depression rotates around a central vortex and winds reach thirty-eight miles per hour.
8. A tropical storm exists when the central vortex starts to become the eye' and the winds range between thirty-nine and seventy-three miles per hour.
9. A hurricane is declared when the eye is easily recognizable and the winds reach seventy-four or more miles per hour.
10. Alfred Thayer Mahan, *The Major Operations of the Navies in the War of American Independence* (Boston: Little, Brown and Company, 1913), 319.

A contemporary etching of the *Egmont* dismasted in the Great Hurricane, October 11, 1780, near the island of St Lucia. (*British Museum*)

in/around the town and nine out of thirteen churches, chapels, and meetinghouses were destroyed. The Barbados Mercury reported that almost all of the plantations—that is, buildings, sugar mills, and fields—were washed away. In the words of Major General Vaughn, Commander in Chief of His Majesty's Royal Forces in the Leeward Islands,

> The strongest colours could not paint . . . the miseries of the inhabitants: on the one hand, the ground covered with mangled bodies of their friends and relations, and on the other, reputable families, wandering through the ruins, seeking for food and shelter: in short, imagination can form but a faint idea of the horrors of this dreadful scene.[11]

According to Major -General Cunningham, the Governor of Barbados,

> a twelve-pounder gun[12] was carried from the south to the north battery, a distance of 140 yards. . . . The Wind forced its way into every part of the Government House, and tore off most of the roof, though the walls were three feet thick, and doors and windows had been well barricaded.[13]

---

11. I. Kimber & E. Kimber, *The London Magazine, or Gentleman's Monthly Intelligencer* (London: 1780), 49:622-23.
12. It weighed 1,380 lbs.
13. Wayne Neely, *The Great Hurricane of 1780* (Bloomington, IN: iUniverse, 2012), 146, 188.

The smaller ships, i.e. sloops, brigs, etc., bore the brunt of the storm. The *Happy Return* was blown out of Carlisle Bay and foundered upon trying to return, the *Mary & Isabella* sank outside of the Bay, the 20-gun storeship, *Britannia*, was blown out of the Bay and was never seen again, and the *Edward*, like the *Happy Return*, was blown out of the Bay and foundered upon trying to reenter the shallows. The longest distance a ship was blown must/ go to the *Albemarle*. Early in the morning on the October 10, the ship was driven by the winds out of Carlisle Bay. The next time she was heard of was on the 15th. The damaged frigate arrived in English Harbor on the island of Antigua, 308 miles away.[14] The only ship that was damaged and arrived in a port even farther away was the *Egmont*. She was outside the Grand Cul-de-Sac when she was struck by the hurricane; it was not until January 4 that she was reported sighted, laying in a bay on the island of Puerto Rico, 477 miles away.[15]

On the morning of October 10, the hurricane moved on to the island of St. Lucia, the home of the other half of the British fleet in the Caribbean. The fleet, moored at the Grand Cul-de-Sac in Port Castries and Gros Islet Bay, was under the command of Admiral George Rodney, however, when Rodney sailed north to New York in late August, he turned command of the fleet over Commodore William Hotham.

The hurricane made landfall around 6:00 am. Six ships, moored either in the Grand Cul-de-Sac or Gros Islet Bay before the hurricane struck, either foundered or were wrecked. They were the 42-gun *Blanche*, the 14-gun *Chameleon*, the 18-gun *Beaver's Prize* (near Vieux, St. Lucia), the 74-gun *Cornwall*, the 24-gun *Deal Castle* and the 14-gun *St. Vincent*. Three Ships of the Line patrolled the entrance to the Grand Cul-de-Sac—the 74-gun *Montagu*, the 74-gun *Egmont*, and the 74-gun *Ajax*. Three more were anchored at their moorings and then forced out to sea were the 32-gun *Alcmene*, the 32-gun *Amazon* and the 74-gun *Vengeance*. All six suffered severe damage to their masts and riggings.[16] The 74-gun *Conqueror*, which had sailed for Jamaica to col-

---

14. William Reid. "Journal of the Proceedings of the HMS *Albemarle*," *An Attempt to Develop the Law of Storms*, 322-27.
15. "From John Laforey, Commissioner of the Navy at the Leeward Islands, January 4, 1781," *Letter-books and Order-books of George, Lord Rodney, Admiral of the White, 1780-1782* (New York: New York Historical Society, 1932), 133.
16. "Letter to Mr. Stephens from Admiral Hotham, October 23, 1780," *The Remembrancer or, Impartial Repository of Public Events for the Year of 1781* (London: Almon and Debrett, 1780), 11:66; "Letter from Rear-Admiral Sir Peter Parker to Mr. Stephens," November 6, 1780," ibid., 11:80; "Letter to Admiral Hotham from Captain William Clement Finch, October 23, 1780," ibid., 11:67.

lect a convoy, took three months to return to the Grand Cul-de-Sac; she had lost her mainmast and one hundred men had to bale water from below every day because her pumps were not operational. The 28-gun *Andromeda* was cruising on the east side of Martinique with the 28-gun *Laurel* and the 44-gun *Endymion*. The *Andromeda* was wrecked eighteen miles east of Martinique, the *Laurel* was wrecked along the coast of Martinique and the *Endymion* lost all of her masts but found a way to reach Port Royal on October 29.[17]

Early on the 11th, the hurricane moved onto the island of Martinique, the home of the French fleet in the Caribbean. It passed the island of Dominica on the 12th, and then struck Guadeloupe, St. Kitts and St. Eustatius before reaching Puerto Rico. The Mona Passage is a body of water that lies between the island of Puerto Rico and the island of Hispaniola (the island shared by Haiti and the Dominican Republic). Two of the last ships to be affected by the hurricane, the *Ulysses* and the *Pomona*, were sailing in the passage when the hurricane arrived. Both suffered damaged to their masts.

On November 14, Admiral Rodney, aboard his ship, the 90-gun *Sandwich*, set sail with a large squadron from New York for the Caribbean. Two days after his departure, his squadron was caught by "a Violent Gale of Wind," in his words, "which continued for forty-eight hours, dispersed the whole, and I greatly fear has occasion'd very great damage to many of His Majesty's Ships."[18] He had left New York with twelve ships but when he arrived in Barbados on December 5, only two were still with him. They were the 74-gun *Triumph* and the 64-gun *Intrepid*. Only two of his ships, the 74-gun *Terrible* and the 28-gun *Cyclops*, was already moored in Carlisle Bay. It is likely that the "Gale of Wind" that had separated all of the other ships was a nor'easter. When Rodney reached Barbados on December 5, he could not believe what he saw,

> It is impossible to express the Dreadful scene it has occasion'd at Barbados and the Condition of the miserable inhabitants; nothing but ocular demonstration could have convinced me it was possible for Wind to have caused so total a destruction of an Island remarkable for its numerous and well-built Habitations ... I am convinc'd the whole Face of the Country appears an entire ruin and the most Beautiful Island in the World has the appearance of a County laid waste by Fire, and

---

17. "The Marine List," *New Lloyd's List* No. 1228 (December 29, 1780).
18. "To Philip Stephens, Secretary of the Admiralty, December 10, 1780," *Letter-books and Order-books of George, Lord Rodney*, 90.

Sword... Not one single Battery in the whole Island but what has been totally destroy'd.[19]

That same day, he also wrote to his wife,

> The strongest buildings and the whole of the houses, most of which were of stone, and remarkable for their solidity, gave way to the fury of the wind, and were torn up to their foundation; all the forts destroyed.
> ... More than six thousand persons perished, and all the inhabitants are entirely ruined.[20]

Over the course of the next two weeks, the ships of his scattered squadron began to appear in British ports throughout the Caribbean. The ships were the 74-gun *Resolution*, the 74-gun *Alcide*, the 74-gun *Shrewsbury*, the 74-gun *Torbay*, the 28-gun *Boreas*, the 28-gun *Triton* dragged themselves into the closest British ports in the Caribbean. Each had suffered extensive damage to their masts.[21] Only one ship foundered; it was the 28-gun *Shark*.

On December 10, Rodney wrote to the Admiralty explaining what had transpired on Barbados.

Nowhere in the letter does it appear that he was aware that a hurricane had also landed on Jamaica.

> I shall... acquaint Sir Peter Parker of the Crippled Condition not only of great part of the Squadron I brought with me from America, but also of those I left under Commodore Hotham who escaped the Hurricane, but remain unserviceable till Masts and Rigging can be procured to refit them... I shall point out to him the necessity of his sending me a large reinforcement of Ships, and hope Sir Peter Parker will be convinced... that it is his duty without a Moments delay to hasten the Reinforcements I shall demand.[22]

On the 22, he wrote to Rear-Admiral Sir Samuel Hood,

> The Situation of His Majesty's Affairs in this Part of the World requiring your speedy Ju[n]ction with me at St. Lucia, I have not a Doubt but upon the Receipt of this Letter you will join me with all possible Dispatch and bring with you all Store Ships and Victualers, notwithstanding their having been order'd to any other part of the World.[23]

---

19. "To Philip Stevens, Secretary of the Admiralty, December 10, 1780," ibid., 91.
20. "To Lady Rodney, December 10, 1780," in William Reid, *An Attempt to Develop the Law of Storms*, 319.
21. *Letter-books and Order-books of George, Lord Rodney*, 97-8.
22. "To Philip Stevens, Secretary of the Admiralty, December 10, 1780," ibid., 93.
23. "To Rear-Admiral Sir Samuel Hood, December 22, 1780," ibid., 105.

And on the 25th, he wrote to Captain John Laforey, Commissioner of the Navy for the Leeward Islands,

> The Terrible Effects of the Hurricane[s] in October and the hard Gale of Wind my Squadron experienced on the Coast of America has so dismantled my Line of Battle Ships, that only nine of them will be capable of going to sea, till Sir Samuel Hood arrives with the Store Ships from England.[24]

Laforey was the officer in charge of overseeing all ship repairs. For the next three months he was the most important British officer in the Caribbean.

Once the second hurricane departed the Caribbean, Rodney, Hotham and Parker had to repair the British fleet. There were no docking facilities in any of the big ports, underwater damage could not be repaired because there were no drydocks and stores were in high demand. Rodney informed the Admiralty in England that no stores could be found in the Caribbean; they would have to be sent from England or New York. On January 4, 1781 he received some good news.

> The Navy Board are taking the utmost Care to replace the Loss of Masts and Stores occasioned by the late dreadful Hurricane at the Leeward Islands, the *Union* of 300 Tons being already loaded at Spithead, and the *King George* of 1150 Tons and the *Flora* of 700 now taking in their Cargoes at Wolwich for that Purpose.[25]

On January 7, he received even better news. Rear-Admiral Sir Samuel Hood had arrived in the Caribbean with eight ships of the line and a convoy of supply ships and victualers. With four warships already refitted and the nine that were "capable of going to sea," Rodney now had a fleet of twenty-one ships of the line. This was important because he had recently been informed that the Count D'Estaing had just arrived from France with a fleet of twenty-two ships of the line.

It would take the British fleet in the Caribbean another four to five months before things were even close to what they were like before the hurricanes. Some ships had to be sent back to England for repair, while others were sent to the naval yard in New York; supplies and food were constantly needed; French ships ended up in British ports and vice versa. This meant prisoners of war and captured ships had to be ex-

---

24. "To Captain John Laforey, Commissioner of the Navy at the Leeward Islands from Admiral Rodney," ibid., 111.
25. "To Philip Stevens, Secretary of the Admiralty, January 4, 1781," ibid., 139; in the same letter Rodney was informed that two of Hotham's ships, *Egmont* and *Endymion*, had arrived at Port Royal on October 28 and 29.

changed; more sailors need to be procured; naval hospitals had to be built; ships had to be redistributed between New York, Rhode Island, the Delaware River, Chesapeake Bay and the Caribbean; and a war still had to be fought.

POSTSCRIPT

There were additional consequences of the hurricane described in this article: damage to the islands of St. Kitts and St. Eustatius, damage to Capt. Philip Affleck's squadron that patrolled the Chesapeake, and severe damage to the French fleet at Martinique.

To date, the San Calixto II Hurricane of 1780 has been considered the deadliest storm of all time; not the biggest, not the strongest and not the most expensive, but the deadliest. The exact number of deaths has been difficult to determine, but the numbers that are frequently tossed about claim the Hurricane took between 22,000 and 27,000 lives. This number seems low when one looks at the number of deaths each island claims in their records.

Top Ten Weather Interventions

DON N. HAGIST

"In war, as in medicine, natural causes not under our control, do much." Gen. Horatio Gates wrote this about the terrain that so heavily influenced his victory at Saratoga in 1777.

Another natural cause that heavily influenced events of the American Revolution was weather. Here are ten instances where unexpectedly uncooperative weather had a major effect on how a battle or a plan played out, where things might have gone very differently if the weather itself had been different. We didn't include predictable weather like the heat of summer or the onset of winter, only those instances where the weather did not cooperate with otherwise well-laid plans.

QUEBEC, DECEMBER 1775

Bad weather can help an attacking force achieve surprise. When the attackers are fatigued, however, and the attack is timed because of expiring enlistments, poor weather might favor the defenders instead. When it is well known that an attack is likely, the chances for success are even further diminished. When an American army attempted to storm the city of Quebec on the night of December 31, 1775, a snowstorm hindered more than helped. Winds and blinding snow probably made the nighttime advance much slower than it otherwise would have been, allowing the defenders, firing from secure sheltered positions, to stop the attackers in their tracks. Whether clear skies would have changed the outcome is questionable, but the attack on Quebec is first battle during the American Revolution where the weather was a memorable factor. According to one participant, "gloomy the prospect in this tremendous storm—snow not less than six feet deep, while yet a heavy darkness pervaded the earth almost to be felt."[1]

---

1. "Dr. Isaac Senter's Jornal," *March to Quebec*, Kenneth Roberts, ed. (Portland, ME: Down East, 1967), 233.

DORCHESTER HEIGHTS, MARCH 1776

By March 1776, the siege of Boston had been an eleven-month stalemate. Commanders on both sides knew that a bold move was required to change the situation, and the obvious place was Dorchester Heights, an eminence across the water to the south that overlooked the city and which was well within range of heavy cannons. Americans seized those heights on the night of March 4-5, 1776, and began building fortifications. Knowing that an American battery there would make the town untenable, the British immediately embarked nine battalions—nearly 5,000 men—to retake the position before it was made too strong to assault. But a sudden squall on March 5 made it too dangerous for the British boats to cross the harbor and effect a landing. By the time the weather cleared, the works had been strengthened enough to make an attack impossible. The weather prevented a major battle and left the British no choice but to abandon Boston. In the words of a British private soldier, "the wind blowing hard and it rained very heavy, so that it was Impossible for the troops to land on the intended place. For the two days and two nights we were on board, the storm lasted and the wind blew right a head. During that time the Enemy were hard at work."[2]

LONG ISLAND, AUGUST 1776

After the Battle of Long Island on August 27, 1776, George Washington's army was hemmed in on Brooklyn Heights. Although their fortifications were strong, their position was perilous; it was unlikely they could stand up to an assault by Gen. William Howe's army, once it had a day or two to recuperate and regroup after the long, arduous fight on the 27th. Washington decided to retreat, but with the British navy in control of the waters separating Long Island from the mainland, prospects of an unopposed withdrawal were slim. Their salvation was a thick fog on the night of August 29-30 that covered their careful, silent withdrawal to Manhattan. "What was our astonishment upon the morning of the 30th," wrote a British officer, "to find those stupendous works, which had been constructed with so much care and labour, and which were to have been destroyed with so much danger and expense, utterly abandoned and deserted by the poorest mean-spirited scoundrels that ever surely pretended to the dignity of Rebellion."[3]

---

2. Thomas Sullivan, 49th Regiment of Foot, in *From Redcoat to Rebel: the Thomas Sullivan Journal*, Joseph Lee Boyle, ed. (Bowie, MD: Heritage Books, 1997), 34.
3. Capt. James Murray, 57th Regiment of Foot, in Eric Robson, ed., *Letters from America 1773 to 1780* (New York: Barnes & Noble, no date (circa 1950)), 35-36.

WHITE PLAINS, OCTOBER 1776

The Battle of White Plains, New York raged on October 28, 1776, leaving the opposing armies bruised but the British victorious on Chatterton Hill. The American army took positions just a short way to the north and prepared for another assault that they knew was imminent. By October 31, the British were ready to advance, the Americans were anticipating the attack, but weather disrupted all of their plans. Heavy rains prevented a British advance, and the Americans took the opportunity to retreat still farther. Lt. William Carter of the 40th Regiment of Foot wrote, "Every necessary disposition was also made for attacking them on the morning of the 31st, but we were obliged to abandon the design, owing totally to the violent rain which fell during the preceding night and that morning."[4]

TRENTON, DECEMBER 1776

When General Washington proposed to attack the Hessian garrison at Trenton, New Jersey in December 1776, he knew that surprise was essential. His opponents were professional soldiers who had kept his army on the run for four months. With the American army on the brink of collapse, victory was imperative but not assured. Washington came up with a bold, well-conceived plan. A violent snowstorm on the night of December 25-26 almost derailed the attack by preventing two of three attacking forces from crossing the Delaware River. But it also served to ensure the element of surprise, and the attackers rapidly overwhelmed the Trenton garrison. In the words of a Hessian officer, "our weapons, because of the rain and snow, could no longer be fired, and the rebels fired on us from all the houses. There remained no other choice for us but to surrender."[5]

ATLANTIC OCEAN ON THE EASTERN SEABOARD, AUGUST 1777

Usually it is stormy weather that impedes military operations, but in the age of sailing ships, calm weather could also have an adverse effect. In mid-July 1777 British troops boarded ships in New York and sailed for the Chesapeake Bay to make a landing south of Philadelphia and advance on the city from the landward side. Once the city was taken, some troops could return to New York to cooperate with another army advancing from Canada to Albany. It was a sound plan, but a stretch

---

4. William Carter, 40th Regiment of Foot, *A Genuine Detail of the Several Engagements, Positions, and Movements of the Royal and American Armies, during the years 1775-1776* (London, 1784), 45.
5. Bruce E. Burgoyne, ed., *Enemy Views: The American Revolutionary War as Recorded by the Hessian Participants* (Bowie, MD: Heritage Books, 1996), 116.

of calm days while the fleet was at sea caused the voyage to take much longer than expected. The troops didn't land until the last week of August, and by the time they finally reached Philadelphia, the northern army was already in trouble at Saratoga. "The fleet made no progress this day," wrote a British army engineer at sea with the fleet on August 6.[6]

MALVERN, PENNSYLVANIA, SEPTEMBER 1777

Although the British won a tremendous victory at the Battle of Brandywine, they needed time to regroup after a long and arduous fight. The defeated American army also needed to regroup, and encamped less than a dozen miles away. When this disposition became clear, the British planned an attack on September 16, 1777, and the Americans girded for defense. The British army moved out in the morning, and their advanced elements soon met and defeated parties of American soldiers. Before a major battle developed, heavy rains thwarted the efforts of both sides, soaking ammunition, turning roads into mud, and causing the abortive engagement to be called the Battle of the Clouds. Recalled a British officer, "a most heavy Rain coming on frustrated the good Effects which were expected from this Capital Move & sav'd the Rebel Army from a more compleat Over throw than they had met with at Brandywine."[7]

RHODE ISLAND, AUGUST 1778

The major battle fought in Rhode Island on August 29, 1778 was nothing compared to the battle that everyone thought would happen, not on land but at sea. A powerful French fleet was cooperating with American land forces to besiege the British garrison in Newport. A large British fleet came to the garrison's relief, and the two naval lines of battle began maneuvering to get the best wind advantage. As the two fleets vied for tactical advantage before closing in to engage, a hurricane pressed upon them. Two days of mountainous seas scattered the ships, causing enough damage that both navies made for ports where repairs could be made—Boston for the French, New York for the British. The journal of the French warship *Engageante* recorded, "the wind blew from the NE with violence accompanied by continual rain. . . . This terrible gale had had no diminution."[8]

6. John Montresor, "The Montresor Journals," *Collections of the New York Historical Society* (New York: Printed for the Society, 1881), 434.

7. Anonymous British Journal, 1776–78, ms. no. 409, September 16, 1777, Sol Feinstone Manuscripts Collection, American Philosophical Society Library, Philadelphia.

8. *Naval Documents of the American Revolution* Volume 10, ed. Michael J. Crawford (Washington, DC: Government Printing Office, 2019), 806.

STONY POINT, JULY 1779

The dramatic American victory in storming the British fort at Stony Point on the Hudson River is well known. The midnight attack was well-planned and expertly executed, but was abetted by an often-overlooked contribution by the weather. The southern end of the fort's outer defenses, a line of abatis that extended into the river, was anchored by a well-armed gunboat. The American plan called for surprising and overwhelming this vessel in order to get around the defenses, perhaps the riskiest part of the entire operation. An unexpected rain squall forced the gunboat to leave her station and move farther out into the river; when the American attackers came during the night, they found the flank unprotected. "Had the Gun Boat been at her station, and the People in her Vigilant," testified a British officer at a court martial concerning the fort's capture, "I do not think it possible for a Column of Men to have waded thro' the water without being heard."[9]

YORKTOWN, OCTOBER 1781

Hemmed in by a joint American and French army and without support from the Royal Navy, the British forces at Yorktown, Virginia had one last chance to avoid capitulation. Like the Americans had done so many times during the war, they could escape during the night of October 16, crossing the York River to Gloucester Point, and then moving north to who knows where. Whether this gambit would have prolonged the war for hours or years will never be known, for a sudden and violent squall disrupted the operation. Out of options, Gen. Charles Cornwallis initiated surrender negotiations the following day. He wrote to his superior, "at this crucial moment the weather, from being moderate and calm, changed to a most violent storm of wind and rain and drove all the boats, some of which had troops on board, down the river. It was soon evident that the intended passage was impracticable."[10]

---

9. Testimony of Ensign Henry Hamilton, 17th Regiment of Foot, in Don Loprieno, *The Enterprise in Contemplation: the Midnight Assault of Stony Point* (Westminster, MD: Heritage Books, 2009), 141.
10. Charles Cornwallis to Henry Clinton, October 20, 1781, in Ian Saberton ed., *The Cornwallis Papers: The Campaigns of 1780 and 1781 in the Southern Theatre of the American Revolutionary War*, 6 vols (Uckfield: The Naval & Military Press Ltd, 2010), 6:127.

The Fruits of Victory: Loyalist Prisoners in the Aftermath of Kings Mountain

WILLIAM CALDWELL

The Battle of Kings Mountain was fought on October 7, 1780 in the upcountry of South Carolina near the border with North Carolina. As the gun smoke dissipated and Patriot officers rallied their men, they found themselves victorious and in possession of the mountain-top; but still in danger. British Gen. Charles, Lord Cornwallis and his army were only thirty-five miles to the east at Charlotte, North Carolina and the Patriots knew that the now-deceased British Major Patrick Ferguson had sent numerous requests for reinforcements over the week prior. The frontier Patriots still had a long way to go before they would return to their settlements in the foothills of the Blue Ridge Mountains and beyond in the Overmountain settlements. Their return journey seemed even more daunting due to the fact they were now burdened with roughly 700 Loyalist prisoners. What were they to do with so many prisoners? Where could they safely house these men away from British rescue? The fate of these 700 Loyalists began forming the next day as the Patriots started retracing the long trail homeward.

The morning of Sunday October 8, the weary Patriot soldiers awoke on the ridge of Kings Mountain. They had slept on the battlefield as best they could amid rain and the sounds of wounded men, and had been busy gathering captured supplies and guarding their prisoners. The elected Patriot leader, Colonel William Campbell of Virginia, recorded capturing sixty-eight Loyalist provincials (uniformed soldiers mostly from New York and New Jersey) and 648 Loyalist militia (local men from the Carolinas) for a total of 716 prisoners. 163 of the prisoners had injuries of varying severity. The Patriots gathered the captured equipment of the Loyalist army, disabled the muskets by removing the gun flints, and forced each prisoner to carry one, or sometimes two, of these captured weapons. Loyalist militia who were too wounded to travel were paroled by Patriot officers and left on the battlefield in the care of local people who had been drawn by the sounds of the previous day's fight. At 10:00 a.m. the long line of over 700 marching prisoners and roughly 900 mounted guards began retracing their steps to the west, towards the rest of the Patriot army who were coming from the Cowpens to reunite with them. Colonel Campbell remained on the battleground with a small force to bury the dead and destroy the remaining Loyalist supplies: three shallow mass graves (one for the Patriots, one for the Loyalist militia, and one for the Loyalist provincials) were dug and seventeen supply wagons were pulled over campfires to burn.

That first day of the return march covered twelve miles to a plantation on the east bank of the Broad River near Buffalo Creek. The Loyalist who owned the property is recorded in different sources as "Waldrop," "Waldron," or possibly "Fondren." Patriot Benjamin Sharp recorded that it was here they discovered a patch of sweet potatoes, and that "This was most fortunate for not one in fifty of us had tasted food for the last two days and nights."[1] This meager feast was supplemented when the rest of the Patriot army joined them from the Cowpens driving an unrecorded number of beef cattle. Campbell and his burial detail also reunited with the army here and joined in the needed food and rest. The next day, October 9, the march was delayed by the burial of Patriot Col. James Williams who was mortally wounded in the final moments of the fierce battle, making him the highest-ranking Patriot casualty.[2] The Patriots and their prisoners proceeded to march a few miles and camp was made further west along the banks of the Broad River. Here, the prisoners were finally allowed the first food they had received in two days: a single ear of corn.[3]

Come daylight on October 10, the march quickened to add distance between the Patriots and potential British pursuit. The journals of two Loyalist prisoners record a march of twenty miles, with camp made in

1. Lyman Draper, *King's Mountain and Its Heroes: History of the Battle of King's Mountain, October 7th, 1780, and the Events Which Led to It* (Cincinnati: Peter G. Thomson, 1881), 323.
2. James Williams is referred to here as "colonel" due to his service at that rank. His commission as brigadier general issued by the exiled Patriot government of South Carolina held little if any influence over his South Carolina comrades, and none over the North Carolinians and Virginians.
3. E. Alfred Jones, ed., *The Journal of Alexander Chesney, a South Carolina Loyalist in the Revolution and After* (Columbus: Ohio State University: 1921), 18.

a piece of woods "where we lay contented with our lot on the cold ground."[4] The hatred between Patriots and Loyalists was sometimes ferocious, but Campbell tried his best to control tempers. On October 11, he issued a general order asking his officers to help stop the "disorderly manner of slaughtering and disturbing the prisoners,"[5] threatening punishment to any abusive Patriot guards.

Other than the rare night camping in the woods, this army of starving men and horses tried to encamp at Loyalist farms to confiscate their produce and livestock, a tactic familiar to both sides in this bitter fighting. The night of Wednesday, October 11, the army camped at the plantation of "Colonel Walker" where a wooden pen, previously used by Patrick Ferguson to hold Patriot prisoners, was now used to hold the Loyalists.[6] At this sizable farm with assumedly plenty to eat, the army rested for one extra day. The Loyalist prisoner Doctor Uzal Johnson wrote that he and the other captured officers "had the mortification to see our baggage divided to the different corps."[7] Fellow prisoner Lt. Anthony Allaire recorded that this division of their personal goods was especially insulting as "they had promised on their word we should have it all."[8] Further insult was added when a change of clothes was given to the prisoner officers: five dirty and torn shirts for nine men to share.

As the American frontiersmen continued moving their prisoners northward away from British reinforcements, Continental Army leadership was trying to figure out what to do with this many captured enemy combatants. Continental Gen. Horatio Gates attempted to order Virginia Col. William Preston to take command of the prisoners and build barracks for them at his base at Fort Chiswell in southern Virginia. Preston flatly refused, citing that his men were already stretched too thin guarding forts and lead mines against local Loyalist sabotage and the potential of an attack from British-allied Cherokee warriors. Preston claimed to be incapable of taking on any more duties but suggested Boutetourt County, further up the Shenandoah Valley, would be a safer location to house this many prisoners.[9] Colonel Campbell suggested to General Gates that the Loyalist militiamen be drafted

---

4. Anthony Allaire, "Diary of Lieut. Anthony Allaire, of Ferguson's Corps, Memorandum of Occurrences During the Campaign of 1780," in Draper, *Kings Mountain and Its Heroes*, 493.
5. Draper, *King's Mountain and Its Heroes*, 326.
6. Ibid., 327.
7. Bobby Moss, ed., *Uzal Johnson, Loyalist: Revolutionary War Diary of Surgeon to Ferguson's Command* (Blacksburg, SC: Scotia Hibernia Press, 2000), 75.
8. Allaire, "Diary of Lieut. Anthony Allaire," 505.
9. Draper, *King's Mountain and Its Heroes*, 358.

into the Continental Army in the north under George Washington. The Continental Army was always in need of men, and the great distance from any friends or neighbors would keep these southern Loyalists from being able to easily desert. Gates was unsure of what action to take and sent these suggestions to the Continental Congress to let them decide the fate of the prisoners.

While Campbell awaited directions from Gates, he fought to hold his army together as they marched further into North Carolina. Patriot desertion rampantly increased, making the prisoner-to-guard ratio dangerously close. The exhausted and starving Patriots were reported to rob any homes they passed regardless of the occupants' allegiance. Campbell described it as "leaving our friends, I believe, in a worse situation than the enemy would have done."[10] He ordered that no discharges be issued to soldiers until their prisoners were safely secured.

The fate of some Loyalist prisoners was decided by their captors. On October 14, after marching to the Loyalist plantation of wounded prisoner Aaron Bickerstaff (or Biggerstaff), a court martial was formed of twelve Patriot officers, including at least three magistrates. During the rainy night of October 14 into the pre-dawn morning of October 15, charges and testimonies were heard against some of the Loyalist prisoners. Samuel Chambers and James Crawford, two former Patriots who had deserted and warned Ferguson of the approaching Patriot Overmountain Men, were pardoned by Patriot Col. John Sevier: Chambers was his old friend and neighbor, and it was argued that Crawford was young and had been easily misled. Thirty-six Loyalists were condemned to death on counts of "breaking open houses, killing the men, turning the women and children out of doors, and burning the houses."[11] These described actions were familiar to many of the onlooking Patriots, being both victims and perpetrators of similar acts in the brutal civil war that raged in the southern backcountry. Loyalist accounts of the trial testified that the condemned were hanged "for their Loyalty to their Sovereign. They died like Romans, saying they died for their King and his Laws."[12] One of the condemned men, Isaac Baldwin, escaped from the gallows when his younger brother feigned being distraught with grief and was permitted to hug his brother one last time. During their embrace, the younger Baldwin pulled out a hidden knife, slashed his brother's restraints, and the two boys escaped through the surprised crowd into the dark woods. By 2 a.m., nine of the con-

10. Ibid., 532.
11. Ibid., 544.
12. Allaire, "Diary of Lieut. Anthony Allaire," 511.

demned had been hanged from a large tree outside the Bickerstaff home: Ambrose Mills, Mr. Lafferty, Walter Gilkey, James Chitwood, Mr. Grimes, Robert Wilson, John McFall, John Bibby, and Augustine Hobbs. One Patriot soldier, Paddy Carr from Georgia, was noted to have gestured to the tree limbs decorated with executed Loyalists and remarked that "Would to God every tree in the Wilderness bore such fruit as that."[13] Loyalist prisoner Dr. Uzal Johnson noted how the melancholy scene was worsened by the rain and the presence of the wives and daughters of some of the condemned, who were following behind the army in hopes of their loved ones being released. Johnson noted that "Mrs. Mills, with a Young child in her Arms, set out all Night in the Rain with her Husband's Corpse, and not even a Blanket to cover her from the inclemency of the Weather."[14] The executions ceased in the early morning hours and the army immediately resumed its march north towards the Catawba River.[15] Recent rains had begun to raise the rivers, and time was running out before any further escape northward would be impossible. The bodies of the nine executed Loyalists were left in the tree outside Mrs. Bickerstaff's home for her to bury.

The sunrise of October 15 brought no relief from the pouring rain. For the next eighteen hours, guards and prisoners alike slogged through thirty-two muddy miles, determined to cross the Catawba River before it flooded. Loyalist accounts describe making this march without having bread or meat for two days, but being offered the chance to purchase from the guards one ear of "Indian corn" for thirty-five Continental dollars, or forty dollars for a drink of water.[16] Due to the distraction of fatigue and hunger, poor visibility caused by rain, and desperation among the Loyalists as they headed deeper into Patriot territory, nearly 100 prisoners escaped during that one day's march of October 15. In the darkness of 10 p.m., the prisoners were forced to ford the cold chest-deep waters of the swelling Catawba River to arrive

13. Draper, *King's Mountain and Its Heroes*, 341.
14. Moss., *Uzal Johnson*, 76.
15. Several theories attempt to explain why only nine of the condemned were executed and the other men reprieved. One theory suggests that Mrs. Bickerstaff came to Patriot Col. Isaac Shelby requesting a stop to the executions at her home. Another theory says that the hangings were in retaliation for the execution of Patriots who had violated their paroles and been captured at Augusta, Georgia; after an equal number of Loyalist prisoners had been executed, the trial leaders felt vengeance had been satisfied. Yet another theory says one of the pardoned prisoners told Isaac Shelby that the feared British officer Banastre Tarleton and his British Legion were close on their trail and soon to arrive, and he wanted to warn the Patriots in gratitude for being pardoned.
16. Draper, *King's Mountain and Its Heroes*, 346.

at Quaker Meadows, home of Patriot leaders Charles and Joseph McDowell. Here the Patriot army finally found a breath of relief with the flooding river guarding them from the phantom of any pursuing British cavalry. With the prisoners now secured from immediate rescue, the Patriot army began to disband: Edward Lacey and his men returned to South Carolina, Isaac Shelby and John Sevier's Overmountain Men recrossed the Blue Ridge Mountains, and William Campbell's infantry began their long walk back to Virginia. Remaining to guard the prisoners were the North Carolinians under Joseph Winston, Benjamin Cleveland, and Joseph McDowell, and William Campbell with his mounted Virginians. These guards barely outnumbered the approximately 500 prisoners who remained, but they were determined to see their mission completed. At daybreak, the army pushed northeast deeper into North Carolina.

Over the next several days, the pace of the march slowed as the threat of British rescue faded away. Fear of their unknown fate forced some prisoners to risk escaping. Three Loyalists made a dash for the woods on October 17; two escaped while their third comrade was wounded by a guard and hanged the next morning.[17] News of the decisive action at Kings Mountain spread quickly, and the army with its prisoners drew attention from both local Patriots and Loyalists. Small groups of Patriot militia arrived to join the army and assisted escorting the prisoners. On October 21 relief was provided to the prisoners by some local Loyalist women who brought them "butter, milk, honey, and many other necessaries of life."[18] Some Loyalist officers were allowed to stay in a local tavern with their guards, where they met two Continental Army officers who were traveling through the area. The Continental officers observed the soiled, exhausted, and starved condition of the prisoners, and as one Loyalist recorded, they "pitied our misfortune in falling into the hands of their militia."[19]

October 23 began a new chapter in the struggles of the remaining Loyalist prisoners. The now-roughly 300 prisoners and their Patriot guards arrived at Bethabara, North Carolina, a settlement of the Moravian Church, or the United Brethren. The town diary notes that upon arrival, the prisoners were "placed like cattle in a small fenced off space, where they spent nineteen days and nights, and nearly starved."[20] The army's occupation of the Moravian towns was such a drain on resources

17. Allaire, "Diary of Lieut. Anthony Allaire," 511.
18. Ibid., 511.
19. Ibid., 512.
20. Adelaide Fries, ed., *Records of the Moravians in North Carolina* Volume IV: 1780-1783 (Raleigh, NC: Edward's and Broughton Print Co., 1930).

that aid was needed from the neighboring town of Salem: bread, flour, produce, oxen, and additional manpower were all sent from neighboring farms to assist in feeding this unannounced swarm of starving men and horses. While the Moravians were pacifists, the Patriots did not lower their guard and remained violent and aggressive towards the prisoners. The first night in town saw an armed Patriot storm into the quarters of the Loyalist officers, demanding their bed and refusing to leave until his commanders forced the man out. A snide comment to a Patriot guard almost caused one prisoner to be hanged, but he was able to escape before his execution date. Loyalist Dr. Johnson noted the practice of Patriot officers to cut the prisoners with their swords. While tending the wounds of one of the attacked prisoners, Dr. Johnson was himself assaulted by Patriot Col. Benjamin Cleveland. One social event allowed to the prisoners was when they were forced to attend a large church service in the woods near town, held in honor of the recent Patriot victory at Kings Mountain. As one Loyalist officer wrote, "we heard a Presbyterian sermon, truly adapted to their principles and the times; or rather, stuffed as full of Republicanism as their camp is of horse thieves."[21]

While imprisoned at Bethabara, the number of prisoners dwindled rapidly. Several Loyalists were able to escape and began their long journey to British lines in South Carolina, including Provincials Lt. Anthony Allaire and Dr. Uzal Johnson. Many of the prisoner losses were from Patriot North Carolina civil authorities claiming jurisdiction over North Carolina Loyalists and extraditing them for trial. Other Loyalists were allowed to join the Patriot militia or Continental Army for a period of service varying from several months to two years. One of the only mentions of laundry is from the Moravian diary about one of these groups of new Continental Army recruits: they were allowed enough time to get their clothes cleaned before reporting for service with the Patriot army.

As October rolled into November, the weather turned cold and frost began to cover the field where the Loyalist prisoners were held. Rumors spread among the prisoners that they would be marched over the Blue Ridge Mountains or into the Shenandoah Valley of Virginia, where other British prisoners of war were confined. The thought of another hard, cold, mountainous march drove many Loyalists to desperation. Loyalist Dr. Johnson noted on November 8 that "we received orders to be ready to March. The Militia had most of them enlisted in the Continental service rather than suffer Death by Inches starving with cold

---

21. Allaire, "Diary of Lieut. Anthony Allaire," 512.

and hunger."[22] He further noted the next day, "This morning near Twenty of the soldiers made their escape, being apprehensive of a disagorable March over the Mountains."[23] Filled with fears of mountain marches and hard labor in Patriot lead mines, the remaining prisoners were marched out of Bethabara on November 10, 1780 towards the jail in Salisbury, North Carolina. The few remaining Loyalist officers were led to Salem, North Carolina, where they remained for ten days before heading towards the camp of the Continental Army further northeast in Hillsborough, North Carolina.

Stories of the harsh treatment of the Loyalist prisoners reached General Cornwallis. He wrote to Continental Gen. William Smallwood in November 1780 complaining particularly of the executions at Bickerstaff's. Cornwallis expressed his willingness to exchange captured Patriot militiamen to liberate the Loyalist survivors of Kings Mountain, but no exchange agreement was reached. On November 20, the Continental Congress ordered Virginia Governor Thomas Jefferson to prepare places to receive the Loyalists wherever he saw fit. On November 23, the remaining prisoners arrived at the Continental Army camp in Hillsborough, North Carolina where Gen. Horatio Gates was angered by the result: only 130 prisoners remained of the initial 700. When Gen. Nathanael Greene took command of the Southern Continental Army in December, he was likewise angered by the poor management of the Loyalist prisoners: Cornwallis had been willing to discuss exchange, with British prison ships in Charleston harbor filled with American prisoners, but any chance to redeem a significant number of them had been wasted. General Greene ordered the Salisbury jail better suited to house the remaining Loyalist prisoners with a picketed log wall constructed around the jail and huts built within the compound. As winter ushered in the year 1781, Patriot spies reported that nearly 200 Loyalist prisoner draftees who had joined the Continental Army had already deserted back to the British. This is supported by the research of Dr. Bobby Moss in his work "The Loyalists at Kings Mountain," with numerous Loyalist veterans of Kings Mountain later claiming to have served in the 1781 defense of other British posts including the backcountry fort at Ninety-Six, South Carolina and others throughout the Charleston area. Due to the lack of guards, the civil authorities being allowed to claim jurisdiction, and the practice of allowing the prisoners to join Patriot service, only sixty Loyalist prisoners remained by January 1781 of the original 713 who had surrendered on

---

22. Moss., *Uzal Johnson*, 83.
23. Ibid., 84.

October 7, 1780.[24] Continental Col. Henry Lee summarized the opinion of many Continental officers regarding the handling of these prisoners when in January 1781 he wrote, "The North Carolina government has in a great degree baffled the fruits of victory."[25]

The Patriot victory at Kings Mountain and the accomplishments of the Overmountain Men sent shockwaves through the Southern Campaign of the American Revolution, but many Patriot army leaders felt the results fell short of what could have been accomplished. The escape of hundreds of Loyalist prisoners and their return to British service made some Continental officers view Kings Mountain not so much as a deadly blow to the British campaign in the Carolinas, but only as a delay that temporarily slowed British progress. General Cornwallis was forced to abandon his plan to invade North Carolina upon hearing of the Patriot victory, but after resting at winter quarters in Winnsboro, South Carolina and being reinforced with British regulars, Spring 1781 found Cornwallis prepared for another season of campaigning. But notably absent from this 1781 campaign were large numbers of local Loyalists. Kings Mountain and the devastation of the Loyalist ranks may have seemed miniscule on the maps of Continental Army generals, but along the banks of the Broad, Saluda, Catawba, and Yadkin Rivers, the impact was felt loud and clear. Never again would local Loyalists turn out to support the British army in large enough numbers to sway the loyalty of entire districts in the western backcountry. For the next twenty-six months until the British evacuated the southern states, Loyalist militia were relegated to supporting roles in small garrisons and raiding parties. For the rest of the war, the shadow of Overmountain Patriots haunted the plans of British commanders who sought to hold the western backcountry. The Overmountain Men, the Yadkin Valley Patriots, and all those who joined in the destruction of Major Patrick Ferguson and his Loyalist army may not have completely chopped down the tree of Loyalism in the South, but they undeniably sank their axes deep.

---

24. It is presumed that the remaining Loyalist prisoners were escorted to the Shenandoah Valley where they joined other British prisoners of war being held there. This is supported by the pension applications of Thomas Lewis and James Stagel, both who describe escorting prisoners from Kings Mountain into Virginia: Lewis to "Woodstock in Shenandoah County" and Stagel to Albemarle Barracks.

25. Draper, *King's Mountain and Its Heroes*, 360.

Top Ten Quotes by Francis Lord Rawdon

TODD W. BRAISTED

For the past two years I have had the good fortune to be heading up a project to gather, for eventual publication, the correspondence of one of the more colorful officers on the British side, Francis Lord Rawdon. Rawdon was an Irishman, one of a handful of young officers who catapulted to command ahead of older officers by taking advantage of opportunities to lead Loyalist troops on the Provincial Establishment. Like fellow officers Banastre Tarleton and John Graves Simcoe, Rawdon commanded a regiment while still in his mid-twenties.

Born in December 1754 at Moira, County Down, west of Belfast in what is now Northern Ireland, Rawdon entered the British military at the age of sixteen as an ensign in the 15th Regiment of Foot. Through the influence (and especially the money) of his family, including his very influential uncle and member of the House of Lords, the Earl of Huntingdon, Rawdon began his climb in rank through the British purchase system. With the 5th Regiment of Foot, in which he was then a lieutenant, Rawdon embarked in 1774 for America, where he would spend much of the next seven years.

As an officer of grenadiers, Rawdon was heavily involved in the opening actions of the American Revolution, especially at the Battle of Bunker Hill, where his actions were noted by several senior officers, particularly Generals John Burgoyne and Henry Clinton. Rawdon departed Boston with Clinton in January 1776, a staff officer on Clinton's expedition to the Carolinas, where they met up with the force under Lord Cornwallis in the ill-fated attempt to take Charleston. Rawdon continued with Clinton in the New York City Campaign in 1776, culminating in the British occupation of Newport, Rhode Island. The young Irish captain (promoted to that rank in the 63rd Regiment of Foot in July 1775) accompanied Clinton to London on that general's brief return home in January 1777. Returning to America that summer, Rawdon stayed with Clinton at New York City while the main army under Sir William Howe fought in Pennsylvania. Howe's return to England in early 1778 proved fortuitous for Rawdon, as Clinton succeeded to command of the Army in America. The new British commander in chief appointed Rawdon adjutant general of the Army in America, just in time for the evacuation of Philadelphia and the march across New Jersey. Not only did Rawdon hold the top staff position in the army, he did so as a brevet British lieutenant colonel and a full colonel on the Provincial Establishment as commander of a regiment.

In May 1778, it was thought expedient to try and raise a corps of Irishmen in America, as an enticement to those Loyalist emigrants of that kingdom and especially to lure Washington's Irish soldiers, of whom there were many, to the British side. Clinton named Rawdon colonel of this new regiment, the Volunteers of Ireland. Rawdon quickly lavished money on the corps, supporting its officers and personally paying for distinctive uniforms and accoutrements for the soldiers. These expenses were well above his pay grade, necessitating a near-constant chain of monetary requests to his parents.

As others found while working among Sir Henry Clinton's inner circle, the British commander could prove a thorny boss. Rawdon, who initially thought very highly of Clinton as a person and officer, grew frustrated and confounded by his superior's arrogance and picayune behavior. In the first days of September 1779 this culminated in concerning comments over a diner discussing the drafting of another Provincial unit, Emmerick's Chasseurs. Rawdon resigned the office of adjutant general the next day, although quickly writing to London to solicit the retention of brevet rank in the Army, having arranged for his brother George to succeed him as captain in the 63rd Regiment. Another brother, the Honorable John Rawdon, lost a leg as captain in 4th (or King's Own) Regiment of Foot in 1777 during the Pennsylvania campaign. In both cases, Lord Rawdon showed great attention to looking after the well-being of his uniformed siblings.

Now solely focused on his regiment, the Volunteers of Ireland, Rawdon led his corps in April 1780 as part of the reinforcement for the Siege of Charleston, then underway in South Carolina. After the surrender of that city to Clinton the following month, Rawdon and the Volunteers remained behind as part of the southern army commanded by Lord Cornwallis. Sent into the interior of the province, Rawdon established headquarters at Camden and commanded all the outlying posts in that neighborhood. He commanded the left wing of the army, composed of three Provincial regiments, at the battle fought near Camden there on August 16, 1780, earning praise from Cornwallis. While appreciating the acknowledgement, Rawdon felt slighted that his efforts were not sufficiently commended, thus creating some ill feelings towards Cornwallis.

Rawdon continued in command at Camden and eventually was involved with Cornwallis's army in late autumn. When Cornwallis shifted the army's march to North Carolina that winter, Rawdon returned to Camden with his regiment, where he again assumed command, this time of the entire province. Despite defeating Nathanael Greene's army at Hobkirk's Hill on April 25, 1781 and masterfully relieving the Siege of Ninety-Six later that spring, the state of the army and his own declining health forced an evacuation of the interior of the province. Clinton, still showing some attachment to his former protégée, promoted Rawdon to brigadier general of Provincial forces and granted him leave to return home now that more senior British officers had arrived in the province. Weeks before embarking on his journey, Rawdon, along with Charleston commandant Nisbet Balfour, presided over the execution of rebel Col. Isaac Hayne, who had been taken prisoner while under arms and in battle while, as the British claimed, under a parole not to do so. It was a turbulent end to his career in America.

The journey home, on a packet (mail) ship was cut abruptly short when the vessel was captured by the French fleet. Sent to France as a prisoner, he was quickly paroled to Paris and from thence home to London and then Ireland, having to defend his action regarding Hayne along the way. Exchanged in 1782, Rawdon raised a new regiment in Ireland, the 105th Regiment of Foot, formed around the cadre of commissioned and noncommissioned officers of the Volunteers of Ireland, sent from America in October of that year. This new corps saw no service outside of Ireland and was disbanded shortly after the end of the war.

Rawdon continued on in various military and government roles, most notably as governor general of India. He passed away in 1826 at the age of seventy-one, while serving as governor of the island of Malta, where he is buried still. Below are some classic passages from Rawdon's writings, primarily to his family, where his candor, openness and humor were typically on display.

RAWDON TO HIS UNCLE in London on June 20, 1775, concerning the Battle of Bunker Hill and the shattered remains of his grenadier company: "Only eleven of our Grenadier Company are left; other Grenadier Companys have suffered even more. I received no hurt of any kind; but a ball passed thro' a close cap which I had made in imitation of the foreign travelling caps & wore for convenience sake, for we no longer think of appearances at present. I was every where in the thickest of the fire & flatter myself that I behaved as you could wish."[1]

RAWDON TO HIS UNCLE, from "the heights of Charlestown" on October 5, 1775, where he had been on duty for months: "It is very bleak at present upon these Heights, & the duty of the Officers is severe. At our lines, neither officer or man have the smallest shelter against the inclemency of the weather, but stand to the works all night. Indeed in point of alertness & regularity, our Officers have great merit. I have not seen either drinking or gaming in this camp. If any thing, there is too little society among us: In general every man goes to his own tent very soon after sunset, where those who can amuse themselves in that manner, read; & the others probably sleep. I usually have a Red herring, some Onions, & some Porter about eight o'Clock, of which three or four grave sedate people partake; we chat about different topics, & retire to our beds about nine."[2]

RAWDON TO HIS UNCLE while embarked on board the ship *Mercury* from New York, en route to the 1776 southern campaign, relating what he heard concerning the repulse of the attack on Quebec on New Year's Eve in 1775: "This loss has so dispirited the Yankies that we hear they cannot prevail on the men to march for Canada; altho' Governor Trumbull has assured them, that 'after mature consideration he can promise them success, for the Righteous God loveth righteousness, & of consequence they must succeed.' Such are the arts with which they delude the ignorant bigots of this country. Mr. Trumbull's opinion of these people, & mine, differ widely."[3]

RAWDON TO HIS UNCLE dated from Horn's Hook on Manhattan, September 23, 1776, about a week after the capture New York City, wherein he described the scene of one of the few opposed amphibious landings of the war: "On the 15th, General Clinton embarked early in the morning (in some flat bottomed boats which had been brought past the town in the night) with the Light Infantry, the British, & the Hessian Grenadiers; making between three & four thousand men. Commodore Hotham had the Command of the Boats; Genl. Clinton & I were in his barge with him. We embarked in Newtown Creek, & as soon as we got into the East River, formed the Line, & pushed directly

---

1. The Huntington Library, Hastings Family Papers, mssHA, Box 97, HA 5106.
2. The Huntington Library, Hastings Family Papers, mssHA, Box 98, HA 5110.
3. The Huntington Library, Hastings Family Papers, mssHA, Box 98, HA 5114.

for Kipps's Bay. As we approached, we saw the breastworks filled with men; & two or three large Columns marching down in great parade to support them. The Hessians who were not used to this water business, & who conceived that it must be exceedingly uncomfortable to be shot at whilst they were quite defenceless & jammed together so close, began to sing hymns immediately. Our men expressed their feelings as strongly, tho' in a different manner, by damning themselves & the enemy indiscriminately with wonderful fervency. The Ships had not as yet fired a shot, but upon a signal from us they began the most tremendous peal I ever heard. The breastwork was blown to pieces in a few minutes, & those who were to have defended it were happy to escape as quick as possible thro' the neighbouring ravines. The Columns broke instantly, & betook themselves to the nearest woods for shelter. We pressed to shore, landed, & formed without losing a single man."[4]

FROM WHITE PLAINS, NEW YORK on November 3, 1776, Rawdon described to his uncle the fighting at that place a few days previous, as well as this anecdote of his brother John, then a lieutenant in the 15th Regiment of Foot: "Two days ago, the Rebels having carried off the part of their baggage, & burnt the rest, abandoned their works & retired thro' the mountains. We endeavored to follow them but in vain. We had some Cannonading with their rear guard, by which my brother John (who is an excellent Soldier in every respect) was very near killed. Two men who stood close to him were killed by a Twelve pounder, & a Splinter of one of their sculls stuck in his thigh; but did not hurt him much. This Campaign has been of infinite service to him. He is every thing I could wish him."[5]

LORD RAWDON'S FATHER perhaps had a laugh from this letter dated at New York, September 22, 1778 wherein Rawdon alludes that the corps he raised in America, the Volunteers of Ireland, consisted, at least in great part, of deserters from Washington's army: "My Regiment at present consists of above 400 Men, & is really a fine one. I fancy there are few men in it who have not at one time or other had a shot at their Colonel. They are this day gone into Jersey, as part of a Corps of 6000 Men under Ld. Cornwallis."[6]

ON SEPTEMBER 22, 1779 Rawdon attempted to express to his father the reasons for his resigning as adjutant general, and what Sir Henry Clin-

---

4. The Huntington Library, Hastings Family Papers, mssHA, Box 99, HA 5119.
5. The Huntington Library, Hastings Family Papers, mssHA, Box 99, HA 5120.
6. Public Record Office of Northern Ireland, Granard Papers: Letters from the 1st Marquess of Hastings, 1776-1781, T3765/M/4/2, No. 6.

ton had become: "It is sufficient to say that disappointments of various kinds, have so affected Sir Henry's temper, that it would have been unbecoming both my rank, & character to have remained with him. His rudeness, & want of decency to me as a Gentleman, has been so frequent, that altho' he used to be sensible of it & make apologies for it afterwards, I could not bear the idea of being perpetually subject to such caprice. There is a certain respect invariably due from one man to another."[7]

IN A LETTER DATED FROM Camden, South Carolina on Christmas Eve 1780, Rawdon braced his mother to expect reading negative press on him in the papers, alluding to a captured order of his to the inhabitants in the area to bring in or behead deserters from his corps, or risk severe punishment. Rawdon explained the threats were simply that, in the hopes of stopping desertion: "You must expect to hear me talked of as a monster of cruelty: For the Rebels who have in this Country been guilty of the most atrocious barbarities, never fail to raise the most violent outcries when we punish the treachery of their partisans with the severity due to it. I esteem it highly dishonest to let the fear of vulgar obloquy intimidate one from the performance of what one knows to be one's duty: Therefore, under any circumstances that require stepping beyond the line of precedent, I must always be very liable to incur misrepresentation. Washington, with a view of sowing dissention, sent to Sir H. Clinton a letter of mine which was intercepted by Gates; with a grievous complaint against it's severity; It was a *Lettre Fulminante*, calculated to terrify our pretended friends in the Country, from enticing the troops to desert; & it will give a mighty pretty idea of my character, if it appears in a London news-paper."[8]

THE STRESS AND FATIGUE of his South Carolina command is evident in a letter from Rawdon to his father dated from Camden, March 16, 1781: "The business of my present situation is wearisome to the greatest degree. To military cares, is added all such civil administration as can now take place: and the management of a people who have no sense of Honor, who appear to want every principle of humanity, & who feel no obligation in the most solemn oath, is as ungrateful a task as can be well imagined."[9]

---

7. Public Record Office of Northern Ireland, Granard Papers: Letters from the 1st Marquess of Hastings, 1776-1781, T3765/M/4/2, No. 14.
8. Public Record Office of Northern Ireland, Granard Papers: Letters from the 1st Marquess of Hastings, 1776-1781, T3765/M/4/2, No. 19.
9. Public Record Office of Northern Ireland, Granard Papers: Letters from the 1st Marquess of Hastings, 1776-1781, T3765/M/4/2, No. 22.

Rawdon had no sooner returned to Ireland from France when he was informed by his uncle that the Duke of Richmond, no fan of the war in America, sought to question Rawdon's conduct in the affair of Colonel Hayne. Rawdon rushed to London, where, at noon on February 21, 1782, he fired off this challenge to the Duke: "The expressions, with which you, My Lord, introduced the motion, were as unnecessary to the business, as they are little reconcileable to the dignity of a Senator, the public spirit of a Citizen, or the Candor of a Gentleman: of course, I feel them fit objects for my resentment. I do therefore require, that you, My Lord, shall make a public excuse, in such manner, and in such terms as I shall dictate, for the scandalous imputation which you have thrown on my Humanity; a quality which ought to be as dear in a Soldier's estimation as valor itself. If your Grace had rather abet your malignity with your Sword, I shall rejoice in bringing the matter to that issue."[10]

---

10. The Huntington Library, Hastings Family Papers, mssHA, HA Americana Box 1, Folder 21.

Russia and the Armed Neutrality of 1780

ERIC STERNER

Like a rock dropped into a smooth pond, the American Revolution spread ripples across the European world. French and Spanish entry into the war amplified those ripples to reach the distant shores of the Baltic and White Seas. In 1780, Russia reacted and threatened to upend the entire strategic balance in Europe, which would have thrown British strategy for fighting the American Revolution on its heels. Russia's creation of the League of Armed Neutrality becomes one of those great "what if?" questions of the American Revolution. It highlights the constant uncertainties and contingencies that British strategists faced as the American Revolution impacted European politics. The immediate issue at stake was how Britain treated neutral states in its wars with the Americans, French, and Spaniards.

Prior to the American Revolution, Anglo-Russian relations were peaceful, benign, and built around a mutually profitable trade in raw materials. In particular, the states surrounding the Baltic Sea, including Russia, were reliable sources of naval stores. For their part, British merchant ships carried most Russian exports to overseas markets.

Catherine II, eventually known as Catherine the Great, was a minor German princess who took power in 1762 following a coup against her husband. Catherine initially focused on internal administrative, legal, and economic reforms. To that end, her government signed a commercial treaty with Britain in 1766.[1] The treaty allowed neutral trading with ports of belligerent states so long as the goods did not include contraband. Russia could trade with Britain's enemies during wartime so long as the goods did not include war material, and vice versa. The treaty capitalized on a mutual interest in foiling French policies and

---

1. Samuel Flagg Bemis, *The Diplomacy of the American Revolution* (Bloomington, IN: Indiana University Press, 1935, 1957), 149.

strengthening an already beneficial trade relationship, particularly in naval stores. Russia had little ability or interest in violating the treaty. Due to Russian dependence on Britain, the latter had little need to enforce it. Still, Catherine disliked relying on British merchants and encouraged increased trade with other states. By 1776 the British consul in St. Petersburg noted the growing presence of French and Spanish vessels in port. In 1778, British merchants still carried over half of Russia's cargos: 339 British ships versus 285 from other countries.[2] But, the next year British merchant visits fell to 314, while non-British vessels rose to 379, a growing portion of them Dutch.[3]

In 1775, Britain explored the possibility of hiring Russian troops for use against its rebellious colonies. Catherine dismissed the idea, but predicted American independence in her lifetime.[4] Otherwise, Russia took little interest in Britain's American colonies. The war's spread to France and Spain changed that.

Under evolving standards of international law, Britain's trade embargo against its colonies was legitimate as few European powers questioned a country's right to control colonial trade. Privateers and Royal Navy vessels would stop ships at sea, inspect their cargos, and dispatch those vessels suspected of violating the embargo to a British port for adjudication by an Admiralty court. As Anglo-French tensions increased and war loomed, Britain strengthened and widened its blockade. On July 29, 1778 new orders in council directed the Royal Navy to seize or destroy all French vessels it encountered. A month later, the council expanded the blockade and directed the Navy to bring all vessels, including neutral ships, bound for French ports carrying "Naval or Warlike Stores" into a British port.[5] Worse, British lawyers in the Admiralty began tinkering with the definition of contraband and interpretations of various treaties, sometimes including grain that might find its way to an enemy, sometimes not. At the same time, the burden of proving a neutral vessel was not trading contraband cargo fell on the ship's owners.

2. Isabel De Madariaga, *Britain, Russia and the Armed Neutrality of 1780* (London: Hollis & Carter, Ltd., 1962), 176. Focused on Sir James Harris, Britain's ambassador to Russia, De Madariaga's study is by far the most authoritative examination of political and diplomatic maneuvering in St. Petersburg, largely viewing efforts through the perspective of diplomats "on the ground," in the Russian capital. That perspective, however, often views events through the lens of personal relationships, downplaying matters of strategy.
3. Madariaga, *Britain, Russia and the Armed Neutrality of 1780*, 176,
4. John T. Alexander, *Catherine the Great: Life and Legend* (Oxford: Oxford University Press, 1989), 185.
5. David Syrett, *Neutral Rights and the War in the Narrow Seas, 1778-1782* (Fort Leavenworth, KS: U.S. Army Command and General Staff College, Combat Studies Institute, n.d.), 2-3.

In 1778, Denmark floated the idea of an armed neutrality to defend the doctrine of "free ship, free goods" and the rights of neutral states to trade with countries at war.[6] The Danes noted that none of the north European states could resist British policy unilaterally, but that in combination they might be able to tip the scales against the Royal Navy, thereby securing neutral trade.[7]

While ideas about banding together or adopting a posture of armed neutrality floated around European capitals, Russia was primarily focused on landward events. To the south, Russia and the Ottoman Empire dueled over different puppet regimes in the Khanate of Crimea following their 1768-1774 war. To the west, the War of Bavarian Succession erupted over political influence and power among the German states in central Europe. Eventually, Russia threatened to intervene. The eventual Peace of Teschen in 1779 made Russia a guarantor of the Holy Roman Emperor and introduced a newly powerful player into the political dynamics of central Europe.[8] Still, Russia could not escape the American Revolution, Britain's naval strategy, or its impact on maritime trade.

In August 1778, the American privateer *General Mifflin* sank one British merchant and seized several others carrying Russian goods to Britain.[9] Catherine responded in September by ordering a squadron to the port to convoy British merchant ships.[10] Then, in October, British vessels seized the Russian merchant *Jonge Prins*, bound for France with a cargo of hemp and flax.[11] Count Nikita Panin, Russia's foreign minister, did not believe war with Britain was in Russia's interest, particularly given greater issues at stake in central Europe and the Black Sea. So, in December he proposed that Russia hedge its response and announce an intention to close the White Sea to *all* commerce raiders, whether naval vessels or privateers. Catherine approved and her government formally protested British policy and practice, but little came of it.[12] Britain seized still more Russian vessels in the coming months.

---

6. Grainger, *The British Navy in the Baltic*, 129-130.
7. David Syrett, *The Royal Navy in European Waters During the American Revolutionary War* (Columbia, SC: University of South Carolina, 1998), 118.
8. H.M. Scott, *The Birth of the Great Power System, 1740-1815* (Harlow, England: Pearson Education Limited, 2006), 178-179.
9. Syrett, *The Royal Navy in European Waters*, 119.
10. Dmitrii Katchenovsky, Frederic Thomas Pratt, trans., "Prize Law: particularly with reference to the Duties and Obligations of Belligerents and Neutrals," in James Brown Scott, ed., *The Armed Neutralities of 1780 and 1800* (New York: Oxford University Press, 1918), 123-124.
11. Syrett, *The Royal Navy in European Waters*, 119.
12. Katchenovsky, "Prize Law," 124.

In April, 1779, Britain went so far as to announce that convoys of merchant ships, an innovation adopted by neutrals to deter Britain's Navy, would not be immune to its stop and seize practice. Denmark appealed to the Russian court for support as Britain ramped up its pressure and maintained considerable ambiguity over its embargoes.[13] Although Russia's trade remained modest, British policies grated. In November 1779, Catherine sent instructions to her new ambassador in London referring to British Admiralty court judgments as episodes of "insolence," "insubordination," and "cupidity."[14] While the main Russian complaint referred to the in-expeditious and unfavorable disposition of Russian cargos seized by British privateers, the British government let the matter pass, offering no new instructions to its courts or privateers in response to the Russian complaint.

Catherine's attitude toward the warring parties did not improve when in December 1779 the British seizure of an escorted Swedish convoy became the talk of Europe.[15] Then, she learned in January 1780 that Spain had seized a ship chartered by Russian merchants to carry a cargo of corn to France and Italy.[16] About the same time, news reached her of the Royal Navy's capture of a Dutch convoy. Then, at the end of the month, she learned that the Spanish had seized another vessel charted by Russian merchants.[17] A strong protest was sent to the Spanish government, but the naval free-for-all was becoming intolerable in the Russian court, something the British government did not fully appreciate.

Exactly when and how Catherine II decided to respond to the frequent transgressions against neutral shipping rights, as she—and not the belligerents—understood them, is unclear. However, it does appear that the determination to respond and the concept that emerged originated with her.[18] Although the Russian court was famed for its intrigues and many observers thought policy was determined by that maneuvering, Catherine was intelligent, educated, and knew her own mind quite well. Sometime in the winter of 1779-1780, the Russian response came into focus for her.

In February 1780, without consulting her Council of State or Foreign Minister, Catherine mobilized a portion of the Russian fleet, fif-

13. Madariaga, *Britain, Russia and the Armed Neutrality of 1780*, 142-144.
14. Ibid., 148.
15. Ibid., 155.
16. Syrett, *The Royal Navy in European Waters*, 119.
17. Madariaga, *Britain, Russia and the Armed Neutrality of 1780*, 156.
18. Katchenovsky, "Prize Law," 124-125; Madariaga, *Britain, Russia and the Armed Neutrality of 1780*, 156-157.

teen ships of the line and five frigates.[19] Then, she instructed Count Panin to draft instructions to ambassadors in the neutral states inviting them to make a multilateral declaration about the rights of free trade and invite them into a treaty to enforce those principles. (Conveniently, she learned about this time that her ambassador to The Netherlands had been floating just such an idea in the Dutch government, possibly at her direction but without her government's knowledge.)[20] Finally, in March 1780, Russia's reasons for proposing an armed neutrality and the principles that would guide it were presented to foreign ambassadors in St. Petersburg.

Russia's proposal drew heavily from the principles underlying the posture known as "free ships, free trade." It began first by noting its neutrality in the Revolutionary War and the resulting European War, the violations of its rights as a neutral power, and the impact of interference with Russia's trade. Then the Empress decided to announce her intentions.

"These hindrances to the liberty of trade in general, and to that of Russia in particular, are of a nature to excite the attention of all neutral nations. The Empress finds herself obliged therefore to free it [her trade] by all the means compatible with her dignity and the well-being of her subjects."[21] With that in mind, Russia laid out several principles for Britain, Spain, and France that would guide its behavior:

    1. Neutral vessels were free to navigate from port to port and along belligerent coasts;

    2. Cargos in such vessels, including that owned by subjects of the belligerents, were immune to seizure, with the exception of contraband;

    3. Contraband was defined by the Treaty of Commerce between Russia and Great Britain;

    4. Blockaded ports were defined by a sufficient number of ships stationed outside the port as to render access to others dangerous, i.e., the distant or high-seas blockades common to sailing ships in general and practiced by Britain of necessity, were invalid;

    5. Principles 1-4 would serve as rules regarding adjudications of seized cargos by Admiralty Courts.

---

19. Madariaga, *Britain, Russia and the Armed Neutrality of 1780*, 158.
20. Ibid., 162.
21. "Declaration of the Empress of Russia regarding the Principles of Armed Neutrality, addressed to the Courts of London, Versailles and Madrid, February 28, 1780," in Scott, ed., *The Armed Neutralities of 1780 and 1800*, 273. Russia still used the Julian calendar at this time and the dates in the Scott volume are offered in the older calendar. Under today's calendar, the announcement was made on March 10.

With those principles in mind, Russia announced it was readying a portion of its fleet to enforce them. While the announcement pledged to maintain neutrality, it hinted at the possibility of using force: "This measure ... will observe so long as she is not provoked and forced to pass the bounds of moderation and perfect impartiality. It is only in this extremity that her fleet will have orders to go wherever honor, interest, and need may require."[22]

While word traveled to the courts in London, Versailles, and Madrid and those governments contemplated the Russian declaration, Catherine proposed to the Netherlands, Denmark, Prussia, Sweden, and Portugal in April that they form a League of Armed Neutrality. British diplomats learned of the overtures nearly immediately. The proposal was based specifically on Catherine's conclusion that the British were violating the Anglo-Russian Commercial Treaty of 1766 and the "natural rights" of neutral states. From Russia's perspective, that meant "the other trading Powers will immediately come into her way of thinking relative to neutrality." With that in mind, she invited these powers "to make a common cause with her, as such a union may serve to protect the trade and navigation."[23] It was a moment of extreme vulnerability for Britain's naval power.

France and Spain capitalized on the opportunity quickly. The King of Spain responded by expressing his desire to respect neutral rights and attributed Spanish violations to Britain's refusal to embrace them and neutral violations of their obligations vis a vis contraband. "The King ... will this day have the glory of being the first to give the example of respecting the neutral flag of all the Courts that have consented, or shall consent, to defend it ... and to show to all the neutral Powers how much Spain is desirous of observing the same rules in time of war as she was directed whilst neuter, His Majesty conforms to the other points contained in the declaration of Russia."[24] An exception was made for trade with Gibraltar, then under siege by Spanish forces.

The King of France was quick to embrace the concept as well:

> The war in which the King is engaged having no other object than the attachment of His Majesty to the freedom of the seas, he could not but with the truest satisfaction see the Empress of Russia adopt the

---

22. "Declaration of the Empress of Russia," February 28, 1780, *The Armed Neutralities of 1780 and 1800*, 274.
23. "Russian Memorandum containing a Project for an Armed Neutrality, presented to the States-General of the Netherlands, April 3, 1780," Scott, ed., *The Armed Neutralities of 1780 and 1800*, 275.
24. "Reply of the King of Spain to the Declaration of the Empress of Russia, April 18, 1780," Scott, ed., *The Armed Neutralities of 1780 and 1800*, 279-280.

same principle and resolve to maintain it. That which Her Imperial Majesty claims from the belligerent Powers is no other than the rules already prescribed to the French marine....The King has been desirous, not only to procure a freedom of navigation to the subjects of the Empress of Russia, but to those of all the States who hold their neutrality and that upon the same conditions as are announced in the treaty to which His Majesty this day answers.[25]

It was a de facto recognition of the League of Armed Neutrality, even before the league had come into being. Better still, from Russia's standpoint, France rested its posture on Catherine's concept of neutral rights, again seeking to diplomatically isolate Britain and make entry into a league more attractive.

Russia's proposal was potentially disastrous for London's security, not to mention its strategy. Britain suddenly faced the prospect of an alliance of neutrals created specifically to counter her naval strategy. Worse, they would radically change the naval balance of power. In 1780, Great Britain had roughly 117 Ships of the Line in its fleet, divided among the North Sea, the English Channel, the Mediterranean, the Caribbean, and North America. Combined, the French and Spanish boasted 129 such vessels, although they were similarly divided among multiple theaters. Russia only had thirty Ships of the Line, but the Danes and Swedes together boasted nearly sixty. The Netherlands sported another twenty-six.[26] Even superior ships, crews, and command would not spare the British in the event of such a quantitative mismatch.

The question for Britain, however, was what exactly did Catherine's proposal mean? Was Catherine trying to rewrite international law? Britain relied heavily on notions of legitimate national security and self-defense to justify intercepting and seizing cargo that might aid its adversaries. As a practical matter, its routine of stopping neutral ships at sea and dispatching them to British ports for adjudication was the only way to enforce its policy. Building an international consensus against Britain's concept threatened to undermine one of its greatest advantages in warfare: its maritime edge. Thus, Catherine's principles not only threatened Britain's advantages in its war with America, France, and Spain, but could well do so in any future war it fought. Alternatively, was Catherine laying the groundwork to intervene in the American Revolution as part of some new continental strategy? Russia was in the

---

25. Ibid., 284-285.
26. John D. Grainger, *The British Navy in the Baltic* (Woodbridge, UK: The Boydell Press, 2014), 130-131.

midst of shifting its major alliance from Prussia to Austria and might well have further designs on the Mediterranean. Or, was Russia simply looking to apply economic pressure to improve its position relative to Britain's naval practices? As late as 1780, Britain still relied on Russia for 90 percent of its cordage and nearly 90 percent of its largest masts.[27] The bottom line for policymakers in London was determining how far Catherine was prepared to go to defend her new doctrine.

The answers to those questions were not initially clear to Britain, its ambassador in St. Petersburg, or officials around the world.[28] Fortunately for Britain, they were not clear to the states Catherine invited to join her armed league, either. Sweden quickly sought clarification by requesting information about how such a league would function:

1. How would the league provide reciprocal protection and mutual assistance?

2. Would each member be obligated to protect the commerce of every party to a convention, or would individual states be able to set aside a portion of their own military forces for its own protection. In other words, would the league create joint military forces?

3. How would combined operations be governed when operating together, i.e., who would command and what rules of engagement would apply?

4. Would states complain individually to the belligerents should their trade be interrupted, or must all representations to Britain, France, and Spain be conducted by the league collectively?

5. Who would decide how the league responded when the trade of a single member was interrupted? Might each state be left to its own devices?[29]

They were entirely reasonable matters to discuss as league members might quickly find themselves at war with Britain. Russia's reply was quickly forthcoming. Decisions were expected to be unanimous, usually a formula for inaction. The court at St. Petersburg envisioned a narrow security agreement limited to freedom of the seas. Catherine's government seems to have anticipated a kind of armed convoy escort in which a convoy would pass from the care and protection of one state's national

---

27. N.A.M. Rodger, *The Command of the Ocean: A Naval History of Britain, 1649-1815* (London: Allen Lane, 2004), 347.
28. Syrett, *Neutral Rights and the War in the Narrow Seas, 1778-1782*, 31; Syrett, *The Royal Navy in European Waters During the American Revolutionary War*, 121.
29. "Explanation requested of the Court of Russia by the Court of Sweden relative to the Project for an Armed Neutrality, April 5, 1780," Scott, ed., *The Armed Neutralities of 1780 and 1800*, 276-277.

fleet to another's as the convoy moved from place to place, a bit like a relay race. Indeed, St. Petersburg's orders to its Baltic Squadron limited its protection to Russian merchant vessels, which were few in number.[30] Specifics would be worked out in a written convention. Outside of those principles laid out in the March declaration, members would be left to their own devices.[31] Due to Baltic geography, such a concept would place the greatest burden and risks on those members closest and most vulnerable to British naval power, hardly an incentive for Denmark, Sweden, or The Netherlands to join. They might be better off pursuing bilateral side-deals with Britain.

Still, the confusion persisted. British officials received mixed signals from various Russian officials at St. Petersburg and contradictory intelligence in foreign capitals. So, London generally interpreted Russia's initiative through the eyes of court intrigues. As late as July 1780, Lord Stormont, the British Secretary of State for the Northern Department, could only declare "The more I reflect on all that has passed of late, the more I am inclined to believe that we have not got to the bottom of this strange business."[32] Nevertheless, Russia's lack of adequate political and diplomatic preparation caused delays and created opportunities for others. A number of British citizens officered Russia's Baltic fleet. They used the interregnum to inform Catherine's government that they would not serve in a conflict with Great Britain.[33] In May, the Danes, who had been negotiating with Britain to resolve their conflicts at sea, promptly and secretly proposed revising a trade treaty of 1670 to address British concerns over naval stores. Then it announced it was closing the Baltic to hostile vessels.[34] Yet, different factions in Copenhagen warmed to the Russian proposal. So, Count Bernstorff, essentially the first minister, negotiated with Britain and Russia simultaneously, signing agreements first with Britain and then Russia in July.[35] Sweden similarly negotiated new terms of trade with Britain. Both Denmark and Sweden promised to forego trade in contraband and naval stores

---

30. Syrett, *The Royal Navy in European Waters During the American Revolutionary War*, 122.
31. "Reply of the Court of Russia to the Request of Sweden for Explanations respecting the Project for an Armed Neutrality, April 29, 1780," Scott, ed., *The Armed Neutralities of 1780 and 1800*, 288-289.
32. Syrett, *The Royal Navy in European Waters During the American Revolutionary War*, 122.
33. Ibid., 122.
34. "Declaration of His Danish Majesty Regarding the Neutrality of the Baltic Sea, communicated to the Courts of the Belligerent Powers, May 8, 1780," Scott, ed., *The Armed Neutralities of 1780 and 1800*, 290-291.
35. Madariaga, *Britain, Russia and the Armed Neutrality of 1780*, 187-189.

before entering into a treaty with Russia, essentially giving Britain what it wanted. Thus, Russia's unfavorable terms for creating the league contained the seeds of its failure. Prussia and Austria joined in 1781, followed by others before the American Revolution ended. Catherine had her league, but its existence had been rendered meaningless. Whether British diplomacy in separating Denmark and Sweden from a multilateral alliance with teeth or Russian ineptness was to blame remains a subject of debate. In either case, the potential new threat to the naval component of Britain's war strategy was rendered moot.

Looking back, the tendency is to dismiss The League of Armed Neutrality as unserious or intended for some other purpose. Historians John Grainger and Sam Willis saw it as a Russian attempt to dominate the Baltic powers or mask Russian imperial and mercantile ambitions.[36] David Syrett considered it a prestige project.[37] Yet, the episode demonstrates two important overlooked aspects of the American Revolution. First, its effects traveled to distant shores, well beyond the immediate combatants, be they American or British, Frenchmen or Spaniards. Britain's strategy for winning those wars were essentially the transmission belts forcing consequences onto neutral parties and an eventual reaction.

Second, the league's existence represented a real threat to British strategy and security and London perceived it so. Indeed, when The Netherlands threatened to join in late 1780, Britain promptly declared war to make the Dutch ineligible. Going to war with yet another European power was preferable to risking a strengthened league. Lord Sandwich, First Lord of the Admiralty, concluded "the fact is, that we are at this moment in the most ticklish crisis with the Court of Russia, and that at this instant the giving them the least cause of complaint or entering into any altercation with them, might have the most decisive & fatal consequences."[38] Thus, dismissing the league lightly in hindsight, as we sometimes do, was not something the British could do during the American Revolution. Sandwich's reaction is a reminder of the tenuous and gossamer strands that held Britain's war effort together for so long. After Waterloo, the Duke of Wellington famously remarked "It was the nearest run thing you ever saw in your life." Something similar might be said for the League of Armed Neutrality.

36. Grainger, *The Royal Navy in the Baltic*, Chapter 6; Sam Willis, *The Struggle for Sea Power: A Naval History of the American Revolution* (New York: W.W. Norton & Company, 2015), 402.
37. Syrett, *The Royal Navy in European Waters during the American Revolutionary War*, 129.
38. Quoted in Ibid., 129.

Prelude to Yorktown: Washington and Rochambeau in New York

BENJAMIN HUGGINS

The months leading up to the Battle of Yorktown in October 1781 are often glossed over in histories of the Revolutionary War. But they should not be. They were crucial months of preparation for the campaign to come. The events of late June to mid-August 1781 tell the important story leading up to the most consequential decision made by Gen. George Washington during the Revolutionary War. The resulting march of the allied French and American armies from New York to Virginia to confront the British forces operating in that state would culminate in a battle that would decide the outcome of the war.

During the months of June, July, and August, the two armies and their commanding generals undertook numerous actions that were critical to building trust and confidence in their ability to undertake military cooperation, starting with the movement of the French army from Newport, Rhode Island, to New York's Westchester County. Some of the most interesting of such actions were the joint reconnaissances the two generals conducted of the defenses of British-occupied New York City in anticipation of a siege. In addition to the two generals sharing personal hazards and building trust, these scouting operations involved the joint movement of the two armies—crucial experience for later operations.

In the latter part of June 1781, Washington and Lt. Gen. Jean-Baptiste-Donatien de Vimeur, Comte de Rochambeau, commander of the French army, began putting into operation a plan decided on at their conference held the previous month in Wethersfield, Connecticut. In his diary, Washington summarized the decisions of the conference:

> Fixed with Count de Rochambeau upon a plan of Campaign—in Substance as follows. That the French Land force (except 200 Men) should March so soon as the [French naval] Squadron could Sail for

Boston—to the North River & there, in conjunction with the American, to commence an operation against New York (which in the present reduced State of the Garrison it was thought would fall, unless relieved; the doing which w[oul]d enfeeble their Southern operations, and in either case be productive of capital advantages) or to extend our views to the Southward as circumstances and a Naval superiority might render more necessary & eligable.[1]

In accordance with these plans, Washington shifted the Continental army's position south from West Point to Peekskill, ten miles closer to New York City. By the time Washington issued the orders for this march, Rochambeau had already set his four infantry regiments and one legionary corps—a mixed unit of mounted dragoons and infantry—in motion for the long journey from Newport to Westchester County. The Continental army began its march by divisions on June 21. Within four days the army had set up camp at Peekskill where the commander in chief joined it on June 25.[2]

With the French army on the march and his own army now located closer to New York City, Washington decided to make a surprise attack. He intended to target the city's northernmost defenses—the forts on the north end of Manhattan Island—and a Loyalist outpost at Morrisania, just across the Harlem River from the forts. Brig. Gen. Armand-Louis de Gontaut, duc de Lauzun would lead the raid on Morrisania and Maj. Gen. Benjamin Lincoln the attack on the Manhattan forts. Both would occur on July 3. Washington hoped to capture the forts before the British could react and then use them as a base for the siege. He would march the remainder of the Continental army south to be in position to support the two generals and exploit any success. It would be the first combined military operation of the two armies. Washington set the operation in motion after dark on July 1.

According to plan, Lincoln embarked the attack force at Teller's Point on the Hudson River. The detachment then sailed down the New Jersey side of the river until it reached the site of old Fort Lee, nearly opposite the British forts on Manhattan Island. There, Lincoln disembarked his troops, and after sunrise on July 2 he made observations of the British defenses. Lauzun joined his legion with an American dragoon regiment and some Connecticut state troops and began his march to Morrisania. Washington began marching the main army south at 3:00 A.M. on the 2nd.

1. Donald Jackson and Dorothy Twohig, eds., *The Diaries of George Washington*, 6 vols (Charlottesville, VA: University of Virginia Press, 1976–79), 3:369 (*Diaries*). All dates are 1781 unless otherwise specified.
2. *Diaries*, 3:381–2.

Because of unexpectedly strong British defenses, Lincoln could not attack the forts, and, in accordance with Washington's orders, he moved his force across the river to the area north of King's Bridge to aid Lauzun's attack on Morrisania. A force of German jägers by happenstance met and engaged Lincoln's force and were soon reinforced. Lincoln's men fought hard but were forced to retreat towards the main army, now moving south from Valentine's Hill, a dominating height eight miles from the allied camp and only four miles north of King's Bridge. Observing the approach of the Continental main army, the jägers broke off their pursuit and retreated to King's Bridge. Hearing the firing to the north, Lauzun canceled his own attack and rode to the sound of the guns. But he arrived too late to aid Lincoln. The Loyalists, though, were forced to retreat to Fort No. 8, the only British outpost on the mainland (just across Harlem Creek from the Manhattan forts). After conducting a brief reconnaissance, Washington left some troops near King's Bridge as advanced guards and moved the main army back to the White Plains area, where it set up camp.[3] During the fighting, British Gen. Henry Clinton had ridden "out to Kings Bridge to observe their motions and catch at any advantage that might offer." But he "soon saw that nothing could be attempted—without risking a general action."[4]

---

3. *Diaries*, 3:385–86, 388–89; Washington to David Waterbury, June 30 and July 1, Washington Papers, Library of Congress; Washington to Rochambeau, June 30, Rochambeau Papers, Beinecke Library, Yale University; Washington to Lauzun, July 1, Washington Papers, Library of Congress; Washington to Benjamin Lincoln, July 1, Harvard University; Washington to Elisha Sheldon, July 1, Washington Papers, Library of Congress; Lincoln to Washington, July 2, Benjamin Lincoln Papers, Massachusetts Historical Society; Washington to Samuel Huntington, July 6, Papers of the Continental Congress, National Archives; *New-York Gazette: and the Weekly Mercury* for July 16; Journal of Lieutenant Jean-François-Louis, Comte de Clermont-Crèvecœur, in Howard C. Rice, Jr., and Anne S. K. Brown, eds., *The American Campaigns of Rochambeau's Army, 1780, 1781, 1782, 1783*. 2 vols. (Princeton, NJ: Princeton University Press, 1972), 1:32; Carl Leopold Baurmeister, *Revolution in America: Confidential Letters and Journals, 1776–1784, of Adjutant General Major Baurmeister of the Hessian Forces*. Translated and annotated by Bernhard A. Uhlendorf. (New Brunswick, NJ: Rutgers University Press, 1957), 449–50; *Diary of Frederick Mackenzie Giving a Daily Narrative of His Military Service as an Officer of the Regiment of Royal Welch Fusiliers during the Years 1775–1781 in Massachusetts, Rhode Island and New York*, 2 vols. (Cambridge, MA: Harvard University Press, 1930), 2:556–59. The army's camp was just east of White Plains, New York, and west of Dobbs Ferry on the Hudson River. For a contemporary map of the French and American encampments, see Rice and Brown, *American Campaigns of Rochambeau's Army*, 2:238–39 (map 43).
4. William B. Willcox, ed., *The American Rebellion: Sir Henry Clinton's Narrative of His Campaigns, 1775–1782, with an Appendix of Original Documents* (New Haven: Yale University Press, 1954), 307.

The French army joined the American army at the camp on July 6. The armies remained in this position for over two weeks with no opposition from the British. Clinton, believing himself outnumbered and thinking a siege of New York was imminent, had adopted a defensive mentality, even requesting the return of many regiments from the southern states.[5] The allied generals' strategy was working.

Washington desired to conduct an extensive reconnaissance of the British works on the north end of Manhattan Island, along the Harlem River, and along Long Island Sound. On July 14, he ordered 5,000 men readied to march for King's Bridge to "cover and secure" the operation, but "incessant rain" prevented the march.[6] Nevertheless, Washington and Rochambeau decided to conduct a smaller-scale reconnaissance.

On July 18, the two generals, accompanied by Continental army's chief engineer, the French quartermaster general, and the French chief engineer, rode to the eastern shore of the Hudson River, escorted by 100 dragoons. They then crossed to the New Jersey shore "in order to reconnoitre the Enemy Posts and Encampments at the North end of York Island." There, they met an escort of 150 Jersey troops. Taking "different views" of the British defenses on Manhattan Island and along Harlem Creek, the party went as far south as Fort Lee, before returning and crossing back to the allied camp. Demonstrating his thoroughness and attention to military detail, Washington recorded in his diary his "discoveries," or observations, regarding the forts: their water defenses, potential landing points and access routes from the river, the terrain near their approaches, the strength of their defensive works, and the nearby British camps. His detailed observations span three printed pages in the published diary.[7]

Shortly after this reconnaissance, the two commanders again turned to the plan for the campaign. Admiral Barras, the commander of the small French naval squadron at Newport, wanted Washington and Rochambeau to decide on "a definitive plan of Campaign" that he could send to the Comte de Grasse, the admiral commanding a large French fleet then operating in the West Indies. De Grasse's orders directed him to come to the American coast in the fall. The two generals met in formal conference and agreed on a plan of operations. If de Grasse should "arrive in Season" and could "force the Harbour of N York," and

---

5. *Diaries*, 3:390; Henry Clinton to Lieutenant General Charles, Earl Cornwallis, June 11, 15, and 28, in Ian Saberton, ed., *The Cornwallis Papers: The Campaigns of 1780 and 1781 in The Southern Theatre of the American Revolutionary War*. 6 vols. (Uckfield, UK: Naval & Military Press, 2010), 5:95–98.
6. *Diaries*, 3:393.
7. Ibid., 3:394–96.

if the British army remained divided, Washington wanted to keep "the Enterprize against N York & its Dependencies" as the allies' "primary Object." But the American commander had to acknowledge the "uncertainties" he faced in filling his regiments to full strength and obtaining supplies from the state governments. If de Grasse arrived too late in the season or brought too few land troops with him, Washington agreed that the allies should leave a garrison at the strategically important post of West Point and march with the remainder of their regiments to Virginia.[8]

With this decision made and the weather improved, Washington and Rochambeau decided to conduct the extensive reconnaissance that they had planned for the 14th. Washington ordered 5,000 men made ready to march at 8:00 P.M. on July 21. As a secondary objective, an attack would be made on any troops from Col. James Delancey's Loyalist raiders found outside Fort No. 8. At the appointed time, the French and American soldiers began their march south in four columns, each column on a separate road with a detachment of artillery. Lauzun's legion and Col. Elisha Sheldon's legion also joined the march. The appointed rendezvous for all columns was to be Valentine's Hill. Also, the Connecticut militia and state troops stationed at Horseneck (Greenwich) marched down the coastal road toward Eastchester, where they were joined by Sheldon's cavalry to clear Throgs Neck of enemy troops. Likewise, Sheldon's infantry would join Lauzun's legion to clear out Morrisania. Col. Alexander Scammel's light infantry corps was to cover these advanced troops. The light infantry "were to advance thro' the fields & way lay the Roads—stop all communication & prevent Intelligence getting to the Enemy." The mountainous, wooded terrain with narrow passes and bad roads made the march slow and difficult, but, nevertheless, the French and American infantry formed their junction at Valentine's Hill at 3:00 A.M. on July 22. Led by Maj. Gen. Samuel Holden Parson's division, the army then pushed further south arriving at the heights back of Fort Independence by daybreak and deployed east as far as Delancey's Mills and Williams Bridge.

Washington was pleased with the operation: "The enemy did not appear to have had the least intelligence of our movement or to know we were upon the height opposite to them till the whole Army were ready to display." The British had, in fact, been surprised by the movement. Not until daybreak on the 22nd were they aware that the allied

---

8. Rochambeau to Washington, July 19, and Summary of Conference Held at Dobb's Ferry, N.Y., same date, both in Washington Papers, Library of Congress; Diaries, 3:397, entry for July 20 and notes.

force had arrived and taken up strong positions in their front. Observing the arrival of the French and Americans, the Hessian troops posted just north of King's Bridge quickly retreated to the island and drew up the drawbridge over Harlem Creek.[9]

To establish strong advanced posts, Washington ordered a Continental battalion with three field pieces to advance to the walls of the partially destroyed Fort Independence—just north of King's Bridge—and other troops to take position in front of Fort No. 8. The Continentals came under fire from the British and Loyalists in the fort, but, according to one of Rochambeau's aides-de-camp, they marched under this fire "very valiantly and in very good order." Rochambeau sent a detachment of his grenadiers and chasseurs to support the American battalion. After making these dispositions, the two allied commanders and their aides rode west to Cox Hill to reconnoiter the British fortifications on the north end of the island. Ships anchored where Harlem Creek joins the Hudson River and batteries in the forts fired on the party but without effect. After finishing this reconnaissance, the generals rode back to camp.[10]

While these events were occurring, the columns sent to break up the Loyalist camps proceeded to Throgs Neck and Morrisania, but, according to Washington, had "little effect, as most of the Refugees were fled, & hid in such obscure places as not to be discovered." Others had retreated to adjacent islands, British shipping in the East River, or Fort No. 8. "A few however were caught and some cattle & Horses brought off."[11] As the Loyalists retreated, the allies began a harassing fire on Fort No. 8. At 6:00 A.M. two cannon were brought up to fire on Howland's Ferry (behind the fort) where the Loyalists were trying to cross to Manhattan Island.

Despite these attacks, the British remained in the defensive posture they had exhibited earlier in the month. "No movements were made on our side, except reinforcing No. 8, with 20 men," British officer Maj. Frederick Mackenzie wrote. Expecting a large attack on the fort, the British ordered "the troops stationed near Kingsbridge . . . to be in readiness to move if called upon" but took offensive action. The rein-

---

9. *Diaries*, 3:399; Evelyn M. Acomb, ed., *The Revolutionary Journal of Baron Ludwig von Closen, 1780–1783* (Chapel Hill, NC: University of North Carolina Press, 1958), 97–98 (von Closen includes some events of the morning of the 22nd in his journal entry for the 21st; *Mackenzie Diary*, 2:570.
10. *Diaries*, 3:398–99 (Washington recorded some of the events of the morning of the 22nd in his diary entry for the 21st); Acomb, *Journal of von Closen*, 98-99.
11. *Diaries*, 3:398-99.

forcements for the fort—a troop of dragoons— exchanged shots with American dragoons in the forward post adjacent to the fort.[12]

With the army deployed and the allies firmly in control of the ground, Washington, Rochambeau, and their chief engineers began "to reconnoitre the enemy's position and Works first from Tippets hill opposite to their left." The party, accompanied by aides-de-camp and escorted by a party of light infantry and about eight dragoons, first visited the position of the advanced battalion where they could observe Fort George on Manhattan Island. On the way to reconnoiter Morrisania, the party passed Delancey's Mill, where a battalion of French troops was posted. The generals then proceeded along the bank of Harlem Creek to Morrisania. Washington soon came under fire. The British had observed the reconnaissance column. "Mr Washington was with them, " Mackenzie wrote, "and came so near the point with some Cavalry, that some Cannon shot were fired at him, which soon obliged him to move off."[13]

After this, near Morrisania, the party "surprised a sort of light corps of about 20 Loyalists, including foot and horse, which had not had time to cross the river." Washington, who had ridden about a mile ahead of the light infantry escort, sent forward eight dragoons to charge the Loyalists. The aides-de-camp joined the charge. Setting off at a gallop, the dragoons and aides found that the Loyalists had taken refuge in a house. Taking musket fire from the windows, the dragoons and aides surrounded the house, began returning fire with their pistols and carbines, and called on the Loyalists to surrender, threatening "to give them no quarter and to burn the house if they refused." The Loyalists then called out that they were surrendering and exited the house. Meanwhile, about 200 British soldiers had gathered on the opposite shore and began firing at the Americans and French with muskets and grapeshot fired from four field pieces. Spotting this support, the Loyalists attacked the dragoons and aides. They paid a severe price for their rashness. Many were sabered or shot. Some dived into the Harlem River and were drowned. Ten Loyalists and seven horses were captured. Other than a horse shot from underneath one of the aides, the allied party took no casualties. A participant, French captain Louis-Alexandre Berthier, who would become a marshal of France under Emperor Napoleon I, wrote in his journal that Washington and Rochambeau "watched this little skirmish, which lasted five minutes, at very close range."

12. *Makenzie Diary*, 2:570–71; Acomb, *Journal of von Closen*, 98.
13. *Diaries*, 3:399–400; Acomb, *Journal of von Closen*, 99; *Makenzie Diary*, 570–71.

Washington's observations, which he recorded in his diary, were again very detailed. He noted that Fort Charles, just behind King's Bridge, "would be absolutely at the command of a battery which might be erected" at Tippets Hill. He thought the fort on Cox Hill "was in bad repair, & little dependence placed on it." But from every view he "could get of Forts Tryon, Knyphausen & Laurel hill the Works are formidable." He also recorded extensive notes on enemy camps, potential crossing points for an assault, and potential locations for artillery. The two generals and the engineers then completed their reconnaissance and the party returned to camp.[14]

Since the allies had not attacked Fort No. 8 in force, the British expected them to retire from the area in the night. But at daybreak they discovered that the allies remained in their positions in full force. At 3:00 A.M. on the 23rd, Clinton had ridden out to King's Bridge to reconnoiter the allied positions from several points. Arriving at the fort on Cox Hill, he sent one of his aides-de-camp to Fort No. 8 with directions to the commanding officer to fire several cannon shots into the allied line. "His design," wrote Mackenzie, "was to make the Enemy shew themselves, and enable him the better to judge of their position and numbers." The shots "had the desired effect." Immediately after the shots, the allied "Soldiers, who had been lying down, run up to the nearest heights, and Shewed the whole extent of their lines, and enabled him to form a good judgement of their numbers. " Clinton next went to Fort Charles, the bastion guarding the crossing at King's Bridge, where he could be easily observed by the allied troops posted at Fort Independence. A French or American dragoon was seen riding out from the fort and a cannon was soon brought up. Four or five shots were fired at the column coming up to relieve the garrison at Fort Charles "but without effect." When the cannon in Fort Charles returned fire, the allies withdrew the piece from Fort Independence. But Clinton had left Fort Charles before the artillery began firing. After several hours of observation, he had satisfied himself that the allies "did not intend any immediate attempt" and returned to his quarters to have dinner. The British commander evidently had no thought of attacking the allied lines. He had believed since early June that he was "threatened with a siege" of New York.[15]

---

14. Journal of Captain Louis-Alexandre Berthier, in Rice and Brown, *American Campaigns of Rochambeau's Army*, 1:252–53; *Diaries*, 3:399–400.
15. *Mackenzie Diary*, 571–72; Clinton to Cornwallis, June 8 and 11, in Saberton, *Cornwallis Papers*, 5:123–25. Clinton's spies had intercepted some of Washington's letters that discussed the campaign plan agreed at the Wethersfield conference (Saberton, *Cornwallis Papers*, 5:126–34).

While Clinton was conducting his observations, the allied generals resumed their reconnaissance, but they shifted the location to another point vital to the projected operation. Early in the morning, Rochambeau and his aides-de-camp called on Washington. The two generals, accompanied by the chief engineers and an escort of ninety American dragoons, then set out on a reconnaissance of Throgs Neck, a peninsula southeast of Westchester that juts into Long Island Sound opposite to Whitestone on Long Island.[16] A crossing from Throgs Neck to Long Island would be part of any operation leading to a siege of New York because control of Brooklyn Heights was essential. From Whitestone, a road led south to Flushing and the Jamaica Road that in turn led to Brooklyn Heights. Washington succinctly described the objective: "Went upon Frogs [Throgs] Neck, to see what communication could be had with Long Isld."[17] From Throgs Neck the officers could clearly see the shore of Long Island, just a short distance across the sound. A sixteen-gun British privateer, at anchor in the sound, took the party under fire. During the reconnaissance, the generals and their escort had to cross a low-lying marshy area; a "little connecting bridge" was quickly constructed to allow them to cross.[18]

Arriving at the point where the engineers wished to conduct their observations, the party rested. As Rochambeau later recalled: "While our engineers carried out this geometrical operation, we slept, worn out by fatigue, at the foot of a hedge, under fire from the cannon of the enemy's ships, who wished to hinder the work. Waking first, I called General Washington, and remarked to him that we had forgotten the hour of the tide. We hurried to the [bridge] on which we had crossed this small arm of the sea which separated us from the mainland; we found it covered with water. We were brought two little boats, in which we embarked, with the saddles and trappings of the horses; they then sent back two American dragoons, who drew by the bridle two horses, good swimmers." Rochambeau's aide-de-camp Ludwig von Closen wrote: "After the leaders' horses were over, I must confess that I was astonished to see the 90 horses of the American dragoons ... unsaddled and compelled to swim across at once, without a rope or anything. The American officer assured me *'that he had often had his men swim across, and that the horses were accustomed to this from birth'*" (italics in original). Rochambeau remembered that the crossing "was made in less than an

---

16. Acomb, *Journal of von Closen*, 101.
17. *Diaries*, 3:401.
18. Acomb, *Journal of von Closen*, 101.

hour, but happily our embarrassment was unnoticed by the enemy." Washington rated the ship's fire as "harmless."[19]

The generals and engineers then decided to conduct a second reconnaissance of Morrisania, but, coming that close to the enemy, they needed to boost their escort. Rochambeau sent von Closen to find Lauzun's legion which was stationed some miles north of Throgs Neck. The engineers, though, rode to Morrisania well ahead of the generals so as not to be disturbed in their observations. Von Closen noted that a "few carbine shots were fired at those who reconnoitered too openly."[20] Washington's summary of the reconnaissance was brief and subdued: "Having finished the reconnoitre without damage—a few harmless shot only being fired at us—we Marched back about Six o'clock by the same routs we went down & a reversed order of March and arrived in Camp about Midnight."[21] With the reconnaissances completed, Washington could do little but wait for reinforcements to come in from the states and look forward to the arrival of the French fleet. Between July 24 and 31, he recorded in his diary only comments on his correspondence and minor troop movements.[22]

By the first day in August Washington had come to the realization that a siege of New York would not be possible. On that date the general wrote in his diary that all material preparations had been made for the siege "and every thing would have been in perfect readiness to commense the operation against New York, if the States had furnished their quotas of men agreeably to my requisitions," but only half of the men requested had arrived at camp. He began to shift his strategy: "Thus circumstanced, and having little more than general assurances of getting the succours called for . . . I could scarce see a ground upon wch. to continue my preparations against New York—especially as there was much reason to believe that part (at least) of the Troops in Virginia were recalled to reinforce New York and therefore I turned my views more seriously (than I had before done) to an operation to the Southward." He began making preliminary arrangements for marching the army to Virginia.[23]

---

19. *Diaries*, 3:401; Rochambeau, *Memoires, militaires, historiques, et politiques de Rochambeau*, 2 vols. (Paris, 1809), 1:283–84, quoted in *Diaries*, 3:401-2; Acomb, *Journal of von Closen*, 101.
20. Acomb, *Journal of von Closen*, 101–2.
21. *Diaries*, 3:401. In this instance, he did not record his observations, but Brig. Gen. Louis Duportail, the army's chief engineer, later furnished him with a summary of the engineers' observations (see Duportail to Washington, August 18, 1781, in Washington Papers, Library of Congress).
22. Washington made no entries in his diary on July 24, 25, 26, 27, and 28.
23. *Diaries*, 3:404–5.

In the next two weeks, Washington carried out the routine duties of army commander. He monitored events in Virginia and at New York, continued to familiarize himself with the roads and ground in the region of the camp, urged governors to keep up the militia serving with the army, tended to the organization of the army's light infantry corps, and called in troops from other posts to concentrate his army.[24]

On August 14, the long-awaited message from de Grasse arrived. Washington received dispatches from Admiral Barras announcing that de Grasse intended to sail for Chesapeake Bay from Cap François (in modern Haiti) on August 3 with between twenty-five and twenty-nine ships of the line and 3,200 land troops. De Grasse, Washington wrote in his diary, was anxious "to have every thing in the most perfect readiness to commence our operations in the moment of his arrival." But the French admiral would be obligated to return to the West Indies in mid-October.

Presented with de Grasse's decision for the Chesapeake, Washington did not hesitate in making his most consequential decision of the war. Matters had now "come to a crisis," he wrote, and he had to decide on "a decisive plan." Being limited by de Grasse's short stay, "the apparent disinclination" in the French naval officers "to force the harbour of New York," and "the feeble compliance" of the state governments to his requests for men, he relinquished "all idea of attacking New York" and instead ordered the French army and a large detachment of the Continental army to march for "the Head of Elk to be transported to Virginia for the purpose of cooperating with the force from the West Indies against the Troops in that State."[25] That momentous decision changed the course of the war. A mere five days after Washington made his decision, the French army and half the Continental army in New York were on the march to Virginia to meet de Grasse and join Lafayette's army that had been holding Cornwallis at bay in that state.

The threat of a siege that the operations of the French and American armies had placed in Clinton's mind continued to affect his actions (or lack of action). Even as the allies marched from the Hudson into New Jersey, he remained on the defensive. By the time he realized the allies were marching south through New Jersey, it was too late to do anything

24. Ibid., 3:405–9.
25. Ibid., 3:409–10.

but sail to the Chesapeake with troops to aid Cornwallis.[26] But de Grasse's victory at the Battle of the Chesapeake would soon foreclose that option. Between Rochambeau and Washington, as well as their troops, trust had been established and experience gained in combined operations. Now the allied armies could march with confidence to confront Cornwallis, who had taken post on the York River and begun to fortify an old tobacco port as a base—Yorktown.

---

26. See Clinton to Cornwallis, September 2-4 and 6, in Saberton, *Cornwallis Papers*, 6:32-34. Clinton's letters to Cornwallis throughout June, July, and early August reveal this defensive mindset. See the letters of June 8, 11, 19; July 11 and 15; and August 11 in Saberton, *Cornwallis Papers*, 5:95–97, 123–25, 135–36, 142–43 and 6:20-24. In the letter of July 15, Clinton told Cornwallis he had been "reduced" by detachments to Virginia to a "very bare defensive" at New York. Clinton was preparing at most for a quick offensive in the Philadelphia-Delaware River region to "seize" the supplies stored in that city, but then he planned to bring the troops back to defend New York (see Clinton to Cornwallis, June 28, in Saberton, *Cornwallis Papers*, 5:114–15).

The Abdication(s) of King George III

BOB RUPPERT

On April 1, 2015, Queen Elizabeth II announced the creation of the Georgian Papers Programme. It is a ten-year project to transcribe, digitize, conserve, catalogue, and disseminate close to 425,000 pages related to England's Hanoverian monarchs located in the Royal Archives at Windsor Castle. Most of the papers are personal and official correspondence—the remaining are household administrative records. The process is a collaboration between the Royal Archives, King's College London, the College of William and Mary in Virginia, and the Omohundro Institute of Early American History and Culture. Upon the Programme's completion, all of the papers will be made available online to historians and the public alike. Within the 425,000 pages are 33,000 related to the reign of King George III. Two of those pages, apparently written in March 1783, are entitled "A Draft of a Message of Abdication from George III to the Parliament."[1]

King George had already drafted an abdication on March 27, 1782 titled "Message from the King":

> His Majesty during the twenty one years He has sate on the Throne of Great Britain, has had no object so much at heart as he maintenance of the British Constitution, of which the difficulties He has at times met with from His scrupulous attachment to the Rights of Parliament a re sufficient proofs.
>
> His Majesty is convinced that the sudden change of Sentiments of one Branch of the Legislature has totally incapacitated Him from either conducting the War with effect, or from obtaining any Peace but on conditions which would prove destructive to the Commerce as well as essential Rights of the British Nation.

1. Royal Archives, GEO/MAIN/5367.

> His Majesty therefore with much sorrow finds He can be of no further Utility to His Native Country which drives Him to the painful step of quitting it for ever.
>
> In consequence of which Intentions His Majesty resigns the Crown of Great Britain and the Dominions appertaining thereto to His Dearly Beloved Son and lawful Successor, George Prince of Wales, whose endeavours for the Prosperity of the British Empire He hopes may prove more Successful.[2]

The last thing King George wanted was for Parliament to consider granting the colonies their independence, but with Gen. John Burgoyne's 1777 surrender at Saratoga in the north and Gen. Charles Cornwallis's 1781 surrender at Yorktown in the south; with his Ministry at odds with itself and him, and with his political strategists offering no new ideas as to how to successfully end the war, he knew that everything was coming to a head. On February 22, 1782, Henry Seymour Conway, a general in the British Army, member of Parliament for forty-one years and an opponent of Lord North's administration, introduced a motion in the House of Commons demanding an end to the war; later that day a vote was taken and the motion was defeated 194 to 193.[3] Five days later, Conway introduced a revised version of the motion; this time it passed 234 to 215.[4] Lord North knew that soon his ministry would be subject to (and likely lose) a no confidence vote. If this occurred George III would not have enough support in the House to fend off the Marquess of Rockingham and his Whigs who sought not only to put an end to the war but to grant independence to the American colonies. On March 8, John Cavendish introduced a no confidence, or censure, motion regarding His Majesty's ministers; later that day a vote was taken and the motion was defeated 226 to 216.[5] On March 18, North, believing that he would not survive the next vote, wrote to King George,

> There are no persons capable and willing to form a new Administration except Lord Rockingham and Lord Shelburne with their parties: and they will not act with any of the present Ministry but the Chancellor. It follows then that the present Cabinet must be removed.[6]

---

2. "Draft Message from the King, March 1782," in John Fortescue, ed., *The Correspondence of George the Third from 1760 to December 1783* (London: MacMillan, 1927), 5:447.
3. William Cobbett, *The Parliamentary History of England, from the Earliest Period to the Year 1803* (London: T. C. Hansard, 1814), 22:1028-48.
4. Ibid., 22:1064-1085.
5. Ibid., 22:1114-1150.
6. "Lord North to the King, March 18, 1782," in Fortescue, *The Correspondence of George the Third*, 5:395-96.

On March 19, he informed the King of the revised language in the motion that was scheduled to be brought forth the next day:

> That in the present Distracted state of the Country, it is contrary to the interests of His Majesty to continue the management of Public Affairs in the hands of the Present Ministers.[7]

On March 20, North, not willing to subject the King's ministry to another vote, announced in the House "as the object of the motion was to remove his Majesty's ministers, he could take upon him[self] to say that his Majesty's ministers were no more; and therefore the object being already attained, the means by which gentlemen had intended to obtain it, could no longer be necessary."[8] The House of Commons, the people's legislative body in Parliament, was no longer able to support the Ministry's war position; King George believed the expression of no confidence toward the Ministry was equally an expression of no confidence toward him. He feared that he was the king of a country which had no further use for him. The House adjourned until March 25; two days later, King George appointed the Marquess of Rockingham as the new Prime Minister. Interestingly, Rockingham then asked Edward Thurlow to remain as the Lord Chancellor in his administration.

It is not known why and when King George chose to change his mind about abdication, but the person most likely to have influenced his decision was Thurlow.[9] Thurlow had been handpicked by the King for the office of Lord Chancellor in 1778 and had shared the King's viewpoint regarding granting independence to the colonies. Thurlow also believed that the King should accept the inevitable, that is, that Rockingham and his Whigs would soon control Parliament.

Twelve months later, King George produced a draft of an abdication speech. This time it was not written by another person and was not in the form of a press release. Instead, it was a personal letter to the members of Parliament. Since the draft message in 1782, King George had to deal with the death of Rockingham on July 1, 1782 and the appointment three days later of Lord Shelburne, an ally of Rockingham and the third Prime Minister in less than four months; the resignation of

---

7. "Lord North to the King, March 19, 1781," ibid., 399-401.
8. Cobbett, *The Parliamentary History of England*, 22:1214-1215.
9. Edward Thurlow was the second closest member of the Privy Council to King George III; the closest was Lord North who had wanted to resign as far back as 1778 after Burgoyne's surrender.

Shelburne seven and half months later on February 24, 1783[10]; and the formation of a new political alliance in Parliament between his estranged prime minister, Lord North, and Charles James Fox, someone he strongly disliked. Feelings of "no further Utility" arose again but this time they were stronger. Early in March the King told John Dunning, Lord Ashburton, that he had prepared the letter "without assistance."[11]

The draft letter read:

> I cannot at the most serious, as well as most painful moment of My Life, go out of the Great Assembly, without communicating to You My Intentions, not asking Your Advice.
>
> The first time I appeared as Your Sovereign in this place now above twenty two years, I had the pleasing hope that being born among You, I might have proved the happy instrument of conciliating all Parties and thus collecting to the Service of the State the most respectable and most able Persons this Kingdom produced. Of this object I have never lost sight, though sad experience now teaches me that selfish Views are so prevalent that they have smothered the first of Public Virtues, attachment to the Country, which ought to warm the breast of every Individual who enjoys the advantage of this excellent Constitution, and the want of which Sentiment has prevented the Unanimity which must have rendered Britain invulnerable, though attacked by the most Powerful Combinations.
>
> My own Inclination to alleviate the Distresses of my People, added to the Change of Sentiments of one branch of the Legislature which rendered the real object of the War impracticable, made me undertake the arduous task of obtaining the Blessings of Peace, rendered indeed more difficult by the Resolution above alluded to. I cannot efficiently acknowledge the candour with which the Courts of France and Spain have conducted themselves during the Negociation of the Preliminary Articles, which greatly accelerated that desirable Work.
>
> Circumstances have since arisen that might make those Courts more doubtful of the stability of the Councils of this Country. I have again attempted to collect the most efficient Men of all Parties [who] under My Inspection. But this Patriotic attempt has proved unsuccessful by the obstinacy of a powerful party that has long publicly manifested a resolution not to aid in the Service of their Country.
>
> I must therefore to end a conflict which certainly puts a stop to every wheel of Government make a final Decision, and that I think my self compelled to do in this Assembly of the whole Legislature.

10. Shelburne resigned over the peace terms being negotiated.
11. John Cannon, *The Fox-North Coalition: Crisis of the Constitution, 1782-4* (Cambridge, University Press, 1969), 72n2.

A long Experience and a serious attention to the Strange Events that have successively arisen, has gradually prepared my Mind to expect the time when I should be no longer of Utility to this Empire: that hour is now come; I am therefore resolved to resign My Crown and all the Dominions appertaining to it to the Prince of Wales my Eldest Son and Lawful Successor and to retire to the care of My Electoral Dominions the Original Patrimony of my Ancestors. For which purpose I shall Draw up and Sign an Instrument to which I shall affix my Private Seal. I trust this Personal Sacrifice will awaken the various parties to a Sense of their Duty and that they will join in the Support and Assistance of the Young Successor.

You may depend on my arduous attention to Educate My Children in the Paths of Religion, Virtue and every other good Principle that may render them if ever called in any Line to the Service of Great Britain, not unworthy of the kindness they may hereafter meet with from a People whom collective I shall ever Love.

May that All Wise Providence who can direct the inmost thoughts as well as Actions of Men give My Son and Successor not only every assistance in guiding his Conduct, but Restore that sense of Religious and Moral Duties in this Kingdom to the want of which every Evil that has arisen owes its Source; and may I to the latest hour of my life, though now resolved forever to quit this Island, have the Comfort of hearing that the Endeavours of My Son, though they cannot be more Sincere than Nine have been for the Prosperity of Great Britain, be Crowned with better Success.[12]

The letter has three parts. To start, King George made it very clear that "Unanimity . . . rendered Britain invulnerable though attacked by the most powerful combinations" and inferred that the lack of unity going forward would render her vulnerable. He declared that the governing political class had lost "the first of Public Virtues—attachment to the Country," and replaced it with "selfish views." To him these selfish views represented a lack of unanimity.

Next the letter expressed that King George found it difficult to get "the most Efficient men of all parties" to join his government because many refused to serve unless they were joining others of the same party or faction, or the body they were joining had exclusive management over the affair or issue in question. "The obstinacy of a powerful party . . . has long publicly manifested a resolution not to aid in the Service of their Country." The powerful party he was referring to were the Whigs under Rockingham and then Shelburne. King George called

12. georgianpapers.com/2017/01/22/abdication-speech-george-iii/.

this partisanship "a conflict which certainly puts a stop to every wheel of Government." There is part of a sentence that King George scratched out in the draft that read "to become the tool of a Party neither My Duty to the Station I hold among you nor to my own Character will permit." By aligning himself with a party, he would be acting contrary to his duty and character and risk moving in a direction that could only lead to less unanimity. In his eyes the British polity was broken and he was powerless to do anything about it. He could no longer be of "utility" to his people and his kingdom.

The King concluded by writing, "I am therefore resolved to resign My Crown and all the Dominions appertaining to it to the Prince of Wales my Eldest Son and Lawful Successor . . . I trust this Personal Sacrifice will awaken the various parties to a Sense of their Duty and that they will join in the support and Assistance of the Young Successor." He was hoping that his son would be extended something that had not been extended to him: "I trust this Personal Sacrifice will awaken the various parties to a Sense of their Duty." In the draft of a letter that he never sent to his son, King George referred to "a cruel dilemma." The dilemma was not whether he needed "to take without destruction of my principles and honour; the resigning of my crown" but rather, should he be leaving the crown to his son who had not "yet come of age,"[13] not been schooled in political machinations and could become "the puppet . . . of the House of Commons."[14]

Who then convinced King George not to resign for a second time and why? It appears again to have been Edward Thurlow, the Lord Chancellor, with some help from Thomas Pitt, the cousin of the next prime minister, William Pitt the Younger. Their solution was for him not to resign, but rather to cut back on the patronage available to his ministers and the ranking Whigs in Parliament. This would in time make them unpopular and cost them their offices. It would also give the Prince of Wales more time to be groomed for his eventual position.

Little did anyone know, but George III would threaten to resign for a third time twenty-one months later on December 23, 1783.

---

13. "George III to Prince of Wales, March 1783," in Arthur Aspinall, ed., *Correspondence of George Prince of Wales* (London: Cassell and Company, 1963), 1: No. 71.
14. "George III to Lord Weymouth, March 25, 1783," in Fortescue, *The Correspondence of George the Third*, 6:310.

Jemima Howe, Facts and Fiction

JANE STRACHAN

Jemima Howe (1724–1805), a pioneer woman of the early Vermont frontier wilderness, survived a 1755 abduction along with her seven children ranging from six months to eleven years old, three years of captivity in French-Canada, and three husbands, the first two killed by Abenaki.[1] The early American literary genre of Indian captivity narratives presented the story of Jemima Howe, but cloaked it in myth. As literacy rates rose right after the American Revolution, especially among women, so climbed the popularity of these historical and often religious stories.[2] The burgeoning colonial readership provided the audience for Jemima Howe to become a celebrity, widely known as the "fair captive," alongside a hero of the American Revolution—her rescuer and suggested romantic lead, Maj. Gen. Israel Putnam—in two competing captivity narratives.

The importance of the captivity narrative in American literary history and its role in creating an American literature cannot be underestimated.[3] One of the first best sellers in this literary genre was *The Sovereignty and Goodness of God Being a Narrative of the Captivity and Restoration of Mrs. Mary Rowlandson*, likely arranged and written at least in part by Increase Mather, Puritan clergyman and president of Harvard, with his son, Cotton Mather, a minister and prolific author following in his father's footsteps with a well-known captivity narrative about Hannah Dustan. Mrs. Rowlandson's narrative went through nu-

---

1. Jane Strachan, "Jemimah Howe: Frontier Pioneer to Wealthy Widow," *Journal of the American Revolution*, December 9, 2021, allthingsliberty.com/2021/12/jemima-howe-frontier-pioneer-to-wealthy-widow/.
2. Nancy F. Cott, *The Bonds of Womanhood: "Women's Sphere" in New England, 1780–1835* (New Haven: Yale University Press, 1977), 15.
3. Gary L. Ebersole, *Captured by Texts. Puritan to Post-Modern Images of Indian Captivity* (Charlottesville and London: University Press of Virginia, 1995), 9–10.

merous printings from its initial publication in 1682 well into the 1800s and is considered a colonial classic even today.

During the next wave of this literary genre, authors, publishers and printers kept a particularly close eye on sales and the changing literary tastes of the fast-growing market, especially for sentimental fiction prevalent in captivity narratives such as those about Jemima Howe.[4] The two captivity narratives about her, published during the late 1780s and early 1790s, provide historical context and attest to the significance of these stories in the creation of American literature and myth just after the American Revolution. These founding-era narratives were increasingly secular and partisan, written to reinforce the rejection of British culture and the emergence of one that was uniquely American. They often offered a vision of the universal archetype—the creation of a "potent cultural myth," a hero who represented an American definition of self.[5] The intertwined captivity narratives of Jemima Howe and Israel Putnam that took place during the French and Indian War fit squarely into the later phase of this literary genre.

The first publication to reference the Howe-Putnam captivity narrative was David Humphreys' popular 1778 *The Essay on the Life of the Honourable Major-General Israel Putnam*. A Yale graduate, Humphreys was a confidant and scribe to George Washington, a lieutenant colonel in the American Revolution, foreign statesman, member of the writing group called the Connecticut Wits, and aide de camp to Putnam.[6] In his combined biography, history and romance, Humphreys devoted five pages of *The Essay* to the Putnam-Howe narrative which followed the often-cited story about Putnam nearly being burned alive at the stake by French-allied Caughnawaga, his rescue, and his time as a prisoner of war in Quebec where he met the engaging, yet delicate, Jemima Howe. Even if it was not romance at first sight, Putnam's behavior toward her represented the height of chivalry.

Humphreys portrayed Putnam as Jemima's protector from her French owners' lecherous advances and her personal escort on their

---

4. Frank Luther Mott, *Golden Multitudes: The Story of Best Sellers in the United States* (New York: Macmillan, 1947), 20, 303; Christopher Castiglia, *Bound and Determined* (Chicago: University of Chicago Press, 1996), 107, 208n2.

5. Greg Siemenski, "The Puritan Captivity Narrative and the Politics of the American Revolution," *American Quarterly*, 42, no. 1 (March 1990), 35.

6. David Humphreys, *An Essay on the Life of the Honourable Major-General Israel Putnam* (Indianapolis: Liberty Fund, 2000), xxiii. This reprint was taken from the last published edition of *The Miscellaneous Works of David Humphreys* in 1804. Unless otherwise noted, all references to *The Essay* refer to the 2000 reprint. Edward Cifelli, *David Humphreys* (Boston: Twayne Publishers, 1982), 76, 108.

eventual journey back home to freedom. Humphreys' *The Essay* represented a move away from Biblical or classic archetypes and toward the American-made, born and raised hero. In this popular work, Putnam symbolized cool-headed fearlessness against the jaws of death during wilderness warfare, an unquestioning love of country, and an unwavering sense of duty. On the other hand, Jemima Howe was Putnam's counterpoint, a sentimental heroine, a victim in distress.[7]

The second publication about Mrs. Howe was a supposed *Genuine and Correct Account of the Captivity Sufferings and Deliverance of Mrs. Jemima Howe* by long-time local Vermont clergyman, Rev. Mr. Bunker Gay, first published in volume three of *The History of New-Hampshire* by clergyman and historian Jeremy Belknap in 1792. Later that year and with Belknap's permission, Reverend Gay's account was extracted from this historical opus for further distribution as a pamphlet.[8] Although the title might suggest otherwise, its so-called veracity was a "standard publishing ploy to boost sales."[9]

Reverend Gay's portrayal of Jemima Howe, unlike that of Humphreys, had a psychological orientation that focused on her inner thoughts and fears. In his pen, her role as a mother was paramount, especially her concern for the welfare of her dispersed children during their three years of captivity. It also included several references to "all-powerful providence" as the reason for Jemima's perseverance and survival, as to be expected from a clergyman writing at the time.[10]

Both David Humphreys and Reverend Gay seized the opportunity to spin stories about their captives. Both writers wanted their work to provide "amusement" for readers. Humphreys was especially keen to promote a book about the life of a hero he had a major hand in creating as evidenced by his oversight of the publishing of at least seven editions of *The Essay* during his lifetime. With an obvious intention to sell copies, he also secured advertisements in the *Connecticut Courant and Weekly Advertiser* and the *Connecticut Journal* around the time *The Essay* was first released. The advertisements emphasized historical biography

---

7. Ebersole, *Captured by Texts*, 160–164.
8. Robert W. G. Vail, "Certain Indian Captives of New England," *Proceedings of the Massachusetts Historical Society*, 68, no. 3 (Oct. 1944–May 1947), (113–131), 126–127, detailed publication history of Reverend Gay's narrative.
9. *Women's Indian Captivity Narratives*, Ed. Kathryn Zabelle Derounian-Stodola (New York: Penguin Books, 1998), which uses Bunker Gay's text from *A Genuine and Correct Account of the Captivity, Sufferings and Deliverance of Mrs. Jemima Howe* (Boston: Belknap and Young, 1792), xxvi, 95.
10. Derounian-Stodola, *Women's Indian Captivity Narratives*, 98, 100.

and romance, with language like "authentic account of an American Hero" and stories that surpassed the "bounds of credibility" and "astonishing fictions of romance."[11]

As for Reverend Gay's spin, soon after his account of Jemima Howe appeared in Belknap's *History of New-Hampshire*, he took advantage of the ever-popular pamphlet, another distribution channel to gain readers. But that's not all he did. After all, the good reverend's work, as its title suggested, was authentic and true, thus implying that Humphreys' *The Essay* was not. As Providence would have it, the reverend's work followed that of Humphreys and so he had the advantage of reading an extract of *The Essay* in a Boston newspaper and reciting it to Jemima Howe. At first, she thought it was all true. But for reasons that Reverend Gay never explained, she changed her mind about the truthfulness of several of Humphreys' stories.[12] With that competitive information in hand, Reverend Gay countered Humphreys' romantic tales.

Thus, the stage was set in the battle for readers between David Humphreys, a widely-read American poet, writer and "literary celebrity" of the time; and Reverend Gay, who was Jemima Howe's local pastor, neighbor and a poetic writer of "quaint epitaphs" and eulogies of his long-gone flock.[13]

Despite the undeniable facts about Putnam as a French prisoner of war in Quebec, especially a daring plot to escape with three other adventuresome characters—interesting stories in their own right—they were not included in Humphreys' storyline.[14] Instead, he focused on Putnam's willingness to jeopardize his own safety to protect Jemima Howe from her French masters' repeated attempts to compromise her virtue.

---

11. "David Humphreys to Jeremiah Wadsworth," June 4, 1788 in David Humphreys, *The Essay*, 1–3, about the purpose and nature of his work; Derounian-Stodola, *Women's Indian Captivity Narratives*, 97, for Reverend Gay "speaking" to Belknap in the opening of Mrs. Howe's account; Frank Landon Humphreys, *Life and Times of David Humphreys: Soldier—Statesman—Poet, 'Belov'd of Washington'* (1917, repr., New York and London: Franklin Classics Trade Press, n.d.), 2:Appendix VI, 461–466; *Connecticut Courant* (Hartford), September 1, 1778, 1; *Connecticut Journal* (New Haven), September 3, 1788, 3.
12. Derounian-Stodola, *Women's Indian Captivity Narratives*, 94, 104.
13. Cifelli, *David Humphreys*, 49, for the quotation "literary celebrity;" Abby Maria Hemenway, *Vermont Historical Gazetteer* (Brandon, VT: Published by Mrs. Carrie E. H. Page, 1891), 5:292, 309.
14. For Putnam's adventures in Quebec, see Robert C. Alberts, *The Most Extraordinary Adventures of Major Robert Stobo* (Boston: Houghton Mifflin, 1965), 202–203; Simon Stevens, *Journal of Lieut. Simon Stevens, from the Time of his being Taken, near Fort William-Henry, June 25th 1758* (Boston: Edes and Gill, 1760), 3–5.

In one romantic scene, Humphreys wrote that the young Frenchman was "fired to madness by the sight of her charms ... forcibly seized her hand ... declared that he would now satiate the passion which she had so long refused." Mrs. Howe used "tears, those prevalent female weapons ... while he ... snatched a dagger, and swore he would put an end to her life." She implored him to do so, but finally managed to escape from his clutches. Putnam rushed to her rescue, warning the persistent young man that he would "protect the lady at the risk of his life." According to one literary critic, Humphreys' version of the Putnam-Howe captivity narrative read like a "novel of seduction" rather than history or biography. Even today, reading about Putnam's chivalry and fatherly relationship with Mrs. Howe's young sons, it is easy to imagine that he, too, had not escaped the power of Mrs. Howe's charms.[15]

Humphreys' captivity narrative also served as partisan propaganda to affirm the shift from that of being collective captives of a tyrant king to a collective self-image as citizens of a nascent republic built on American soil. It was not an accident that Humphreys' story had no British officials, officers or regulars to support the colonial prisoners of war in Quebec. Even the French governor-general of New France, Pierre de Rigaud, Marquis de Vaudreuil-Cavagnial, representing America's war-time ally, negotiated an arrangement to release certain prisoners with Col. Peter Schuyler of New York, including Jemima Howe, three of her sons and Israel Putnam. Governor Marquis de Vaudreuil's presence is palpable in Humphreys' story and provides a stark contrast to the absence of British actors.[16]

In Humphreys' pen, once Putnam and Mrs. Howe rediscovered their freedom, they became literary metaphors for the revolutionary sentiment and triumph over British assaults on liberty. By using this story to create Putnam as an early American heroic archetype, Humphreys could showcase the emerging nation's political and cultural independence from Britain and put Israel Putnam and, to a lesser extent, Jemima Howe, on the map of America's early literature and mythmaking.[17]

Humphreys' competition was Reverend. Gay, whose writing about Jemima Howe was not as accurate as his "genuine and correct" title

---

15. Humphreys, *The Essay*, 51–52; Derounian-Stodola, *Women's Indian Captivity Narratives*, 93, for the quotation "novel of seduction;" Helen Hunt Jackson, *Bits of Travel at Home* (1878; repr., Boston: Little, Brown, and Co., 1909), 202–203.
16. Siemenski, "The Puritan Captivity Narrative and the Politics of the American Revolution," 36, 45.
17. Ibid., 36, 45 and 52; Leon Howard, *The Connecticut Wits* (Chicago: University of Chicago Press, 1943), 270; Cifelli, *David Humphreys*, 74.

claimed. From the very first word of his narrative, Reverend Gay is a co-author and editor interjecting his own comments into the story.[18]

As editor, Reverend Gay altered Jemima's voice to embellish her story and exploit the growing popularity of this market. For example, after she was sold by her captors to a Frenchman named Joachim Saccapee and his son, who considered her their paid-for property, they subjected her to their "excessive fondness" and continuous advances. It was through Colonel Schuyler that the Marquis de Vaudreuil learned of her plight, chastised the father and ordered the son, an Army officer, from "the field of Venus to the field of Mars."[19] This was a phrase a Harvard-educated editor would know and use, not one a frontier woman would likely know, let alone use.

To bolster the reverend's truth-bearing title—and despite acknowledging that he had read only an extract of *The Essay* in a Boston newspaper much earlier—it is not until the very end of the narrative when Reverend Gay mentioned Israel Putnam and took umbrage with Humphreys' "romantick and extravagant" tales, claiming that he was "misinformed" about the details.[20] For example, with the full support of Jemima, the reverend countered Humphreys' story about the "amorous and rash lover" whose veins boiled at the thought of her such that "blood would frequently gush from his nostrils." Humphreys detailed the obsession further, adding that the unrequited lover, who had now lost his senses, followed the newly released prisoners to Lake Champlain, jumped into the cold November water and swam after Jemima Howe's boat, never to be seen again.[21]

Although Reverend Gay's version of this story was toned down, it too seems questionable. He countered Humphreys' story with his own and with the full support of his subject. He wrote that when Jemima was enroute from Canada to Albany, she met the young Saccappe while on a boat with Colonel Schuyler. The persistent man boarded, gave her some "handsome presents" and then departed in what appeared to be "tolerable good humour."[22] There is no indication if she rejected his gifts, which would have made the story plausible given his recent threat to kill her with his dagger. It is hard to imagine how or why Saccapee would make such a dramatic shift to a more gentlemanly demeanor, especially after his prized possession was taken from him.

18. Derounian-Stodola, *Women's Indian Captivity Narratives*, 94–95.
19. Ibid., xix, 102.
20. Ibid., 104.
21. David Humphreys, *The Essay on the Life of the Honorable Major-General Israel Putnam: Addressed to the State Society of the Cincinnati in Connecticut* (Hartford: Hudson and Goodwin, 1788), 80, quotations are from the original printing of *The Essay* in 1788.
22. Derounian-Stodola, *Women's Indian Captivity Narratives*, 104.

Reverend Gay continued with a story presumably told by Jemima. When she went to Canada after the French and Indian War to bring her daughter Submit back home, she again met the young Saccapee who showed her a lock of her hair and her name printed in vermilion on his arm. Reverend Gay never explained why Jemima, who claimed to need a "large stock of Prudence" to fend off the frequent encounters with the young man, would ever see him again. Although quick to point out Humphreys' romantic tales, the reverend never explained how the persistent man obtained a lock of her hair or her reaction to seeing her name in bright red painted on his arm.[23]

Reverend Gay gilded the anti-Humphreys lily again, countering another of his misinformed tales. The reverend explained that Mrs. Howe had never been appointed, let alone considered, to be sent to England as her hometown's agent to advocate for a local New Hampshire land claim being superior to that of a New York grant. On the other hand, Humphreys claimed she had been "universally designated" by her neighbors for the trans-Atlantic task. One often-cited expert on Indian captivity narratives has caustically noted that Humphreys' claim was completely "bogus."[24]

Interestingly, the Humphreys stories noted by Reverend Gay as romantic, extravagant and misinformed were omitted from the version of *The Essay* that was included in the last edition of Humphreys' *Miscellaneous Works*, dated 1804. Although we will never know with absolute certainty why Humphreys made these deletions, we can draw several well-founded conclusions. We know that Humphreys oversaw the publishing of this later work and made dramatic revisions throughout to accommodate new knowledge and the changing attitudes of readers. In this later edition of *The Essay*, he likely decided to bow to the competition in favor of a more fact-based, yet perhaps less commercially acceptable, story. This conclusion seems likely as the 1804 publication included a new footnote stating that these stories had come from Putnam himself and were omitted because "on further information, they appeared to be mistakes."[25] Just perhaps, this further information came from a competitive ecclesiastical source.

---

23. Ibid., 102, 104.
24. David Humphreys, *The Essay on the Life of the Honorable Major-General Israel Putnam: Addressed to the State Society of the Cincinnati in Connecticut* (Hartford: Hudson and Goodwin, 1788), 81–82, for the quotation "universally designated." Derounian-Stodola, *Women's Indian Captivity Narratives*, 104, 346n15.
25. Howard, *Connecticut Wits*, 259; Cifelli, *David Humphreys*, 104; Roy Harvey Pearce, "The Significances of the Captivity Narrative," *American Literature* 19, no. 1 (March 1947), 13; Humphreys, *The Essay*, 52, explaining the reason for the deletions.

The narratives of the two writers take different approaches to the literary genre of captivity narratives. Reverend Gay's approach is a story of a frontier woman and her inner thoughts during captivity, a damsel in distress who is a victim of the wilderness. Although Jemima Howe shows signs of assertive behavior, she still must seek out men for assistance. The reverend's story is about Jemima Howe and her concern for her family, reserving any mention of Putnam or criticisms of Humphreys until the end of the narrative.

On the other hand, Humphreys wove together a story about Putnam's capture by Indians and his calm (and, thus, heroic) character while nearly being roasted alive with a second captivity tale that details his intriguing relationship with a melancholy and sentimental (and, thus, sympathetic) heroine. Humphreys' interwoven stories also reflected the promise of optimism regarding what was then the western frontier and the courage and prowess of a newly emerging frontier hero, an American archetype. Humphreys' work is closely aligned with the beginning of Romantic fiction in which the hero of his own Indian captivity narrative steps into another captivity scene to rescue a fair maiden.[26]

In retrospect, it is not surprising that Humphreys would take the approach he did with *The Essay* and have such success with it. One of his Yale peers and member of the Connecticut Wits, the poet and lawyer John Trumbull, created the mold for a successful Romantic narrative. In 1786, Trumbull published a popular, albeit pirated, version of Daniel Boone's story published earlier by John Filson, a Kentucky surveyor and friend of Boone. Trumbull was obviously keen to sell a pamphlet about the increasingly popular western adventure that also included a female captive to cater to readers' tastes for a sensational story. Both Humphreys and Trumbull featured their lead character as the prototype of the frontier hero, thus, placing them squarely in the early stages of American romantic fiction. Both writers, but especially Trumbull, likely far exceeded their wildest expectations with the numerous reprints of their popular stories.[27]

Long after these first stories about Jemima Howe and Israel Putnam, several additional works were written about the "fair captive." The two most notable are a lengthy prose-like poem by Annie L. Mearkle published in 1937 and the more well-known historical novel by the prolific New England writer Marguerite Allis in 1941, *Not without*

---

26. Ebersole, *Captured by Texts*, 160–164; Richard Slotkin, *Regeneration through Violence, the Mythology of the American Frontier*, (Norman, OK: University of Oklahoma Press), 324.
27. Slotkin, *Regeneration through Violence, the Mythology of the American Frontier*, 323, 325.

Peril. In true romantic form, Allis tells of Putnam and Jemima Howe parting ways after their release from French captivity, hardly able to speak as they hold back their tears, even the gregarious and usually outspoken Putnam. These writings, like those from the late Revolutionary era, continue to cloud an authentic account of the life of Jemima Howe, an indefatigable pioneer heroine and well-to-do widow who became a financial matriarch to her family and business partner of influential male neighbors and politicians, well worth knowing about for inspiration today.[28]

---

28. Angela Marco [A. L. Mearkle], "Fair Captive, a Colonial Story" (Brattleboro, VT.: Stephen Day Press, 1937); Marguerite Allis, *Not without Peril* (1941; repr., Charlestown, NH: Old Fort No. 4 Associates, 2004).

The Articles of Confederation– A Silver Lining

RICHARD WERTHER

The Articles of Confederation described the first government of the new United States. As one may imagine from understanding the later debates on the Constitution in 1787, there were a number of points of contention on the Articles that were later re-argued for the Constitution. But there was one issue in the debate on the Articles that would ultimately play a significant role in the way the United States coalesced and grew. It did not have to be "re-litigated" when the Constitution was debated. The issue was the disposition of the continent's western lands, those lands beyond the recognized borders of the British colonies. Who would own them, and how would they be managed? Despite all their failures, the settlement of the western lands question would become the most enduring positive contribution of the Articles of Confederation.

The founders had the foresight to begin design of a new government while the Declaration of Independence was still being drafted. On June 12, 1776, the Continental Congress formed a committee consisting of a single representative from each colony: Josiah Bartlett (New Hampshire), Samuel Adams (Massachusetts), Stephan Hopkins (Rhode Island), Roger Sherman (Connecticut), R. R. Livingston (New York), John Dickinson (Pennsylvania), Thomas McKean (Delaware), Thomas Stone (Maryland), Thomas Nelson, Jr. (Virginia), Joseph Hewes (North Carolina), Edward Rutledge (South Carolina), Button Gwinnett (Georgia), and Francis Hopkinson (New Jersey). It delivered an initial draft just one month later, penned by John Dickinson. The Articles were debated by the full Congress until November 15, 1777, and that month the President of Congress sent a circular letter with the Articles to the state legislatures for their review and approval.

Yet the Articles were not fully ratified until February 2, 1781! Why so long? Besides the fact that there was a war going on that naturally occupied people's time, the western lands issue held up the Articles for nearly four years after the draft was issued. To place this timing in some context, the Articles were finally approved only about seven months before the British surrender at Yorktown and two years and six months before the formal ending of hostilities in September of 1983. The new nation got through most of the war without a fully approved structure of government. In the interim, the Continental Congress ran things, and while it probably hewed closely to the principles outlined in the Articles, the Articles were not the official law of the land.

When Dickinson delivered his draft, many debates arose, both before the document left Congress and after it went to the states for review. Two major issues involved apportionment of costs and representation in Congress. These two foreshadowed similar debates on the Constitution.

The argument on the apportionment of costs hinged on a familiar issue that would arise again—slavery, and whether enslaved people should be counted if the allocation was based on population. Benjamin Harrison of Virginia offered a compromise that two slaves count as one free laborer, presaging the three-fifths compromise later incorporated into the Constitution. Although a vote along sectional lines would have favored the counting of enslaved people in some manner, Congress eventually abandoned headcounts altogether and decided to allocate costs based on relative land values (a seemingly difficult and subjective number to quantify).[1] A parallel discussion emerged on voting rights by state and whether they should be weighted in some way or simply be one state, one vote. This time the fault line was between the large states and the small states. Roger Sherman of Connecticut proposed that two votes be taken on each question, one with voting weighted by state population and the other being one vote per state. Apparently, the delegates were not yet ready for the Connecticut Compromise of 1787 and voted to go with one vote per state.

This brings us to our main event—the debates over western land holdings. This is where things bogged down, at least for one state. The new lands acquired in the 1783 Treaty of Paris represented a vast territory stretching from the Appalachian Mountains to the Mississippi River between the southern shores of the Great Lakes and Spanish Florida. To whom did these lands belong? Initially seven states claimed them based on old colonial grants and Indian treaties: Massachusetts, Connecticut, New York, Virginia, North Carolina, South Carolina, and

---

1. William J. Watkins, Jr., *Crossroads for Liberty* (Oakland, CA: Independent Institute, 2016), 31.

Georgia. These states supported this stance by claiming that the state of war with Britain meant that their borders reverted to those specified by their original colonial charters, which were expansive although still limited by the proclamation line of 1763 which limited expansion to the Appalachians. Many of these state claims were overlapping. The other six states had no claims beyond their existing boundaries.[2] Termed "landless" states, they feared that the other states, enlarged by western territories, would become economically and politically dominant.[3]

In the initial comment period for the Articles, Maryland, one of the landless six, proposed the following change to Article IX: "the United States and Congress assembled shall have the power to appoint commissioners, who shall be fully authorized and empowered to ascertain and restrict the boundaries of such confederated states which claim to extend to the River Mississippi or the South Sea."[4] This amendment was deferred and then voted down. So began Maryland's battle.

"Maryland's refusal to agree to the Articles of Confederation until Congress should be given some portion of the West," writes one historian, "was interpreted as a result of the 'farsighted policy of Maryland in opposing the grasping land claims of Virginia and three of the Northern States.'"[5] This sentiment grew, frankly, less out of any noble patriotic aim or idealistic long-term vision than it did out of a straight-up jealousy of Virginia and the hopes and speculative dreams of the land companies within it.[6]

The landless states wanted the Articles to stipulate that Congress limit the boundaries of those states claiming western lands. Under their proposal, Congress would take ownership of the western lands and sell off them off, using the money to benefit all by paying off war debts. Beyond pure economic concerns, the landless states had concerns that Virginia, already the most influential state in the union, would raise its influence even more given its massive western holdings (230 million acres, over 60 percent of the total western acreage claimed by the seven states).[7] Figure 1 shows the land holdings and claims of the colonies at the time the Articles were adopted.

---

2. Farley Grubb, *Founding Choices—American Economic Policy in the 1790s* (Chicago and London: University of Chicago Press, 2011), 261.
3. Ibid.
4. The Library of Congress: Journals of the Continental Congress, June 22, 1778.
5. Merrill Jensen, "The Cession of the Old Northwest," *The Mississippi Valley Historical Review*, Vol. 23, No. 1 (June 1936), 27.
6. Ibid.
7. Watkins, *Crossroads for Liberty*, 32.

Figure 1: Land holdings and claims of the colonies in 1781. (*Wikimedia Commons*)

Some states such as Virginia claimed that their borders extended all the way to the South Sea (the Pacific Ocean), which included land claimed both by the United States and the Indians, and land claimed by Spain.

Dickinson's first draft of the Articles provided, though weakly, for Congressional governance over the western lands. The Articles implied that Congress had the authority to judge matters related to the boundaries of states or their jurisdiction, but only as a last resort. Adding to the uncertainty of this arrangement, Congress lacked the executive power to enforce such decisions. Even if Congress were to rule in matters of interstate conflict, it would be up to the states to abide by that ruling.

Samuel Chase of Maryland was a particularly strong supporter of vesting the power of controlling state borders in Congress. Benjamin Harrison of Virginia countered that Virginia's large claims were simply based on its charter, just as Maryland's were based on its. Harrison warned that "gentlemen shall not pare away the Colony of Virginia."[8] Along the same lines, Benjamin Huntington of Connecticut, a state with western lands (albeit much smaller than Virginia's) questioned whether the landless states could prove that Virginia's claims and associated power posed a threat to the landless states and, even if they did, it didn't follow that Congress could claim the right to alter the chartered borders of a colony. He urged unity against what he termed "mutilating charters."[9]

At this stage, the power of Virginia won out. The delegates realized that, if stripped of its vast territories, Virginia would likely opt for disunion. They relented and Dickinson's provision giving Congress power over the western lands was struck. But the battle was not over for the landless states, and they searched for other ways to solve the problem. But they had little defense other than to withhold approval of the Articles. In October they made a final attempt to write their desires into the Articles of Confederation. They offered a series of motions designed to give Congress power to fix the western limits of the landed states. Each of the motions failed.[10] Eleven states approved the Articles between late 1777 and late 1778. Virginia, perhaps not surprisingly, was the first to approve. Delaware held out for a year, approving in 1779. Maryland, now the lone non-approver, kept on sparring with Virginia.

Virginia's General Assembly pushed back, after it signed but Maryland still hadn't, against what it considered unlawful interference by the nascent national government in an independent state's internal affairs. The legislature issued a "remonstrance" on December 14, 1779

> Should congress assume a jurisdiction, and arrogate to themselves a right of adjudication, not only unwarranted by, but expressly contrary to the fundamental principles of the confederation; superseding or controuling the internal policy, civil regulations, and municipal laws of this or any other state, it would be a violation of public faith, introduce a most dangerous precedent which might hereafter be urged to deprive

---

8. Ibid., 33.
9. Ibid.
10. Jensen, *The Cession of the Old Northwest*, 33.

of territory or subvert the sovereignty and government of any one or more of the United States, and establish in congress a power which in process of time must degenerate into an intolerable despotism.[11]

But Maryland remained stubborn. By 1780 they were still flatly refusing to ratify until this issue was solved by the states claiming western lands ceding them to the national government for "the general benefit." The problem of western land claims was clearly the only obstacle to final ratification of the Articles of Confederation.[12] Besides Maryland withholding its approval, the only other tactic for the landless states was to press states with such claims to cede their claims to the national government, despite a lack of any real negotiating leverage.

One concern that surfaced in the debate was that the states with western land holdings would move toward empire at some point. On the frontier westerners worried about the imperial or colonial intentions of the East, and they talked about it quite freely. It would be difficult to disabuse those states of the visions of their own colonial holdings.[13] With freebooters on the loose like Aaron Burr and James Wilkinson, the latter (and perhaps the former) under the pay of the Spanish, anything was possible. It is not overstating the case to say that the "conflicts over which governments had jurisdiction over these lands created the first crisis of disunion."[14]

Examples of this had surfaced already. In 1784 the North Carolina Assembly entertained a proposal for three counties of its western lands to be organized as the state of Franklin. The state even went so far as to hold a constitutional convention, agreeing on things like a unicameral legislature and guarantees of religious freedom. John Sevier was appointed governor, and a delegate was dispatched to Congress to request that Franklin be admitted to the union as the fourteenth state. There were no real processes or rules for this. Due to a number of complications with land treaties with the Cherokees, the state of Franklin teetered; by 1787 new leaders rallied for a return to North Carolina sovereignty. Sevier tried but failed to interest the Spanish governor in New Orleans to annex the state and was as a result arrested for treason. He was rescued from prison by a heavily-armed gang of followers before he could be tried. In February of 1789, Franklin leaders including

---

11. Virginia's Cession of the Northwest Territory, www.virginiaplaces.org/boundaries/cessions.html.
12. Grubb, *Founding Choices*, 263
13. Robert V. Remini, "The Northwest Ordinance of 1787: Bulwark of the Republic," *Indiana Magazine of History*, Vol. 84, No. 1 (March 1988), 17.
14. Grubb, *Founding Choices*, 259.

Year	State	Acres	Notes
1781	New York	202,187	jointly claimed by Massachusetts
1784	Virginia	229,917,493	some acres jointly claimed by other states, excludes Kentucky, and includes lands reserved in Ohio to Virginia
1785	Massachusetts	34,560,000	jointly claimed by other states
1786	Connecticut	25,600,000	jointly claimed by other states, but with 3,800,000 of Ohio held back as a reserve
1787	South Carolina	3,136,000	solely claimed
1790	North Carolina	26,679,600	mostly Tennessee which had already been alienated and so is typically not counted
1802	Georgia	56,689,920	solely claimed
Gross Total		376,785,200	simple sum
Net Total Ceded To the National Government		221,989,787	minus overlapping claims, the North Carolina cession, and Virginia and Connecticut reserve lands in Ohio

Figure 2: Cessions of land from each state, 1781—1802. Used with permission of Farley Grubb, National Bureau of Economic Research.

a repentant Sevier took an oath of allegiance to North Carolina, clearing the way for North Carolina to include the Franklin land as part of their state in the session of Congress. The short existence of the state of Franklin, if nothing else, provides a representation of how Congress did not want the process for new states to work.[15]

When Maryland's resistance finally broke, it wasn't because Virginia wore them down. Instead, it was precipitated by a series of raids by the British navy and privateers throughout the Chesapeake Bay region in 1780. When Maryland asked the French to provide ships to block the raids, the French responded with a suggestion that Maryland should ratify the Articles of Confederation first.[16] The ongoing campaign by landless states also had slowly worn down opposition to those states' proposals, and later in 1780 Congress resolved that all lands ceded by states to the national government should be "disposed of for the common benefit of the United States." As these conditions were hammered

15. Michael Toomey, "The State of Franklin," northcarolinahistory.org/encyclopedia/state-of-franklin/.
16. Virginia's Cession of the Northwest Territory, www.virginiaplaces.org/boundaries/cessions.html.

out, states one by one from 1781 through 1802 ceded their western lands to the national government. The commitment to cede these lands in 1781, along with the practical considerations of French defense support, opened the door to the final ratification, by Maryland, of the Articles of Confederation on March 1, 1781.[17] On March 1, 1784 Congress accepted Virginia's cession of western lands, three years after the completion of the Confederation.[18]

The avalanche of state cessions is shown in Figure 2.[19]

Between 1780 and 1787, Congress affirmed its authority over the ceded lands and established the basic principles and policies of land distribution and governance for decades to come. This was accomplished by the passage of three great ordinances—the Ordinance of 1784, the Ordinance of 1785, and the Northwest Ordinance of 1787—the first initiated under Thomas Jefferson and then fleshed out and carried forward by others in Congress, with the 1785 and 1787 Ordinances superseding the 1784 Ordinance.[20] The cessions happening simultaneous to this are depicted in Figure 3, overleaf.

Particular attention should be paid to the Northwest Ordinance of 1787, which historian Robert Remini has dubbed the "Bulwark of the Republic." The signature achievement of the Articles of Confederation government, this Ordinance was one of the most important, progressive, and far-reaching legislative acts in the nation's history.[21] The Northwest Ordinance, along with the Land Ordinances of 1784 and 1785, set up the structure for the orderly addition of states to the union. Until these Ordinances, there had been significant dangers of states setting up their own colonial empires or territories coming under foreign influence.

Dr. James White, a North Carolina congressman who in the words of one recent historian had a dream of empire for "Greater Franklin," told Don Diego de Gardoqui, the Spanish minister to the United States, that the western settlements would separate from the United States if Spain would reopen the Mississippi River, provide a military alliance and commercial concessions, and permit them to expand their territory down the Tennessee River past the Muscle Shoals to the headwaters of the Alabama and Yazoo Rivers.[22] Another such threat in-

---

17. Grubb, *Founding Choices*, 264, as discussed in Journals of the Continental Congress 19: 208-24.
18. Jensen, *The Cession of the Old Northwest*, 48.
19. Grubb, *Founding Choices*, 264.
20. Ibid., 282-283.
21. Remini, "The Northwest Ordinance of 1787: Bulwark of the Republic," 15.
22. Ibid., 20.

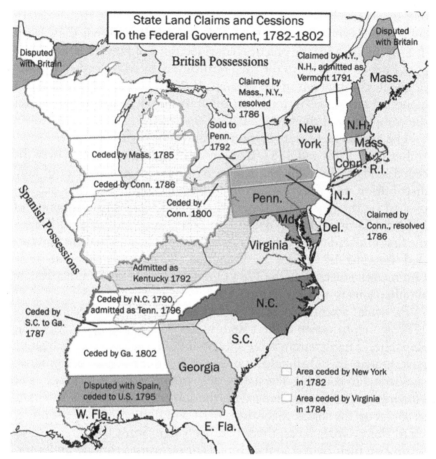

Figure 3: Land cessions from 1782 thru 1802. (*Wikipedia Commons*)

volved the ever-scheming Wilkinson. He came to Kentucky from Maryland around 1783 and quickly established himself as a leader of the movement to separate Kentucky from Virginia. He demanded radical action, and there was plenty of talk about establishing an independent nation. Wilkinson and his friends called for a declaration of independence from Virginia and from the United States. It was decided to take the issue to the people and the question of separation was narrowly rejected, a little too close for comfort.[23]

What made the difference, what completely turned the situation around, was the passage of the Northwest Ordinance. It was passed by a skeleton crew of only eighteen congressmen as all the big guns were

23. Ibid., 21.

either at the Constitutional Convention or out of the country on diplomatic missions. But the backbenchers came through, passing the ordinance on July 13, 1787.[24] Now the West knew that Congress had a policy with respect to the territories and that that policy meant colonial rule until such time as the settlers were prepared to take their place as co-equals with the other states in the Union. The United States could now expand, not as an empire with subject peoples and territory but by the orderly addition of new, sovereign states; and these states, in the words of the Ordinance, would be "on an equal footing with the original States in all respects whatsoever."[25] At the Constitutional Convention, delegates approved Article IV, section 3, paragraph 2 of the Constitution which stated, "The Congress shall have Power to dispose of and make all needful Rules and Regulations respecting the Territory or other property belonging to the United States."[26]

So, was the Articles of Confederation the major failure it has been known as? Well, maybe, but what was achieved here was worth the price of admission so to speak. It set the stage for an orderly growth of the American republic and ultimately secured the achievement of its destiny.

---

24. The Ordinance had to be revisited and tweaked to be in compliance with the new Constitution when the latter went into effect in 1789. This was accomplished without incident, and it became The Northwest Ordinance of 1789.
25. Ibid., 23.
26. Grubb, *Founding Choices*, 265.

Undeceived: Who would Write the Political Story of the Revolution

JAMES M. SMITH

In July 1783 John Jay, one of the Americans negotiating a treaty of peace between Great Britain and the United States, was sitting at his desk. The negotiations, taking place in Paris, France had been going on for some months with much quibbling over language, borders, trading rights and fishing rights. Sentences were being written and rewritten over and over again. Now as the negotiations were entering their final stage, Jay sat down and thought of the future. He had some concerns and he wrote to Charles Thomson, Secretary of the Continental Congress about them.

Jay had met Thomson when he was a member of the First Continental Congress that met in August 1774. Jay was a delegate from New York and was considered a moderate. John Adams, a radical from Massachusetts, did not think much of Jay at the time. A number of colonies had chosen radicals in the resistance to Britain as their delegates, with the most radical delegates coming from Massachusetts and Virginia. There quickly developed an alliance between the Adamses of Massachusetts and Virginians Richard Henry Lee and Patrick Henry. There were moderates like John Jay of New York and John Dickinson of Pennsylvania as well as conservatives like Joseph Galloway of Pennsylvania and James Duane of New York.

On the first day of the congress, it was decided that someone needed to be the secretary. The conservatives had centered on James Duane, the moderates on Silas Deane, but the radicals reached outside the membership of the congress and chose Charles Thomson. He was the most radical leader in Philadelphia and had been deliberately left off the Pennsylvania delegation by the Pennsylvania legislators, thinking they would isolate him from any influence in the congress. Instead, the conservatives found that the radicals had, behind the scenes, already rounded up enough votes to make him the offer of secretary by a wide margin. Thus, Charles Thomson became a central part of the congress. He was the only one to stay in his position throughout the whole fifteen years of the Continental Congress. No document was official without his signature. Many times, especially after the war, there were days and weeks when he was the only one in attendance. When the others went home, he alone was the government of the United States. He sat on many committees as the secretary. He undoubtedly had influence in unofficial discussions on the issues facing the congress. Over the years he developed a reputation for honesty and fairness.

It was natural for Jay to consider that Charles Thomson was particularly well suited for the special task he had in mind. Jay was concerned that with the coming of peace, Americans would start competing for credit about winning the revolution. He knew only too well that the Continental Congress had been full of factions and partisanship throughout the revolution. He himself had, during the early days of the first Continental Congress, belonged a faction believing in moderation on independence and dealing with Great Britain, while fellow peace negotiator John Adams had been a leader in the radical group, primarily from Massachusetts and Virginia, who wanted an aggressive posture and were early in calling for independence. During the ensuing years members of Congress had sparred over issues such as the abolition of slavery, the extent to which the United States should be subservient to France—a nation that had provided essential financial and military support—and a host of other issues. Now with independence won, everyone would be writing histories and memoirs each claiming that they or their favorite persons, or the faction that they belonged to, was the most influential and important in the victory.

Charles Thomson, Jay thought, was the one person to set the record straight. So Jay picked up his pen and wrote,

Passy, France, July 19, 1783
Dear Sir,

When I consider that no person in the world is so profoundly acquainted with the rise, conduct and conclusion of the American Revolution as yourself, I cannot but with wish that you would devote one hour in the four and twenty to giving posterity a true account of it. I think it might be comprised in a small compass. It need not be burdened with a *minute* account of battles, retreats, evacuations, etc.; leave those matters to more voluminous historians. The political story of the Revolution will be most liable to misrepresentation, and future relations

of it will probably be replete with intentional and accidental errors. Such a work would be highly important to your reputation, as well as to the cause of truth with posterity ... With every sincere esteem and regard, I am Sir, your friend and servant.[1]
John Jay

Whether Charles Thomson considered Jay's proposition at this time is not known; he was still busy in his role as secretary. The war was over and now a nation had to be built. Laws had to be formed, a system of finances arranged, diplomatic missions abroad maintained, a peace time army and navy regulated, a system of territories west of the Appalachian Mountains arranged and most important, a system for dealing with the Native Americans in this new nation established. The Continental Congress had lots of work to do. Charles Thomson remained at his post.

When, finally, a new government was formed in 1789, many of the old Continental Congress members were elected to positions within the new government. As such, many of the old feuds and factions and political disputes went with them. Charles Thomson, who had sided with none and made no political alliances, was left out. His last official act was to go to Mount Vernon and deliver the last message from the Continental Congress, that the new constitution had been properly ratified and that George Washington had been elected president and should report to New York City, the new capital. Thomson accompanied Washington to New York and there presented him with the official journals of the Continental Congress and all official papers and the seal of the United States. With that act Charles Thomson became unemployed.

As the new government took form, John Jay, who had become the first Chief Justice of the Supreme Court, again wrote to Charles Thomson to remind him of his earlier commission.

New York, November, 1791
Dear Sir,

As we enter this, our new beginning in the history of our nation and have reflected on the fact that you are not a part of our new government, I know that you are disappointed in that omission. However, upon reflection I wonder if that may not turn out for the best. My friend, you have been at the very center, the heart of our Revolution, from the beginning to the end. Indeed, there have been times when all have let

---

1. John Jay to Charles Thomson, July 19, 1783, *The Revolutionary Diplomatic Correspondence of The United States*, Francis Wharton, ed. (Washington, DC: Government Printing Office, 1889), Volume 6.

loose the responsibilities of government and duty. When others have absconded and abandoned their duties, you have remained at your post. During the fifteen years of our government in which the Continental Congress was our government and led us through the revolution and early days of peace and hard times, you have never failed your duty.

Then Jay reminded Thomson of his fears that the histories of the revolution would be inaccurate and full of partisan views, fears that since the end of the war had already begun to play out.

As you know, a number of persons, none of which have been as faithful from the beginning to the end, have written histories of our revolution. I have found them all wanting, either in completeness, candor, or truthfulness. They are almost all full of faction and point of view. You, my friend, who have been at the very center of it all, from the beginning to the end, can set the record straight. I am persuaded that heaven in its mysterious ways, have spared you of further employ to our country in order that you may perform one more, great and lasting service. You, my friend, should be the one to tell the story of our struggles as a nation. Only you were there from the beginning to the end, only you have the reputation to tell the story as it really happened without regard to faction or personality. Do this, my friend, do his great service for your country and posterity.

Your obedient Servant. John Jay

This time Thomson gave Jay's letters some thought. He did start his history. But he must have wondered if his narrative would have any place in America. Americans had already written their history based on what they saw with their hearts rather than their minds. The truth would have no place in American history. After burning all his papers in 1815 he wrote to John Jay, "No . . . I ought not, for I should contradict all the historians of the great events of the Revolution . . . Let the world admire the supposed wisdom and valor of our great men. Perhaps they may adopt the qualities that have been ascribed to them, and thus good may be done. *I shall not undeceive future generations.*"[2]

With the destruction of Thomson's papers one of his biographers wrote that "much of the truth about the revolutionary period is gone forever."[3] Another wrote that "Whatever the cause which inspired [Thomson] to destroy his papers, the loss to history was an irreparable one."[4]

2. Boyd Stanley Schlenther, *Charles Thomson: A Patriot's Pursuit* (Newark: University of Delaware Press, 1990), 204-205. Italics by author.
3. Ibid., 205.
4. Lewis R. Harley, *The Life of Charles Thomson* (Philadelphia: George W. Jacobs & Co., 1900), 160.

Partisan Politics and the Laws which Shaped the First Congress

SAMUEL T. LAIR

Admirers of the Founders are prone to adopt a romantic view of them as men of sheer principle who would scoff at the petty partisan squabbles and maneuvering that define our modern politics. No doubt, the men of that blessed generation approached politics with a unique commitment to first principles. At the same time, however, they were also deeply familiar with the less noble side of statesmanship and can be counted as amongst the shrewdest political tacticians of any age. This duality is exemplified by the period of ratification. A far cry from the spirit of fraternity which defined the Revolutionary period, it was a bitter partisan slugfest that continued long after the bell. In turn, the implementation of the infant Constitution's improved science of politics was forced to coincide with this lingering partisan contest. As state legislatures grappled with how to implement the Constitution's often vague mandates in the lead up to the first Congressional elections, the high browed theory expounded by the *Federalist* quickly became sacrificed on the altar of "party spirit." The result was a patchwork of elections laws that were just as much the product of political gamesmanship as Constitutional construction. To this end, this essay presents an overview of the state election laws for the First Congress and the political precedents they established. It will begin with a brief summary of the Constitution's overarching theory of Congressional representation, followed by an explication of how that theory was interpreted and often supplanted by partisan considerations in each state.

THE INTENTION OF THE FRAMERS

The Constitution is rather vague on how members of the House of Representatives are to be elected. The only guidance provided is in Article 1, Section 4, which gives a general pronouncement of power to state legislatures to determine the "times, places, and manner" of holding congressional elections, subject to the authority of Congress to "at any time by law make or alter such regulations."[1] The choice to allow state legislatures the freedom to regulate their congressional elections as they pleased was deliberate. As explained by James Madison during the Constitutional Convention of 1787, "whether the electors should vote by ballot or vivâ voce, should assemble at this place or that place; should be divided into districts or all meet at one place, shd all vote for all the representatives; or all in a district vote for a number allotted to the district . . . would depend on the Legislatures."[2] Nonetheless, despite this leeway, it seems that the Framers largely expected states to adopt regionally centered districts represented by a single individual—otherwise known as single-member districts. For example, Rufus King, a member of the Philadelphia Convention, predicted in the Massachusetts's Ratifying Convention that Congressional apportionment would involve having "this State thrown into eight districts, and a member apportioned to each," with the number and size of the districts periodically adjusted as the population increased.[3]

This assumption, or at least the preference for single-member districts, was collaborated by Madison in the *Federalist*. Madison argued that the purpose of representation in the extended sphere is to create a system in which the representatives will "refine and enlarge the public views."[4] It was essential to this scheme that representatives have "an immediate dependence on, and an intimate sympathy with, the people."[5] The best way to accomplish this, Madison argues, is through single-member districts. To this point, in defending the House against the charge that "it will be too small to possess a due knowledge of the interests of its constituents," he described such a system.[6] "Divide the largest state into ten or twelve districts," Madison explained, "and it will be found that there will be no peculiar local interest in either, which will not be within the knowledge of the representative of the district."[7]

---

1. U.S. Constitution, art. 1, sec. 4, cl. 1.
2. *The Records of the Federal Convention of 1787*, ed. Max Farrand (New Haven: Yale University Press, 1911), 2:241.
3. "Rufus King in the Massachusetts Convention, January 21, 1788," in *Records of the Federal Convention of 1787*, 3:267.
4. James Madison, "Federalist 10," in *The Federalist*, Gideon Edition, ed. George W. Carey and James McClellan (Indianapolis: Liberty Fund, 2001), 46.
5. James Madison, "Federalist 52," ibid., 273.
6. Ibid.
7. James Madison, "Federalist 46," ibid., 292.

Nevertheless, the authors of the *Federalist* also understood that partisan considerations would greatly influence the laws regulating congressional elections. As noted by Madison in *Federalist 10*, the "latent causes of faction are thus sown in the nature of man," meaning that "the spirit of party and faction" would always be a part of the "ordinary operations of government."[8] All that it required was the impulse to do so, which one of Madison's co-authors, John Jay in *Federalist 3*, aptly identified as "the prospect of present loss or advantage," which would "often tempt the governing party in one or two states to swerve from good faith and justice."[9] Indeed, Madison predicted during the Convention that these influences would likely be brought to bear on the Republic's system of representation. He noted that because of the license granted to the state legislatures to regulate elections, it could be expected that whenever they "had a favorite measure to carry" in Congress they would "mould their regulations as to favor the candidates they wished to succeed."[10] Accordingly, it was this very expectation of partisan influence that necessitated the safeguard of granting Congress the Constitutional authority to "at any time by law make or alter such regulations."

Madison's and Jay's expectation of "party spirit" influencing the operation of state governments would prove prescient during the creation of the laws that governed the elections for the First Congress. In fact, Madison himself expressed the justification for the partisan machinations that would soon play out in the election laws of several pro-Federalist states. In a letter to George Washington, Madison predicted that with ratification secured, the Antifederalist "plan will be to engage of the Legislatures in the task of undoing the work [of ratification]; or to get a Congress appointed in the first instance that will commit suicide on their own Authority."[11] Agreeing with Madison's assessment, Washington urged "all the advocates of the Constitution ... to combine their exertions ... in order that the Republic may avail itself of the opportunity for escaping from Anarchy, Division, and the other great national calamities that impended."[12] Many other likeminded proponents shared Madison and Washington's view that the fight over the adoption of the Constitution was far from over after ratification. As a result, Federalist

---

8. James Madison, "Federalist 10," ibid., 44.
9. John Jay, "Federalist 3," ibid., 11.
10. *Records of the Federal Convention*, Farrand, 2:241.
11. "James Madison to George Washington, June 27, 1788," in *The Papers of George Washington*, Confederation Series, vol. 6, 1 January 1788–23 September 1788, ed. W. W. Abbot (Charlottesville: University Press of Virginia, 1997), 356–357.
12. Ibid.

legislatures across the young nation would respond by passing election laws that would ensure their victory and, in turn, secure the Constitution.

THE STATE ELECTION LAWS

Pennsylvania was the first state to pass a law regulating their elections for the First Congress. Motivated by the proceedings of the Harrisburg Convention within their own state, the state's Federalists met in Philadelphia in the fall of 1788 to deliberate on the best mode for electing Federalist congressional representatives and presidential electors before the next state elections could threaten their majority.[13] Within several days, the Federalist dominated legislature rushed through an elections bill. The impetus of this law was expressed months earlier by one of the soon-to-be Federalist Congressman, Thomas Fitzsimons, who explained that the "representation of this state in the new Congress will in great measure depend upon the plan that may be adopted for choosing them. A good mode might now, I believe, be obtained, which in another Assembly would not be practicable."[14] Accordingly, rather than adopt the single-member district model advocated by *Federalist*, the legislature chose to elect its members of Congress through a general ticket, with the people submitting a written ballot with eight names and the eight individuals with the most votes receiving the appointment to the First Congress.[15] In conjunction, Pennsylvania Federalists also engaged in an early form of party organization, reconvening a second time to nominate a slate of Congressional candidates and Presidential electors under what was likely the first party ticket in United States history.[16]

Further evidence of the partisan motives behind the legislature's election law was expressed by Benjamin Rush, who observed in a private letter that "by obliging the whole state to vote in one ticket, it is expected the Federalists will prevail by a majority of two to one in the choice of Representatives."[17] Another Pennsylvania Federalist, Thomas Hartley, also admitted the plan's partisan motives, noting how the Antifederalists were "taking all the pains in their power to obtain a ma-

---

13. "Proceedings of a Philadelphia Meeting, October 1," in *The Documentary History of the First Federal Elections*, 1788-1790, ed. Merrill Jensen, Robert A. Becker (University of Wisconsin Press, Madison: 1976), 1:297.
14. "Thomas Fitzsimons to Samuel Meredith, Philadelphia, August 20," ibid., 1:253.
15. "The Pennsylvania Election Law, October 4," ibid., 1:299-301.
16. "James Wilson's Report of the Proceedings of the Lancaster Conference, November 3," ibid., 1:324-327.
17. "Benjamin Rush to Jeremy Belknap, Philadelphia, October 7," ibid., 1:302.

jority in the federal legislature," which required, in turn, "equal exertions" on the Federalists' side to prevent "the government [from becoming] embarrassed, and the wheels prevented from moving."[18] Beyond these partisan considerations, Hartley also noted some general advantages to the system, arguing that by electing representatives "at large you have a better chance of obtaining good men."[19] Interestingly, Madison spoke favorably of the Pennsylvania Legislature's decision, contradicting his position in the *Federalist* written only nine months earlier. He remarked that the mode of election adopted by Pennsylvania "will confine the choice to characters of general notoriety, and so far favorable to merit."[20] Nevertheless, he also admitted the system was "liable to some popular objections," likely resulting in some states, such as Virginia, to opt for the single-member district model.[21] Rather than lament this disparate standard, Madison suggested that perhaps it was to be desired so the best mode of election could be ascertained through experience.

In Massachusetts, leading up to the legislature's passage of its first election law, several Federalists advocated in print for following Pennsylvania's lead in electing its representatives at large. One Federalist, writing under the pseudonym Honorius, echoed the arguments of Hartley, stating that the general ticket provided the "fairest chance of selecting the best and most competent characters."[22] He also proclaimed it was the system most congenial to the spirit of the Constitution since it had a "happy tendency to nationalize the citizens, and to blend the interests of towns, districts, counties, and the whole commonwealth, into one great and general concern."[23] Nevertheless, when the Massachusetts legislature decided on the issue in November, it adopted the single-member district model without much disagreement within the Federalist caucus. However, the legislature's decision did not preclude them from ensuring a partisan advantage. The districts were drawn to provide an outsized influence to the Federalist urban strongholds along the eastern seacoast. Accordingly, despite only possessing a mere 35 percent of the state's population, the eastern counties received half of the state's eight representatives, compared to only one representative for 20 percent of the population in the counties within modern day Maine, and three representatives for the remaining 45 percent of

---

18. "Thomas Hartley to Tench Coxe, York, October 6," ibid., 1:304.
19. Ibid.
20. "James Madison to Thomas Jefferson, New York, October 8," ibid., 1:302.
21. Ibid.
22. "Honorius, Herald of Freedom, November 3," ibid., 1:469-470.
23. Ibid.

the state's population in the Western counties.[24] A more equitable distribution of seats would have seen the Antifederalist dominated western counties with four seats, the Maine counties with two seats, and three seats for the coastal counties.

In Maryland, a pseudonymous writer echoed the arguments made by Federalists throughout the republic, stating that the general ticket method was more representative of the spirit of the Constitution and best suited to choosing men of great character and independence of principles. By contrast, he charged the single-member districts would result in representatives who "will not be too proud to court what are generally called the poor folks, shake them by the hand, ask them for their vote and interest, and, when an opportunity serves, treat them to a can of grog, and whilst drinking it, join heartily in abusing what are called the great people."[25] The anonymous Federalist's jab was almost certainly directed at the Anti-Federalists, who often argued for a form of representation more closely associated with direct democracy and whose constituency consisted largely of the yeoman class.

The Federalist sentiments against single-member districts in print carried over to the state's election laws, where the Federalist-dominated legislature chose to forgo the system.[26] Instead, the legislature opted to adopt a peculiar hybrid between a single-member district and general ticket system. The Maryland law established that the state would still be divided into six districts with residency requirements for candidates. However, it also allowed voters to cast a ballot for a candidate in each of the six districts. By turning the elections into a statewide contest, these laws allowed the Federalists to draft and disseminate a unified party ticket, as was done in Pennsylvania.[27] Combined, the Federalists' rudimentary party organization and the state's general ticket election system all but ensured a Federalist sweep by allowing the predominantly pro-Constitution western Maryland counties to neutralize the Antifederalist strongholds of Anne Arundel, Baltimore, and Hartford counties. The results led one Antifederalist to publicly question whether "any honest, virtuous citizen, not a Slave to Party, could maintain, that the Act regulating the late Election, is constitutional, just, or wise?"[28] In his estimation, "the three counties (of) Frederick, Cecil, and

---

24. "The Passage of the Massachusetts Election Resolution, November 1-20," ibid., 1:476-477.
25. "A Pennsylvanian, reprinted in the *Maryland Journal*, Baltimore, November 14," ibid., 1:125.
26. "Maryland Election Law, December 22," ibid., 1:136-140.
27. "*Maryland Journal* (Baltimore), December 26," ibid., 1:161-162.
28. Ibid.

Washington have chosen Representatives for the whole State."[29] He also questioned the validity of the results themselves, arguing that it would be impossible for 1,161 out of 1,200 eligible residents of Washington County to have voted without fraud. Regardless of whether these claims are true, the sentiment represents a general view that the state's election laws were more motivated by partisan advantage than ensuring a proper system of representation.

A few states adopted election laws without much evidence of partisan politics having a significant influence. Of these states, South Carolina adopted the single-member district model, though it did not require residency to be nominated within any of the districts.[30] New Hampshire elected its three representatives at large, allotting the nomination to any candidate which received more than one-sixth of the popular vote and providing for a run-off election with the six top-ranked contenders if any candidate failed to cross that threshold, a safeguard which proved necessary.[31] Meanwhile, in Georgia, where the state ratified the Constitution unanimously and Federalists enjoyed a comfortable majority, national politics also had a minimal influence on the state's election laws. However, these facts did not preclude local prejudices from influencing their electoral system. To this point, Edward Telfair, a representative from the upcountry, included an amendment that would allow voters in each of the state's three districts to vote for one Representative in each district. The amendment passed on nearly strict regional lines, with thirty-seven up-country and five low-country delegates voting in favor and twenty-seven low-country delegates opposed.[32] In the end, the legislature adopted the same hybrid model used in Maryland.

Connecticut adopted a modified version of the general ticket system that it had used since 1779 to nominate representatives to the Confederation Congress. In perhaps the earliest use of primary elections in America, when the freeman of the state met in early November to elect members of the General Court, they would also nominate no more than twelve individuals for Congress. A representative from each

---

29. "A.B., *Maryland Journal*, Baltimore, February 3," ibid., 1:211-212. This opinion led to a lively print debate by Federalist sympathizers who took issue with the article's observations and calculations. For the debate, see "Publius, February 6," ibid., 1:214-215; "A.B., February 13," ibid., 1:216-218; "A Friend to Truth, February 20," ibid., 1:221-223; "An Inhabitant of Washington County, February 24," ibid., 1:223-225; "A.B., March 3," ibid., 1:225-227."
30. "South Carolina Election Law, November 4," ibid., 1:167-169.
31. "New Hampshire Election Law, November 12," ibid., 1:790-792.
32. Ibid., 2:453.

county would then meet and forward a list of the twelve individuals who received the highest number of votes to the legislature, who would then disseminate a printed ballot to every town. The following month, the freeman of each town would then cast their votes for no more than five of the twelve individuals, with the five individuals receiving the greatest number of votes elected to office.[33]

Federalist dominated legislatures were not the only ones to participate in partisan chicanery, under the leadership of staunch Antifederalist Patrick Henry, Virginia's election laws were also influenced by party spirit. Virginia adopted the single-member district model, including a provision that required candidates to be residents of their districts for at least twelve months.[34] In the words of Francis Corbin, a delegate to the Convention, Virginia's election law was "not so much in Conformity perhaps to the Spirit of the new Constitution as in Conformity to the genius, the habits & the Prejudices of the people of Virginia."[35] To this end, Federalist commentators conjectured that the legislature's actions were designed to provide a general advantage to the Antifederalists and prevent the election of prominent Federalist figures, namely, James Madison.

Supporting this view, George Lee Tuberville wrote in a letter to Madison that "the object of the majority of to day has been to prevent yr. Election in the house of Representatives... first by forming a district (as they supposed) of Counties most tainted by antifederalism... then by confining the choice of the people to the residents in the particular districts."[36] Agreeing with Tuberville, Edward Carrington, in another letter to Madison, also speculated that the Antifederalists inserted the residency requirement with the direct purpose of preventing the election of Madison to the House of Representatives.[37] However, the plan failed. Madison comfortably defeated his future Secretary of State and Presidential successor, James Monroe, and Federalists successfully captured seven of Virginia's ten congressional seats.[38]

New Jersey chose to elect its representatives using the general ticket method and by ballot, creating a system in which citizens would submit a written ballot with four names, with the four highest-ranked candidates receiving the nomination.[39] Prior to the election, one observer

---

33. "The Connecticut Election Resolution, October 15," ibid., 2:24-25
34. "The Virginia Election Law for Representatives, November 19," ibid., 2:293-295
35. "Francis Corbin to James Madison, Richmond, November 12," ibid., 2:370-371.
36. "George Lee Tuberville to James Madison, Richmond, November 13," ibid., 2:372.
37. "Edward Carrington to James Madison, Richmond, November 9-10," ibid., 2:367.
38. "James Madison to Thomas Jefferson, New York, March 29," ibid., 2:408.
39. "The New Jersey Election Law, November 21," ibid., 3:14-18.

expressed his pessimism regarding the system and, particularly, the process of electing by ballot, arguing that it would result in too many candidates receiving votes. The observer argued that this system would prevent voters from the opportunity to conduct "a proper scrutiny ... into the conduct and general character of each candidate."[40] He also lamented that this large pool of candidates combined with the incentive for county residents to vote for their favorite sons would likely result in an outcome in which "a man might happen to be returned who had not perhaps more than a twentieth part of the votes of the whole State."[41] Helping to prevent this outcome, however, was a concerted effort by several Federalist assemblymen to form a unified ticket between two east and two west Jersey candidates, affectionally referred to by their opponents as the "junto ticket."[42] The ticket proved successful and all four members were elected.[43]

In New York, the debate over the state's election law reflected the state's status as the center of the Federalist-Antifederalist debates during ratification. In both instances, the debate began in print. One such view, published in the *Daily Advertiser*, provided a novel argument that directly contradicted Madison's reasoning in the *Federalist*. Accordingly, responding to the contention that representatives should be intimately acquainted with the interests and feelings of their constituents, the anonymous author rejected that this led to the necessary endorsement of single-member districts. One reason, argued the author, is that everyone cannot personally be acquainted with their delegates. Rather, people can only know their reputation and public character, which is sufficient for the purpose of representation. The author's interpretation of the Constitution was that representatives were meant to act for the good of their state and not their district. Hence, elections were ultimately subject to control by the state legislature, "where all the interests, feelings, partialities and errors of all corners of the state are collected into a point."[44] The author concluded by noting how the general ticket method had been in use in Connecticut for years. To this end, he praised Connecticut's innovative use of primaries, which he believed best insulated representatives from "the violence of party."[45] In response, an author under the pseudonym Publius Secundus Americanus provided a point-by-point refutation of the anonymous Federalist. Among

40. "John Stevens Jr. to Benjamin Van Cleve, Hoboken, November 21," ibid., 3:19-20.
41. Ibid.
42. ibid., 3:36.
43. ibid., 3:109.
44. "Daily Advertiser, New York, November 7," ibid., 3:209-210.
45. Ibid.

his rebuttals, Publius argued that it was the general ticket method that would more likely result in the "forming [of] state parties." Moreover, he believed that the general ticket method would only advantage those already elected while concealing the "men of real merit," who would likely "live and die in oblivion."[46]

The dispute over which method New York should adopt carried over into the state legislature, where control was split evenly between Federalists and Antifederalists. As was generally seen throughout the other states, the Federalist assemblymen supported the general ticket method, while the Antifederalists supported single-member districts. Federalist Henry Brockholst Livingston attempted to introduce an amendment that provided for the hybrid system adopted by other states. In support of his motion, he argued that "the constitution gave every man a right to vote for six men, and that it would be an arbitrary stride of power to restrain him to vote only for one."[47] Opposing Livingston, Antifederalist John Lansing responded that if the Constitution had intended to not provide for single-member districts, it would not have given the state legislatures the unqualified authority to do so. "As to the propriety of electing by districts," Lansing argued, single-member districts were the "most likely way to obtain a representation of the people" since voters are more likely to be acquainted with a single candidate from his locality than six men from throughout the state.[48]

In the end, the New York legislature decided to adopt the single-member district model.[49] On its face, it seems New York's election law was among the least influenced by partisan politics since it did not blatantly favor one political party. On the contrary, New York's adoption of the single-member district demonstrates just how great of an influence party politics had in shaping the congressional election regulations of the early republic. Among the states whose election laws were blatantly tilted to favor a single party —such as Pennsylvania, Massachusetts, Virginia, and Maryland — the smoking gun was either adopting the general ticket/hybrid method or drawing districts that heavily favored urban centers. The reason for these laws was that they were adopted by legislatures with clear partisan majorities, representing both the opportunity and the prospect of present loss or advantage articulated by Madison and John Jay in the *Federalist*. New York's legislature,

---

46. "Publius Secundus Americanus, *Daily Advertiser*, New York, November 10," ibid., 3:210-211.
47. "Assembly Debates, Thursday, December 18," ibid., 3:233.
48. Ibid.
49. "The New York Election Law, January 27," ibid., 3:361-364.

by contrast, was split between a Federalist Senate and an Antifederalist Assembly. In turn, this power-sharing arrangement had a formative impact on the state's decision to adopt the single-member district since any attempt by either party to pass a bill favoring only one side's interest would undoubtedly fail. As a result, the legislature adopted the only model which allotted both parties a moderate chance of success.

THE FIRST ELECTION LAWS IN RETROSPECT

In all, of the eleven states which participated in the first congressional elections, one state only had one representative, making the method of choice moot; four states adopted the general ticket method, four states adopted the single-member district model, and two states adopted a hybrid model, which split the state into districts but allowed voters to cast votes for a representative in each.[50] Meanwhile, the election laws and party tactics adopted in response to the laws marked several significant milestones in American democracy and party development. For example, Connecticut's election law utilized the first instance of a primary system for congressional office. In Massachusetts and Virginia, legislatures engaged in the first instance of drawing districts with the explicit purpose of providing a lopsided partisan advantage, a practice that would become known as gerrymandering. Meanwhile, Federalists in Maryland and New Jersey promulgated the nation's first party tickets.

A key trend that defined the election was the diversity of opinions within the Federalist coalition regarding the modes of congressional selection. As articulated by Madison in the *Federalist* and echoed by other framers like Rufus King, single-member districts seem to be the method of congressional selection most consistent with the spirit of the Constitution. However, a consistent theme of Federalists throughout the debates over the first election laws was that it was rather the general ticket method that is most consistent with the spirit of the Constitution. Further evidence of this supposed dissonance within the Federalist coalition was the opposing methods adopted by states predominated by Federalists. For example, both Georgia and New Jersey unanimously ratified the Constitution, yet the former adopted the single-member district method, while the latter adopted the general ticket method. Moreover, in Virginia, Edward Carrington observed that the state's election laws were adopted by a "union of Feds. & Antifeds, so that no proposition could be offered agt,"[51] suggesting that the Virginia Federalists accepted the single-member district without any qualms.

50. Neither Rhode Island nor North Carolina participated in the first congressional elections, having not yet ratified the Constitution.
51. "Edward Carrington to James Madison, Richmond, November 9," ibid., 2:367.

In making sense of these contradictions among the Federalists, James Madison's aforementioned observations during the Convention and within the *Federalist* that party spirit would likely influence the operations of government provides the most cogent explanation. Indeed, this view was corroborated by Francis Corbin's opinion that Virginia's election laws were primarily influenced by the "habits & prejudices of the people of Virginia."[52] Accordingly, the decisive influence on the first state election laws seemed not to be the pure theory of the Constitution, but party politics. In Pennsylvania, the adoption of the general ticket method was widely regarded at the time as adopted to ensure the election of Federalist representatives. In Virginia and Massachusetts, the single-member districts allowed both sides to draw districts that favored their party and disenfranchise the opposition. Georgia and Maryland adopted the hybrid system on strictly regional lines, with the Maryland legislature's motives also aligning with their Federalist sympathies. Three different electoral systems, five instances of partisan advantage playing a decisive role in the formation of election law. Meanwhile, in New York, where the parties were forced to compromise due to a split legislature, the election law created a system that provided both sides with a fair opportunity for electoral gain. Of course, as shown above, partisans on both sides justified their actions on Constitutional grounds, but the electoral advantage of many of the laws was a blatant and recurrent feature.

This trend is consistent with the development of congressional selection throughout the early republic. For instance, New Jersey adopted the general ticket method under the stewardship of a Federalist majority in 1788. In the three subsequent legislative sessions, Republicans attempted to pass an election bill for district elections. In 1798, Republicans finally succeeded in adopting the single-member district method, transforming a 0-5 representation disadvantage to a 3-2 majority. Two years later, a newly minted Federalist majority reversed Republicans' gains and reverted the state back to the general ticket method. This time, however, the Federalist's gambit failed, and the surging Republican party won every seat. As noted by historian Richard P. McCormick, "once in control, the new party abandoned its earlier advocacy of district elections and capitalized to the fullest extent on its power."[53]

In all, as expressed by the authors of the *Federalist,* any time partisans are given the impulse and the opportunity to affect institutional change

---

52. "Francis Corbin to James Madison, Richmond, November 12," ibid., 2:371.
53. Richard P. McCormick, *The History of Voting in New Jersey: A Study of the Development of Election Machinery, 1664-1991* (Rutgers University Press, 1953), 108.

to gain an advantage, they are likely to do so. During the first federal election, partisans were awarded such an opportunity through the Constitution's failure to stipulate a particular method of congressional selection and an impulse from the posturing between Federalists and Antifederalists following the Constitution's ratification and the unfolding debate over amendments. Though the Founders on both sides of the debate were undoubtedly committed to their principles, they also recognized that victory in politics often requires shrewd maneuvering. The typical narrative of the Founding would have one believe that the partisan squabbles and political machinations of the era did not arise until well into the Washington administration. On the contrary, the debates over the first election laws prove that partisan politics and the friend-enemy distinction have influenced the implementation of the Constitution from the very outset of its ratification.

"Characters Pre-eminent for Virtue and Ability": the First Partisan Application of the Electoral College

SHAWN DAVID MCGHEE

Scholars typically cast the outcome of the second presidential election as either a forgone conclusion or a non-event.[1] After all, George Washington ran unchallenged and once again received unanimous support from the Electoral College.[2] Shifting academic focus from the first magistrate to the second, however, reframes the 1792 contest as a struggle for the soul of the republic rather than a forgettable victory for the incumbent. As the first Washington administration drew to a divisive close, Republicans sought to unseat Vice President John Adams and replace him with a candidate they felt embodied republican virtue. If they succeeded, these actors felt they could exorcise Adams's perceived monarchical influence on President Washington and return the nascent republic to its revolutionary principles. Federalists, however, supported Adams in order to protect the integrity of the national government. From their perspective, Republican rule would undermine the federal architecture and return the republic to the instability of the 1780s or worse. Yet efforts to vanquish or vindicate Adams required careful consideration of the Electoral College and represent the earliest attempts at weaponizing that institution for national partisan purposes.

Writing in September 1792, physician Benjamin Rush confidently reported to New York's rising star Aaron Burr that the republican spirit continued to strengthen among the American people. He then urged Burr to take a more active role in "removing the monarchical rubbish

---

1. An exception is James Roger Sharp, *American Politics of the Early Republic: A New Nation in Crisis* (New Haven: Yale University Press, 1993).
2. Stanley Elkins and Eric McKitrick, *The Age of Federalism: The Early American Republic, 1788-1800* (New York: Oxford University Press, 1993), 288-92.

of our government."³ For Rush, monarchy ran contrary to Christian virtue and he feared monarchical influence on the national government threatened "all our ideas of republicanism."⁴ He was not alone. Writing in the *New York Journal*, one activist predicted Washington would win the upcoming election but cautioned the vice presidency remained an open contest that would determine whether "true republicanism shall prevail . . . or the seeds of aristocracy be permitted to take deep root in this soil of freedom." During this crisis, the writer warned, some designing men remained "anxious to overthrow the glorious fabric of freedom, and erect on its ruins that deformed monster, Aristocracy."⁵ These clear attacks on the sitting vice president encapsulated Republicans' growing distrust of John Adams and, more broadly, fear that hereditary government might supplant the American Constitution. The federal republic, according to these observers, was young, unsteady and vulnerable to the seduction of monarchy.

Federalists also anguished over the nation's immediate future. According to Alexander Hamilton, no aristocratic cabal plotted to monarchize the republic. The "only enemy which Republicanism has to fear in this Country," he declared, "is the Spirit of faction and anarchy" and the "demagogues" sowing the aforementioned discord for their own advancement.⁶ Abigail Adams, for her part, grew increasingly frustrated by public accusations of her husband's alleged attachment to monarchy. She warned a correspondent that Republicans were engaged in a sustained effort to overthrow the government and claimed there were "no falsehoods too barefaced" for antifederalists to promote.⁷ An equally alarmed contributor to the *Columbian Centinel* theorized Republicans sought to replace Adams because his principles challenged their avarice. That party, this writer continued, would consider Adams's potential defeat as a victory over the Constitution.⁸

In this paranoid political environment, unsettled observers of all persuasions pleaded with President Washington to stand for reelection de-

---

3. Benjamin Rush to Aaron Burr, September 24, 1792, in L.H. Butterfield, ed., *Letters of Benjamin Rush*, 2 vols. (Princeton: Princeton University Press, 1951), 1: 623.
4. Benjamin Rush to Jeremy Belknap, June 21, 1792, in Ibid., 1: 620.
5. "To the Citizens of the United States," in *New York Journal*, September 1, 1792.
6. Alexander Hamilton to Edward Carrington, May 26, 1792, in Harold C. Syrett, ed., *The Papers of Alexander Hamilton*, 27 vols. (New York: Columbia University, 1961-87), 11: 426-45.
7. Abigail Adams to Thomas Welsh, November 15, 1792, in James C. Taylor, et al., eds., *The Adams Papers*: Adams Family Correspondence, 14 vols. (Cambridge: Harvard University Press, 1963-), 9: 326-28.
8. *Columbian Centinel*, November 17, 1792.

spite the president's desire to return to private life.⁹ Thomas Jefferson, sensing an early sectional crisis, went so far as to tell Washington that "North and South will hang together if they have you to hang on."[10] Attorney General Edmund Randolph offered an even darker assessment of the partisan atmosphere on the eve of the election: Only Washington could prevent the nation from descending into chaos. "Should a civil war arise," he gloomily remarked, "you cannot stay home."[11] No one could envision another candidate for chief magistrate in 1792. Filling the vice presidency, however, became a partisan contest over the principles of the American Revolution.

Historian Stephen Wilhelm traced the origins of the vice presidency to the deputy governor of Massachusetts, an office outlined in that colony's 1628 charter. Architects of that covenant designed the position to fill potential executive voids should a governor be rendered incapable of executing his duties. Other colonies emulated this model and, though the concept of a junior executive caused some controversy during the Constitutional Convention, American delegates fashioned the vice presidency for similar purposes.[12] Yet the method for electing the vice president, as noted by scholar Harry Thompson, also forced state actors to think beyond the boundaries of their home states. The framers assumed no future statesman would enjoy the national esteem Washington earned during the Revolutionary War. In light of this, directing electors to consider presidential candidates from two separate states compelled voters to be aware of and comfortable with the very real possibility of an alternative contestant. In this respect, the framers aimed to nationalize the presidency.[13] Alexander Hamilton expected both the

---

9. Tobias Leer to George Washington, August 5, 1792, in Dorothy Twohig, et al., eds., *The Papers of George Washington*: Presidential Series, 20 vols. (Charlottesville: University of Virginia Press, 1987-), 10: 628-32; Memorandum on a Discussion of the President's Retirement, May 5, 1792, in William T. Hutchinson, et al., eds., *The Papers of James Madison*: Congressional Series, 17 vols. (Chicago: University of Chicago Press, 1962-91), 14:299-304; Alexander Hamilton to George Washington, July 30, 1792, in Syrett, ed., *Hamilton Papers*, 12: 137-39; Sharp, *American Politics*, 54-55; Elkins and McKitrick, *Age of Federalism*, 290-92.
10. Thomas Jefferson to George Washington, May 23, 1792, in Julian P. Boyd, et al., eds., *The Papers of Thomas Jefferson*, 44 vols. (Princeton: Princeton University Press, 1950-), 23: 535-41.
11. Edmund Randolph to George Washington, August 5, 1792, in Twohig, et al., *Washington Papers*, 10: 622-27.
12. Stephen J. Wilhelm, "The Origins of the Office of the Vice Presidency," *Presidential Studies Quarterly* 7, no. 4 (1977): 208-14.
13. Harry C. Thompson, "The Second Place in Rome: John Adams as Vice President," *Presidential Studies Quarterly* 10, no. 2 (1980): 171-78.

chief and second magistracies to be occupied by "characters pre-eminent for ability and virtue." The Electoral College, according to Hamilton, safeguarded those offices from the intrigue of foreign courts and corruption of popular politicking.[14] Since most delegates viewed Washington as the ideal president and that office's likely first occupant, preparing to fill his shoes must also have been on their minds.[15] As Washington was nearing sixty, the creation of the vice presidency may equally reflect an effort to imbed political stability and continuity into the very fabric of the Constitution.

As the election of 1792 neared, Republicans began plotting to replace John Adams with a man of solid republican principles. In early June, Thomas Jefferson discovered some northern Republicans intended to secure New York governor George Clinton's election over Adams.[16] Days later, Hamilton learned of this scheme and alerted the vice president, writing "the plot thickens ... [and] a serious design to subvert the Government discloses itself."[17] But Clinton's tarnished victory in New York's gubernatorial race two months earlier caused at least some Republicans to distance themselves from his potential candidacy.[18] In the shadow of that controversial election, New York's Melancton Smith and Marinus Willett contacted Virginia's James Monroe "soliciting the friends of republicanism in your State" to join them in supporting Aaron Burr.[19] After careful consideration, James Madison, writing on behalf of Virginia's Republicans, responded cryptically that his state intended to support the more experienced man, meaning Clinton, who was "more likely to unite a greater number of electoral votes." Supporting a lesser-known character (Burr), he warned, would only jeopardize their shared goal of removing Adams.[20]

---

14. Alexander Hamilton, "Federalist 68," in Clinton Rossiter, ed., *The Federalist Papers: Alexander Hamilton, James Madison, John Jay* (New York: New American Library, 1961), 411-15.

15. Elkins and McKitrick, *Age of Federalism*, 45; Clinton Rossiter, *The American Presidency* (New York: Harcourt, Brace, World, 1960), 81.

16. James Madison to Thomas Jefferson, June 10, 1792, in Hutchinson, et al., *Madison Papers*, 14: 315-16.

17. Alexander Hamilton to John Adams, June 25, 1792, in Syrett, *Hamilton Papers*, 11: 559-60.

18. Thomas Jefferson to James Madison, June 21, 1792, in Boyd, et al., *Jefferson Papers*, 6: 89-91; Tench Coxe to John Adams, July 8, 1792, founders.archives.gov/documents/Adams/99-02-02-1356; see also Alfred F. Young, *The Democratic Republicans of New York: The Origins, 1763-1797* (Chapel Hill: University of North Carolina Press, 1967), 277-341.

19. James Monroe to James Madison, October 9, 1792, in Hutchinson, et al., *Madison Papers*, 14: 377-81.

20. James Madison to Melancton Smith and Marinus Willet, October 19, 1792, in Ibid., 14: 387.

The very survival of republican government, according to Madison, hinged on the incumbent's defeat.

Alexander Hamilton suspected his opponents of even deeper machinations. He described Clinton as a known enemy of the federal government and Burr as an unprincipled actor unworthy of public confidence. Those assessments aside, Hamilton speculated that Republicans planned to split northern electoral votes between Burr, Clinton and Adams and unite the South around Jefferson to secure his elevation.[21] Jefferson, keeping a watchful eye on electoral politics, considered the upcoming contest the proper channel to gauge "the public sense of the doctrines of the Monocrats." And despite his personal revulsion to Adams's politics, the calculating Virginian predicted the vice president's years of public service would "prevail over the demerit of his political creed."[22] For Republicans, the election of 1792 offered electors a choice between republican government and monarchy. For Federalists, it asked voters to select either respectable government or anarchy. Both proto-parties viewed their rivals as enemies of the republic and an existential threat to the nation's future.[23] And both equally considered themselves the true custodians of the American Revolution, intensifying the struggle to replace or retain Adams.

The contest for the vice presidency also raged in American newspapers. One pseudonymous observer, writing as "Lucius," decried Adams as an opponent of the American republic due to his perceived attachment to kings and lords.[24] "Marcus" countered, citing the vice president's *Defense of the Constitutions of the United States of America* as "the best defense of a free republican government in the English language."[25] Even after the election, one contributor to the *National Gazette* accused Adams of "giving the government a twist toward royalty," while another warned readers that if "you wish not a king . . . abandon Mr. Adams [and] annihilate his political existence."[26] Still another defended Adams as "a firm and true republican."[27] Opponent "Wat Tyler" railed that if Americans re-elected Adams, "monarchy men" would force voters to refer to the president and vice president as

21. Alexander Hamilton to Charles Cotesworth Pinkney, October 10, 1792, in Syrett, *Hamilton Papers*, 12: 543-45.
22. Thomas Jefferson to Thomas Pinckney, December 3, 1792, in Boyd, et al., *Jefferson Papers*, 24: 696-97.
23. James Roger Sharp introduced the term "proto-party" to describe the developing factions during the Washington administration. See Sharp, *American Politics*.
24. *Philadelphia Daily Advertiser*, November 24, 1792.
25. *Gazette of the United States*, November 21, 1792.
26. *National Gazette*, December 5, 1792.
27. *Gazette of the United States*, November 10, 1792.

"*Thee* and Thou."[28] Another critic argued that any friend of public tranquility must choose Clinton over Adams due to the incumbent's support of hereditary distinctions.[29] For most partisan observers, the political environment surrounding the second presidential election radiated with suspicion and apocalypticism.

Partisan operatives worked tirelessly to keep abreast of electoral developments, but in 1792 news moved at four-miles per hour and it took observers time to gather reliable information. Madison learned in late November that the entire South favored Clinton. If the governor could peel off eight eastern votes, Madison's informant reasoned, "I think he will be elected."[30] An elector from Virginia informed Madison that, since Adams openly disdained the southern states, "Clinton . . . appears to be the only alternative." He then announced his intention to vote for the governor.[31] Madison, ever cautious, prudently recorded he lacked the data "to calculate with certainty the event of the contest."[32] Jefferson anxiously kept a careful state-by-state account of the returns as they came in to him.[33] Charles Adams warily predicted that, as far he understood the returns, his father would hold the office.[34] Abigail Adams expressed shock that New York led Virginia "by the Nose," and described both states as openly hostile to the vice president and national government.[35] Another partisan enthusiastically reported that Adams had carried all of New England, delivering what he dubbed a mortal blow to Republicans' nefarious designs. The American public, this writer explained, refused to permit Adams "to retire to obscurity."[36] The *National Gazette* received a report predicting (correctly) Washington and Jefferson had carried Kentucky.[37] Acting the part of disinterested gentleman, John Adams claimed to have little interest in the election's outcome. Yet he carefully inventoried for his wife the electoral returns he had gleaned from his vast correspondence, drawing out where he

---

28. Ibid., December 29, 1792.
29. *National Gazette*, December 1, 1792.
30. John Dawson to James Madison, November 27, 1792 in Hutchinson, et al., *Madison Papers*, 14: 417-18.
31. William Overton Callis to James Madison, November 19, 1792, in Ibid., 14: 409-10.
32. James Madison to Edmund Pendleton, December 6, 1792, in Ibid., 14: 420-21.
33. Thomas Jefferson to John F. Mercer, December 19, 1792, in Boyd, et al., *Jefferson Papers*, 24: 757-58.
34. Charles Adams to Abigail Adams, December 5[?], 1792, in Taylor, et al., *Adams Papers*, 9: 336-37.
35. Abigail Adams to John Adams, December 29, 1792, in Ibid., 9: 360-62.
36. Henry Marchant to John Adams, January 1, 1793, founders.archives.gov/documents/Adams/99-02-02-1395.
37. *National Gazette*, January 1, 1793.

expected the most support and where Clinton might prove an attractive alternative.[38] One refreshingly candid observer admitted that, while Adams appeared unpopular, election returns "All seem to depend on Vague rumours."[39]

When Congress officially tabulated electoral returns on February 13, 1793, Adams won reelection handily with seventy-seven votes. He drew his support mainly from New England and the Mid-Atlantic states. Clinton received fifty, predominantly from New York and the South, while Jefferson yielded Kentucky's four votes. Aaron Burr, who according to Hamilton aggressively campaigned for the position, garnered one electoral vote from South Carolina.[40] In late December, some Adams supporters hailed his likely victory as a complete triumph for federalism. For Adams, however, earning more votes than Clinton hardly seemed a victory. If some Americans considered the sacrifices and suffering the current vice president endured on the nation's behalf comparable to those of Clinton, Adams lamented, "it is high time to Quit Such a service. There is not the Smallest degree of Vanity in this."[41]

Equally stung by the results, Republicans could only claim monarchy no longer threatened the nation's future. Artificial aristocrats, they rationalized, dared not advance their haughty designs before a watchful citizenry after such a close call.[42] Yet the election actually exposed some sobering political realities about the American electoral system. It revealed that Washington's universal acclaim was unique; no other statesman held the public's trust in virtually every corner of the union. And historically, no other republican form of government had ever dared govern so vast and diverse a realm. Alarmingly, these realities constrained any future national candidate to navigate hardening sectional divisions in an increasingly polarized atmosphere over an ever-expanding nation. Partisan actors would consider this political arithmetic when factoring in the Electoral College for future elections during the Early National Period.

---

38. John Adams to Abigail Adams, December 10, 1792, in Taylor, et al., *Adams Papers*, 9: 343-44.
39. Robert Gamble to Thomas Jefferson, December 4, 1792, in Boyd, et al., *Jefferson Papers*, 24: 698-99.
40. Alexander Hamilton to George Washington, September 23, 1792, in Syrett, *Hamilton Papers*, 12: 418.
41. John Adams to Abigail Adams, December 19, 1792, in Taylor, et al., *Adams Papers*, 9: 351-52.
42. *National Gazette*, January 2, 1793; Abigail Adams to John Adams, January 7, 1793, in Taylor, et al., *Adams Papers*, 9: 372-74.

Weaponizing Impeachment: Justice Chase and President Jefferson's Battle Over the Process

AL DICKENSON

There was much discussion over the impeachment process during the Constitution's ratifying debates. Many Federalists argued that the ability to impeach an individual gave disproportionate power to the House of Representatives, while some Antifederalists favored more provisions to prevent tyranny from taking root, especially in the Executive Branch. Some individuals liked the idea of having a body other than the Senate try impeachment cases. Most delegates, if not all, feared impeachment could be weaponized. Early in Thomas Jefferson's presidency, this fear became real with the impeachment of Samuel Chase, a Federalist-affiliated Supreme Court Justice. Some historians might ask if this impeachment was a political move. Many Federalists thought so. Chase was an ardent Federalist, and vocally supported America's first Federalist president, John Adams, even throughout Chase's tenure on the Supreme Court bench. Jefferson did not like Chase's behavior, but the third president disliked Chase's politics even more. Hence, Jefferson, with an Antifederalist majority in the House of Representatives, had Chase impeached.

To better understand the objections of the impeachment clause, historians first have to understand the debate over impeachment and the fear that it could be used to increase the power of the party in charge of the House of Representatives. Federalists were afraid that there was too much power being given to the House. If the House did not like an individual or their actions, it was thought that the House could simply impeach that person.[1]

---

1. John Kaminski and Richard Leffler, eds., *Federalists and Antifederalists: The Debate Over the Ratification of the Constitution* (Madison, WI: Madison House Publishers, Inc., 1998), 38.

Many Founding Fathers thought that impeachment would give pause to politicians attempting to commit certain unsavory acts, or even acts that might seem unsavory, even if they were not. However, Pennsylvania Antifederalist William Petrikin, writing under the pseudonym Aristocrotis, countered, "this entirely vanishes, when it is considered that the senate hath the principal say in appointing these officers, and that they are the sole judges of all impeachments."[2]

Petrikin wrote that too much power was consolidated in Congress.[3] He feared how much power the Senate had to appoint and remove cabinet members, judges, ambassadors, and other unelected officials.[4] Under the name Aristocritis, Petrikin wrote, "it would be absurd to suppose that they would remove their own servants for performing their secret orders. . . . For the interest of rulers and the ruled will then be two distinct things."[5] While Aristocritis may seem to have been paranoid, he was rightfully so. Aristocritis, along with many Antifederalists, thought that power corrupts people.[6] While he feared that the Senate might appoint people that the majority in that body liked, it does not seem that he considered that the powers vested in Congress could be used against those they did not like. This separation of power is exactly what the framers of the Constitution wanted and precisely why they established checks and balances to the system.[7] No single group of people, be it legislative, judicial, executive, the states, or some amalgamation of these groups, could fully enforce what they wanted, at least not without support from the rest.

New York state also had issues with the impeachment clause, insisting that a separate court, other than the Senate, be used in trying impeached individuals.[8] On July 26, 1788, the New York convention,

---

2. Aristocritis, "The Government of Nature Delineated; or An Exact Picture of the New Federal Constitution, Carlisle, Pa., c. 27 April 1788," in *The Documentary History of the Ratification of the Constitution (DHRC)*, vol. XXXIV, Pennsylvania Supplemental Documents [3], eds. John Kaminski, et. al. (Madison, WI: Wisconsin Historical Society Press, 2019), 1255.
3. An Old Whig, "Philadelphia Independent Gazetteer, 12 October," in *DHRC*, vol. XIII, Commentaries (I), eds. John Kaminski, et. al. (Madison, WI: Wisconsin Historical Society Press, 1981), 376.
4. Aristocritis, "The Government of Nature Delineated," 1255-1256.
5. Ibid., 1255.
6. Reformation, "Philadelphia Independent Gazetteer, 29 September 1787," *DHRC*, vol. XXXII, Pennsylvania Supplemental Documents [1], 248-249, ; "Pennsylvania Mercury, 28 June 1788," *DHRC*, vol. XXXIV, Penn. Suppl. Docs. [3], 1308.
7. Kaminski, *Federalist and Antifederalists*, 68.
8. Pauline Maier, *Ratification: The People Debate the Constitution, 1787-1788* (New York: Simon & Schuster, 2010), 397-398; New York Convention, "New York Declaration of Rights, Form of Ratification, and Recommendatory Amendments to the Constitution,

headed by New York governor and future Vice President George Clinton, signed the Constitution into ratification in their state. They included several amendments including how they did not want the Senate to preside over the trial of impeached officials. When the announcement of the New York convention's decision came, the members made it clear that they all had taken issue with at least some part of the Constitution, but they felt comfortable with the ongoing ratification process. The New York convention hoped a better-measured and tempered Constitution would become the final version of the document.[9] The basis of their fear was reasonable and the New Yorkers echoed their southern neighbors in Virginia with similar objections.[10] The objection was that the Senate would be unlikely to convict the people they confirmed for various positions should they be impeached. William Grayson, a staunch Virginia Antifederalist and one of Virginia's first two senators, once wrote "since [the Senate] was also charged with advising the president, it would be his partner in crime."[11] But there was no other viable court to try impeached officials.[12]

The debate over how impeachment was to work continued among the states and federally even as it was laid out in its original form by Madison and other creators of the Constitution. Furthermore, three of the country's largest states, Virginia, Pennsylvania, and New York, all had serious objections to the clause regarding the Senate trying cases of impeachment. While the clause by itself may not have been enough to stop ratification in these states, the discourse on it certainly cast a shadow over three states that were essential to the Constitution's success.

Before the ratification of the Constitution by a majority of the states by 1789, there was great debate over the impeachment clause. Historian Jonathan Gienapp states that the silence of the Constitution on the removal process of members of the Executive Branch was a dangerous affair.[13] Gienapp refers specifically to a South Carolinian politician,

---

26 July 1788," in *DHRC* vol. XXIII, New York [5], eds. John Kaminski, et. al. (Madison, WI: Wisconsin Historical Society Press, 2009), 2333.
9. Maier, *Ratification*, 398.
10. James Madison, "Impeachment of the Executive, [20 July] 1787," founders.archives.gov/documents/Madison/01-10-02-0066.
11. New York Convention, 286; William Grayson, "The Virginia Convention Wednesday 18 June 1788," in *DHRC* vol. X, Virginia [3], eds. John Kaminski, et.al (Madison, WI: Wisconsin Historical Society Press, 1993), 1373-1375; 1387.
12. James Madison to an Unidentified Correspondent, May 29, 1805, founders.archives.gov/documents/Madison/02-09-02-0466.
13. Jonathan Gienapp, *The Second Creation: Fixing the American Constitution in the Founding Era* (Cambridge, MA: Harvard University Press, 2018), 126-127.

William Loughton Smith, who objected to the fact that the only way for an executive officer to be removed, as laid out in the proposed Constitution, was by impeachment.[14] Smith wanted more ways to remove an officer, should it be necessary, although no other proposal was made. Smith further objected that in the Constitution, it only allowed the executive to be impeached for "treason, bribery, or other high crimes and misdemeanors."[15] The ensuing debate did not focus so much on whether the president could be impeached or how to impeach a president, but instead, the debate revolved around executive officers such as various department secretaries, ambassadors, judges, and others. While most members of the ratifying conventions found it laughable that impeachment was the only method of removing a non-elected executive official, it seems as though those same committee members could not agree on how the officers of the executive branch should be removed.[16] This debate lasted long into the First Federal Congress, particularly with the proposed Foreign Affairs Act of 1789. The failed bill reignited a debate on how "good behavior" should impact a potential impeachment, and if impeachment could be enacted solely for a lack of "good behavior."[17] For Jefferson and the impeachment of Samuel Chase, the idea of "good behavior" became an important, albeit minor, factor in the trial of the judge.

The term "good behavior" did not mean that judges needed to uphold societal standards, such as not being publicly drunk or not being corrupt. Instead, as *The Federalist 78* suggests, "good behavior" is based on the ability "to secure a steady, upright, and impartial administration of the laws."[18] As is perhaps obvious, this term of "good behavior" is somewhat nebulous, as it will depend on an individual to determine what judicial decisions are "steady, upright," and most important and difficult, "impartial."[19] Nonetheless, it might have been a stretch for Chase to be considered impartial. In 1796, the year Chase was appointed to the Supreme Court by outgoing President George Washington, the judge made speeches supporting fellow Federalist John Adams. That

---

14. Ibid., 127.
15. Ibid., 126-127; US Constitution, art. 2, section 4.
16. Gienapp, *The Second Creation*, 127-128.
17. Ibid., 133-134; 386.
18. Publius (Alexander Hamilton), *The Federalist 78, May 28, 1788*, reprinted in the New York *Independent Journal*, June 14, 1788, as quoted in Kaminski, *Federalists and Antifederalists*, 136-137.
19. Ibid., 136-137; Irving Dillard, "Samuel Chase," in Leon Friedman and Fred L. Israel, eds., *The Justices of the United States Supreme Court, 1789-1969: Their Lives and Major Opinions* (New York: Chelsea House, 1969), 1:189.

same year, 1796, is the year Adams won the presidency.[20] These missteps were only Chase's first. At this time, Chase came into the spotlight as being a Federalist ally, regardless of his attempts to be impartial as a judge.

One of the next steps that Chase took to further his reputation as a Federalist was participating in the enforcement of Adams' controversial Alien and Sedition Acts.[21] Jefferson's dislike of Chase started with the judge's prosecution of James Callender, an Antifederalist newsman, who continuously wrote scathing opinion pieces about John Adams.[22] From the bench, Chase scolded Callendar and impartially conducted a trial. Chase soon convicted, sentenced, fined, and imprisoned Callender because of the latter's contempt for Federalist doctrine and President Adams.[23] The Callendar case, along with the John Fries trial from 1800, where Jefferson considered Chase's actions improper in court, were among the eight articles of impeachment leveled at Chase in March 1804.[24] Chase defended his judicial choices regarding these cases, one against Callender and the other referring to Fries, a man who led an armed revolt regarding taxes in his home state of Pennsylvania, as being under the protection of and by right of the Sedition Act of 1798, which forbade disloyal, profane, or otherwise improper language from being spoken or published.[25]

Antifederalists under Jefferson strongly objected to the Sedition Act, as well as its sister act, the Alien Act. Jeffersonians felt these laws, passed by Federalists, imposed tyranny on the American people.[26] As renowned scholar of early American political history Adrienne Koch writes, "despite the diplomatic tone of his Inaugural Address, Jefferson had no intention of abiding by the dictatorial rulings made under the Alien and Sedition Acts. The new President had not forgotten the dangers and abuses to which some of his most respected friends had been subjected in the brief 'reign of witches,' which he was now ready to dispel... Those who were still in jail for 'seditious' writing, Jefferson

---

20. Dillard, "Samuel Chase," 193.
21. R.B. Bernstein, *Thomas Jefferson The Revolution of Ideas* (New York: Oxford University Press, 2004), 154.
22. James Madison to Thomas Jefferson, August 5, 1797, founders.archives.gov/documents/Madison/01-17-02-0026.
23. Bernstein, *Thomas Jefferson*, 154; Jefferson to James Monroe, May 26, 1801, founders.archives.gov/documents/Jefferson/01-34-02-0147.
24. Dillard, "Samuel Chase," 192-194, 196; Jefferson to Edmund Pendleton, April 19, 1800, founders.archives.gov/documents/Jefferson/01-31-02-0436.
25. Dillard, "Samuel Chase," 196.
26. Ibid., 194-195; Adrienne Koch, *Jefferson & Madison The Great Collaboration* (London, England: Oxford University Press, 1950), 184.

pardoned."²⁷ The Alien and Sedition Acts were heinous to not only Jeffersonian Democratic-Republicans, but also to many Federalists, like James Madison, who generally favored government oversight in public affairs. Madison even proposed counter-legislation to combat Adams' acts.²⁸ It is important to note that while the Alien and Sedition Acts were considered by many, even today, to be unconstitutional violations of First Amendment rights, the Acts were law and Chase did have the responsibility to follow the law as a judge on the Supreme Court and lower court benches. After all, that is what a judge on "good behavior" was supposed to do.²⁹

The crux of the controversy lay in the question of whether Samuel Chase acted on "good behavior" by upholding the rule of law as it was presented. To most, except some of the most ardent Antifederalists, Chase's actions were justifiable since he was doing his job as a Supreme Court justice, even though he was following laws that overlooked an individual's rights. Jefferson, on the other hand, took Chase's actions a different way. On May 13, 1803, the president sent a letter to Maryland Representative and strong Antifederalist ally Joseph Nicholson, asking that Nicholson start an investigation into Chase's "good behavior," ideology, and court rulings.³⁰ Though it had backing from a sitting United States president, the investigation started slowly. A House Committee gathered to inspect Chase's history in 1804. On March 12, the House of Representatives voted to impeach Chase on eight articles. Six of those articles dealt with specific issues in Chase's handling of the trials of both Callender and Fries. A seventh charge examined Chase's attempt to have a Wilmington newspaper editor indicted for sedition, while the eighth and final article of impeachment focused on Chase's perceived meddling in a grand jury in Baltimore.³¹ It would be almost a whole year before Chase faced a Senate trial for his impeachment.

It is important to note that Chase was doing his job as a judge. According to William Rehnquist, Chief Justice of the United States Supreme Court from 1986-2005, "more moderate Republicans saw no

---

27. Koch, *Jefferson & Madison*, 218; "Thomas Jefferson to Dr. Joseph Priestly, 21 March 1801," *The Writings of Thomas Jefferson*, ed. Paul Leicester Ford, vol. VIII, 21: quoted in Koch, *Jefferson & Madison*, 218.
28. Koch, *Jefferson & Madison*, 184; Irving Brant, *James Madison: Father of the Constitution, 1787-1800* (Indianapolis: Bobbs-Merrill Company, Inc., 1950), 421.
29. Publius, *The Federalist 78*, 136.
30. Dillard, "Samuel Chase," 195; Jefferson to Joseph H. Nicholson, May 13, 1803, founders.archives.gov/documents/Jefferson/01-40-02-0278.
31. Dillard, "Samuel Chase," 195-196.

need for structural change in the government."³² Rehnquist continues, citing that if Chase had been convicted, this would have given Jefferson and the Antifederalists an opening to reshape the judiciary in a way that would better suit them and their agenda.³³ Then-Senator John Quincy Adams, son of the former president John Adams, wrote to his father stating the same thing: "the assault upon Judge Chase; as this in its turn was unquestionably intended to pave the way for another prosecution, which would have swept the Supreme Judicial Bench clean at a stroke."³⁴ According to Senator Adams, even Jefferson's push for an investigation that would lead to an impeachment was an overstep of power. Writing to his father the following week, Senator Adams said the articles of impeachment levied against Chase were more about the Antifederalists perceiving "evil intent" in Chase's choices rather than points of law and order and "good behavior."³⁵ Senator Adams' claims were hyperbolic as the articles of impeachment did deal with actual legal issues and not just "evil intent," but Senator Adams' thoughts on the matter, particularly in his first letter to his father, were not far from the truth.³⁶

One need not look far to find evidence of Rehnquist's point about how many Jeffersonian Democratic-Republicans did not want to proceed with Chase's impeachment. Turning to some of Jefferson's own correspondences with his political allies, Representative Caesar A. Rodney, in a letter to Jefferson, stated that "Judge Chase was extremely moderate here in his charge. I suppose he was ashamed of the [charge] he gave in Maryland."³⁷ Rodney continued, writing that while Chase tried the patience of Antifederalists, and should not have issued his rulings on a couple of cases, impeaching Chase was not the solution to change the judiciary.³⁸ It seems Rodney later changed his mind, however, writing, "I find the impeachment of Chase is a popular thing even with some Federal lawyers who can not but admit its justice &

---

32. William Rehnquist, *Grand Inquests: The Historic Impeachments of Justice Samuel Chase and President Andrew Johnson* (New York: Quill William Morrow, 1992), 53-54.
33. Ibid., 54.
34. John Quincy Adams to John Adams, March 8, 1805, founders.archives.gov/documents/Adams/99-03-02-1391.
35. John Quincy Adams to John Adams, March 14, 1805, founders.archives.gov/documents/Adams/99-03-02-1395.
36. Ibid.: John Quincy Adams to John Adams, March 8, 1805; Rehnquist, *Grand Inquests*, 75-76.
37. Caesar A. Rodney to Jefferson, July 7, 1803, founders.archives.gov/documents/Jefferson/01-40-02-0518.
38. Ibid.

propriety."³⁹ Rodney also supported chief Chase prosecution manager and Virginian John Randolph's issue of orders to inquire about Chase's activities.⁴⁰ Even though Rodney changed his mind, Rehnquist's point is proven that there were some that did not support Jefferson's attempts to rewrite the judicial branch's authority. In fact, the Antifederalists who did not support Jefferson, either for philosophical or practical reasons, would put an end to Samuel Chase's trial.⁴¹ On February 26, 1805, Samuel Chase was acquitted on all accounts. One charge had Chase face nineteen votes in favor of conviction versus fifteen, the largest majority the Senate could muster. Another charge had zero votes for impeachment. The other six were all similar to one another, being in the mid-teens for conviction or innocence on each charge. A two-thirds majority vote is required for conviction. In 1805, 23 senators would have had to cast "guilty" votes to remove Chase from office.

The impeachment and failed trial of a United States Supreme Court Justice could have broken the Constitution. Although the trial was held on the grounds of impropriety, it was about political power. Chief Justice Rehnquist argues that this event set up the independent judiciary that the United States still has.⁴² Some of Chase's actions were also supportive of judicial independence, like his support of *Marbury v. Madison*, which in effect gives the Supreme Court say over Congressionally passed laws.⁴³ While Chase's impeachment trial served to strengthen the Supreme Court's hold over America, the Supreme Court could just as easily have gone from "the least dangerous branch" to a branch that was not even a consideration for danger if the Jeffersonian Antifederalists had gotten their way.⁴⁴ In the immediate aftermath of Chase's acquittal, there were calls from House impeachment managers and various Senators for new alterations to the Constitution. Both Randolph and Nicholson offered resolutions to make removing federal officers easier.⁴⁵ According to Rehnquist, the only thing that stopped these resolutions from possibly becoming amendments was the soon-expiring lame-duck session of Congress. When the House reconvened, the resolutions were never spoken of again.⁴⁶

39. Rodney to Jefferson, April 9, 1804, founders.archives.gov/documents/Jefferson/01-43-02-0172; Jefferson to Nicholson, May 13, 1803.
40. Ibid.
41. Rehnquist, *Grand Inquests*, 99; 104-105; Dillard, "Samuel Chase," 196.
42. Rehnquist, *Grand Inquests*, 114.
43. Ibid., 115.
44. Ibid., 106: Publius, *The Federalist 78*, 136.
45. Rehnquist, *Grand Inquests*, 106-107.
46. Ibid., 106.

Though Jefferson's partisan tactics to remove a judge failed, he and other Antifederalists succeeded in ensuring that federal judges in the future would be more careful in their personal rhetoric, as well as ensuring more fairness from the bench.[47] As Rehnquist puts it, the Senate saw that Chase perhaps acted unethically in how he issued sentences as a lower court judge and also in his personal rhetoric, but found nothing but solidity in his judicial rulings and proceedings, particularly during his time as a Supreme Court Justice, the position for which he had been impeached and was being tried.[48] Renquist does not excuse Chase's behavior, but indicates that perhaps Jefferson overplayed his hand in his effort to reform the nation's highest court. At times during the trial, up to six Jeffersonian Democratic-Republican Antifederalists voted not to convict Chase for various reasons. Dr. Samuel Mitchill, a senator from New York who voted not to convict Chase, once wrote, "this tedious and important trial is brought to an end. All this mighty effort has ended in nothing. On this occasion myself and my colleague . . . acted with the Federalists. But we did so on full conviction that the evidence, our oaths, the Constitution, and our conscience required us to act as we have done."[49] The six Democratic-Republicans that broke away from Jefferson are notable, and Mitchill is possibly even more so, as he and the president had some correspondence. Jefferson and Mitchill were friends, with Mitchill regularly sending Jefferson reading materials.[50] The six dissenting Democratic-Republicans are important because they show that the Constitution's ratifiers were correct—the impeachment process could potentially be weaponized for political gain, as President Jefferson attempted with his efforts against Justice Chase.

Oftentimes there is very little that stands between tyranny and liberty, or, according to some, Federalism and Antifederalism.[51] It appears as though the Constitution's framers and their opposition had

---

47. Dillard, "Samuel Chase," 197.
48. Rehnquist, *Grand Inquests*, 107-109.
49. "Samuel Mitchill to Catherine Mitchill, 26 February 1805," *Harper's New Weekly Magazine*, vol. LVIII, no. CCCXLVII (April 1879), "Dr. Mitchill's Letters from Washington: 1801-1813": quoted in Rehnquist, *Grand Inquests*, 109-110; "Samuel Mitchill to Catherine Mitchill, 1 March 1805," *Harper's New Weekly Magazine*, vol. LVIII, no. CCCXLVII (April 1879), babel.hathitrust.org/cgi/pt?id=coo.31924080772068&view=1up&seq=759&q1=this%20tedious%20and%20important%20trial%20is%20brought%20to%20an%20end, 749.
50. Jefferson to Samuel Mitchill, September 8, 1805, founders.archives.gov/documents/Jefferson/99-01-02-2354.
51. Aristocritis, "The Government of Nature Delineated," 1255.

reason to argue and deliberate. If Chase had been impeached, it is likely that a whole new meaning would have been given to the separation of powers, namely one where the Legislative Branch held control over almost everything. It does seem odd, however, that while the Antifederalists were so afraid of impeachment not working in favor of the people, they were the ones that first used it and for attempted political gain, no less. Moreover, this is what various Antifederalists feared, that the impeachment process could be weaponized. Indeed, in the case against Samuel Chase, it was.

Insurrection and Speculation: How a Farmer, Financier, and Surprising Sharper Seeded the Constitution

SCOTT M. SMITH

The January 6, 2021 assault on the Capital rocked America, but it was by no means the largest, or even the most threatening, armed rebellion in the post-Revolutionary War era. In 1786 and 1787, Daniel Shays, a middle-class farmer and decorated Continental Army captain, was one of several leaders of as many as four thousand men against the state of Massachusetts, whose fiscal policies were dictated by the demands of the coastal elite. The Shaysites believed they were well within the rights enumerated in the Declaration of Independence to alter or abolish any form of government that had become destructive of the consent of the people. After an army of mercenaries hired by James Bowdoin, the governor of Massachusetts, decisively routed the rebels, the Founding Fathers scapegoated Shays, in particular, in order to incite the citizenry to replace the weak Confederation Congress (1781-88) with the powerful tripartite national government that has endured to this day.

Born in 1747 to landless Irish immigrants, Daniel Shays toiled as an itinerant farm worker around Pelham in western Massachusetts. When war appeared imminent, he enlisted in Woodbridge's militia which quickly became part of the 5th Massachusetts Regiment of the Continental Army.[1] Joining his father and brother, Shays fought at Bunker Hill, rapidly gaining his lieutenancy. By 1777, he was promoted to captain in what had become the 27th Continental Regiment.[2] He

---

1. Steven Danver, *Revolts, Protests, Demonstrations and Rebellions in American History* (Westport, CT: Greenwood Publishing, 2011), 220.
2. en.wikipedia.org/wiki/5th_Massachusetts_Regiment.

participated in the victory at Saratoga and remained with his unit in the New York region afterwards. General Lafayette awarded a ceremonial sword to Shays in recognition of his bravery in the assault on Stony Point in July 1779.

Since the Continental Congress had no taxing authority, it could only come up with the cash to pay, clothe and feed Continental Army soldiers by printing paper money. Over the course of the war, Congress emitted 240 million dollars of currency (and the British counterfeited millions more), setting off an inflationary spiral that drove the value of a Continental dollar below three cents by 1780.[3] An index of wholesale prices skyrocketed from 78 in 1775 to 598 in 1778, peaking in 1780 at 10,544.[4]

Unsurprisingly, farmers and merchants were reluctant to accept Continental currency in payment for army supplies, setting the stage for the disastrous winters at Valley Forge and Morristown. Just settling into camp in December 1777, General Washington wrote to Congress: "I am now convinced beyond a doubt, that unless some great and capital change suddenly takes place ... this Army must inevitably be reduced to one or other of these three things. Starve—dissolve—or disperse, in order to obtain subsistence in the best manner they can."[5]

In addition, many prominent politicians feared both George Washington and his standing army, refusing support on moral as well as fiscal grounds. After surviving the Pennsylvania winter, Washington wrote to a friend, "the jealousy which Congress unhappily entertain of the Army, and which, if reports are right, some Members labor to establish ... there is nothing more injurious—or more unjustly founded ... no history, now extant, can furnish an instance of an army's suffering such uncommon hardships as ours have done, and bearing them with the same patience and Fortitude."[6] In 1780, John Jay, president of Congress, requested three million dollars from the states but received less than forty thousand.[7] Despite these financial hardships, the commander in chief still expected his officers to dress, ride and reside

---

3. "Congress issues Continental currency, June 22, 1775," www.politico.com/story/2018/06/22/congress-issues-continental-currency-june-22-1775-652244.
4. Peter Mathias, *The Transformation of England: Essays in the Economics and Social History of England in the Eighteenth Century*. (Milton Park, UK: Taylor & Francis, 2013).
5. George Washington to Henry Laurens, December 23, 1777, founders.archives.gov/documents/Washington/03-12-02-0628.
6. Washington to John Bannister, April 21, 1778, founders.archives.gov/documents/Washington/03-14-02-0525.
7. Joseph Ellis, *The Cause: The American Revolution and its Discontents: 1773-83* (New York: LiveRight Publishing), 212.

in camp like gentlemen, an expensive proposition. Accordingly, after five years of essentially unpaid service, Daniel Shays retired in 1780, sold his ceremonial sword, and returned home.

Over the next few years, Shays bought a 100 acre hardscrabble farm (likely with money borrowed from other veterans),[8] joined the Committee of Safety to root out Tories, and was elected town warden. With the state legislature sitting 100 miles away in Boston, unreachable in winter, frontier towns had a history of self-governance. Pelham, for example, provided a ballot to all male adults even though the state constitution mandated a minimum net worth for voting. A literacy rate approaching 90 percent, the highest in the world, as well as a locally elected clergy, also contributed to a culture of independent opinion throughout rural Massachusetts.

Hard money loans from France helped ease inflation in America in the early 1780s, but prices escalated again after the Revolutionary War ended in 1783, setting off a nationwide recession. From 1775 to 1790, per capita gross national product fell 46 percent due to the need to repay war debts, property devastation wreaked by the war, and the trade embargo forcibly imposed by the British Navy, lurking off America's coastline (by comparison, GNP fell 48 percent during the four years of the Great Depression in the twentieth century).[9] Without international trade, the United States and its citizens could not replenish their coffers of gold and silver, further exacerbating the cash crunch.

Under the Articles of Confederation, each state by design was essentially a sovereign entity left to its own devices to raise revenues. Tremendously fearful of a return to a monarchical government (with Washington as the likely King), supporters of the Articles, particularly Arthur Lee of Virginia, glorified them as a "rope of sand" vastly preferable to a "rod of iron."[10] Despite the sorry condition of the balance sheet of every state, voters still demanded debt and tax relief—and politicians complied, implementing a variety of debtor-friendly measures:[11]

> Close the courts temporarily to prevent lawsuits
> Allow payment in goods or property
> Eliminate interest payments

---

8. Leonard Richards, *Shays's Rebellion: The American Revolution's Final Battle* (Philadelphia: The University of Pennsylvania Press, 2002), 5.
9. allthingsliberty.com/2015/02/how-was-the-revolutionary-war-paid-for/.
10. Ellis, *The Cause*, 290.
11. Abner Linwood (Woody) Holton, *Unruly Americans and the Origins of the Constitution* (New York: Hill and Wang, 2007), 55.

Only pay original bondholders, not speculators
Pay back bonds at purchase price, not par (and calculate interest the same way)
Use state tax revenue to buy and retire bonds
Print more paper money

Debtholders countered by waging publicity campaigns and creating "anti-luxury" associations, impugning the spending habits of the masses, particularly on goods such as frilly women's clothes.

With four million dollars of debt[12] and thirteen million dollars in paper money outstanding (ten times the emission of neighboring Connecticut),[13] Massachusetts was in worse fiscal shape than almost any other state. In fact, cash was so low that Massachusetts began paying its militia in 1780 with commodity certificates redeemable for "5 bushels of corn, 68 pounds of beef, 10 pounds of sheep's wool, and 16 pounds of sole leather."[14] In 1785, the popular, and populist, governor, John Hancock resigned rather than yield to pressure from wealthy debtholders to collect more taxes.

James Bowdoin, a prosperous shipowner involved in the "triangle" trade, large landowner, and bitter Hancock rival, assumed the governor's seat. Massachusetts promptly passed an incendiary bill that not only imposed tax rates significantly higher than neighboring states, but also required that taxes be paid in hard currency, not paper or commodities (as the state had been paying its soldiers!).[15] To his credit, Hancock was one of the few merchants who continued to accept paper money despite its deflated value. Overall, the tax burden on the ordinary citizen actually quadrupled compared to pre-war levels under British rule.[16] Daniel Shays, like hundreds of other cash-poor backwoodsmen, was taken to court several times by local retailers for failure to meet his obligations, one as low as three pounds.[17] Fees for lawyers, sheriffs and administrators added to his frustration.

On the polar opposite of the economic spectrum, Robert Morris was believed to be the richest man in America. Born into modest circumstances in Liverpool in 1734, he immigrated to Virginia at age thirteen first to join his father, a successful tobacco trader, shortly

12. en.wikipedia.org/wiki/Funding_Act_of_1790.
13. David M. Roth, *Connecticut's War Governor: Jonathan Trumbull* (Guilford, CT: Globe Pequot, 2017), 41.
14. www.masshist.org/collection-guides/view/fao0004.
15. Danver, *Revolts*, 222.
16. Holton, *Unruly Americans*, 28.
17. David Szatmary, *Shays Rebellion: the Making of an Agrarian Insurrection* (Amherst, MA: University of Massachusetts Press 1980), 66.

thereafter moving to Philadelphia to apprentice in the banking firm of Charles Willing. When his father died in 1750, Morris inherited enough capital to launch his career. Personally sailing to Caribbean ports, Morris traded in agricultural commodities including tobacco, flour, and wheat, as well as enslaved people. His work ethic, global contact network, trading acumen, and willingness to make highly leveraged bets fueled his ascent.

As war approached, Morris took a more active role in politics, serving on Pennsylvania's Committee of Safety and then as a delegate to the Second Continental Congress. A "moderate" businessman, Morris at first abstained in the vote for independence, but finally signed the Declaration of Independence in August 1776, stating, "while I do not wish to see my countrymen die on the field of battle nor do I wish to see them live in tyranny."[18]

Over the course of the war, Morris became the most powerful politician in America, and the Continental Army's best friend. His "secret" committee secured gunpowder and munitions overseas despite British blockades and seizures. He was a signatory to the Articles of Confederation, becoming America's de facto chief executive for the next three years as the federal congress simply withered away, often failing to seat a quorum. In 1784, Thomas Jefferson noted in conversation with a visiting Dutch baron: "The men of Congress are no longer men of distinction."[19] Abigail Adams referred to congressmen as "beardless boys."[20] Since Congress was essentially bankrupt, Morris issued "Morris Notes," backed by his own fortune, enabling Washington to purchase crucial supplies and pay the soldiers at least a pittance of what they were owed.

Although Morris clearly supported the nation's soldiers, he was always a capitalist at heart, strongly advocating that all government debts must be paid in full if the country was to achieve "power, consequence, and grandeur."[21] In a letter circulated to all governors, Morris blistered Arthur Lee's analogy, noting that if the states did not pay their share, then "our enemies will draw strong arguments that our

---

18. Robert Morris to Horatio Gates, October 27, 1776, *The Founders on the Founders*, ed. John P. Kaminski (Charlottesville: University of Virginia Press, 2008).
19. Ellis, *The Cause*, 323; *Letters of Delegates to Congress*, ed. Paul Smith (Washington, DC: Government Printing Office, 1976-2000), 21:494.
20. Abigail Adams to John Quincy Adams, March 20, 1786, *Adams Family Correspondence Volume 7* (Cambridge, MA: Harvard University Press, 2005), 98, 114.
21. E. James Ferguson, *The Power of the Purse* (Chapel Hill: University of North Carolina Press, 1961), 120.

Union is a rope of sand ... No words [alone] will induce men to risk their property on the security of a nominal union."[22]

When Gov. Jonathan Trumbull of Connecticut balked, Morris admonished him: "As to the complaint made by the people of a want of money to pay their taxes, it is nothing new to me ... the complaint is quite as old as taxation and will last as long ... Hundreds who cannot find money to pay taxes, can find it to purchase useless geegaws, and expend much more in gratification of vanity, luxury, drunkenness and debauchery than is necessary to establish the freedom of their country."[23]

Unsurprisingly, Morris developed a slew of political enemies who objected to his clout as well as his occasional intermingling of personal and national business. Joseph Reed, President of the Supreme Executive Council of Pennsylvania, the nation's most populated and powerful state, called Morris a "pecuniary dictator," further noting that Congress had forfeited "all business of deliberation and executive difficulty"; nevertheless, Reed added that "humiliating as this power is ... the public has received a real benefit from Mr. Morris' exertions."[24]

Under Morris's guidance, Congress established the first national bank, the Bank of North America, but the states still dragged their heels. As the war wound down, mutinies over back pay by Continental Army officers and enlisted men flared. In 1783, Morris personally signed 6,000 "Morris notes" as the Continental Army retired from the field. In 1784, Morris resigned all his government posts, noting that he would not be the "Minister of Injustice."

Although Morris stepped away, his notes circulated widely. Eliphat Dyer, a congressman from Connecticut, wrote from Philadelphia: "the Financier's [Morris] notes and bills are in full credit and paid on sight, and are rather preferred to money by the merchants here, and yet a shameful discount is placed on them and large speculations made by traders."[25] Abigail Adams, long revered as a matriarch of liberty, was one of many prominent speculators, or "sharpers," on the other side of the bond trade.

---

22. Charles Rappelye, *Robert Morris: Financier of the American Revolution* (New York: Simon and Shuster, 2010), 250; Morris circular, July 27, 1781, *Papers of Robert Morris Volume 1* (Pittsburgh, PA: University of Pittsburgh Press, 1973) 1:464.
23. Rappelye, *Robert Morris*, 248.
24. Rappelye, *Robert Morris*, 251-2; Joseph Reed to Nathanael Greene, November 1, 1781, cdm16694.contentdm.oclc.org/digital/collection/p16124coll1/id/50415/rec/2.
25. Eliphat Dyer to Trumbull, July 29, 1782, *Collections of the Massachusetts Historical Society* 7th series volume 3 (Boston: Massachusetts Historical Society, 1902), 344-348.

In 1776, tasked with running the family farm outside Boston while her husband was in Congress in Philadelphia, Abigail purchased her first Congressional Loan Office certificates, trading at roughly 75 percent below par but promising 6 percent interest on the full face value. At worst, she reasoned, these bonds would depreciate more slowly than the paper money she was forced to accept in rents from her tenants; the upside was huge if Congress could pay the interest and eventually redeem the bonds at par. In September 1777, Congress voted to back these bonds with bills of exchange drawn on French loans, essentially guaranteeing their creditworthiness. Demonstrating his integrity, John Adams, well aware of his wife's investments, was one of the few congressmen to vote against this proposal.[26] Abigail continued to invest in bonds for the next twenty years.

While the profitability of the bond trade became well known, only a small percentage of the population in the 1780s had the hard cash necessary to speculate. In Massachusetts, half the state debt was held by thirty-five men who had close ties to its legislature. Although outside of this elite circle, the Adams were able to invest John's salary (elected officials and civil administrators were consistently paid during the war, while soldiers were not), as well as Abigail's gains. Abigail further supplemented her coffers by launching her own retail business, selling fashionable pins, textiles and fine china that her husband shipped from his ambassadorial posts in Europe. Given the British blockades, these luxury items were scarce in America, fetching several times their pre-war prices.

In 1784, Abigail joined her husband in Paris and then moved with him to London later that year. While they resided overseas until the summer of 1788, Abigail kept abreast of the rebellion brewing in Massachusetts which she knew had depressed bond prices. In a letter to Thomas Jefferson, she explained: "Ignorant, restless desperadoes, without conscience or principals, have led a deluded multitude to follow their standard, under pretense of grievances which have no existence but in their imaginations . . . you will see the necessity there is of the wisest and most vigorous measures to quell and suppress" the rebellion. In a hypocritical twist, given Abigail's own import operations, she added: "Luxury and extravagance both in furniture and dress had pervaded all orders of our countrymen and women, and was hastening fast to sap their independence . . . Vanity was becoming a more powerful principle than Patriotism."[27]

26. Abner Linwood (Woody) Holton, *Abigail Adams* (New York: Free Press, 2009), 132.
27. Abigail Adams to Thomas Jefferson, January 29, 1787, founders.archives.gov/documents/Adams/04-07-02-0181.

Abigail Adams was conveniently out of touch with the situation at home: equity, not vanity, motivated Daniel Shays and his fellow rebels. Veterans who had been paid for their service with bonds, not cash, were compelled to sell their paper at 70 to 90 percent discounts to feed their families—and then were taxed heavily by Massachusetts so that the state could pay back the speculators at par plus interest. Furthermore, many in the financial/merchant class, like Adams, who had never set foot on a battlefield, actually resented the veterans, fearing that they would form a permanent standing army and corrupt the "glorious cause" of the Revolution.

Popular backlash against the Army gained momentum in 1780 when Congress voted to guarantee back pay plus a pension for life for officers. Although the pension was later commuted to five years, the damage was done. Negative sentiment gathered more appeal in 1783 when Continental officers formed the Society of the Cincinnati (ironically named after a victorious Roman general who retired and returned to his farm) to preserve their memories and provide funds to widows, orphans and disabled veterans. Membership in the Cincinnati would be passed down from father to son. Aghast at the creation of a hereditary military aristocracy, Jefferson (clearly an aristocrat himself) wrote to Washington that the Cincinnati "is a cancer planted in the heart of the Republic."[28] In 1786, the Massachusetts legislature went so far as to formally assert that the battles at Lexington, Concord and Bunker Hill were fought by local militia, not the Continental army.[29]

Hounded by debt collectors, scammed by lawyers, thrown in jail by sheriffs, and scorned by the well-to-do, Shays and his fellow farmers gathered at Conkey's Tavern in Pelham on July 18, 1786 to draft a petition to the state legislature.[30] They adopted the moniker "Regulators" (first used by rebellious farmers in North Carolina twenty years earlier[31]), because they sought to rein in the excesses of the ruling class and level the economic playing field. Their petition called for a new state constitution granting more representation to the working class, lower salaries for legislators, and that the seat of government be moved out of Boston.

After the legislature adjourned for the year without responding, fifty western towns banded together to form a Committee of Safety, reminiscent of pre-Revolutionary times. On August 29, fifteen hundred

28. Ellis, *The Cause*, 287.
29. Ibid., 287.
30. Richards, *Shays's Rebellion*, 4.
31. allthingsliberty.com/2021/05/william-tryon-and-the-park-that-still-bears-his-name/.

armed Regulators marched towards the Northampton courthouse, the state's primary outpost in its western territory, where they were joined by several hundred more sympathizers. The elders of Pelham wanted Shays to lead this "army" but he initially refused, preferring to serve in the ranks. Confronted by a hostile mob, the three judges adjourned the court.

When the tribunal tried to reopen in September in Worcester to issue foreclosure notices and arrest warrants to delinquent debtors, the judges faced the same angry opposition. The scope of the insurgency should not have been surprising given that debt lawsuits in Worcester had jumped fourfold in the past decade and now involved one third of the adult male population.[32] Unsurprisingly homogeneous, the list of Regulators included only three Blacks and three women; almost all the white males considered themselves yeomen and were members of the Congregational church.[33]

As local newspapers carried accounts of the Regulators' success, the rebellion steadily spread to courthouses in Concord, Taunton, and Great Barrington throughout the fall. Enraged, Governor Bowdoin called out the state militia but many "minutemen," particularly veterans, resisted the call. In Great Barrington, the militia put the issue to a formal vote with 80 percent electing to join the Regulators.[34]

Meanwhile, the neighboring state of Rhode Island placated its Regulators by printing more paper money and mandating its acceptance, driving down the price of bonds throughout New England. Abigail Adams argued that "debt was the price of freedom" and demanded to be repaid in full.[35] Terrified that the clarion call of the Regulators might spread nationwide, the Continental Congress moved to raise an army officially to fight Indians, not American citizens, but the poorly cloaked effort never gained traction with the states who would have had to foot its bill.

By late November, Bowdoin finally raised a large enough force to venture out of Boston. The troops arrested five Regulators, including Job Shattuck, the wealthiest farmer in the west, and four of his compatriots, shepherding them to Boston for trial. This sortie only served to further radicalize the countryside. Much to Bowdoin's surprise, the Regulators marched on the court in Springfield in late December and shut it down. To their ultimate detriment, the

---

32. Szatmary, *Shays Rebellion*, 29.
33. Ibid., 58-61.
34. Richards, *Shays's Rebellion*, 12.
35. Holton, *Abigail Adams* 88.

Regulators did not seize the largely undefended federal arsenal at Springfield at this time.

Thoroughly angered and embarrassed, Bowdoin raised funds from 153 Boston bondholders (but not Abigail or John Adams who were still overseas) to hire a four-thousand-man army of mercenaries, primarily from eastern Massachusetts and territories north. William Phillips, namesake of Andover and Exeter academies, was the single largest contributor.[36] Bowdoin handed the reins of his army to Massachusetts native Benjamin Lincoln, a retired Continental Army general and merchant/speculator in his own right.

Lincoln had fought well, sustaining a serious ankle wound, at Saratoga in 1777, but was overshadowed by the exploits of Benedict Arnold. Washington placed Lincoln in command of the Southern Department in 1779 culminating in the siege of Charleston, South Carolina in 1780. Here, Lincoln overestimated the strength of his position, vowing to fight "until the last extremity," and missed the window to evacuate his troops safely. Two weeks later, Lincoln surrendered the key city, dooming 2,500 soldiers to British prison ships, the largest such loss of Continental Army forces in the war.[37]

Washington immediately replaced Lincoln with Nathanael Greene as head of the Southern Department; but Lincoln, exchanged for a captured British general in November 1780, returned to the field, playing an important role in the victorious siege of Yorktown. When Lord Cornwallis, pleading illness, sent his second-in-command to the formal British surrender on October 19, 1781, Washington appointed Lincoln to represent the American side.

After Yorktown, Lincoln moved into politics, becoming Secretary of War under Robert Morris from 1781 through 1783. He joined the Society of the Cincinnati as an original member in 1783 but had little empathy for his fellow veterans who were in rebellion three years later, an opinion held by Washington, Knox, and other senior officers as well. Determined to regain lost glory, Lincoln marched west at the head of Bowdoin's mercenaries on January 19, 1787.

Incensed by the "invasion" of their homeland, the Regulators crossed the Rubicon separating political protest from outright rebellion; however, they were loosely organized and poorly armed. At this point, Daniel Shays stepped up to lead the Regulators' largest regiment as part of a concerted action to capture the Springfield armory. If successful, the Regulators would have been the best-armed military force in North America.

36. Richards, *Shays's Rebellion*, 23.
37. www.nps.gov/articles/siege-of-charleston-1780.htm.

While the rebels beat Lincoln's troops to the armory, a local militia general and Cincinnati member, William Shepherd, got there first. Shepherd feared that Shays would "set up a military government ... and declare himself dictator."[38] His 1,200 men armed themselves from the federal till and dug in. As important, Shepherd intercepted Regulator communications that would have postponed the attack. In the fog of war, Shays charged the armory on January 25, 1787. Shepherd first ordered his cannons to fire over the heads of the rebels but, when they did not halt, his men lowered their aim, leaving four dead and twenty wounded.[39]

The Regulators scattered north, uncharacteristically terrorizing local merchants in their panic along the way. Shays regrouped his men in the town of Petersham, forty miles from Springfield, a few days later. By that time Lincoln had arrived in the west, pursuing the Regulators and itching for battle. He marched his troops twenty miles through an overnight blizzard, catching Shays completely off guard on February 4, sending the rebels scattering into the hills. A hundred-man coterie of Regulators launched one more unsuccessful foray in April in Sheffield, purportedly trying to kidnap Lincoln, but he narrowly escaped, further cementing his status as a hero in his home state.[40] Shays' Rebellion was effectively over.

Ironically, Samuel Adams, the instigator of rebellion against the British monarchy only a decade earlier, became the loudest voice in Boston demanding severe punishment for the Regulators who had dared rebel against his cherished ideal of an elected, "republican" government. Adams spearheaded the passage of the Disqualification Acts which stripped rebels of their right to hold office or own property, suspended *habeus corpus*, mandated jail time and public whippings for the common rebels, and recommended the death penalty for the leadership. Other wealthy merchants, however, proclaimed that they would prefer a return to a monarchy over the tyranny of the mob.[41]

After Petersham, fourteen Regulators, including Shays, were sentenced to death, but none were actually executed at the time (although two were hanged, primarily for looting, at year-end). Recognizing the grass roots popularity of the rebellion, Bowdoin relaxed enforcement of the Acts, allowing four thousand Regulators to simply swear oaths of allegiance and return to their farms. Daniel Shays escaped to the Vermont wilderness, never to return to Massachusetts.

38. Szatmary, *Shays Rebellion*, 74.
39. Ibid., 102.
40. Richards, *Shays's Rebellion*, 36.
41. Szatmary, *Shays Rebellion*, 82.

With Robert Morris retired from public life, Alexander Hamilton, former right-hand man to George Washington, assumed the mantle of advocacy for a powerful federal government and central bank. Hamilton had established a successful legal practice in New York City, gaining notoriety for his defense of the property rights of the wealthy, including Tories who had stood firm against the fight for independence. In this vein, he preached that bondholders were property owners whose gold and silver had rescued the Revolution in its darkest hour. Like Morris, Hamilton believed that they needed to be repaid in full if our fledgling nation ever hoped to attract the new investment necessary to grow.

After Lincoln's defeat of the Regulators, Hamilton painted Shays as a desperate anarchist intent on overthrowing the government. The fear of a second revolution actually motivated Washington himself to come out of retirement in Mount Vernon. Not only did Washington preside over the Constitutional Convention in Philadelphia in June 1787, but he also volunteered to command troops to defeat any future insurrections.

Arguing that the country suffered from "too much democracy,"[42] Hamilton and his fellow Federalists vociferously advocated replacing the Articles of Confederation with a new Constitution. Shays' influence is readily apparent in the widely-read Federalist Papers, written by Hamilton, Madison, and Jay under the common pseudonym Publius. These Papers, eighty-five in total, exhorted the citizenry to implement a national government armed with executive, legislative, and judicial powers that actually suppressed the rights of both state legislatures and common citizens.

In *Federalist #9*, Hamilton wrote:

> A Firm Union will be of the utmost moment to the peace and liberty of the States, as a barrier against domestic faction and insurrection. It is impossible to read the history of the petty republics of Greece and Italy without feeling sensations of horror and disgust ... at the rapid succession of revolutions by which they were kept in a state of perpetual vibration between the extremes of tyranny and anarchy.[43]

James Madison subtly seconded the anti-Shays opinion in *Federalist #10*:

> The influence of factious leaders may kindle a flame within their particular States, but will be unable to spread a general conflagration

---

42. Holton, *Unruly Americans*, 5.
43. resources.utulsa.edu/law/classes/rice/Constitutional/FedPapers/Fed09.htm.

through the other States ... A rage for paper money, for an abolition of debts, for an equal division of property, or for any other improper or wicked project, will be less apt to pervade the whole body of the Union."[44]

Newspapers like the *Pennsylvania Gazette* followed suit, bellowing that "every state has its Shays"[45] and "should the federal government be rejected none other than Daniel Shays would seize control of Massachusetts."[46] In fact, Bowdoin was overwhelmingly defeated by Hancock in the 1787 gubernatorial election and 75 percent of the state legislators were voted out of office. Massachusetts immediately pardoned Job Shattuck and cut taxes; bond prices dropped 30 percent.[47]

While the "people" would not rise again, the spirit of Shays' Rebellion would ultimately force the Federalists to compromise. When 90 percent of the western towns in Massachusetts voted against the proposed Constitution, threatening its ratification, Hancock and Samuel Adams reconciled to support amendments, known collectively as the Bill of Rights (applicable only to white men at the time), which guaranteed critical freedoms to the farmers. As significantly, Federalist leadership caved to the Southern states' demands to maintain slavery. By June 21, 1788, nine states, including Massachusetts, had accepted these amendments and ratified the Constitution, ensuring its passage. Rhode Island became the thirteenth and final state to ratify on May 29, 1790. By then, bond prices had skyrocketed more than 50 percent from their lows.[48]

Did Daniel Shays and the Regulators represent the true spirit of the American Revolution? Or did Abigail Adams, Robert Morris, Alexander Hamilton, and their fellow financiers/merchants? What if the Boston capitalists had not raised their own army? Would the rebels have toppled Bowdoin's government? Would overtaxed farmers in every state have followed suit? Would Indigenous Peoples, fleeced out of their homelands by speculators, have joined the revolt? Would the Southern states have seceded, forming their own nation to protect the profits imbedded in the institution of slavery?

If so, the United States as we now know it might have remained a wishful dream, while a loose confederation (or several feuding confederations) of states, lacking any clout on the global stage, lingered

---

44. resources.utulsa.edu/law/classes/rice/Constitutional/FedPapers/Fed10.htm.
45. *Pennsylvania Gazette*, September 5, 1786.
46. *Pennsylvania Gazette*, February 5 and 12, 1787; Richards, *Shays's Rebellion*, 139.
47. Richards, *Shays's Rebellion*, 119.
48. Ibid., 150

on. Alternatively, the Regulators might have captured Boston and unleashed a Reign of Terror like French revolutionaries did just a few years later.

In fact, the quashing of Shays' Rebellion benefited the entire country (albeit white men in particular). The federal government arising from the Constitution gained the faith of the world's financial community, sparking investment in the United States and its westward expansion. From 1790 until the War of 1812, the United States economy boomed: gross domestic product growth averaged 3.9 percent per year while inflation remained low at only 2 percent per year.[49] On the economic front, at least, Morris, Hamilton, and Abigail Adams were right.

EPILOGUE

Robert Morris signed the Constitution on September 17, 1787 and served as the first United States Senator from Pennsylvania from 1789 to 1795. George Washington asked Morris to become his initial Secretary of the Treasury, but Morris declined, recommending Alexander Hamilton in his stead. Unfortunately, Morris's business dealings turned sour in the late 1780s. He then compounded his problems by over-speculation in western lands. While he was right in concept, his timing was too early and his debts massive. Morris was incarcerated in 1798, serving over three years. He died in poverty in 1806.

Riding the electoral success of her husband, Abigail Adams became the nation's first Second Lady in 1789 and the second First Lady in 1796. It was, however, her financial speculation that ensured the couple's comfortable retirement while other founders, notably Jefferson and Madison, who had elected to invest in land and slaves, not bonds, fell into pecuniary distress. She died in 1818 at the age of seventy-four.

Daniel Shays was pardoned by Massachusetts in 1788 and later granted a military pension by the federal government. He wandered around New York and Vermont, often drunk, for almost thirty years, dying with little but his pension in 1825. After his ignominious passing Shays' stature grew steadily. Poems were written, ballads sung, monuments erected, and highways named in his honor.[50] On the two hundredth anniversary of the assault on the Springfield armory, President Ronald Reagan declared January 25, 1987 Shays' Rebellion Day, noting in his proclamation: "Shays' Rebellion was to have a

---

49. 5minuteeconomist.com/history/1790-1811-the-founding-years.
50. www.youtube.com/watch?v=1QssCPx8t5I.

profound and lasting effect on the framing of our Constitution and on our subsequent history."[51]

While these profound, lasting effects were all actually achieved through peaceful, democratic processes, would they have gained momentum without the kickstart of a violent insurrection? Several months after Shays' Rebellion had ended, and the new Constitution was well on its way towards ratification, Thomas Jefferson wrote: "And what country can preserve its liberties if their rulers are not warned from time to time that their people preserve the spirit of resistance? Let them take arms. The remedy is to set them right as to facts, pardon and pacify them. What signify a few lives lost in a century or two? The tree of liberty must be refreshed from time to time with the blood of patriots and tyrants. It is its natural manure."[52]

---

51. www.reaganlibrary.gov/archives/speech/proclamation-5598-shays-rebellion-week-and-day-1987.
52. Jefferson to William Stephens Smith, November 13, 1787, founders.archives.gov/documents/Jefferson/01-12-02-0348. For the record, the author heartily disagrees with Jefferson here. While democracy was a novel concept in 1787, we now have 235 years of proof that it works, albeit clumsily at times. I would hate to see the United States march violently backwards.

Natural History in Revolutionary and Post-Revolutionary America

MATTEO GIULIANI

In the second half of the 1700s, French natural historian Georges-Louis Leclerc, Comte de Buffon, formulated what would be dubbed the "New World degeneracy" or the "American degeneracy" theory. His work, *Histoire Naturelle, Générale et Particulière*, included a vast array of facts about natural history from around the world as well as the Count's many ideas about the history of the Earth and the organisms that inhabit it. According to Buffon, a set number of distinct types of life generated near a central point. He suggested that species then underwent change as they migrated, affected by their new environments. In a way, Buffon was proposing a sort of proto-evolutionary hypothesis nearly one hundred years before Darwin.

The Count argued that all animals in the New World were degenerate compared to those in the Old World. "Animated nature, therefore is less active, less varied, and even less vigorous," Buffon wrote, "for by the enumeration of the American animals we shall perceive, that not only the number of species is smaller, but that in general, they are inferior in size to those of the old continent."[1]

Buffon had never been to North America, and instead based his claims on specimens in the French King's Cabinet of Natural History, prior published material on North America, accounts from travelers who had been to the New World, and a small menagerie he kept at his summer home, which included some New World and Old World animals.

Cold and humid environments, Buffon maintained, led life to degenerate. The land mass of the New World, Buffon believed, had been under water for a much longer period than the Old World. Therefore,

---

1. Georges-Louis Leclerc de Buffon, *Historie Naturelle, Générale et Particulière*, vol. 9, Quadrupèdes VI (Paris: Imprimerie Royale, 1761), 87, gallica.bnf.fr/ark:/12148/bpt6k1067248h/f11.item.

North America was a relatively new continent that had not had time to heat up or dry out. The result was a cold continent with an extraordinarily humid land and stagnant swamps everywhere. According to the Count, only insects and reptiles could flourish in such an environment. Consequently, humans—whom the Count thought had migrated to the continent via a land bridge that once connected Eurasia with North America—and domesticated animals brought to America were doomed to be smaller and feebler.

American Indians, Buffon affirmed, were responsible for the increase in humidity and the rate of degeneration, as they had failed to drain the swamps: "In these melancholy regions Nature remains concealed under her old garments, and never exhibits herself in fresh attire; being neither cherished nor cultivated by man, she never opens her fruitful and beneficent womb."[2] For the Count, American Indians were:

> A kind of weak automaton, incapable of improving or seconding her [Nature's] intentions. She treated them rather like a stepmother than a parent, by refusing them the invigorating sentiment of love, and the strong desire of multiplying their species. For, though the American savage be nearly of the same stature with men in polished societies; yet this is not a sufficient exception to the general contraction of animated Nature throughout the whole Continent. In the savage, the organs of generation are small and feeble. He has no hair, no beard, no ardour for the female ... He has no vivacity, no activity of mind ... He remains in stupid repose, on his limbs or couch, for whole days ... They have been refused the most precious spark of Nature's fire: They have no ardour for women, and, of course, no love to mankind ... Their love to parents and children is extremely weak. The bonds of the most intimate of all societies, that of the same family, are feeble; and one family has no attachment to another ... Their heart is frozen, their society cold, and their empire cruel. They regard their females as servants destined to labour, or as beasts of burden, whom they load unmercifully with the produce of their hunting, and oblige, without pity or gratitude, to perform labours which often exceed their strength. They have few children, and pay little attention to them. They are indifferent, because they are weak.[3]

Histoire Naturelle was well received in Europe, where Corneille de Pauw's *Récherches philosophiques sur les Americains*, published in 1768, and Guillaume-Thomas François Raynal's *Histoire philosophique et politique*, published in 1770, extended Buffon's ideas to Creoles—Euro-

---

2. Ibid., 110.
3. Ibid., 104-105.

peans born in America. According to de Pauw, degeneracy had and would continue to affect Europeans emigrating to North America and their descendants:

> The Europeans who pass into America degenerate, as do the animals: a proof that the climate is unfavorable to the improvement of either man or animal. The Creoles, descended from Europeans and born in America . . . have never produced a single book. This degradation of humanity must be imputed to the vitiated qualities of the air stagnated in their immense forests, and corrupted by noxious vapours from standing waters and uncultivated ground.[4]

Raynal, for his part, proclaimed that "America has not yet produced a good poet, an able mathematician, one man of genius in a single art or a single science."[5]

When these ideas reached the shores of North America, the backlash was swift. Both James Madison and Alexander Hamilton expressed their disapproval, but it was Jefferson who came up with an effective rebuttal.[6]

The French government had instructed the secretary of the French legation in Philadelphia, François Barbé-Marbois, to gather as much information as possible on the former thirteen British colonies. Barbé-Marbois prepared a list of twenty-two queries to be distributed to the governors of each state. The questionnaire, through Joseph Jones, Virginia delegate to the Continental Congress in late 1780, got to Thomas Jefferson, the then governor of Virginia. Jefferson's response, *Notes on the State of Virginia*, was an overview of his home state. The longest chapter, titled "Productions mineral, vegetable, and animal," precisely confuted the New World degeneracy theory.

Before delving into Jefferson's answer, it is necessary to understand what prompted him to answer in the first place. First off, Jefferson did not deny that climate could affect the size of animals. Instead, he maintained that climate, even when it affected the size of animals, worked within defined limits. In particular, he believed animals to have a max-

---

4. Cornelis de Pauw, *A General History of the Americans, of Their Customs, Manners, and Colours* (Rochdale: T. Wood, 1806), 17-18, archive.org/details/generalhistoryof00pauwarch/page/n3/mode/2up.
5. Guillaume-Thomas François Raynal, *Histoire Philosophique et Politique*, vol. 6 (Amsterdam, 1770), 376, gallica.bnf.fr/ark:/12148/bpt6k109692c.texteImage.
6. James Madison to Thomas Jefferson, June 19, 1786, founders.archives.gov/documents/Madison/01-09-02-0017; Alexander Hamilton, "Federalist No. 11: The Utility of the Union in Respect to Commercial Relations and a Navy," *The Independent Journal*, November 24, 1787, avalon.law.yale.edu/18th_century/fed11.asp.

imum and a minimum size, both set by their "Maker." "What intermediate station they [animals] shall take," Jefferson wrote, "may depend on soil, on climate, on food, on a careful choice of breeders. But all the manna of heaven would never raise the mouse to the bulk of the mammoth."[7]

Furthermore, Jefferson pointed out that there was no evidence that differences existed in the climates of the two worlds that would lead to life in the New World being degenerate:

> The opinion of a writer [Buffon], the most learned too of all others in the science of animal history, [is] that nature is less active, less energetic on one side of the globe than she is on the other. As if both sides were not warmed by the same genial sun; as if a soil of the same chemical composition, was less capable of elaboration into animal nutriment; as if the fruits and grains from that soil and sun, yielded a less rich chyle, gave less extension to the solids and fluids of the body, or produced sooner in the cartilages, membranes, and fibres, that rigidity which restrains all further extension, and terminates animal growth. The truth is, that a Pigmy and a Patagonian, a Mouse and a Mammoth, derive their dimensions from the same nutritive juices.[8]

As Benjamin Franklin presented Jefferson with data that showed that London and Paris were more humid than Philadelphia, the Virginian convinced himself even more that additional studies and facts were needed to draw an accurate conclusion:

> As to the theory of Monsr. de Buffon that heat is friendly and moisture adverse to the production of large animals, I am lately furnished with a fact by Doctr. Franklin which proves the air of London and of Paris to be more humid than that of Philadelphia, and so creates a suspicion that the opinion of the superior humidity of America may perhaps have been too hastily adopted. And supposing that fact admitted, I think the physical reasonings urged to shew that in a moist country animals must be small, and that in a hot one they must be large, are not built on the basis of experiment. These questions however cannot be decided ultimately at this day. More facts must be collected, and more time flow off, before the world will be ripe for decision. In the mean time doubt is wisdom.[9]

---

7. Thomas Jefferson, *Notes on the State of Virginia* (Philadelphia: Prichard and Hall, 1788), 45, docsouth.unc.edu/southlit/jefferson/jefferson.html.
8. Ibid.
9. Jefferson to Chastellux, June 7, 1785, founders.archives.gov/documents/Jefferson/01-08-02-0145.

Another factor that made Jefferson question the Count's theory was the reliability of some of the sources—Frenchmen who had traveled to the New World. Specifically, he asked whether those people were reliable and trustworthy like Buffon and his colleagues working in the king's garden, whether they had natural history as the "object of their travels," and whether they measured or weighed "the animals they speak of." "A true answer to these questions," he concluded, "would probably lighten their authority, so as to render it insufficient for the foundation of an hypothesis."[10]

Overall, regarding the validity of the theory, Jefferson wrote:

> I am induced to suspect, there has been more eloquence than sound reasoning displayed in support of this theory; that it is one of those cases where the judgment has been seduced by a glowing pen: and whilst I render every tribute of honor and esteem to the celebrated zoologist [Buffon], who has added, and is still adding, so many precious things to the treasures of science, I must doubt whether in this instance he has not cherished error also, by lending her for a moment his vivid imagination and bewitching language.[11]

Last but not least, a practical rather than a theoretical question made it imperative to push back against the accusation of degeneracy coming from the Old World. Jefferson was aware that a prosperous future for America would depend heavily on economic relations with other countries and, above all, on a continuous influx of immigrants from Europe. Buffon's theory, which argued that the climate of the New World made life degenerate, cast a bad light on the nascent republic.

Whether claims of American degeneracy were made in Europe with the intention of targeting and hurting American affairs—supposedly with the goal of preventing America's economic and geographic expansion—this is impossible to establish with certainty. What is certain is that the idea that subjects could easily obtain vast tracts of land overseas was not very appealing to European monarchs.

Jefferson began his response by defining the fundamental points of Buffon's thought and by summarizing his reasons:

> The opinion advanced by the Count de Buffon, is 1. That the animals common both to the old and new world, are smaller in the latter. 2. That those peculiar to the new, are on a smaller scale. 3. That those which have been domesticated in both, have degenerated in America:

---

10. Jefferson, *Notes*, 55.
11. Ibid., 68.

and 4. That on the whole it exhibits fewer species. And the reason he thinks is, that the heats of America are less; that more waters are spread over its surface by nature, and fewer of these drained off by the hand of man. In other words, that heat is friendly, and moisture, adverse to the production and development of large quadrupeds.[12]

To counter the Count's claims, he used tables to compare the size of a small sample of animals found in both the New and the Old World (table 1), the size of animals found only in the New World with those found only in the Old World (table 2), and the size of animals domesticated in both (table 3).[13] Jefferson's conclusions were as follows:

> The weights actually known and stated in the third table preceding will suffice to shew, that we may conclude, on probable grounds, that, with equal food and care, the climate of America will preserve the races of domestic animals as large as the European stock from which they are derived; and consequently that the third member of Mons. de Buffon's assertion, that the domestic animals are subject to degeneration from the climate of America, is as probably wrong as the first [the animals found in both continents are smaller in America] and second [the animals peculiar to the New World are on a smaller scale] were certainly so.
>
> That the last part of it is erroneous, which affirms that the species of American quadrupeds are comparatively few, is evident from the tables taken altogether. By these it appears that there are an hundred species aboriginal of America. Mons. de Buffon supposes about double that number existing on the whole earth.[14]

As for Buffon's evidence of the degeneracy of American Indians, nothing Jefferson read in European writings struck him as accurate. Not familiar with the Indigenous peoples of South America, his defense mainly concerned the Indians of North America, of whom Jefferson said he could speak based on his own knowledge and "the information of others better acquainted with him, and on whose truth and judgment" he could rely:

> From these sources I am able to say, in contradiction to this [Buffon's] representation, that he [the Indian] is neither more defective in ardor, nor more impotent with his female, than the white reduced to the same diet and exercise: that he is brave, when an enterprise depends on bravery; education with him making the point of honor consist in the de-

---

12. Ibid., 45–46.
13. Ibid., 49–52.
14. Ibid., 60.

struction of an enemy by stratagem, and in the preservation of his own person free from injury; or perhaps this is nature; while it is education which teaches us to honor force more than finesse: that he will defend himself against an host of enemies, always chusing to be killed, rather than to surrender, though it be to the whites, who he knows will treat him well: that in other situations also he meets death with more deliberation, and endures tortures with a firmness unknown almost to religious enthusiasm with us: that he is affectionate to his children, careful of them, and indulgent in the extreme: that his affections comprehend his other connections, weakening, as with us, from circle to circle, as they recede from the center: that his friendships are strong and faithful to the uttermost extremity.[15]

To provide his readers with an example that disproved the idea of Indian degeneracy, Jefferson resorted to an eloquent speech by Logan, an Iroquois leader whose family was murdered in retaliation by a group of Virginia militia. The militia's punitive expedition, caused by the robbery and murder of a frontiersman in the spring of 1774 by two Shawnees, ruined the good relations that had been established between the tribes and the settlers, leading to Lord Dunmore's War. When the Shawnee lost a decisive battle, peace negotiations began. Logan "disdained to be seen among the suppliants. But, lest the sincerity of a treaty should be distrusted, from which so distinguished a chief absented himself," he sent by a messenger a speech that was later reproduced and very much admired in Europe:

> I appeal to any white man to say, if ever he entered Logan's cabin hungry, and he gave him not meat; if ever he came cold and naked, and he clothed him not. During the course of the last long and bloody war, Logan remained idle in his cabin, an advocate for peace. Such was my love for the whites, that my countrymen pointed as they passed, and said, 'Logan in the friend of white men.' I had even thought to have lived with you, but for the injuries of one man. Col. Cresap, the last spring, in cold blood, and unprovoked, murdered all the relations of Logan, not sparing even my women and children. There runs not a drop of my blood in the veins of any living creature. This called on me for revenge. I have sought it: I have killed many: I have fully glutted my vengeance. For my country, I rejoice at the beams of peace. But do not harbour a thought that mine is the joy of fear. Logan never felt fear. He will not turn on his heel to save his life. Who is there to mourn for Logan?—Not one.[16]

15. Ibid., 62-63.
16. Ibid., 66-68.

Abbé Raynal himself, upon reading it, exclaimed *"Que celà est beau"* (How beautiful it is) and *"comme celà est simple, energétique et touchant"* (How simple, energetic and touching it is).[17]

Buffon, in describing the American Indians, acknowledged that they were about the same stature as Europeans, but argued that they were unable to reason, feel, and love. This, according to the French naturalist, was the cause behind their less developed civilizations. According to Jefferson, this added to the long list of things that did not make sense:

> But if cold and moisture be the agents of nature for diminishing the races of animals, how comes she all at once to suspend their operation as to the physical man of the new world, whom the Count acknowledges to be '*à peu près de même stature que l'homme de notre monde*' [about the same stature as the man in our world], and to let loose their influence on his moral faculties? How has this 'combination of the elements and other physical causes, so contrary to the enlargement of animal nature in this new world, these obstacles to the developement and formation of great germs,' been arrested and suspended, so as to permit the human body to acquire its just dimensions, and by what inconceivable process has their action been directed on his mind alone?[18]

In other words, Jefferson wondered how it was possible for nature to affect animals and humans in such different ways. In the absence of facts, the American concluded that "to form a just estimate of their [the Indians'] genius and mental powers, more facts are wanting, and great allowance to be made for those circumstances of their situation which call for a display of particular talents only. This done, we shall probably find that they are formed in mind as well as in body, on the same module with the 'Homo sapiens Europæus.'"[19]

To the accusation that America had not produced any brilliant mind, Jefferson argued that the country was relatively young and needed time to cultivate great poets. Rome and France, he said, needed time to produce a Virgil and a Voltaire, consequently the same time had to be given to America.

Population, Jefferson pointed out, was an important factor as well:

> Of the geniuses which adorn the present age, America contributes its full share. For comparing it with those countries, where genius is most cultivated, where are the most excellent models for art, and scaf-

---

17. Edward D. Seeber, *Modern Language Notes*, vol. 61, no. 6 (Johns Hopkins University Press, 1946), 415, doi.org/10.2307/2908929.
18. Ibid., 66.
19. Ibid.

foldings for the attainment of science, as France and England for instance, we calculate thus. The United States contain three millions of inhabitants; France twenty millions; and the British islands ten. We produce a Washington, a Franklin, a Rittenhouse [David Rittenhouse, Philadelphia astronomer, instrument craftsman and patriot]. France then should have half a dozen in each of these lines, and Great-Britain half that number, equally eminent.[20]

Jefferson completed *Notes* in 1781, initially sharing it with Marbois and just a few other colleagues. Soon, others learned about the work and asked for copies. Hence, in 1784, while serving as a member of the Continental Congress in Philadelphia, Jefferson discussed *Notes* with a local publisher, but was dissatisfied with the time it would take to print the copies and the price it would cost him. As a result, he took the manuscript with him to Europe that same year, when the Confederation Congress appointed him as Minister Plenipotentiary to France, directing him to join Benjamin Franklin and John Adams in Paris.

Here Jefferson had the first copies of *Notes* printed in English by a Parisian printer in 1785. He then discreetly distributed these among a small circle of friends and acquaintances in France (one copy was transmitted to Buffon, whom Jefferson had yet not met) and America. The decision to keep the distribution of *Notes* under his control was due to Jefferson's concern for the outrage that his liberal ideas (particularly that of the separation of church and state in a new Virginia Constitution and his anti-slavery stance) would have caused in his home state.

Jefferson's statements of belief in political, legal, and constitutional principles, such as individual freedoms, checks and balances, and constitutional government, were what preoccupied him:

> I had 200 copies printed, but do not put them out of my own hands, except two or three copies here, and two which I shall send to America, to yourself and Colo. Monroe, if they can be ready this evening as promised ... I beg you to peruse it carefully because I ask your advice on it and ask nobody's else. I wish to put it into the hands of the young men at the college, as well on account of the political as physical parts. But there are sentiments on some subjects which I apprehend might be displeasing to the country perhaps to the assembly or to some who lead it. I do not wish to be exposed to their censure, nor do I know how far their influence, if exerted, might effect a misapplication of law to such a publication were it made. Communicate it then in confidence to those whose judgments and information you would pay respect to:

---

20. Ibid., 70.

and if you think it will give no offence I will send a copy to each of the students of W.M.C. and some others to my friends and to your disposal. Otherwise I shall only send over a very few copies to particular friends in confidence and burn the rest. Answer me soon and without reserve. Do not view me as an author, and attached to what he has written. I am neither. They were at first intended only for Marbois. When I had enlarged them, I thought first of giving copies to three or four friends. I have since supposed they might set our young students into a useful train of thought and in no event do I propose to admit them to go to the public at large.[21]

Despite Jefferson's precautions, a certain Monsieur Barrios managed to obtain a copy of the book and planned to translate it into French without permission. To avoid this, Jefferson worked on a French edition with the help of Abbé Morellet, a member of the Académie française. This edition, however, did not please Jefferson at all. The Virginian was forced to publish an English edition in order to prevent the public from thinking that the French version, which often changed the meaning of the original, was accurate.

Therefore, in 1787, the book's first public edition, issued in London, began to be sold, while a year later, an American edition was published in Philadelphia. By the turn of the century, *Notes* was used as a popular handbook for natural history and geography and reprinted in newspapers all over the United States. The battle with Buffon, however, was not over. Jefferson was not satisfied; he wanted more—he wanted to change the Count's mind.

Sometime in late 1785, Jefferson, while dining with Buffon, realized that the Count had mischaracterized the American moose for a reindeer. Buffon, open to confrontation, told Jefferson that if he could present him with proof that the American moose was indeed as imposing as the Virginian claimed, he would correct his mistake. It is impossible to know whether the Count intended to retract his theory of degeneration. It is very likely, however, that Jefferson left the dinner meeting convinced of this.

At this point in the story, Jefferson's task was to bring an American moose to France. To do this, he enlisted the help of John Sullivan. Sullivan, a prominent New Hampshire figure, despite countless difficulties, managed to get Jefferson the carcass of a moose. Jefferson thanked him and wrote that he hoped that "Buffon will be able to have him [the

---

21. Jefferson to James Madison, May 11, 1785, founders.archives.gov/documents/Jefferson/01-08-02-0094.

moose] stuffed and placed on his legs in the king's cabinet."[22] Unfortunately, the Count died shortly after receiving the carcass. There was no retraction and the New World degeneracy theory outlived both Buffon and Jefferson.

The two engaged in a scientific debate in a field that was relatively unexplored at the time, yet their contribution to natural history was remarkable, as *Histoire Naturelle, Générale et Particulière* and *Notes on the State of Virginia* continued to influence generations of naturalists and philosophers decades later. The American degeneracy theory finally vanished in the 1850s, when the death of its key players and advancements in science rendered it obsolete.

22. Jefferson to John Sullivan, October 5, 1787, founders.archives.gov/documents/Jefferson/01-12-02-0208.

A Great Englishman? British Views of George Washington, from Revolution to Rapprochement

SAM EDWARDS

In June 1921, George Washington, the victor of Yorktown, arrived in London. His journey across the storm-tossed Atlantic had not been without difficulty, and when he landed on British shores there were some concerns over his condition. But after a careful check and a clean bill of health he was able to proceed to the capital where his anticipated presence had already provoked engaged comment. Lord Curzon, the Foreign Secretary, was amongst those keen to extend a warm welcome (Curzon was married to an American heiress). But others were less sure. Indeed, when news of his imminent arrival became public some Britons expressed clear displeasure. One angrily declared that:

> George Washington was a rebel against the Crown, the slayer of thousands of British troops, the cause of ruin to hundreds of loyalists ... to excite national feeling by putting up a statue of such a person is an act of official dementia.[1]

Despite such comments, the ceremony accompanying the president's arrival went ahead as planned, and on June 30 he was officially installed in a prestigious spot overlooking Trafalgar Square, within sight of another famous military hero of the eighteenth century: Admiral Horatio Nelson. Washington stands there still today, gazing out across the capital of the nation he so humbled, the result of an enduring British fas-

---

1. C.L. Hales to the Office of Works, May 19, 1921, Works 20/123, The National Archives, Kew, UK. At one point there was talk of the statue being placed in or near Westminster Abbey, but this too provoked an angry repost. See "Washington Not Wanted in Westminster Abbey," *Literary Digest* (March 28, 1914), 689-690.

cination with the first president that reaches right back to the Revolution itself.

A HERO OF THE AGES: THE BRITISH VIEW OF GENERAL WASHINGTON

The outbreak of the American Revolution did not instantly rent asunder all transatlantic ties, and in some quarters British sympathies lay firmly with the colonists, perceived as fighting for the time-honored rights of Englishmen.[2] In fact, for some commentators (including Thomas Jefferson), the American rebellion against the "tyranny" of George III was inspired by those English Barons who similarly held to account King John at Runnymede in 1215. Little wonder that many English Dissenters asserted a "profound sympathy" for their American brethren, whilst elsewhere some prominent Britons—most famously Edmund Burke—even actively advocated on their behalf.[3] In 1775, Burke went so far as to call for the "repeal of all legislation offensive to the Americans" in the hope that this might avert the impending crisis.[4]

Nonetheless, once hostilities commenced opinion in Britain hardened, and several of the Revolution's leaders were duly identified as villains and vagabonds. Thomas Paine, for instance, whose fiery words did so much to sustain the Continental Army during the savage winter of 1777-78, became the subject of sustained British scorn. By the 1790s, he was widely ridiculed in Britain as "Mad Tom," with one pamphleteer remarking that the author of *Common Sense* was "an enemy to his king and country, a traitor, a swindler, equally destitute of principles and abilities."[5] John Paul Jones, the father of the United States Navy—made infamous by his 1778 attack on the northern English port of Whitehaven—similarly met with British opprobrium for his afront to the nation's security and sovereignty.[6] News of his death in 1792 did

---

2. See K. Phillips, *The Cousins' Wars: Religion, Politics, Civil Warfare, and the Triumph of Anglo-America* (New York: Basic Books, 2000).
3. C.C. Bonwick, "English Dissenters and the American Revolution" in H.C. Allen and Roger Thompson (ed.), *Contrast and Connection: Bicentennial Essays in Anglo-American History* (London: G. Bell & Sons Ltd., 1976), 88. See also T. Bickham, "Sympathizing with Sedition? George Washington, the British Press, and British Attitudes during the American War of Independence," *The William and Mary Quarterly*, Third Series, 59, 1, (2002), 101-122.
4. Quoted in S. Conway, *The War of American Independence, 1775-1783* (London: Edward Arnold, 1995), 18.
5. See W.A. Speck, "The Image of Tom: Paine in Print and Portraiture" in S. Edwards and M. Morros, eds., *The Legacy of Thomas Paine in the Transatlantic World* (Abingdon: Routledge, 2018), 17-33.
6. The choice of Whitehaven was somewhat ironic, for though Jones did not know it, it had in fact been home to Washington's great-grandmother.

little to assuage such sentiment, and the London press took every opportunity to slander. In one report, Jones was dismissed as "a man of mean birth" who was "savage and cruel, to a degree of barbarity."[7]

And then there was the rebel-in-chief himself, Gen. George Washington, initially seen by some in Britain as the commander of a "despised" and "undisciplined rabble" and a man whose treatment of the Loyalist community long remained a sore point in London. Washington's military qualities likewise provoked occasional British comment, with his previous record in the King's colonial militia, especially his 1754 surrender to the French, a particular focus of attention. Here, claimed at least one British periodical, was proof of his martial failings, for the surrender was due to a basic tactical error: the "want of a good-look-out."[8] Later, Washington's 1780 execution of the British spy, Maj. John André, also drew censure in the British press.

In the long term, however, pointed press criticism of Washington proved unsustainable because it could not accommodate a clear and indisputable fact: if Washington really was no battlefield commander, and if the troops he led were indeed little more than a rabble, then how was it that he and they kept winning against a British Army widely touted in Parliament has amongst the best ever put into the field? It was in response to this rather awkward question that British views of Washington shifted, and for much of the conflict he was in fact portrayed as a "model of citizen virtue and an ideal military leader."[9]

For instance, one issue to garner attention in the London press was the courteous and respectful manner in which Washington treated captured British officers. Following his victory at Yorktown, he allowed them to retain their side arms and personal baggage, and he happily entertained to dinner defeated British Gen. Charles O'Hara, Lord Cornwallis's designated deputy. Such actions were used by some Britons to assert the fundamental decency of the colonists in cause and conduct. Here was clear evidence of Washington the Officer and Gentleman, a natural "aristocrat" and "commander on the European model" who had previously been proud of his English identity (at one point he had been destined for an education there).[10] As Troy Bickham has shown, two

---

7. "Death of Paul Jones," *Evening Mail*, July 27, 1792. See also R. Hornick, *What Remains: Searching for the Memory and Lost Grave of John Paul Jones* (Amherst: University of Massachusetts Press, 2017), 46-47, 56-61.
8. R.C. McGrane, "George Washington: An Anglo-American Hero," *Virginia Magazine of History and Biography*, 63, 1, (1955), 5-9.
9. Bickham, "Sympathizing with Sedition?," 101.
10. M. Cunliffe, *George Washington: Man and Monument* (London: Collins, 1959), 68; R. Chernow, *Washington: A Life* (London: Penguin, 2010), 5-9.

key themes thus developed in British depictions of Washington. The first asserted his status as a "quintessential English-American gentleman."[11] The second further affirmed this by identifying him as a "paragon of Republican virtue."[12] And crucially, these were not partisan views. In 1776, for example, even a Tory paper well-known for being hostile to the American cause declared Washington to be "The Flower of American Chivalry."[13]

No wonder therefore that British Arms had been bested on the field of battle: His Majesty's Redcoats had been conquered by one of their own who had led to victory an army of free-born Englishmen (at least, so went the theory). When this American Cincinnatus was subsequently elevated to the presidency many British liberals and dissenters happily declared their warm approval. After all, the system of government chosen by the Americans was pleasingly familiar in essential form albeit with an important improvement: the addition of a chief executive chosen on merit rather than by the accident of birth. Washington's subsequent conduct in office secured him still further British plaudits, and so too did his efforts to re-establish diplomatic ties with the Empire.

It is thus notable that in 1797, at the end of his presidential career, the dinner Washington hosted for close friends and colleagues included the resident British minister—Sir Robert Liston—whose wife, also in attendance, was famously overcome by tears at the first president's impending retirement.[14] Two years later, when Washington passed away, the Empire's capital went into mourning. A memorial service for those American sailors then in London was held in St. John's Church, Wapping, whilst the British Fleet, busy blockading the French channel ports, lowered the White Ensign to half-mast as a mark of respect.[15] In the London press, meanwhile, Washington was eulogized as a man of "genius, integrity and genuine patriotism" who acted "from the purest principle" and who was nothing less than a "hero of the ages."[16]

THE ANGLO-AMERICAN RAPPROCHEMENT

In the years that followed the esteem in which Washington was held in Britain only intensified, a development which now turned attention towards the question of his lineage. This was something in which Washington himself had always evinced little interest, not least because

---

11. Bickham, "Sympathizing with Sedition?," 101.
12. Ibid.
13. *Jackson's Oxford Journal*, December 7, 1776 quoted in Bickham, 113.
14. McGrane, "George Washington: An Anglo-American Hero," 8.
15. Ibid.
16. *London Morning Chronicle*, January 24, 1800.

the Revolution was a rejection of established ideas of birth and status. Pursuing his English ancestry was thus not a good "look" for a man simultaneously intent on severing political ties with London. As a result, when questioned about his "pedigree" in the 1790s Washington could only reply that he believed his family "came from some one of the northern counties of England; but whether from Lancashire, Yorkshire, or one still more northerly, I do not precisely remember."[17]

For others, however, such uncertainty demanded further research, and in due course the subject of the Washington family line, especially the precise location of its English "roots," drew engaged interest. Leading the way was Sir Isaac Heard, a heraldic "officer at arms," whose energetic pursuit of Washington's ancestry again reveals the first president's high standing in Britain. This pursuit continued across the nineteenth century, being taken up in the 1860s by the pioneering American genealogist Joseph Lemuel Chester, and then by Henry Waters in the 1880s. As the latter put it in 1889:

> On the American side of the water we had a complete chain running back from the President to the first settler of the name. There the chain, like the vast majority of American pedigrees, was broken short off, at the water's edge.[18]

By the end of the century, however, and as a result of the efforts of Heard, Chester, and Waters, this "chain" had at last been re-connected, and the Washington line was traced to four specific corners of England: Washington (County Durham), Sulgrave (Northamptonshire), Warton (Lancashire), and Purleigh (Essex). Even so, as the twentieth century approached the letters pages of the *London Times* still often bore witness to claim and counter-claim regarding some of the fine details.[19]

Crucially, such engaged British interest was shaped and sustained by the various assumptions then informing the so-called "Great Rapprochement."[20] First identified by the historian Bradford Perkins, this was an era in which politicians and diplomats on both sides of the Atlantic enthusiastically celebrated the "ties that bind," a development

---

17. George Washington to Sir Isaac Heard, May 2, 1792. Quoted in A. B. Hart, "The English Ancestry of George Washington," *Proceedings of the Massachusetts Historical Society*, 63 (October 1929—January 1930), 3.
18. H. Waters, *An Examination of the English Ancestry of George Washington* (Boston: New England Historic Genealogical Society, 1889), 7.
19. See, for example, *The Times*, August 29, August 31, September 8, September 13, September 22, October 4, October 15, October 24, and October 29, 1894.
20. B. Perkins: *The Great Rapprochement: England and the United States, 1895-1914* (New York: Antheneum, 1968).

prompted by shifting geo-political realities as well as contemporary obsessions regarding the imagined unities of the "Anglo-Saxon" race.[21] As another scholar has succinctly put it, by the turn of the twentieth century "articulate Englishmen and Americans at all levels of society declaimed about the supposed racial affinity of their two countries and described Great Britain and the United States as natural allies because of the racial bond."[22]

This represented a marked change from the state of Anglo-American relations over much of the preceding century. The Revolution itself was of course something of a nadir, but even in its aftermath lingering disagreements remained, not least over the continued British presence in North America. Amongst other things, this fact was behind persistent Anglo-American disputes regarding the future of the Empire's still loyal northern provinces (Canada) as well over the rights to settling the vast tracts of the Pacific north-west. To this extent, the War of 1812—which famously led to the burning of the White House by British troops—was merely a very public expression of some of the underlying tensions straining the relationship between London and Washington and which persisted long into the post-Revolution period.

The Treaty of Ghent, signed in 1814 by Baron Gambier and John Quincy Adams, resolved some of the outstanding issues, although there were still occasional flare-ups (perhaps most famously the 1861 Trent Affair). But by the 1890s many of the lingering points of contention—especially regarding the British presence in the western hemisphere—had at last been settled. The stage was thus set for a new era of close Anglo-American connection, cultural as much as political and diplomatic. And, as such, the stage was also set for the celebration of Washington's English ancestry, for how better to assert the idea of a deep-rooted transatlantic "racial" connection than by proclaiming the "Englishness" of George Washington?

LONDON'S WASHINGTON

London's Washington statue is an expression of this idea. An exact replica of the one by Antoine Houdon in the State Legislature at Richmond, it was a gift of the Commonwealth of Virginia intended to mark an important occasion: the Centennial of the Treaty of Ghent. Transatlantic plans for this anniversary first emerged in 1911, and by 1914 a

21. For a discussion of turn of the century racial Anglo-saxonism, see D. Bell, *Dreamworlds of Race: Empire and the Utopian Destiny of Anglo-America* (Princeton: Princeton University Press, 2020).
22. S. Anderson, "Racial Anglo-Saxonism and the American Response to the Boer War," *Diplomatic History*, 2:3 (1978), 222.

Statue of George Washington (cast of a marble original of 1788 by Jean-Antoine Houdon; erected 1921) on the lawn in front of the east wing of the National Gallery, Trafalgar Square, London. (*Ham/Wikimedia Commons*)

full schedule of pageants and ceremonies had been devised, culminating with a grand ball to be hosted in Ghent itself shortly before Christmas 1914.[23] But the outbreak of war in Europe intervened and so all was put on hold for the duration of the conflict.

It was only after the Armistice, therefore, that some of the original projects were finally realized, amongst which was the London statue of Washington. To be sure, the subject of where exactly it should be erected certainly drew lively discussion, with some outspoken Britons—like the one quoted above—revealing that the first president's "traito-

---

23. 1st Meeting of the Executive Committee (British), February 21, 1912, Minutes of the Executive Committee, Feburary 21, 1912 to October 17, 1918, Sulgrave Manor Archives.

rous" rebellion against Crown and Empire had neither been forgotten nor forgiven. But such views were always in the minority, and a prominent location outside the National Gallery was soon approved by King George V, namesake and great-grandson of the man who had "lost" the American colonies in the 1780s.

Washington was unveiled before an applauding crowd and with some soaring oratory in June 1921.[24] For many of those in attendance, the first president's English ancestry clearly revealed the underlying unities which bound Americans and Britons into a single family. As Dr. Smith of Washington and Lee University put it:

> our universal Anglo-Saxon instinct for justice and passion for liberty, our common recognition of the imperative of conscience, the rights of the individual, the fatherhood of God, and the essential brotherhood of man—with these multiplied and mighty bonds, so recently softened in the furnace of common suffering and welded anew on the hard anvil of war, this is a world of friendship that has come to stay, and may the God of England and America doom to speedy destruction every effort and agency that attempts to weaken or undermine it.[25]

Lord Curzon, Secretary of State for Foreign Affairs and a Trustee of the National Gallery, clearly agreed, remarking in reply that the "very fact of setting up this statue here was a sign that the two great branches of the English-speaking race were now indissolubly one." Curzon concluded his short address with a final flourish, declaring that he was happy to "gratefully and proudly accept this wonderful statue of a great Englishman."[26]

Notably, the very same sentiment was apparent just a few days earlier at the dedication of Washington's ancestral home—Sulgrave Manor in Northamptonshire—as an Anglo-American "shrine." Much like the statue, the origins of this endeavor also lay in the years shortly before the First World War and indeed involved a similar cast of Anglo-American luminaries, including Viscount Byrce (a former British Ambassador to the United States) and Walter Hines Page (Ambassador to the Court of St. James from 1913-1918). The dedication was a suitably grand occasion and included a procession from the parish church as well as the unveiling of a bust of the first president under the branches of a large walnut tree on the manor's lawn.[27] All those who spoke took

---

24. For details of the statue dedication, see *The Times*, July 1, 1921.
25. *The Times*, July 1, 1921.
26. Ibid.
27. For the dedication of Sulgrave Manor see *Banbury Guardian*, June 23, 1921.

the opportunity to identify Washington's "English" roots as expressive of the deep ties joining Americans and Britons.

Today, a century later, the language used to describe the Anglo-American relationship has of course changed and simplistic and reductive appeals to "racial" connections are—very rightly—beyond the pale. But the details of Washington's English connections nonetheless continue to draw interest across the pond. His ancestral home at Sulgrave remains a memorial to the Anglo-American relationship; the grave of the last Washington of Warton in Lancashire still draws American pilgrims; and various other English communities—from Durham in the north to Purleigh in the south—continue to celebrate proudly their links to the man who so roundly defeated the British Empire all those years ago.[28]

---

28. For some further details, see S. Edwards, "A Great Englishman": George Washington and Anglo-American Memory Diplomacy, c.1890-1925 in R.M. Hendershot and S. Marsh, eds., *Culture Matters: Anglo-American Relations and the Intangibles of "specialness"* (Manchester: Manchester University Press, 2021), 158-188; S. Edwards, "Warton, George Washington, and the Lancashire Roots of the Anglo-American Special Relationship, c1880-1976," *Northern History* 55:2 (2018), 206-234.

AUTHOR BIOGRAPHIES

Todd W. Braisted
Todd Braisted is an author and researcher of Loyalist military studies. Since 1979, Braisted has amassed and transcribed over 40,000 pages of Loyalist and related material from archives and private collections around the world. He is author of *Grand Forage 1778: The Battleground Around New York City* and has been a guest historian on episodes of "Who Do You Think You Are?" (CBC) and "History Detectives" (PBS). He is the creator of royalprovincial.com, the largest website dedicated to Loyalist military studies. Braisted is a Fellow in the Company of Military Historians and member of the State of New Jersey American Revolution 250th Advisory Commission.

William Caldwell
William Caldwell is the Park Ranger for the Overmountain Victory National Historic Trail; a 330-mile motor route stretching across Virginia, Tennessee, and the Carolinas shadowing the trail used by Patriots to the Battle of Kings Mountain. He is a graduate of Clemson and North Greenville University and has taught about the era of the American Revolution since 2008 with county historic sites, North Carolina State Historic Sites, and the National Park Service.

James M. Deitch
James M. Deitch is a Pennsylvania native who grew up in Bucks County surrounded by some of the biggest battlefields of the American Revolution. He holds a master's degree in military history from Norwich University where he is currently a Writing Fellow and is a doctoral candidate at Liberty University. His research focuses on the role of ethnic Germans in the American Revolution and their role in shaping the nation. After retiring from the United States Marine Corps as a combat veteran, he focused his attention on military history and all matters related to logistics for the military in combat.

Al Dickenson
Al Dickenson works as a writer and historian in Milwaukee, Wisconsin, his hometown, where he lives with his wife. He has a desire to showcase content

about American history and politics, as he believes we cannot know where we are going without first understanding where we came from. A graduate of Wisconsin Lutheran College with three Bachelor of Arts degrees in history, communication, and English, Al currently uses his talents in the development department of a local college. Al has been published in the Sage Scholars Newsroom and on WisPolitics.org, among other outlets. More of Al's work can be found at adickensonwriting.wordpress.com.

SAM EDWARDS

Sam Edwards is a Reader (Assoc. Prof) in History at Manchester Metropolitan University in the UK. His research explores war, commemoration, and transatlantic relations, and he has published widely on these subjects, including a book, *Allies in Memory* which was shortlisted for the Royal Historical Society's Gladstone Prize. A recognized authority on Anglo-American relations, Sam has provided expert commentary to BBC TV and Radio, Sky News, and CNN, and he writes and blogs for various outlets, including *The Independent* (UK). Sam is a Fellow of the Royal Historical Society and a Fulbright Scholar (2010), and in 2022 he was a Research Fellow in Residence at the Fred. W. Smith National Library for the Study of George Washington, Mount Vernon, Virginia

MATTEO GIULIANI

Matteo Giuliani is a history enthusiast with a particular interest in the American Revolution, the Gilded Age, and Ancient Rome. He studies Political Science and International Relations at Università degli Studi della Tuscia di Viterbo.

DON N. HAGIST

Don N. Hagist is the managing editor of *Journal of the American Revolution*. His research is focused on the demographics and material culture of the British Army in the American Revolution. He maintains a blog about British common soldiers (redcoat76.blogspot.com) and has published a number of articles in academic journals. His books include *Noble Volunteers: the British Soldiers who fought the American Revolution*, *These Distinguished Corps: British Grenadier and Light Infantry Battalions in the American Revolution*, and *The Revolution's Last Men: the Soldiers Behind the Photographs*. Don is an engineer for a major medical device manufacturer, and also writes for several well-known syndicated and freelance cartoonists.

PATRICK H. HANNUM

Patrick H. (Pat) Hannum served for forty-five years the Department of Defense, twenty-nine years as a U.S. Marine (Assault Amphibious Vehicle Officer), including battalion command, and sixteen years as a civilian professor at the Joint Forces Staff College, National Defense University, where he specialized in operational-level warfare and Phase II Joint Professional Military Education. He continues to study and promote the history and relevance of the American Revolution through membership in the Norfolk Chapter of the Sons of the American Revolution and the Great Bridge Battlefield & Waterways History Foundation, including staff rides, battlefield tours and other educational venues.

Timothy C. Hemmis

Timothy C. Hemmis is Assistant Professor of History with a specialization in Early American History at Texas A&M University–Central Texas, Killeen, Texas. His research focuses on empire, identity, war and society in Revolutionary America (1750-1815). He is also a Regional Coordinator for the Society for Military History for the Southwest United States. He is currently working on a biography of the first and only Geographer of the United States, Thomas Hutchins.

M. Andrew Holowchak

M. Andrew Holowchak is a professor of philosophy and history, who taught at institutions such as University of Pittsburgh, University of Michigan, and Rutgers University, Camden. He is editor of the *Journal of Thomas Jefferson and His Time* and author/editor of over fifty-five books and over 200 published essays on topics such as ethics, ancient philosophy, science, psychoanalysis, and critical thinking. His current research is on Thomas Jefferson, and has published nearly 180 essays and twenty-three books on the subject. Like Jefferson, he has a passion for "putting up and pulling down," but his putting up and pulling down is not architectural, but done on a landscape or in a garden.

Benjamin Huggins

Benjamin Huggins is an associate professor and editor at the Papers of George Washington project at the University of Virginia, where he has edited five volumes of The Papers of George Washington, Revolutionary War Series. In addition to his articles for the Journal of the American Revolution, he is the author of *Washington's War, 1779* and *Willie Mangum and the North Carolina Whigs in the Age of Jackson*. He received his Ph.D. in history from George Mason University in January 2009.

Samuel T. Lair

Samuel is a PhD student at the Hillsdale College, Van Andel School of Statesmanship, Hilldale, Michigan, where he studies the political theory and statesmanship of the American Founding.

Alexander Lenarchyk

Alexander Lenarchyk is a graduate of History from Southern New Hampshire University. He also is involved in an American Revolutionary War living history regiment, the 3rd New Jersey Gray's Regiment. Alexander's historical interests range from early European exploration of North America to the American Revolution. Furthermore, Alexander enjoys researching Native American history of his state of Connecticut and other New England Native groups. Alexander puts a great emphasis on learning history and advocates for living history as well as encouraging people to visit historical locations.

Christian McBurney

Christian McBurney resides in the Washington, D.C. area and is an independent historian. He is the author of six books on the Revolutionary War, including *Dark Voyage: An American Privateer's War on Britain's African Slave Trade*, *George Washington's Nemesis: The Outrageous Treason and Unfair Court Martial of General Charles Lee during the Revolutionary War*, *The Rhode Island Campaign: The First French and American Operation of the Revolutionary War*, and *Kidnapping the Enemy: The Special Operations to Capture Generals Charles Lee & Richard Prescott*. His book website is at www.christianmcburney.com. He is President of the George Washington American Revolution Round Table of the District of Columbia, and is also the founder, publisher, and editor of the *Review of Rhode Island History*, at www.smallstatebighistory.com.

Shawn David McGhee

Shawn McGhee earned his PhD from Temple University. His main areas of interest include the politics of the American Revolution, print culture, political identity formation and Early National political intrigue. He is a professional educator and adjunct professor of history in the Philadelphia Metropolitan area.

Aaron J. Palmer

Aaron J. Palmer, Ph.D. (2009) Georgetown University is Associate Professor of History, Wisconsin Lutheran College and Co-Director of the college's Honors Program. He was a fellow of the Harvard International Seminar on the History of the Atlantic World and the author of *A Rule of Law: Elite Political Authority and the Coming of the American Revolution in the South Carolina Lowcountry, 1763-1776*. He lives in West Allis, Wisconsin, and continues to research and write on colonial politics and the revolutionary era.

Jim Piecuch

Jim Piecuch earned his BA and MA degrees at the University of New Hampshire and his PhD at the College of William & Mary. He is a former history professor and has written extensively on colonial and Revolutionary history. His books include *The Battle of Camden: A Documentary History*, *Three Peoples, One King: Loyalists, Indians and Slaves in the Revolutionary South*, *Cool Deliberate Courage: John Eager Howard in the American Revolution*, co-authored with John Beakes, and *Cavalry of the American Revolution*.

David Price

David Price is the author, most recently, of *The Battle of Harlem Heights, 1776*, and a trilogy about the "Ten Crucial Days" of the American Revolution—*John Haslet's World*, *The Road to Assunpink Creek*, and *Rescuing the Revolution*. David has been awarded the National Society of the Sons of the American Revolution Bronze Good Citizenship Medal in recognition of his work as an author, speaker, and historical interpreter at Washington Crossing Historic

Park in Pennsylvania and Princeton Battlefield State Park in New Jersey. He holds degrees in political science from Drew University and Rutgers University, and lives in Lawrence Township, New Jersey. More information about David and his work, including his Revolutionary War blog "Speaking of Which," can be found at dpauthor.com.

Bob Ruppert

Bob Ruppert is a retired high school administrator from the greater Chicagoland area. He received his undergraduate degree from Loyola University and his graduate degree from the University of Illinois. He has been researching the American Revolution, the War for Independence, and the Federal Period for more than two decades.

Marvin L. Simner

Dr. Marvin L. Simner is Professor Emeritus of Psychology at Western University in London, Ontario. Throughout his academic career his research focus was on the investigation of many long-held but rarely examined theories in the areas of School Psychology, Developmental Psychology, and Psychological Testing. In 1996 he received the Award of Merit from the Ontario Psychological Association, in 2003 he was made a Fellow of the Canadian Psychological Association, and in 2007 he received the Member of the Year award also from the Association. Since his retirement his research has centered on the examination of many long-standing issues in the fields of Canadian and American history.

James M. Smith

James M. Smith graduated with BS degree from Virginia Commonwealth University and lives in Southern Pines, North Carolina. It is his hope to write a political, not military, history of the revolution—the history that John Jay asked Charles Thomson, the secretary to the Continental Congress, to write, but which never got written—telling the story from the point of view of the Loyalists as well as the Patriots. He believes it is important to understand that the American Revolution was as much a civil war as it was a revolution.

Scott M. Smith

After a thirty-year career on Wall Street, Scott retired in 2014 to pursue a lifelong passion to write. His cybersecurity novel, *Darkness is Coming*, won Distinguished Favorite in the Thriller category in the NYC Big Book Award competition. In 2017, he began researching the life and times of Nathan Hale, the official hero of his adopted home state of Connecticut. The effort resulted in *The Spy and the Seamstress*, a historical novel, as well as whetted Scott's appetite to further explore this tumultuous period in American history.

Eric Sterner

Eric Sterner is author of *Anatomy of a Massacre: The Destruction of Gnaddenhutten, 1782*. He worked in the fields of national security aerospace in the public and private sectors. He held senior staff positions on the Committees on Armed Services and Science in the House of Representatives and served in the Department of Defense and as NASA's Associate Deputy Administrator for Policy and Planning. He earned a BA from American University and two MAs from George Washington University.

Jane Strachan

Jane Strachan is an attorney with a background in information technology and intellectual property matters. She is also a former professor and speechwriter who has turned writer of history. She is well-versed in both the French and Indian War and the American Revolution and is working on a book project about the legend of one of Washington's major generals. She also has a keen interest in women spies who served in the Office of Strategic Services and the French Resistance during World War II. Jane is a member of the Daughters of the American Revolution.

Nancy Rubin Stuart

Nancy Rubin Stuart is an award-winning author whose eight nonfiction books focus upon women and social history. Among her books are *Poor Richard's Women: Deborah Read Franklin and the Other Women Behind the Founding Fathers*, *Defiant Brides*, named one of the best books on Revolutionary-era women by the *Wall Street Journal*, *The Muse of the Revolution*, and *American Empress*. Nancy's journalistic work has appeared in the *New York Times*, *Huffington Post*, the *Washington Post*, the *New England Quarterly*, and national magazines.

Richard J. Werther

Richard J. Werther is a retired CPA and history enthusiast living in Novi, Michigan. He studied business management at Bucknell University in Lewisburg, Pennsylvania. He has spent the better part of three decades reading, researching, and writing about various topics pertaining to the American Revolution.

Eric Wiser

Eric Wiser earned a BA in history from Loyola University-Chicago where he was a member of the Phi Alpha Theta National Honor Society in History. He taught at the secondary-education level and is a certified public accountant in the state of Illinois having also studied accountancy at DePaul University.

Joseph E. Wroblewski

Joseph E. Wroblewski, received a BA ('67) and MA ('72) in Social Studies from Trenton State College and earned a Doctorate in Education from Temple University ('87). He served in the Peace Corps in Western Samoa, ('67-'69), worked for the School District of Philadelphia in the Office of Research and Evaluation, and taught Social Studies at the S. A. Douglas High School, until retiring from the School District of Philadelphia in 2002. At present he is a volunteer docent at Morven (Princeton, NJ), the home of Richard Stockton.

INDEX

Abenaki, 85-87, 253
Abigail, 170-180
Académie française, 330
Adams, Abigail, 41, 44, 76, 290, 294-295, 310-315, 318-319
Adams, John, 40-44, 76, 106, 108, 115, 168, 272-273, 289-296, 299-302, 312, 315, 329
Adams, John Quincy, 302, 337
Adams, Samuel, 26, 41, 43, 262, 316, 318
Affleck, Philip, 203
Agress, Bill, 83
Ajax, 199
Albemarle, 199
Alcide, 201
Alcmene, 199
Alden, John R., 150
Alexander, William (Lord Stirling), 193
Alien and Sedition Acts, 300-301
Allaire, Anthony, 215
Allen, Ethan, 100-101, 109
Allis, Marguerite, 94
Allis, Marguerite, 94, 260-261
Allison, Francis, 2
Alsop, John, 118-119
Amazon, 199
Ancrum, William, 130
Andover Academy, 315
André, John, 81, 185, 192-193, 334
Andromeda, 200
Anen, James, 35-36
Anglo-Russian Commercial Treaty, 230
Antifederalists, 278, 281, 283-286, 288, 290, 296-305
Appalachian Mountains, 8, 12, 263-264, 274
Aquidneck Island, 170
Arbuckle, Matthew, 158-159
Archer, John, 152

Argall, Samuel, 33
Argyll Highlanders, 182
Aristocritis, 297
Arnold, Benedict, 56, 81, 131-132, 193, 315
Articles of Confederation, 262-271, 308, 310, 317
Asia, 128
Assunpink Creek, 73, 77-79, 83
Austin, Samuel, 106, 108

Bacchus, John, 152-153
Bache, Richard, 24-25
Bahamas, 196
Baird, Robert, 153
Baldwin, Cyrus, 106
Baldwin, Isaac, 212
Balfour, Nisbet, 220
Bank of North America, 311
Banyar, Goldsboro, 97, 109-110
Barbadoes, 196
Barbados, 30, 196-201
Barbé-Marbois, François, 323, 329-330
Barrett, John, 106
Barrett, Lushington, 152-153
Bartlett, John Russell, 175
Bartlett, Josiah, 262
Basset, Burwell, 68
Bass, James, 52
Beaver's Prize, 199
Becker, Carl, 71
Becker, Marshall, 38
Beham, James, 163
Belcher, Jonathan, 35
Belden, Samuel, 180
Belknap, Jeremy, 255-256
Bennington Mob, 102
Berthier, Louis-Alexandre, 241
Berwick, 197
Bethabara, 214-216

Bibby, John, 213
Bickerstaff, Aaron, 212
Bickham, Troy, 334
Big Shabakunk Creek, 78
Billings, Denison, 180
Bill of Rights, 318
Blanche, 199
Blane, Gilbert, 197
Blenheim, Joseph, 152
Block Island, 173
Blue Ridge Mountains, 92, 214-215
Board of Trade, 26
Bobrick, Benson, 41
Bond, Thomas, 25
Boone, Daniel, 260
Boreas, 201
Boston Common, 26, 151
Boston Harbor, 107
Boston Massacre, 153
Bowdoin, James, 306, 309, 314-318
Braddock, Edward, 3
Brandywine, 50, 207
Bridges, George Wilson, 196
Bristol, 197
Britannia, 199
British 14th Regiment of Foot, 55
Broad River, 210, 217
Brodhead, Daniel, 161-166
Brooklyn, battle of, 122
Brooklyn Heights, 195, 205, 243
Brooks, John, 147
Brown, Beriah, 175-180
Brown, Moses, 168-169
Brush, Crean, 96-110
Bull's Ferry, 185, 187, 190-194
Bunker Hill, 41, 49-50, 111, 218, 220, 306, 313
Burgoyne, John, 124, 129, 134, 155, 181-182, 206, 218, 248
Burke, Edmund, 100, 333
Burr, Aaron, 267, 289, 292-293, 295
Butler's Rangers, 132
Butler, Walter, 132-134
Byrce, Viscount, 339

Callender, James, 300-301
Campbell, John, 157, 159
Campbell, William, 209-214
Canada Creek, 134
Carlisle Bay, 197, 199-200
Carlisle Peace Commission, 126
Carrington, Edward, 283, 286
Carr, Paddy, 213
Catawba River, 213, 217

Catherine the Great, 225-228, 230-234
Causes of the Alienation of the Delaware and Shawnese Indians, 4
Cavendish, John, 248
Cayua, 6
Chamberlain, Mason, 19
Chambers, Samuel, 212
Chameleon, 199
Charles II, 19
Chase, Samuel, 266, 296-297, 299-305
Chatham Barracks, 111, 154
Chelsea Hospital, 181
Cherry Valley Massacre, 81
Chesapeake Bay, 203, 206, 245-246, 268
Chester, Joseph Lemuel, 336
Chitwood, James, 213
Clarke, Arthur, 97
Clark, George Rogers, 164
Cleveland, Benjamin, 214-215
Clinton, George, 133, 135, 292-295, 298
Clinton, Henry, 136-138, 141, 148-149, 185, 188, 190-192, 195, 208, 218-219, 221, 223, 237-238, 242-243, 245-246
Close, John, 183-184
Closen, Ludwig von, 243-244
Clouds, battle of, 207
Colden, Cadwallader, 90, 102-103
College of New Jersey, 78
College of William and Mary, 247
Collegiate Dutch Reformed Church, 97
Columbian Centinel, 290
Committee of Grievances, 100
Committee of Safety, 308, 310, 313
Common Sense (Paine), 333
Commons House of Assembly, 58-59
Concord, 46-47, 49, 51, 104, 313-314
Confederation Congress, 282, 306, 329
Congregation of Notre-Dame, 89-90
Congressional Loan Office, 312
Congress of Confederation, 82
Conkey's Tavern, 313
Connecticut Courant and Weekly Advertiser, 255
Connecticut Journal, 255
Connecticut River, 84-86, 88, 94-95, 98-100, 104-105
Connecticut Wits, 254, 260
Conqueror, 199
Constitution, 1-2, 17, 25, 42, 250, 262-263, 267, 271, 274, 276, 280-288, 290-292, 296-299, 303-304, 317-320, 329
Constitutional Convention, 271, 291, 317

Index

Continental Congress
  alliance with France and, 118-126,
  authority over ceded lands and, 269
  Charles Thomson and, 1-2, 11
  colonial resistance efforts and, 102
  deciding fate of prisoners and, 212
  effectiveness of long rifle and, 76
  examining Morgan's alleged corruption and, 158
  forming a committee consisting of a single representative from each colony and, 262-263
  guarantee of back pay plus a pension for life for officers and, 313
  importance of the Western Department and, 156-157
  Jefferson's excised passage on slavery and, 71-72
  judging boundaries of states and, 265-266
  Penn's description of John Rice and, 170
  printing paper money and, 307
  Secret Committee and, 116-117
  signatures needed for official documents and, 11
  Washington's appointment as commander of the Continental Army and, 67
Conway, Henry Seymour, 248
Corbin, Francis, 283, 287
Cornstalk, 158-159, 161
Cornwall, 199
Cornwallis, Charles, 56-57, 77-79, 82-83, 91-92, 208-209, 216-220, 222, 242, 245-246, 248, 315, 334
Council of Safety, 58-59, 116
Count Bernstorff, 233
Court of Oyer and Terminer, 32, 36
Court of St. James, 339
Cox Hill, 240, 242
Crawford, James, 212
Crawford, William, 161, 165-166
Creeks, 134-135
Cross, John, 172-174
Cuba, 196
Cumberland Committee of Correspondence, 102
Cushing, Thomas, 26
Cyclops, 200

Daily Advertiser, 284
Darling, John, 196
Dashwood, Samuel, 106

Dawson, Henry B., 143-144
Deal Castle, 199
Deane, Silas, 118-121, 126, 272
Declaration of Independence, 2, 40, 69-71, 120, 122, 156, 262, 270, 306, 310
Defense of the Constitutions of the United States of America, 293
Delancey, James, 239
De Lancey, Oliver, 127
Delaware Indians, 3-11, 13, 29-30, 33-34, 157, 159-166
Delaware River, 5-6, 8, 33-34, 122, 203, 206, 246
Denmark, 227-228, 230, 233-234
Deschambault, Jeanne-Charlotte de Fleury, 88-89
desertion, 31, 47, 49, 132, 138-139, 154, 186, 205, 212, 216, 222-223
d'Estaing, Conte, 89, 202
Dick, Alexander, 56
Dickinson, John, 262-266, 272
Dominica, 200
Doolittle, Amos, 49
Doty, Edward, 41, 44
Downes, Elizabeth, 30
Drayton, Henry, 126
drummers, 29th Regiment of Foot, 151-155
Duane, James, 272
dueling, 58-59, 61-66, 141, 150
Duffy, Patrick J., 109
Duke of Richmond, 224
Duke of Wellington, 234
Duke of York, 99
Dummer's War, 84
Dunlap, William, 19
Dunning, John, 250
Dustan, Hannah, 253
Dyer, Eliphat, 311

Earl, Ralph, 131
Edisto Island, 59
Edward, 199
Egmont, 198-199
18th Regiment of Foot, 46, 51, 73
Eight Mile Run, 77-78
Electoral College, 135, 289, 292, 295
Elizabeth, 107-108
Elizabeth II, 247
Elliot, Robert, 91
Emmerick's Chasseurs, 219
Endymion, 200
Engageante, 207

The Essay on the Life of the Honourable Major-General Israel Putnam (Humphrey), 254-256, 258-260
Ewing, Katherine, 74
Exeter Academy, 315

Federalist #9, 317
Federalist #10, 317
Federalist 78, 299
Federalist, 276-280, 284-287, 299, 317
Federalist Papers, 317
Federalists, 135, 276-290, 292-293, 296-305, 317-318, 323
Ferguson, Patrick, 209, 211-212, 217
Fermoy, Matthias-Alexis de Roche, 77-78
15th Regiment of Foot, 218, 222
5th Regiment of Foot, 46, 50, 218
5th Massachusetts Regiment, 306
59th Regiment, 46, 50
Filson, John, 260
First Congress, partisan politics and, 276-288
First Federal Congress, 299
1st New York Regiment, 128, 131-132
1st Pennsylvania Brigade, 186
1st Pennsylvania Continental Regiment, 75, 186-187, 189-190
1st Rhode Island Regiment, 172
Fitzgerald, James, 153
Fitzgerald, John, 146
Fitzsimons, Thomas, 279
Fiva, Anthony, 136-138
Flora, 202
Flora, William (Billy), 52
Fordyce, Charles, 55
Foreign Affairs Act of 1789, 299
Fort Bridgman, 85-86
Fort Charles, 242
Fort Chiswell, 211
Fort Dayton, 131-132
Fort Detroit, 160-164
Fort Dummer, 85, 88
Fort George, 241
Fort Hinsdale, 85
Fort Independence, 239
Fort Laurens, 161-162
Fort McIntosh, 161-162
Fort No. 4, 85, 88-89
Fort No. 8, 237, 239, 240, 242
Fort Pitt, 74, 79-80, 156-165
Fort Pitt Treaty of 1778, 162
Fort Randolph, 157-159
Fort Stanwix, 128-132

Fort St. Johns, 88, 128
Fort Ticonderoga, 87
4th Regiment of Foot, 46, 50, 219
4th Light Dragoons, 186
4th New York regiment, 131
Fox, Charles James, 250
Foxcroft, John, 22
Franklin, Benjamin, 2-3, 12, 14-29, 40, 125, 324, 329
Franklin, Deborah Read, 14-27, 29
Franklin, Francis, 17-18
Franklin, Sally, 18, 21, 24-25, 29
Franklin, William, 2-3, 6, 17, 21, 27, 28-33, 37-39
French–American alliance, 114-126
French and Indian War, 3-4, 12, 19, 28, 31, 68, 85-86, 99, 127-128, 254, 259
French King's Cabinet of Natural History, 321
Friends Public School, 2
Fries, John, 300-301

Gaffield, Benjamin, 86
Gage, Thomas, 90, 104-106, 109
Galloway, Joseph, 29, 272
Gambier, Baron, 337
Gansevoort, Peter, 128, 130, 132
Gardoqui, Don Diego de, 269
Gay, Bunker, 87-88, 255-260
General Mifflin, 227
A Genuine and Correct Account of the Captivity, Sufferings and Deliverance of Mrs. Jemima Howe (Gay), 87, 255
George III, 59, 69-72, 192, 247-249, 251-252, 333
George V, 339
Georgian Papers Programme, 247
Gerlach, Larry, 28
Germain, George, 192
German Continental Regiment, 77
Gervais, John Lewis, 63
Gibson, John, 165
Gienapp, Jonathan, 298
Gilkey, Walter, 213
Gilmore, Robert, 158
Girty, Simon, 157, 159
Gnadenhutten, 34, 165-166
Gontaut, Armand-Louis de (duc de Lauzun), 236-237, 239, 244
Graeme, Elizabeth, 29
Graeme, Thomas, 29
Grafton, 197

Index

Graham, Stephen, 53-54
Grainger, John, 234
Grand Cul-de-Sac, 199-200
Grayson, William, 298
Great Bridge, battle of, 52, 55-56
Great Depression, 308
Great Seal, 1
Green, Dennis, 51
Greene, Nathanael, 79, 216, 220, 311, 315
Green Mountain Boys, 101
Grey, Charles, 185
Gridley, Richard, 91
Grimké, John Faucheraud, 58-66
Grimké, John Paul, 58-59
Gros Islet Bay, 199
Grout, Hilkiah, 86
Grubb, Farley, 268
Gwinnett, Button, 160, 262

Half Pipe, 157, 160, 164
Hamilton, Alexander, 60, 135, 290-295, 317-319, 323
Hamilton, Henry, 156, 160, 208
Hancock, 107
Hancock, John, 41, 43, 309, 318
Hand, Edward, 73-83, 157-162, 166
Hand, Katherine, 80
Happy Return, 199
Harlem River, 236-241
Harrisburg Convention, 279
Harrison, Benjamin, 263, 266
Harrison, Robert, 145-147
Hartley, Thomas, 279-280
Harvard, 253
Harvey, Robert, 43
Haussegger, Nicholas, 77
Haymour, Mathew, 50
Hayne, Isaac, 220, 224
Hazard, Carder, 171-175
Heard, Isaac, 336
Heath, William, 76-77
Hector, 197
Helme, Arnold, 176
Helme, Rouse J., 176
Henry, Patrick, 41-42, 272, 283
Henry VIII, 26
Herkimer, Nicholas, 128-129
Hessians, 77-81, 136-139, 206, 222, 237, 240
Hewes, Joseph, 262
Hewson, Polly, 20-21, 25, 27
Hill, Richard, 105
Hinsdale, Ebenezer, 88

Hispaniola, 200
Histoire Naturelle, Générale et Particulière (Buffon), 321-323, 331
Histoire philosophique (Raynal), 322
The History of New-Hampshire (Belknap), 255-256
Hobbs, Augustine, 213
Hobkirk's Hill, 220
Honorius, 280
Hood, Samuel, 201-202
Hopkinson, Francis, 262
Hopkins, Samuel, 168
Hopkins, Stephen, 168-169, 262
Hotham, William, 199, 201-202, 221
Houdon, Antoine, 337-338
House of Commons, 248-249, 252
House of Lords, 218
Howe, Caleb, 86-87, 89, 91-93
Howe, Jemima, 84-95, 253-261
Howell, David, 176
Howell, Richard, 146
Howe, Martha, 93
Howe, Squire, 86-94
Howe, William, 76, 108-109, 152, 205, 219
Hudson River, 98, 105, 185-188, 192, 208, 236-238, 240, 245
Hume, David, 42
Humphreys, David, 254-260
Humpton, Richard, 187
Hunter, William, 197
Huntington, Benjamin, 266
Huntington, Samuel, 126
Hunt, Jonathan, 94
hurricanes, 195-203
Hutchinson, Thomas, 26

impeachment, 296-305
The Independent Chronicle and the Universal Advertiser, 108
Inns of Court, 29
Intrepid, 200
Ireland, 1, 51, 73, 96-97, 108, 111, 115, 151, 157, 169, 218-220, 222-224
Iris, 182
Iroquois, 6, 31, 34, 81, 327
Irvine, James, 187
Irvine, William, 165-166
Isis, 154
Islands, Leeward, 202
Izard, Ralph, 63-65

Jamaica, 153, 196, 199, 201
James River, 56

Jay, John, 135, 272-275, 278, 285, 292, 307, 317
Jefferson, Thomas, 40-41, 44, 69-72, 156, 216, 269, 291-296, 299-304, 310, 312-313, 319-320, 323-331, 333
Johnson, John, 129
Johnson, Susannah, 89
Johnson, Uzal, 211, 213, 215
Johnson, William, 31, 37
Jones, Jeremiah, 53
Jones, John Paul, 333-334
Jones, Joseph, 323
Jonge Prins, 227
Joy, Mathias, 91
Jubo, John, 154
Juniata River, 8

Karr, George, 64
Keimer, Samuel, 16
Keith, William, 14-15
Kelly, John, 109
Kenawa River, 159
Killbuck, John, 159-162
King George, 202
King, Rufus, 277, 286
King's County Court of Common Pleas, 171, 179
Kings Mountain, battle of, 209, 214-217
Knott, Elvington, 55
Knox, Henry, 79, 91-92, 315

Lacey, Edward, 214
Lafayette, Marquis de, 135, 140, 143-144, 150, 245, 307
Laforey, John, 202
Lake Champlain, 87, 98, 104-105, 154-155, 258
Lamb, John, 127
Lancaster County Associators, 75
Lancaster County Central Park, 83
Land cessions (1782-1802), 270
Langdon, John, 118
Lansing, John, 285
Lassiter, Henry, 53
Laurel, 200
Laurens, Henry, 58-66, 126, 307
Laurens, John, 141
League of Armed Neutrality, 225, 231, 234
Leclerc, Georges-Louis (Comte de Buffon), 321-322, 324-326, 328-330
Lee, Arthur, 43, 308, 310
Lee, Charles, 133, 140-150

Lee, Henry "Light Horse Harry", 193, 217
Lee, Richard Henry, 148, 272
Lee, Samuel, 51
Lee University, 339
Leeward Islands, 198
Lemay, J. A. Leo, 17
Lenape, 3, 28, 33-36, 39, 161, 164, 166
Lender, Mark Edward, 144
Lewis, Cron, 89
Lexington, 49, 104, 313
Lincoln, Benjamin, 236-237, 315-317
Liston, Robert, 335
Little Shabakunk Creek, 78
Livingston, Henry Brockholst, 285
Livingston, Philip, 102, 118-119
Livingston, R. R., 262
Logan, 327
London Times, 336
Long Island, battle of, 77
Long Island Sound, 238, 243
Lord Ashburton, 250
Lord Curzon, 332, 339
Lord North, 115-116, 126, 248-250
Lord Sandwich, 234
Lord Stormont, 233
Lovell, Timothy, 109
Loyalist Claims Commission, 109
Loyalists, 28, 56, 91, 93, 105, 108-109, 127, 129, 132, 134, 136, 157-158, 185, 187-193, 209-219, 236-241, 332, 334
Loyal Refugee Volunteers, 187-188
Lucius, 293

Mackenzie, Frederick, 240-242
Macnell, James, 153
Madison, James, 277-278, 280, 283-287, 292-294, 298, 300-301, 303, 317, 319, 323, 330
Marbury v. Madison, 303
Marchant, Henry, 180, 294
Marcus, 293
Marquess of Rockingham, 248-251
Marquise, B. De La, 128
Martin, Joseph Plumb, 145
Mary & Isabella, 199
Maryland Council of Safety, 116
Mason, Thomas, 51
Massachusetts Provincial Congress, 41
Massachusetts's Ratifying Convention, 277
Mather, Cotton, 253
Mather, Increase, 253

Index

Maxwell, William, 141, 146-148
Mayflower, 41, 44
McCormick, Richard P., 287
McCullough, David, 41
McDougall, Alexander, 128
McDowell, Charles, 214
McDowell, Joseph, 214
McFall, John, 213
McGillivray, Alexander, 135
McHenry, James, 145, 147
McIntosh, Lachlan, 160-162, 166
McKean, Thomas, 262
McKee, Alexander, 157, 159
McKinsey, James, 35-36
Meade, Richard Kidder, 147
Mearkle, Annie L., 260
Mercer, John, 147
Mercury, 221
Mills, Ambrose, 213
Miscellaneous Works (Humphreys), 259
Mississippi River, 263-264, 269
Mitchill, Samuel, 304
Mohawks, 6, 8, 31
Mona Passage, 200
Monmouth, battle of, 132, 135, 140-150
Monroe, James, 283, 292, 300, 329
Montagu, 199
Montego Bay, 196
Montgomery, Richard, 128
Montreal, 85, 87-90, 154
Montressor, Frances, 97
Moravians, 34, 159, 164-165, 214-215
Morellet, Abbé, 330
Morgan, George, 156-162
Morgan, Zachwell, 158-159
Morrisania, 236-237, 239-241, 244
Morris, Robert, 118-122, 309-311, 315-319
Mosely, John, 50
Moss, Bobby, 216
Mount Vernon, 1, 274, 317
Moylan, Stephen, 186-187, 190
Muller, Nicholas, 109
Murray, James, 91, 205
Muscle Shoals, 269

Nansemond County, 52-57
Napoleon I, 241
National Bureau of Economic Research, Cessions of land from each state and, 268
National Gallery, 338-339
National Gazette, 293-294
natural history, 321, 325, 330-331

naval blockade, 115-122, 125, 226, 229, 310, 312
Nelson, Horatio, 332
Nelson, Jr., Thomas, 262
Nelson, Paul David, 193
New Jersey Continentals, 147
Newport, battle of, 81, 111-112, 168, 170, 172, 195, 207, 218, 235-238
New York Evening Post, 135
New York Journal, 35, 290
New York Mirror, 135
Nicholson, Joseph, 301, 303
Ninety-Six, 216, 220
95th Regiment, 51
Noble, Frances, 90
Norman, Thomas, 109-110
North Carolina Assembly, 267
Northwest Ordinance of 1787, 269-270
Notes on the State of Virginia (Jefferson), 323, 329-330
Notre Dame High School, 83
Not without Peril (Allis), 260-261
Nova Scotia, 49, 96, 111, 182, 184
Noyes, Joseph, 177-179
Nutting, Lydia, 84

Ogden, Matthias, 147
O'Hara, Charles, 334
Old Bailey, 181
Old Burial Hill, 44
Oliver, Andrew, 26
Omohundro Institute of Early American History and Culture, 247
105th Regiment of Foot, 220
Oneida, 6, 28-33, 37-39, 134
Onion River Land Company, 101
Onondagas, 6, 31
Ordinance of 1784, 269
Ordinance of 1785, 269
Oriskany, battle of, 128-132
Othello, Joseph, 154
Othello, Thomas, 152, 154-155
Othello, Walter, 155
Ottoman Empire, 227
Overmountain Men, 209, 212, 214, 217

Page, Walter Hines, 339
Paine, Thomas, 333
Panin, Nikita, 227, 229
Parker, Peter, 196-202
Parliament, 2-3, 25-26, 70-74, 167, 247-252, 334
Parson, Samuel Holden, 239
Partridge, Samuel, 106

Paterson, William, 103, 105
Pauw, Corneille de, 322-323
Paxton Boys, 30, 39
Peggy, 107
Pell's Point, 76
Penn, John, 170
Pennsylvania Assembly, 18-19, 22, 29, 82
Pennsylvania Constitutional Convention, 82-83
Pennsylvania Gazette, 16-18, 35, 318
Pennsylvania Packet, 190-191
Pennsylvania State Artillery, 77
Penn Treaty Museum, 34
Penn, William, 2, 19
Perkins, Bradford, 336
Perrine Hill, 148
Perry, Freeman, 180
Petrikin, William, 297
Petry, William, 132
Petty, William (Earl of Shelburne), 37-38, 100, 248-251
Philadelphia Convention, 277
Phillips, William, 56, 315
Phipps, William, 85
Phoenix, 196
Pike, Zebulon, 188-189
Pip Pot Swamp, 56
Pitchkettle Creek, 56
Plumb, Thomas, 111-113
Point Judith, 171
Polly, 107
Pomona, 200
Pontiac's Rebellion, 28, 30, 35, 156-157
Poor Richard's Almanack, 18
Port Royal Harbor, 196
Praying Indians, 30
Preston, William, 211
Prince of Wales, 248-252
Princess Anne District Militia, 55
Princeton University, 78
Pringle, John, 25
Privy Council, 12-13, 26, 249
Proclamation of 1763, 12-13
Prohibitory Act, 115
Provance, James, 152, 153
Providence Abolition Society, 176, 177
Provincial Circuit Court, 32
Publius, 317
Publius Secundus Americanus, 284-285, 317
Puerto Rico, 196-200
Putnam, Israel, 89, 136-138, 253-261

Quakers, 2-4, 9-10, 127

Quebec, 6, 85, 87, 89, 104, 128, 154, 204, 221, 254, 256-257
Quebec Act, 104
Queen's Rangers, 56, 91-92

Rall, Johann, 77
Ralph, James, 15
Ramsey, John, 107
Randall, Joshua, 174
Randolph, Edmund, 291
Randolph, John, 303
Rawdon, Francis Lord, 218-224
Ray, David, 31-32
Raynal, Guillaume-Thomas François, 322-323, 328
Read, Charles, 32
Read, John, 14
Read, Sarah, 14, 16
Reagan, Ronald, 319
Récherches philosophiques sur les Americains (Pauw), 322
Records of the State of Rhode Island and Providence Plantations in New England (Bartlett), 175
Reed, Joseph, 67, 191, 311
Regulators, 313-319
Rehnquist, William, 301-304
Remini, Robert, 269
Rennison, James, 50
Resolution, 201
Retford, Thomas, 155
Rhode Island, antislavery bills and, 167-178
Rhode Island, battle of, 113
Rhode Island Resolves and Acts, 175
Rice, John, 170-180
Richelieu River, 87, 128
Rigaud, Pierre de (Marquis de Vaudreuil), 87-89, 257-258
Rittenhouse, David, 329
Robertson, James, 105-109
Rochambeau, Comte de, 82, 235-246
Rock Ford, 82-83
Rodney, Caesar A., 302-303
Rodney, George, 199-202
Rogers, Catherine, 51
Rogers, Daniel, 51
Rogers, John, 15
Ross, John, 134
Rowe, John, 106
Rowley, Joshua, 197
Royal Archives, 247
Royal Navy, 170, 226-228, 308
Ruby, 197

Index

Rush, Benjamin, 279, 289-290
Russell, John, 152
Russell, Jonathan, 41
Russia, 139, 225-234
Rutledge, Edward, 262

Saccapee, Joachim, 87-88, 258-259
Sagorighweyoghsta, 3, 29, 39
San Calixto II Hurricane, 197, 203
Sandwich, 200
Saratoga, 124, 134, 136, 204, 207, 248, 307, 315
Sartwell Farm, 93
Sartwell, Obadiah, 85
Savanna-la-Mar, 196
Sawtell, Richard, 84
Scammell, Alexander, 81-82
Scarborough, 196
Schuyler, Peter, 87-89, 100, 127, 131-132, 135, 257-258
Scollay, John, 106
Scott, Charles, 140-145, 147
Sears, Isaac, 127
Second Continental Congress, 156, 310
2nd New Jersey Regiment, 146
2nd Pennsylvania Brigade, 186-187, 189-190
2nd Virginia Regiment, 55
Secret Committee, 116-119, 310
Seneca, 6, 9, 31, 163
7th Pennsylvania regiment, 187
74th Regiment, 182
Seven Years' War, 157, 182
Sevier, John, 212, 214, 267-268
Seymour, Robert, 31-33
Shabakunk Creek, 83
Shark, 201
Sharlow, James, 152-153
Shattuck, Job, 314, 318
Shawnee, 3, 6-9, 11, 29, 157-160, 162, 327
Shays, Daniel, 306-309, 313-320
Shays' Rebellion, 314-316, 318-320
Shelby, Isaac, 214
Sheldon, Elisha, 81-82, 239
Shenandoah River, 92
Shenandoah Valley, 211, 215, 217
Shepherd, William, 316
Sherman, Roger, 262-263
Shipetaukin Creek, 77
Shreve, Israel, 146
Shrewsbury, 201
Simcoe, John Graves, 56, 91, 218
Simonds, Robert, 30-31

Six Nations, 3, 6-9, 29, 31, 81, 153
16th Light Dragoons, 182
6th Regiment of Foot, 51
6th Pennsylvania regiment, 187
63rd Regiment of Foot, 218-219
slavery, 22, 52-57, 69-72, 82, 107, 167-180, 263, 273, 281, 310, 318-319, 329
smallpox, 18, 29, 90, 161
Smallwood, William, 216
Smith, Melancton, 292
Smith, Thomas, 154
Smith, William Loughton, 299
Snyder, Jr., John J., 83
Society of the Cincinnati, 313-316
Sons of Liberty, 106, 127
South Carolina Gazette, 59
Southern Department, 315
The Sovereignty and Goodness of God Being a Narrative of the Captivity and Restoration of Mrs. Mary Rowlandson, 253
Spaulding, Leonard, 104
Stamp Act, 24-25
Stanton, Joseph, 172
Stanton, Lodowick, 172-174, 177-180
Stark, John, 81
A State of the Right of the Colony of New-York, 100
Sterner, Eric, 165
Steuben, Baron von, 141
St. Eustatius, 200, 203
Stevenson, Margaret, 20-24
Stevens, Phineas, 86
St. Francois River, 87
Stirling Castle, 197
St. James Episcopal Cemetery, 83
St. John's Church, 335
St. Kitts, 153, 200, 203
St. Lawrence River, 8, 87
St. Leger, Barry, 128-131
Stockton Hollow, 79
Stockwell, George, 130, 132
Stockwell, Mary, 142
Stone, Garry Wheeler, 144
Stone, Thomas, 262
Stony Point, 185, 208, 307
Strahan, William, 20-22
Streater, Ned, 52-57
Streater, Willis, 53
Stuart, John, 158
Stukes, Benjamin, 88-89
St. Vincent, 199
Sugar Act, 25

Sulgrave Manor, 339
Sullivan, John, 81, 163, 330-331
Supreme Court, 274, 296, 299, 301-304
Supreme Executive Council of Pennsylvania, 311
Susquehanna River, 8, 34
Sussex County Jail, 31
Sussex Courthouse, 31
Syrett, David, 234

Tarleton, Banastre, 213, 218
Teedyuscung, 9-10, 13
Telfair, Edward, 282
Teller's Point, 236
Ten Crucial Days winter campaign, 73
Tennessee River, 269
10th Pennsylvania regiment, 187, 189
Thacher, James, 75
Thames River, 184
Thayer, Theodore, 147
13th Virginia Regiment, 162
38th Regiment, 46, 51
Thompson, Harry, 291
Thompson's Island, 163
Thomson, Charles, 1-13, 272-275
Three Cantos (André), 192
Three Rivers, battle of, 154
Throgs Neck, 76, 239-240, 243-244
Thunderer, 197
Thurlow, Edward, 249, 252
Tilghman, Tench, 146-148
Timothy, Peter, 59
Tomkins, Daniel D., 143
Torbay, 201
Tories, 158-159, 308, 317
Townsend, Micah, 94
Townshend Duties, 25
Trafalgar Square, 332, 338
Treaty of Alliance, 124, 126
Treaty of Amity and Commerce, 124, 126
Treaty of Commerce, 229
Treaty of Ghent, 337
Treaty of New York, 135
Treaty of Paris, 54, 82, 166, 263, 272
Trent Affair, 337
Trenton, 73, 77-79, 83, 206
Trident, 197
Trinity College, 73-74
Triton, 201
Triumph, 200
Trumbull, John, 260
Tryon County Committee of Safety, 132
Tryon, William, 97, 100, 104, 109, 136, 139, 313

Tuberville, George Lee, 283
Turgot, Anne-Robert Jacques, 124-125
Turtle Clan, 33, 164
Tuscarora, 6, 31
Tute, Amos, 90
12 Bloody Acts, 101
29th Regiment of Foot, 151-155
22nd Regiment of Foot, 111, 113
27th Continental Regiment, 306
23rd Regiment, 46-47, 50

Ulysses, 200
Union, 202
United Brethren, 214
United States Geologic Service Maps, 56
University of Pennsylvania, 2

Valcour Island, battle of, 154
Valentine's Hill, 188, 237, 239
Valley Forge, 144, 307
Varnum, James Mitchell, 180
Vengeance, 199
Victor, 196
Virginia Constitution, 329
Virginia Minute Battalion, 52
Virginia, population estimates for, 55
Virginia Tax Lists Censuses, 54
Volunteers of Ireland, 222

Walker, Thomas, 152-155
Walking Purchase, 6
Wallace, David, 61
Ward, Christopher, 77
Ward, Harry, 143
Ward, John, 181-184
Ward, Samuel, 118
Ward, Thomas, 187
War of 1812, 54, 144, 155, 319, 337
War of Bavarian Succession, 227
Warren, James, 40-45, 168
Warren, Mercy Otis, 40-45
Warren, Richard, 41, 44
Washington, George
  appointment as commander of the Continental Army and, 67-68
  battle of Brooklyn and, 122
  battle of Monmouth and, 132, 135, 140-150
  British views of, 332-340
  calling a council of war and, 185-186
  commendation for Marinus Willett and, 133
  confronting Charles Lee and, 140-150
  early success and, 114

Index [357]

elected to the presidency and, 1, 274
feud between McIntosh and Morgan, 161-162
letter to congress on condition of his army and, 307
Madison's letter on Antifederalist plan and, 278-279
Mercy Otis Warren description of, 42-43
Morris Notes and, 310
prelude to Yorktown battle and, 235-246
prisoners examined by the General Court and, 107
Rawdon letter and, 223
replacing Hand with more aggressive commander and, 160
replacing Lincoln with Nathanael Greene and, 315
road to Assunpink Creek and, 77-83
unanimous support from the Electoral College and, 289
Valley Forge and, 144, 307
Washington, Martha, 43
Waters, Henry, 336
Wat Tyler, 293
Wayne, Anthony, 141-142, 148, 185-193
weather interventions, 204-208
Wedderburn, Alexander, 26
Weekly Post Boy, 35
Wells, Robert, 59
Wells, Samuel, 98, 101-104
Wentworth, John, 88, 99-100
Weslager, Clinton, 30, 34
Western Department, 156, 160-165
West Indies, 15, 123, 152, 169, 196, 238, 245
Westminster School, 60
West Point, 81, 185, 193, 236, 239
Wetzel, Martin, 164
Whately, Thomas, 26
What Is Sauce for the Goose Is Sauce for the Gander, 22
Wheelwright, Esther, 89
Whigs, 102, 248-252
White Eyes, 157-164
White, James, 269
Whiting, Nathan, 88
Wilhelm, Stephen, 291
Wilkins, John, 157
Wilkinson, James, 267, 270
Willard, Charlotte, 93
Willard, Jonathan, 93
Willett, Edward, 127

Willett, Marinus, 127-135, 292
Willett, Samuel, 127
William Pitt the Younger, 252
Williams, James, 210
Williamson, David, 165
Willing, Charles, 310
Willing, Thomas, 118
Willis, Sam, 234
Wilson, Benjamin, 19
Wilson, John Lyle, 65
Wilson, Robert, 213
Windsor Castle, 247
Winston, Joseph, 214
Wolf Clan, 33
Wood Creek, 131
Woodford, William, 55
Wood, Gordon S., 41
Woodhull, Nathaniel, 102
Wyandot, 165

Yadkin River, 217
Yale, 254, 260
Yazoo River, 269
Yeates, Jasper, 160
York River, 92
York, Thomas, 154
Yorktown, 57, 82, 91-92, 208, 235, 246, 248, 263, 315, 332, 334

Zeisberger, David, 159